Fredric March

Fredric March, 1932.

Fredric March

Craftsman First, Star Second

Deborah C. Peterson

Contributions in Drama and Theatre Studies, Number 65

GREENWOOD PRESS
Westport, Connecticut • London

Library of Congress Cataloging-in-Publication Data

Peterson, Deborah C.
  Fredric March : craftsman first, star second / Deborah C. Peterson.
    p. cm.—(Contributions in drama and theatre studies, ISSN
  0163–3821 ; no. 65)
  Filmography: p.
  Includes bibliographical references and index.
  ISBN 0–313–29802–5 (alk. paper)
    1. March, Fredric, 1897– . 2. Actors—United States—Biography.
  I. Title. II. Series.
  PN2287.M48B65 1996
  791.43′028′092—dc20   95–19584
  [B]

British Library Cataloguing in Publication Data is available.

Library of Congress Catalog Card Number: 95–19584
ISBN: 0–313–29802–5
ISSN: 0163–3821

First published in 1996

Greenwood Press, 88 Post Road West, Westport, CT 06881
An imprint of Greenwood Publishing Group, Inc.

Printed in the United States of America

The paper used in this book complies with the
Permanent Paper Standard issued by the National
Information Standards Organization (Z39.48–1984).

10 9 8 7 6 5 4 3 2 1

To my parents, Carl and Frances Peterson
and J. Vincent Hood (Vinnie)

Contents

Acknowledgments ix

1. Racine 1

2. The Bank and the University 11

3. World War and the University 15

4. New York, New York 21

5. My Name Is Fredric March 29

6. Florence 33

7. Barrymore 43

8. Jekyll and Hyde 57

9. Popularity 67

10. Romantic Leading Man 75

11. Romantic Leading Man, Part II 83

12. *The Road to Glory* and Free-Lancing 95

13. Back to Broadway 107

14. Communist!   123

15. The War Years   133

16. USO and Victor Joppolo   145

17. The Best Years of Our Lives?   153

18. *Columbus* versus *Counterattack*   165

19. The Horrors of a Successful Play   183

20. *Inherit the Wind*   199

21. The Great Orator Plays God   211

22. Fredric March in a Western?   225

23. Illness   233

     Epilogue   237

     Appendix A—Selected Plays   243

     Appendix B—Narration/Radio/Television   249

     Appendix C—Motion Pictures   253

     Bibliography   279

     Index   291

     Photoessay—*follows page 131*

Acknowledgments

In the course of preparing this book, I have incurred debts personal and professional. Therefore, I would like to offer my heartfelt appreciation to Margaret Budd, Leslie Aller, Gary Busha, LuAnn McBride, Dr. Stephen Meyer, Russ Einwalter, Lawrence Quirk, the staff of the Racine County Historical Society and Museum, the staff of the State Historical Society of Wisconsin, Dr. Rodney Sheratsky, Kathryn Davis, Jean Bickel Owen, Jane Carpenter Post, Penelope March Fantacci, and Stanley Mallach for their assistance and support. I also wish to thank Cynthia and Roger for moral support during this process.

Fredric March

1

Racine

What you are about to see is a secret you are sworn not to reveal. And now, *you* who have sneered at the miracles of science; *you* who have denied the power of man to look into his soul; *you* who have derided your superiors. Look! . . . Look! . . . Look!   (Mr. Hyde to Dr. Lanyon, *Dr. Jekyll and Mr. Hyde*—1931)

Hyde drains the contents of the beaker in his hand, letting it fall to the floor, collapses into a nearby chair, and begins that well-known transformation from savage brute into suave, attractive, if harried, Dr. Jekyll. Released December 31, 1931, *Dr. Jekyll and Mr. Hyde* frightened and astounded audiences fresh from two other horror films of that year—*Dracula* and *Frankenstein*. With his original depiction of the romantic but doomed Jekyll and sinister alter ego Hyde, the actor portraying the dual role was immediately projected into stardom. In addition, he won the Academy Award for Best Actor—the only time an Oscar was awarded the lead in a horror film: to a monster portrayed by Fredric March. March managed to mature into one of the best actors in America between 1929 and 1973, an actor of surprising versatility and durability, one of those rare performers who had gone from juvenile leads to the crustiest of old characters.

Though generally respected, March has yet to receive his full due, for he is not as well remembered as his contemporaries, Spencer Tracy and Gary Cooper, with whom he shared the distinction of achieving two Best Actor Oscars. Why did he not leave his mark upon the present generation, as Tracy or Cooper have? March's career was certainly as praiseworthy as theirs. In fact, he advanced beyond them by garnering, along with his two Oscars, two Best Actor Tony Awards, an accomplishment yet to be matched. Unfortunately, the current generation, if they remember March at all, may only recall his second Oscar performance, that of the returning World War

II army sergeant, Al Stephenson, in *The Best Years of Our Lives* (1946).

Then, who was this man, craftsman first, star second? Screen stars of the 1930s were always something one read about in newspapers or the fledgling movie magazines. People to shake the head over, perhaps, and to furnish juicy morsels of conversation, thought of as members of a lighthearted, utterly wild band whom no one could picture in a Racine, Wisconsin, home, or much less at an everyday Racine, Wisconsin, family dinner table. Yet, from just such a home came Fredric March, born Frederick McIntyre Bickel before the turn of the century. The Bickels were ever a conservative crew, simply an average American family, doing average American things. No broken home, divorced parents, child abuse or trauma: just a childhood that bears an uncanny resemblance to several hundred thousand others.

Frederick McIntyre Bickel made his first appearance on August 31, 1897, in an upstairs bedroom at 1811 Park Avenue in Racine, Wisconsin. He joined a family of two boys, Harold LeRoy, ten, and John M., five; one girl, Rosina Elizabeth, eight; one father, John Frederick, president and treasurer of Racine Hardware Manufacturing Company (wagon hardware and office supplies); and one mother, Cora Brown Marcher Bickel. Frederick was born, amid a dead silence of church bells and cheering. His parents were excited, but the rest of the world maintained a great calm. Even among the neighbors, there was little news value in the fact that the Bickels had had another baby.

Frederick was of German and English stock. His father, known popularly as John F., was born in the town of Caledonia, Wisconsin, September 8, 1859, to Johann F. Bickel and Regina Vetter Bickel, natives of Germany who had settled in Caledonia as children. John F. was the only son of four children and spent his childhood and youth on the family farm. Moving to Racine at age fourteen, he worked for his board while attending a local public school. John F. soon began learning the machinist's trade in the shops of the A. P. Dickey Manufacturing Company, where he spent three and a half years while attending night school studying bookkeeping. In November of 1879 at age twenty, he secured a position as assistant bookkeeper in the office of the Racine Hardware Manufacturing Company, becoming assistant treasurer by 1884. Another 1884 event was the meeting of John F.'s future wife, one Cora Brown Marcher, a twenty-one-year-old schoolteacher. She was the daughter of Thomas Scott and Samantha VanDusen McIntyre, originally from Onarga, Illinois, and the English half of Frederick's ancestry. John F. and Cora wed in Racine on January 23, 1886. John F. was soon elected director to the Racine Hardware Manufacturing Company, allowing him to acquire the house on 1811 Park Avenue to start a family. This was not long in coming, for Harold LeRoy was born April 11, 1887, with Rosina Elizabeth (Bessie) two years after on April 2, 1889. On February 21, 1892, another son, John M., called Jack, was added to the Bickel family, while John F. joined yet another company, the Racine Junction Building and Loan Association, as director. In addition to holding a deaconship with the First Presbyterian Church, John F. was vice president of the YMCA, an active Republican, and a member of the Royal Arcanum, Royal League, Modern Woodmen, National Union, and Total Abstinence Societies, all of Racine. He also became treasurer and manager of the Racine Economy Spring Company and held the same position for the Racine Seed Company. His youngest son, Frederick, would inherit John F.'s penchant for "joining."

After Frederick McIntyre was born, it was soon evident that a considerably larger home was needed. Cora's mother had been recently widowed and rattling around a huge Victorian on College Avenue, so she invited the burgeoning Bickel family to move in the fall of 1902. Grandmother Marcher moved to the lower first floor apartment. Next door lived the DuFour family, with five-year-old Lillian being the closest to Fred in age. Lillian related that the Bickels were always such a close-knit family, although she didn't remember Mrs. Bickel as well as she did Bessie (sister Rosina Elizabeth). Apparently, Bessie always looked out for Fred, directing all his birthday parties.

In a *Photoplay* article published in 1932, daughter-in-law Mary Dupuy Bickel (married to older brother, Jack) commented about the Bickel family, describing them as the closest family group that she had ever known. No member of that circle—three boys and a girl and their parents—could, or wanted to, decide anything of importance without a conclave of all the others. Father and Mother Bickel would ask each other in their soft, sweet voices: "What do you think, Cora?" "What do you think, John?" This was followed by the oft-repeated "You know best, dear" (March Papers).

Fred recalled his parents fondly during a 1932 *Screenland* magazine interview: "I ran into luck at the start—it was a swell family. My mother was gay, charming, very naive. We kidded her and adored her" (March Papers). Cora Bickel wrote both prose and poetry and had a great love of the beautiful in literature, art and life, but was quite formidable. Fred's first cousin remembered a very stern Cora: "I never felt comfortable around Cora" (Interview, Kathryn Davis, 17 September 1990). She tried to teach her children the finer, nobler things. Fred continued to *Screenland*; "My father was head of a manufacturing concern and a pillar of the Presbyterian Church. But that doesn't describe him at all. He has always had such wise understanding and tolerance, such humor. The most unforbidding sort of father, and yet we had infinite respect for him even though we looked upon him as an equal in companionship." Mr. Bickel had a full, rich sense of humor and was a born entertainer. Bedtime in the Bickel house when the children were young was eased by a story from their father. Jewish, Irish, Italian and Black dialects would flow from his lips, while his face would take on the lines of the character. Impressionable Frederick loved it, lapping it up, but then he was always attracted by speaking and would listen intently to everything people told him, studying them as they talked.

Much to Cora's dismay, young Frederick's proclivity for mimicry was well developed by the time he was four. Racine pedestrians had to be careful when walking past the Bickel household or they would soon see a three-and-one-half-foot caricature of themselves. Luckily for some of the men and women, they never knew what went on behind their backs as they passed a certain group of children huddled in front of the massive Victorian on College Avenue. For among them was a young boy with a keen eye for oddities who would spot peculiar walks and nasal voices and tiny quirks of conduct. Once, Cora actually had to spank seven-year-old Frederick for imitating a tottering old man passing their residence.

Frederick was not always blessed with the command of the English language and diction he eventually became famous for in Hollywoodland. Once, a secretary of the YMCA visited the Bickel household and Cora was talking to the caller in the front parlor. Frederick had been playing outside. Suddenly, there was a great commotion and a glowing faced little boy dashed in, scattering grubby bits of paper all over.

> "Tickets to hell!" he shouted. "Tickets to hell!" An aghast Cora hastened
> to explain, "Freddie is having a hard time with his 'esses.' He can't say
> 's' at all. It sounds like an 'h' when he says it."(*The Milwaukee Journal*,
> 13 February 1933, March Folder, Racine, WI)

Fred was a crowd pleaser because of his antics in front of anyone and everyone who would stop to listen to him. He commented about his proclivity to recite during the interview to *Screenland*:

> My one and only distinguishing feature was a revolting one. I recited.
> I couldn't be kept from reciting. You know the occasions—church
> bazaars, school entertainments, Sunday School parties. I wasn't
> precocious. Just plain obnoxious. I was ungodly "stuck-up" about it,
> and mistaken teachers and Sunday School teachers were constantly
> having me do it. With gestures—you know the kind. I remember one
> typical one, starting: "In a dark and dismal attic, where the sunshine
> never came, dwelt a little boy named Tommy, sickly, delicate and
> lame." I remember my excitement when I found that one. I locked the
> door of my bedroom and stayed up all night, memorizing in case I
> should get a chance to inflict it on my public. I'm afraid I eventually
> got the chance. (March Papers)

Fred's first speaking "piece," delivered with a vim that almost toppled the boy over, was, "From Greenland's Icy Mountains to India's Coral Strand." He did so well that his parents allowed him to "speak the pieces" later in the family parlor when relatives or company came. He gradually developed into a reliable family actor. Fourth grade schoolteacher Mary Gallagher wrote of the young Fred in 1961, "We all remember his 'Po Lil' Moe.' As he was on his way to his seat he would look at me and mimic in the class (on the sly so no one but we two would know) 'pull an ear' or 'twist a curl on top of his head' as one girl in the class would do when called upon to recite" (letter to Charles Carpenter, 6 October 1961).

It was at the 1635 College Avenue residence that this youthful actor was to meet and join the group of young boys that would comprise the College Avenue Gang. Vinnie Hood, Charlie Carpenter, Jack Ramsey, Jimmy Huguenin, and Vernon Crane either lived on College Avenue or were within walking distance. All were one and a half to two years older than Fred but in the same grade at Winslow Grammar School, which Fred started at age four, the others were five or six. This age difference never hindered Fred, who learned at a young age to endear himself to all individuals who mattered. Fred reminisced about his gang in the *Screenland* magazine article:

> As I look back, we must have been a pleasure to have around. Particularly at that age. If people spoke to us, we wriggled and mumbled incoherently. We walked either with a shambling gait or else bounded, tripping over furniture. Around our elders, we were alternately belligerent and, if we wanted something, maddeningly polite and servile. Boys are strange, inexplicable little animals.

Vinnie Hood, the last living member of Fred's gang, described a small barn in the back of the Bickel property, inhabited by a pony. Apparently, every summer in their youth the College Avenue Gang would hold a Wild West Circus attended by boys and girls of various ages from their immediate neighborhood. Vinnie recalled one summer, the summer of 1907, in particular, when he was eleven years old. Charlie Carpenter, Vernon Crane and Jimmy Huguenin would mount the pony, trying to stay astride while waiting for the starting signal from the sophisticated one of the group, John Ramsey, nicknamed Jack, who always positioned himself by the barn front door in order to catch sight of the "star" of their little production, Fred.

Vinnie remembered that a silence would descend on the crowd of children as they moved back from the pony corral to make room for the shortest member of the College Avenue Gang, being propelled from behind by his sister, Bessie. Fred would always hesitate until he knew he had all the children's attention and would then climb under the corral gate with utmost dignity, heading for an overturned soda pop case, left over from a double header where his gang sold soda pop at 25 cents apiece. Mounting the precarious pop case, Fred would motion to Jack his readiness. He would then turn slowly to face the crowd, glancing first right and then left. Vinnie next recalled Fred's unusually resonant voice for one so young, describing a typical speech to the crowd. "Welcome one and all to our annual Wild West Circus! (uproarious clapping). I would like to start with my latest recitation." Fred would then bow his head for effect, wait for his audience to silence, which they did obligingly, raise his eyes to scan the group slowly, and commence:

> Parson Brown came across the street and asked me, "Little Boy, will you sing for me at Church next Sunday? I'll give you half a crown."
> And I said, "I can't sing at church; I haven't a decent suit to wear."
> He said, "Well, I'll buy you a brand new suit."
> Next Sunday after church, the Parson stood me up on a little table in front of the congregation. I began to sing. "As I went down to the field one day, to see the farmers making hay, I saw the Parson dressed so gay and saw him kiss Miss Molly!"
> Well, the congregation all laughed and clapped their hands and the Parson said, "It's false, little boy!" I ran out of the church singing, "How I cheated Parson Brown, a brand new suit and half a crown, telling the people all around, how he kissed Miss Molly." (Interview, Lillian Dufour Perkins, 27 January 1990)

While the audience laughed, Fred would then nod to Jack, who in turn signaled Charlie and Vinnie—the Wild West Circus had officially started! Forty-five funfilled minutes later, Fred, hanging onto his wagon, would slide down the barn chute from the loft to the ground in a grand finale, the "Spectacular Death Defying Slide for Life!" After the audience departed for home, Vinnie clearly remembered the gang of young boys engaging in a paint fight with leftovers from signs they had made to advertise the circus. Unfortunately, the paint was oilbase and all the boys gained severe verbal punishment by their respective parents that summer evening in 1907.

Vinnie affectionately reminisced about the young boy he called Fred: "Fred pushed ahead in school, scholastically, but wasn't much in athletics, being shorter and smaller than all the other boys. He wouldn't like to hear me say that, for Fred loved sports. Well, anyway, instead of sports, Fred recited, poems, etc.; in our annual Wild West Circus, at Sunday School, and twice every month in the Friday afternoon school plays" (Interview, J. Vincent Hood, 13 January 1990). Fred remembered, "I harangued with such heat that I was one of the regular stars of school and Sunday School entertainment" (*Screenland*, 1932, March Papers). His pals all thought it was pretty smart of him to be able to recite. In fact, his public appearances were so chronic that his gang knew half his repertoire by heart and if he, standing on the platform and carried away by his own effulgence, forgot a line, one of them would prompt him loudly from the audience and neither one of them would be the least abashed. As he grew older, Fred continued to imitate citizens for the amusement of his gang. He would still detect points about individuals he met casually and then would drag them back to life when the unwitting subject had left the area.

Apart from reciting, there were also many other activities a young boy might engage in. Since Racine is on Lake Michigan, the gang used to go swimming inside the breakwater and steal lumber from houses under construction to build rafts. They would also steal their fathers' favorite garden spades and dig tunnels in the lake bank, making all sorts of "secret passages" and "chief's caves," totally impractical places where they were always being submerged in collapsing wet sand. Once, their penchant for thievery got them onto the local police blotter. They were about thirteen years old, though Fred was younger, of course, when the gang walked to nearby Kenosha one late summer afternoon. On the way back they passed by a farm and decided to steal a muskmelon apiece. The farmer, unfortunately, saw the boys and started yelling as they took off running. Fred could not keep up with the rest, so the older boys slowed down, resulting in their capture. Even though they apologized and promised to pay for the melons, the farmer swore out a warrant for their arrest. Fred's father fixed it up, though, buying the melons with the boys paying him back $1 apiece, which was big money back then. However, all Fred's childhood activity was not in shady business. He mowed lawns, shoveled snow, sold magazine subscriptions, collected old paper and sold it to the ragman—all the things a kid did to make a quarter or so.

Fred had outgrown the usual dislike of girls some time before he would admit it. He liked girls before the rest of his gang, and the girls, in turn, "loved" him, christening him "Freddie" and clamoring for his attention at the mandatory dancing classes that all young men and women of that era had forced on them early in their lives. While most of his gang hated these enforced gatherings, Fred, this budding young womanizer, enjoyed them, becoming the best dancer in his class. Fred confessed to *Screenland* later, "Sheepishly, secretly, I fell desperately in love with one girl after another. It wasn't until high school that I openly manifested a liking for a girl. Still fickle, I transferred my affections every couple of months. During the romance, the principal signal of attention was escorting her to dancing class" (March Papers).

One young lady recalled his escorting her to Mrs. William's dancing class and some parties. But she had to move away in tenth grade, to Canada, so the romance ended. Much to her regret. Plainly, Fred never had trouble acquiring a date. His special girl senior year was a petite, small-boned young lady named Julia Burns. The Racine High annual placed silly quotes under each senior's picture; Julia's read, "Julia likes pickles, That's why she likes Bickels." Fred's read, "He oft hath 'Burned' the mid-night oil, But never, I aver, in toil" (*The KIPIKAWI*, 1914). They went steady after high school, but the relationship ended when she got serious and he didn't.

High school was uneventful except that Fred was elected president of his class as he had been the last year of grammar school and was again in college. Fred commented to *Screenland*, "That chronic presidency misled my parents into high hopes for me, poor dears. And except for my debut into oratory, orations being the unavoidable offshoot of recitations" (March Papers). As a sophomore, Fred decided Racine was too small and the rest of the world should not be deprived of his talents as a great orator. Therefore, he entered and won the Racine High School preliminary oratorical contest with "Spartacus to the Gladiators." Next, traveling to Sheboygan, April 19, 1912, to represent his school in the district contest, self-confidently assuming he would win, he only captured second place barring him from competing in the finals. Fred could not understand why he had not won for he had always been star boy at home and this sudden downfall was humiliating. One of the judges consoled him by pointing out the fact that Fred was still in short pants. His parents admitted their folly and immediately bought Fred long pants.

In the next year, he chanced upon Grattan's "Invective against Corry," where Grattan spoke for the liberty of Ireland and against Corry, another Irishman opposed to home rule. Fred prepared for battle anew. On April 29, 1913, now in proper long pants, he won the school contest easily. Advancing next to the district contest in West Allis on May 9, he won again, picked to represent the Oratorical League of Southern Wisconsin. Tomahawk was the site on June 1, 1913, with Fred pitted against eight contestants one from each Normal School district, all carefully trained and considered the best orators in the state. He was the youngest and smallest declaimer at the contest, but his convincing method of delivery and general bearing won out. Showing a finish of interpretation and polish with a fire of enthusiasm that was evident in no other speaker, fifteen-year-old high school junior Frederick Bickel was unanimously given the honor by three judges. He received a gold medal and carried the title of Champion Wisconsin School Orator for a year. That month's school paper, appropriately named *ENICAR* (*Racine* spelled backward), printed: "There is a young fellow named Bickel, who before each oration eats a pickle, though in stature he's small he makes them all fall, when he shows them his medal of nickel," and "Fred Bickel—Loves to hear himself talk." The *Racine Journal* exclaimed, "Fifteen-Year-Old Racine Boy Orator Wins" (March Folder). Fred felt like visiting royalty. Through all the flattering fuss, he moved with stately dignity somewhat marred by the fact that the excitement had broken out in a rash all over his chest and stomach and he wriggled constantly with an acute attack of hives!

Fred's older brothers both attended the University of Wisconsin in Madison at this time, with Harold a member of the Alpha Delta Phi fraternity. Jack, as yet, was not sure what fraternity he would join. This bothered Fred, for he wanted his brothers to be in the same fraternity. In a letter written on March 12, 1913, to brother Jack (five years his senior), Fred revealed his opinion:

Dear Jack:

Kindly forgive and forget my not writing you before, especially at the time when you reached your majority. *Many of 'em!*

Don't know whether you knew that I saw Maude Adam's in "Peter Pan" last month or not. Sat in pit. (50 cents) *Gee!* It was *fine.*

As to your choice of fraternity I wish you wouldn't go Psi U. I hope you will not consider anything but Alpha Delt. If I ever get as far as you are, and have to decide between two fraternities, yours and Harold's, you can readily see it might be a little hard.

With lots of love from your kid brother. Fred (March Papers)

Fortunately for Fred, Jack chose Alpha Delta Phi.

Senior year found Fred president of his class (again), sales manager of the Racine Annual plus business manager for the 1914 monthly school paper. This popularity and sense of "joining in" were to become habits for Fred. His gang thought he would compete in oratory for a third time in spring of 1914 but Fred felt he had already gone to the top in that field, so instead he captured the part of Tillford Wheeler, second male lead in the senior class play, *The County Chairman*, presented at the Racine Theater on May 15, 1914. He also decided to try debating as part of the negative team representing Racine High in the Lawrence Triangular Debating League. He stated to *Screenland* magazine, "And I was rotten! That may have been an omen of my future, a flair for reading someone else's lines but no ability to create my own" (March Papers). They lost, a discovery that knocked any plans for being a lawyer out of his head.

It was now time for Frederick McIntyre Bickel to graduate and seek out his future. A description of the young man at his graduation would include such adjectives as well-liked, affable, confident, extremely handsome even as a youth, self-reliant, outgoing, and top-flight grades in school. All molded and prepared Fred for a successful future, possibly, he thought, in banking. Of course, when he thought about it, it was always "in banking," never as a "bank clerk."

2

The Bank and the University

Fred and his gang graduated from Racine High School at the Orpheum Theater in Racine on June 18, 1914. Charlie Carpenter (who now preferred to be addressed as Chuck), the tallest member of their group and the senior class football star, had to earn money first to go to college, as would Jack Ramsey. Vinnie Hood planned on selling real estate, something he had constantly harangued his friends about throughout their senior year. Vernon Crane was going to move to Detroit and attend a school of engineering. Jimmy Huguenin had recently died of spinal meningitis; the boys had been pall bearers at his funeral the previous month, lending an air of sadness to the otherwise happy occasion.

Most of the gang expected Fred to marry his high school sweetheart, Julia, but Fred had other ideas. He did not want to get married until after college, and felt he could not succeed at the School of Commerce in Madison with a family trailing around after him. Fred fully expected to attend college the fall of 1915 until Mr. Bickel's announcement that the bank his firm dealt with had failed, announcing, "We're not poor, but I just can't afford to send you to college right now. I've made arrangements for you to see Mr. Carson at Manufacturers Bank downtown. A few months ago, he told me to send around any son of mine who might turn into as good a mathematician as myself. That's you, Fred. With your help I'll be in a better position to send you to school" (March Folder).

Fred got the job, at no surprise to him. Starting as a draft clerk and general flunky, he gradually moved up through Christmas savings clerk to teller to discount clerk. He had a pleasant face and nice manners and he knew the folks who did business with him. And banking wasn't so bad. He liked the business, in a mild way, and continued to think perhaps he might become a banker. But it was very vaguely that he thought about it, for at night he went home and loosened all his repressed facial expressions—bankers are supposed to have but one. Fred would stomp around the parlor, sparing no gestures, mimicking whoever impressed him at the bank that day, entertaining Mr. Bickel immensely, with Mother Bickel valiantly ignoring her youngest and most vociferous child.

Fred worked at the bank until fall of 1916, earning $75 a month and leading a wholly uneventful life. The only excitement during this interval was on an August afternoon in 1915 when a Chicago film company arrived in Racine to shoot *A Summer Day in Racine*, in which seventeen-year-old Fred Bickel had a small part. In his film debut, Fred rode in a car, wearing the popular straw hat of that era, and waved. An awesome beginning. Life persisted in moving slowly. Fred taught Sunday School, went to local dances and regularly attended live theater at the Orpheum, or if he was lucky, at the ornate Davidson Theater in Milwaukee. Weary of waiting for Fred, Julia married another boy. Finally, during the summer of 1916, Mr. Bickel decided it was high time Fred went to college. On his oldest brother Harold's advice, he applied and was accepted at the University of Wisconsin in Madison, but would keep his ties to the bank by working summers and Christmas breaks, thereby helping to fund his education.

Jack Ramsey and Chuck Carpenter also planned on attending the university, majoring in letters and science, while Fred would enter the School of Commerce. Landing in Madison early September 1916, the first item on their college agenda was to gain acceptance into a fraternity, the same one Fred had written to his brother Jack about a few years back, Alpha Delta Phi. Fortunately for the remnants of the College Avenue Gang, all were "rushed" and welcomed into the Alpha Delts, remaining in that fraternity for their college duration and attending many Alpha Delt reunions throughout the rest of their lives.

Fraternities, like families, wanted their boys to be "somebody," or "a big man on the hill." A young man might shine either on the hill or on Langdon Street where the various sorority houses were. However, if you shone on the hill it often happened you fell woefully short in accomplishments with the ladies. A "good dater" to a fraternity was sometimes rated equally as valuable to chapter prestige as a "grind" on the hill, a chap who could be counted upon to drag up the fraternity average at those crucial moments —final exams. Fred belonged to neither group but spanned both. Enrolled in the School of Commerce, one of the most difficult on the hill, he made superior grades. He was not a constant shadow at sorority parties but when he did appear he was affable and entertaining. Fred Bickel was a man the fraternity brothers knew would fail at nothing, whether in his big man on the hill duties, his grades, *or* scoring with his current "girl," for he was still forever falling in and out of love.

Continuing in the tradition he had established in high school, that of joining anything and everything, Fred was the assistant manager of the 1917 varsity football team, accountant for the 1918 *Badger Annual*, honor member of the Sophomore Society of the Skull and Crescent, plus active in the university's Corps of Cadets, attaining Sergeant of Company I January 9, 1917, and advancing to First Sergeant of Company G on November 1, 1917. During his freshman year, Fred wanted to act again and joined one of the two male dramatic clubs, the Edwin Booth Society, a group that had broken away from the older drama society, Haresfoot. A rule was in effect at that time preventing membership in both, so Chuck Carpenter joined Haresfoot. Much has been written and recorded about Fred's assumed membership in Haresfoot. During the thirties, a framed photograph of him hung in the Haresfoot office, autographed by him, "It is nice of you to want my picture, but I was never a member of Haresfoot" (March Papers). However, he did compete in the Haresfoot Follies, acting vignettes sponsored by the Haresfoot Club, on December 8, 1917, singing "Whenever I Think of You." Fred inclined more toward comedy routines, especially acting out popular songs of the day.

At that time the university did not promote theater, hence, the only opportunity one had to emote was in the junior or senior plays, in which one had to *be* a junior or senior in order to qualify for the cast. Of course, Fred was only a lowly freshman, so he turned to the activities that the various theater societies held, small plays sponsored either by the male groups, Haresfoot and Edwin Booth, or by their female counterparts, Red Domino and Twelfth Night. The theater group's dramas or comedies, as the case may be, were relegated to the women's gym in Lathrop Hall—that is, if you were careful to arrange a time when the women weren't practicing volleyball in their bloomers. However, these groups tended to place the more advanced members of their societies into these plays, rather than an unknown such as Fred Bickel.

That left only debating, which Fred already knew he was a failure in, and freshman declamatory (the university equivalent to oratory). Now, here was an area he could *shine* in, and why not inflict Grattan's "Invective against Corry" upon yet another set of judges. The date was February 19, 1917, and Fred M. Bickel won first place in the preliminary Open Freshman Declamatory contest. This earned him the right to compete against nine other freshmen, all representing the various men's literary societies. On March 8, 1917, Fred had no trouble competing on the university level and won the freshman "Dec," receiving a gold fob medal for his efforts. The university student paper, *The Daily Cardinal*, reported the next day, "A rich oratorical voice accompanied by perfect platform poise" (March Papers).

Another event that the drama societies sponsored and competed among themselves in was Union Vodvil, held annually at the Fuller Opera House in downtown Madison. Each club would put together various acts, practicing wherever they could find an empty room. The acts were then allowed only *one* rehearsal on the actual Fuller stage and this was after 11:00 p.m., when the movie was over, lasting until 4:00 a.m., under the watchful eye of the dean of women to make sure there was *no* frivolity! Fred first ventured into Union Vodvil in a combined Haresfoot and Edwin Booth Dramatic Society production called *The Unseen Host,* by Percival Wild (with Paul Rudy, the female impersonator Haresfoot half) on January 26, 1918, with Fred acting the surgeon. They won second prize.

By spring 1918, everyone on campus knew who Fred Bickel was, either through Vodvil appearances, his continued good grades or his success with the various sororities. He was dubbed "the actor" at the fraternity house, although he had no idea at the time of becoming one. After class and after campus organizations had met, Fred would sometimes stride into the Frat house with a mimic mood upon him. He was, for the moment, the president of the university; he was Teddy Roosevelt; he was any figure who created current talk. Fred would strike dramatic poses and go through various contortions of pantomime that sent his brethren into gales of laughter. "Big men on the campus" were also given responsibilities and those that came to Fred Bickel were not lightly discharged, especially those of the man-to-man sort. After the hours of study were over, many of the younger boys invariably drifted to Fred's room for a little jawing, wanting advice on courses, on "the right girl for a date" or "other reasons" and on the unraveling of some personal entanglement.

Methodical by mind and training, Fred had a college room that could have been inspected at any time by the president of the national chapter. Fred believed that objects had places, and should be in them. He had a set time for rising in the morning—and arose. He had an allotted time for study, for his campus activities, for his recreation. He never let one or the other get out of hand. "Fred accomplished such an enormous lot of things," one of his fraternity brothers said, "just because he planned his day" (March Papers). When Fred Bickel studied, he studied. When he wanted fun, he had that, too.

On at least one occasion, however, Fred did forget his standard operating procedure. A fellow student remembered that an entertaining Fred knew how to get into the good graces of the English instructor. Apparently, one day, she called for Fred Bickel to read his theme in class. Fred stood up, read from some papers in his hands, and promptly received an 'A.' However, when he sat back down, it was noticed by his classmate that he had not done his homework, for there was not a word written on those papers. He had made it up as he went along! Obviously, the beginnings of an actor.

3

World War and the University

World war loomed large in the lives of Fred Bickel, Chuck Carpenter and Jack Ramsey as they were busy studying for final exams during the spring of 1918. In fact, Jack planned on going to Fort Sheridan for a preliminary one month training camp for infantry officers on June 3. Fred wanted to apply for Officer's Candidacy hoping to impress his newest girlfriend, Aline Ellis, a flour mill heiress from Indiana, and her more stern mother, a widow who felt Fred too immature for her daughter. In fact, Fred had delayed asking Aline to marry him because of his inability to get along with her mother. He seemed to feel that if he joined the army, becoming an officer of merit, winning medals, *overwhelming* Mrs. Ellis with his ability, then how could she stand in his way?

As it turned out, Fred did join up and went first to Fort Sheridan June 3 to July 3, 1918, then applied for Officers' Candidacy with the Field Artillery Central Officers Training School. Heading for Camp Zachary Taylor July 17, 1918, Fred was commissioned a second lieutenant in the artillery and looked forward to seeing some action overseas. However, instead of going overseas he was retained as an instructor of equestrianism. He recalled to *Screenland*, "Heaven knows why, because up to that time my only riding had been done on the fat indolent pony we had as children" (March Papers). After serving a period there, during which time the Armistice was declared and all hopes of covering himself with military glory went glimmering, he was sent to Fort Sill, Oklahoma. The war ended on February 7, 1919, with Fred mustered out in time for the second semester of the 1918–1919 year at Wisconsin (discharged February 10, 1919).

Aline Elizabeth Ellis, also a junior in 1919, majoring in letters and science and hailing from Evansville, Indiana, was Fred Bickel's college sweetheart. Most likely, Fred met Aline during their sophomore year during the small staged dramas their respective societies sponsored, for Aline was a member of the women's drama society, Twelfth Night. She had also been an army nurse for six months while Fred was at Fort Sill. Aline was quite a bit shorter in stature than Fred but they were a stunning couple together and most congenial. She had very black hair that accentuated the clearness of her skin and formed a decided semiframe for her regular features. She dressed very well and knew how to wear her clothes, using practically no makeup, never wearing electric colors, and yet she was the kind of person one noticed and remembered. Her unusually large dark eyes had something to do with this; they were fascinating, but seemed to be always sad. Fred and Aline would take long walks along Madison's Lake Mendota or sometimes he would bring a book and the evening would be spent reading together. Occasionally they attended a movie and stopped at a chocolate shop afterward. Fred's first cousin, Kathryn Davis, recalled how Fred worshiped Aline. "She was so dear to him, such a darling shy person, when I met her. Fred adored her—he was wonderful to Aline" (Interview, Kathryn Davis, 17 September 1990). They were in love.

One comment about their relationship from the senior *Badger Annual* of 1920 in the humor section related a nonsensical conversation of the various Gamma Phi Betas (Aline's sorority) during a chapter meeting. The chapter president was teasing Aline, "That reminds me, the girls are complaining that you and Fred are getting more than your fair share of the parlor!" Fred escorted Aline to the Junior/Senior Prom in 1920—Wisconsin veterans of these proms know that that is almost like announcing the engagement. They went steady during their last two years at the university, becoming engaged by the end of their senior year. After all his girl chasing, Fred Bickel had finally settled on the young woman who was to be his wife.

About this time Fred and his steadfast friend and fraternity brother, another 'big man' on campus, Chuck Carpenter, started amusing the other brethren at the chapter house with jokes and songs to relieve the boredom of continued study. Chuck was clever at the piano and Fred made a perfect straight man or foil for him plus he sang ditties well. The boys were persuaded to make a real team of it and do the act for Union Vodvil under the name Carpenter and Bickel. They entered the Union Vodvil competition presenting a sketch called "Undertones" by the Assassins of Sorrow (alias Carpenter and Bickel) on April 24, 1919, chattering, singing and joking their way into third place. "It was a grand act," a classmate remembered. "Chuck was one of the campus funny boys and Bickel had swell stage presence, also poise and popularity. The act was big stuff in those days. All you had to do was to lug on a piano and the act was ready made. And the boys weren't bashful" (March Papers).

Fred next decided to try his luck in the junior play tryouts for the romantic lead of Percinet in *The Romancers* by Rostand, a play that had all the necessary ingredients for success: duels, abductions, conspiracies, parental quarrels and a love affair. With the experience afforded him in past Union Vodvil productions, plus his exceptional good looks, Fred was the obvious choice. The *Daily Cardinal* student paper started advertising for the play on May 23, 1919: "'Kiss me, Sylvett.' 'Never!' But she does a minute later. All this occurs in the first act of *The Romancers*, the three act comedy which the Juniors will present in the open-air theater next Friday evening. Fred Bickel is the amorous swain and sweet, demure, Helen Colby is the girl in question. This, perhaps, is why Fred is the only man in the cast who has never cut a rehearsal!"

On May 26, 1919, Fred received his first review from the *Daily Cardinal*: "Fred Bickel was burdened with a wordy part but came through well. His scenes with Miss Colby, while they discussed the 'abduction,' was like the Fred of Union Vodvil and Edwin Booth. Subtle, sly humor fits Bickel well." One fellow classmate remembered a dedicated young actor who was very earnest about parts he took, wanting every detail right, putting everything into a part, becoming the part. Even when arguing about a set, the answer was always, "That's the way Fred wants it and that's the way it was!" That summer Fred also became one of the founding members of the National Collegiate Players, Pi Epsilon Delta, the honorary dramatic fraternity founded at the University of Wisconsin on June 2, 1919.

Because he had spent so much time away during the war, Fred was unable to go home to his bank job in summer of 1919, having instead to attend classes to qualify for senior status by fall of 1919. Therefore, he waited on tables at various fraternity houses to earn spending money. Oswald Peters, also majoring in Commerce and a graduate of the 1920 class, recalled in a 1990 interview.

> I waited on table several times with Fred Bickel. Fred knew I needed help financially. It was all I could do one meal to the next. So Fred got me some extra jobs waiting on table in his fraternity. When there was a break between courses, we would sit in the kitchen and talk. He was usually quite serious and would talk about such things as the importance of the "human element" and integrity in our future careers.

Peters also commented on the inherent comic side of Fred's character, "One time, Stephen Gilman, Professor of Commercial Law, was late for a lecture session. While we were waiting, Fred took the podium for several minutes and impersonated the professor. His performance —the gestures, frowns, scowls, grimaces and piercing eyes—had the place in an uproar. We should have known then that he was a born actor" (Interview, Oswald Peters, 18 February, 1990).

As Fred's senior year approached, he contemplated running for class president, which would be a hefty job, outside class work, table waiting and his managing the football team that fall. He would be the obvious candidate, nonetheless, for he had a wonderful outgoing personality. He liked everybody and everybody liked him and was the most popular member of the class, even above any athlete. Deciding to run, Fred won by a large margin in one of the most spiritedly contested university elections, in which more votes were cast than in any previous competition for offices at the university. Elected October 28, 1919, he announced long lists of committees, which, like all senior committees, past and present, did nothing. He did, however, manage to launch the first student fund-raising campaign to build a student union. Previous campaigns canvassed the alumni only, while Fred's petitioned all university students. One out of every two students became a life member of the student union fund, contributing $50 per student. He was helped in this effort by fellow student Larry Hall, a cheerleader and roommate while on the road during football season. Larry was to remain one of Fred's lifelong friends.

As seniors, Fred and Chuck continued their popular partnership of Carpenter and Bickel. Feeling for one last time the pull of the stage, they put together a final Union Vodvil act, "The Gloom Picklers present 'The Sunshiners in Unsuppressed Desires.'" On April 3, at the Fuller Opera House, Chuck Carpenter and Fred Bickel broke up the scenery and set the stage for their own number. They opened informally by shoving in the piano and from then on kept up a steady line of lighthearted chatter, a happy combination of wit and satire on preceding acts, winning third prize.

Fred was one of the few students who qualified scholastically to join the Honorary Commerce Fraternity and the Iron Cross, the Honorary Senior Society. He had also been a member of the Honorary Junior Society, an organization, unfortunately, named "Ku Klux Klan," something that would plague Fred years later. During the spring of 1920 Professor Gilman nominated Fred Bickel for a special banking scholarship. Frank Vanderlip of the National City Bank in New York was launching an experiment that would take a number of college boys and train them as apprentices in the main branch for eventual work in the foreign branches. As Fred remembered in the *Screenland* interview: "It sounded romantic—one might be sent to Berlin or Rio or Singapore or anywhere. One saw oneself—'the young foreign banker,' in sun helmet and trailed by admiring natives, driving along picturesque streets in carriages, a potentate of finance" (March Papers). His previous two years with the Racine bank gave him an additional advantage—the scholarship was his.

Fred Bickel had a future beyond Racine, Wisconsin, and was eager to start that future, with Aline, of course. With the Vanderlip Scholarship in hand, all that remained was graduation. His life looked promising, for the moment. On May 15, 1920, he was to escort Aline to the large men's gymnasium at the

University of Wisconsin to the annual Junior/Senior Prom, where Aline displayed her new engagement ring. Unfortunately, it was at the prom that Aline broke the news to Fred that her mother wanted to know what their future exactly entailed, asking him pointedly to prove his worth.

Fred explained to Aline that after the scholarship program was through he fully expected to become the *greatest* banker New York had ever seen, with an appointment in London, Paris or perhaps Rome. Aline's mother, however, wanted her to stay in Indiana near her family, rather than traipsing after Fred until he was a success. In other words, delay their marriage. Apparently Mrs. Ellis worried about how Fred would take care of Aline, especially in New York. It can only be guessed at how Fred accepted this news but according to his first cousin he did ask Aline what she wanted to do. Aline felt they should postpone their marriage until he became more established. She would go home to Indiana and they would write. That way, her mother could not possibly object to their marriage. Fred, however, wanted to marry Aline immediately, stating that he already felt old at age twenty-two and that most couples had already started families. His almost perfect senior year seemed to be collapsing, all in one night, a night that had now taken on a somber overtone. Aline, however was adamant, stating, "If we wait, Fred, it will give me more time to convince Mother. Don't you love me enough to wait?"

"Of course I love you." Then, one can imagine Fred turning away from Aline, staring at the dancers in the gaily decorated but crowded gymnasium. "I'll wait." Then, dejectedly, "I'll wait."

4

New York, New York

Needless to say, Aline had dampened Fred's spirits. He had no time to dwell on this, for he had speeches and farewell addresses to write plus commencement exercises to organize. These activities kept his mind off Aline's unwillingness to get married, for the moment.

The monthly *Commerce Student Business Magazine* carried some remarks by Fred to fellow students: "Too many undergraduates in the Commerce School become discouraged and decide to change their course. If they feel they desire an entirely different kind of education, this is undoubtedly the right thing to do, but often the change is made because of a lack of stick-to-itive-ness. While we maintain our loyalty to the finest Commerce Course any university offers, let us remember always that there are no quitters at Wisconsin" (March Papers). Fred graduated with honors June 21, 1920, kissed Aline good-bye, with promises to write, and headed for Racine to begin packing for New York. Chuck Carpenter and Jack Ramsey were home, too, before they embarked on their separate courses. The College Avenue Gang had now shrunk to one member, Vinnie Hood, who had remained in Racine selling real estate as he had planned back in 1914.

The National City Bank scholarship involved employment for a year in the New York City office preparatory to a post in the National City's foreign branch service. Fred lived in a nice old rooming-house in Brooklyn Heights overlooking all New York, working in the bank during the daytime and studying the banking program at night. He had a sweet old landlady who was an ex-vaudeville actress, nutty about actors and always talking about the acting profession. The atmosphere of New York on the brink of what was eventually referred to as the "Roaring Twenties," must have been an exciting one for the Wisconsin youth, a decade of sensations. Never has a modern people been so recklessly dedicated to thrills or to keeping itself amused. The whole nation was becoming restless, dissatisfied, hectic, and it was smart to mock everything that had once seemed sacred. In such an environment, the bank program soon became tedious to Fred. His postgraduate existence as an important cog in a financial machine translated to just another post in a cage of the New York branch of the National City Bank. After Fred had been at the bank about two months, there was a shake-up in the bank personnel and James Stillman took over the directorship. Stillman was not as enthusiastic about Vanderlip's experiment and the college apprentices became a little uneasy about their futures. None was being sent to a foreign branch. What was more likely to follow was a long apprenticeship with perhaps the final reward of becoming assistant cashier. Another Wisconsin graduate located in New York who occasionally saw Fred remarked, "His attitude toward life in general was different than in college; he was definitely bored by the routine of bank life" (Interview, Oswald Peters, 18 February, 1990).

For diversion, Fred managed to attend as much theater as his small salary and the bank hours would allow. He eventually began to think about acting as a career at this time, but hesitated, knowing what Aline's mother might do, not to mention his own parents' disappointment. But the decision was made for him fall of 1920 at noon, when Fred doubled over in acute pain while at his job. Fellow bank employees took him home, not realizing that Fred was undergoing an appendicitis attack. His landlady immediately sent for a doctor, who sent for an ambulance. As Fred waited for the ambulance, his landlady distracted him from the pain and fear by relating anecdotes from her days in the theater. When he went under the anesthetic before his operation, those stories were the last things he thought about. Hours later, he awoke with a new resolve—to be an actor or else!

Throughout convalescence, Fred devoured books on the history of the theater. All notions of becoming a financier were quietly interred after months of debilitating bank routine. He knew his family would be opposed to his appendix born idea, so he confided only in his sister-in-law, Mary, wife of his older brother, Jack, who lived in New Jersey. She supported him in this but questioned him about how Aline might feel. This had worried Fred but he felt their love for each other would see them through any crisis. Unfortunately, he had not bargained on Aline's strong-willed mother, for there was no way that her daughter would marry an impoverished, just-starting-out "actor." Fred, though, was adamant about his chosen future as he had been adamant in all things, once he made up his mind, and alienated Aline. For whatever reason, she chose her mother's side. Aline was to never see Fred again in her lifetime. She followed her mother's advice, marrying a prominent Indianapolis businessman. During a 1990 interview, her daughter commented that it annoyed her mother if anyone found out that she had once been engaged to Fredric March. In fact, Aline *never* talked about him, *never* even went to his movies. Fred did not quite recover from his love of Aline, though, for years later in 1970 at his fiftieth college reunion, he asked his hosts, hopefully, "Is Aline here? (Interview, Virginia Hall, 18 May 1990).

Methodical and farsighted as ever, Fred wrote the bank, asking for a six-month leave of absence. He would burn no bridges behind him, would this aspiring young actor. Another letter, far more difficult to write, went to Racine. It was thoughtfully received, carefully read. The Bickels were somewhat bewildered. Their son had never shown a real outward desire to go on the stage before; life seemed so pleasantly cut out for him. The stage presentations they had seen in Racine—well, the Bickels thought them cheap if they considered them at all. It all seemed so perilous. They advised him to take the time off to get it out of his system. Fred promised to be the same when he left the theater as he was now.

Nineteen twenty! Fred thought of it less as the beginning of that decade than as the year that "Banking lost Bickel to Broadway." All his nice conventional desires for big business had vanished as if they had been extracted along with his appendix. He was reborn, and felt so *special* that he had few qualms about the theaters' ability to recognize that here was something rather remarkable. All idea of doing anything but securing a job in the theater left Fred. He had no notion of how one went about it, but suddenly he saw very clearly that this was what he had always, subconsciously, wanted and intended. The fact that he didn't have the faintest idea *how* he was going to be an actor troubled him not at all. Fred beat the pavements and made the rounds of casting offices, who promptly threw him out because he had no photographs. So, he had some cheap pictures made—shirt open at the throat, two fingers contemplatively against the temple. Seeing them, he thought, "Why, I really look just like an actor already!" (*Screenland*, 1932, March Papers). He proceeded to leave an attractive photo of himself at the various agents with the following statistics typed on the back:

Bickel, Fred M.	32 waist	Main 9938 Home
12 Sidney Pl.	9 1/2 shoe	Bryant 16 Office
Bklyn.	8 glove	23 yrs.
5-11"	will not pose in underwear	
158 lbs.	(March Papers)	

He then waited, and waited, and waited—until his monetary situation forced him to find other jobs. Until his big break happened, for he was sure it would happen soon, Fred took full advantage of his striking John Barrymore –like profile by posing for such famous artists as Charles Dana Gibson and Howard Chandler Christy and for Arrow collar advertisements.

Finally, one of the theatrical agencies he besieged gave him a bit part in a silent movie. This was a jolt for Fred, as he was having quite a spell of Shakespeare at the time and his hopes had been centered on Shakespearean drama as the ultimate in theater, especially after he saw John Barrymore in that actor's first Shakespearean role in *The Tragedy of Richard III*. Therefore, this fooling around in the low commerce of movies was distasteful to Fred, but he went along anyway, assuring himself that this was merely one of the exigencies of art. He worked as an extra in a movie called *Pay the Piper* being made in Astoria for Paramount Pictures. He became one of a group of "supes," actors needed for crowd scenes, one of the mob and not very happy about it—until the paychecks were passed out and he discovered that he had made $7.50 a day, of which 75 cents went to the agent. That was a horse of an entirely different hue and the crasser half of his nature responded in delight. Seven and a half a day—that made forty-five dollars a week—one hundred and eighty dollars a month! Movies weren't so low after all. The future loomed ahead in a rosy glow of prosperity and it was not long before Fred got to know the ropes of mob acting. With such an orderly mind, he soon became leader of the "supes." When someone was needed to cut in on the heroine dancing in a ballroom, Fred was the boy chosen. He was, however, only a black shoulder and arm to frame the pretty face of the star.

On other occasions he played an extra in *The Great Adventure*, starring Lionel Barrymore, and again in *The Education of Elizabeth* with Billie Burke, plus *The Devil* with George Arliss. It was some time during this interval that Fred met the distinguished silent film director D. W. Griffith, a biographical event notable only for its futility. Fred saw the great man at a theater and rushed him—diffidence not being one of his weaknesses. Introducing himself, using mutual friends in Kentucky as a weapon, Fred hardly gave the poor man time to answer. He called Griffith's attention to his supposed resemblance to Richard Barthelmess and asked whether Griffith would like to make a test of him as a possibility for Barthelmess's double and stand-in. Griffith politely and briefly suggested Fred call his assistant at Mamaroneck about it. He did, but nothing ever came of it.

In between decorating the far backgrounds of movies, and not wanting to overlook any means of keeping a little cash in his pocket, Fred went back to immortalizing cravats, shoes, shaving cream and the like, plus renewed posing for the various commercial artists. Fred commented to *Screenland*,

Don't let anyone tell you that posing for artists is a sissy job. I think my interlude of modeling was as good for me as those strenuous working-out exercises I heard about and was too lazy to take. Muscular control is necessary if you hope to get through one morning without falling off the stand. Standing straight and taut for two and three hours does a lot for coordination of the nervous system. What I'm getting at is it's darned hard work and doesn't deserve the stigma that is on it. (March Papers)

It was not long after that Fred heard David Belasco was preparing a new production, *Deburau*, a tragicomedy in four acts adapted by Granville Barker from the French of Sacha Guitry, and needed at least fifty "supes." Of 300 hopeful candidates, Fred was rejected, so he went back to modeling, dreaming of his eventual discovery, which came quite by accident. While he was posing for Leon Gordon, his first important opportunity came, unexpectedly. Gordon had asked him to stop by a theater to obtain some seats for *Lady of the Lamp*. On his way from the box office he saw the agent who had sent him on his first silent film job for Paramount. Since it never seemed to bother Fred to jump at people he hardly knew, he accosted him breezily and asked whether he had anything yet. Fortunately, he did, and at the Belasco Theater on Forty-fourth Street. It seemed that *Deburau*, the same play Fred had tried to get into as a supe, needed someone right away for the very small part of Victor Hugo, no experience necessary. Fred looked near enough to their idea of Hugo to get by so he was hired *and* in a prestigious *Belasco* production for $30.00 a week. He had to play the Victor Hugo bit, work as third assistant stage manager, understudy, and play the prompter, a man who appeared but once and had one line to say. But the learning of one line was not enough for a chap who became president of everything he joined; Fred learned *all* the male parts at rehearsals. He remarked once, "Victor Hugo had no lines, but I foraged in the Public Library going through every record of Hugo I could find for material for my 'characterization!'" (March Papers).

Fred Bickel made his stage debut at Ford's Theater in Baltimore, December 7, 1920. This was the first time he had his name on a theater program outside Wisconsin. When the play moved later that month to New York, Bickel went with it and premiered on December 23. Fred felt that *Deburau* and his modest function in it were the finest training camp he could possibly have fallen into. He no longer saw himself as a gift from heaven but as a very raw novice with a devil of a lot to learn. And high time, too. In the daytime, he was still posing, or, on other occasions, doing extra work in movies. At night, he was first to arrive at the theater and last to leave—a dynamo of activity, on duty to see that all props were in the right place, rushing into his Hugo makeup, then downstairs and up again as the prompter. Fred's big moment arrived when the juvenile lead of the show had to have his tonsils out: Fred played the part for ten days. He vividly remembered to *Screenland*, "The exquisite terror and grandiloquence of that moment when I left the dark protection of the wings and stepped into the glare of the footlights, alone on the stage with an entire audience looking to me for entertainment!" (March Papers).

With such steady employment, and on some friends' advice, Fred decided to invest in some acting lessons with Madame Eva Alberti, who taught at the American Academy of Dramatic Arts. Madame Alberti directed Fred to imitate people (something he was already a class act at) he had seen on the streets or subways, telling him that the world is your workshop. When interviewed in 1935 after he had been placed first by speech experts as the most accomplished in his speaking voice and stage accent, Fred remarked about his earlier experiences in New York:

> I was mildly surprised to learn that my diction was not good enough for the stage. You see, when I went to New York I took with me my middle-Western form of speech, with its thorough pronunciation of the letter "r," and its "noo" instead of "new" as well as countless other characteristic examples of style in speech. My "r's" had to be "softened." It's "Neuspapuh" according to my teachers. Believe me, it's hard to keep on speaking good English. As a matter of fact, off-stage I slip right back into my Wisconsin dialect, with its "tuhnight," "tuhday," "meetcha tuhmorrow," and all the rest. (*Los Angeles Sunday Times*, 26 December 1935, March Papers)

When the run of *Deburau* ended, Belasco invited Fred to become understudy for the following season, but friends counseled him to look for juvenile roles in other plays rather than risk the vague chances of an understudy. So, at the age of twenty-three, after *Deburau* closed, Fred secured a part in a non-Broadway production of George Ade's show *The County Chairman*, a play he was familiar with because of his second male lead in that same play when he was a senior in high school. He then obtained the second juvenile lead in a road company of *Shavings*. Back in New York by winter of 1921, Fred had a small part in Al Jolson's *Lei Aloha* and then procured his first "real" part on Broadway in a William Brady production of Jules Eckert Goodman's *The Lawbreaker*, which opened February 1, 1922. Fred's first New York review was for his performance in *The Lawbreaker*. "A remarkable unaffected performance of the banker's weak and troubled son by Frederick Bickel" (March Papers). It was during the run of *The Lawbreaker* that Fred met and became life long friends with John Cromwell, also acting in the production, who felt Fred should change his name from Frederick Bickel to something more appropriate. From Fred's diary, January 9, 1922—"Ate with Mr. Collins and Mr. Dempsey who agrees with Mr. Cromwell (John) that my name should be changed" (March Papers). However, he would not officially change it for two more years.

Brady next offered Fred a long-term contract, which bowled him over, thinking he had finally "arrived." Fortunately, he checked himself in time with "Here, here, Bickel. You've still got a terrific lot to learn." Therefore, he decided a Midwest stock company would benefit from his thespian talents (*he* would profit from the experience, too). In 1918 a new stock company was based in Dayton, Ohio, the Brownell-Stork Company (married couple Mabel Brownell and Clifford Stork). From April 1 to October 2, 1922, the company played summer stock at the Victory Theater and the following summer found the Dayton Players Starring Mabel Brownell at the Victory once more, opening July 9 and closing October 8, 1923. All told, Mabel Brownell spent six summers in Dayton. Two of those summers, 1922 and 1923, included in their stock of actors a young juvenile named Frederick Bickel, who, with a regretful glance at the salary Brady offered, went off to Dayton, Ohio, for twenty-three weeks playing, on the whole, pretty dumb juveniles. But even that, in a stock company, was good training. Acting then wasn't difficult for him because he was playing young men his own age. When the Brownell Players presented their Premiere Play, *Enter Madame*, April 22, 1922, the *Dayton Journal* of April 25 recognized a new talent with "Next among the new ones was Frederick Bickel, the new juvenile. Mr. Bickel shows promise that cannot be overlooked." And again in *The Men She Married*, it was Fred the audiences remembered. "Mr. Bickel, the juvenile, is a 'comer' in his profession—can we say more? His youth and experience we shall always remember with more affection then the play" (March Papers).

While at Dayton Fred met visiting actress Ellis Baker, daughter of the playwright Edith Ellis. Ellis Baker was born in Muskegon, Michigan, October 26, 1898. She was the third generation representative of a theatrical family, also being the niece of Edward Ellis. Making her stage debut at age five in *The Point of View*, she was also featured in such plays as *Beatrice and the Blackguard*, *The Arabian*, *The Firebrand*, *I Like It Here*, *The Little Foxes*, *A Man's House*, *Fallen Angels*, and *Some Call It Madness*. Most of these offerings were performed while she was stock at Great Neck, Long Island. Fred, still unsophisticated plus extremely impressionable, looked up to Ellis as she had already made a name for herself in stock. Ellis remarked in a February 1937 *Picture Play* interview; "He was sweet and enthusiastic and terribly romantic—and Fred was so terribly earnest about becoming a really good actor. Not just an actor, or even just a very highly paid actor—but a good actor" (March Papers). They started 'seeing' one another, first in Dayton, then back in New York, becoming an "item." Ellis, and, of course, her mother, were invaluable mentors to a young man with such lofty ambitions, advising him to continue stock until he had mastered sufficient theater technique. The nature of their work, naturally, caused Ellis and Fred to endure long separations but he made even absences seem pleasant. Determined, Fred sent Ellis love letters every day. Even when she went to Europe, he arranged for her to receive a letter and some little present daily, causing Ellis to remark that he was the most romantic man she had ever met before or since. Their long-distance courtship developed into an engagement by the end of 1923.

After another summer season with the Brownell Players in Dayton, Fred secured a part in *Zeno* to open first in Chicago. *Zeno* broke the house record December 7, 1923, at the Hempstead Theater, but when it moved on to New York, it flopped, and was soon canceled. John Cromwell, who was now producing and directing plays, happened to see Fred in *Zeno*'s short Broadway life and, remembering him from *The Lawbreaker*, offered him a contract. Fred accepted with characteristic enthusiasm.

By now, the Bickels realized Fred had no intention of going back to banking. They still were not totally sold on his being an actor, but they understood his drive for perfection and dug in for the duration.

5

My Name Is Fredric March

John Cromwell, fellow actor, director, but more often than not, a good friend, was promoting Fred in early 1924 and often complained about his last name Bickel. Ellis, too, did not like his last name. They set about concocting various stage names. One story related that Ellis wanted him to use his middle name and her first name: McIntyre Ellis. But he could not abide a name like that, being too used to "Fred," so stood his ground. Finally, they settled on his idea, Fredric March. Another story has it that since twelve was a lucky number for him, he shortened his mother's maiden name from Marcher to March, and changed Frederick to the phonetic form. Regardless, Fred sent the following piece (March Papers) to all the agents he could find.

> This is 1924,
> I won't be Bickel any more!
> Fredric March is now my name,
> Wishing everyone the same,
> Happy New Year!

Fred was soon off to fulfill theater commitments by May. He made use of his new stage name, "Fredric March," in his first assignment under Cromwell's supervision, May 13, 1924, as the juvenile in *The Melody Man*, a comedy by Herbert Richard Lorenz and opening at the Ritz Theater in New York. *The Melody Man* only ran for fifty-six performances but afforded Fred two soon-to-be-life time friends: John Cromwell, of course, and the young Richard Rodgers, who had a few tunes in the show. After it closed, Fred took some time off to consider his future, especially where Ellis Baker figured into it. By this time, college love Aline had yet to respond to any of his letters, and he had heard through some college friends that she had become recently engaged to a prominent Indianapolis businessman, someone that Aline's mother approved of. Bitter, Fred made up his mind. While Ellis was playing Chicago in *The Show Off*, spring of 1924, he determined to cut their engagement short and marry before he was to start in John Cromwell's August production of *Tarnish*, also in Chicago. They eloped to Milwaukee and secretly married. Surprising Fred's parents the next day in Racine, Ellis was met with stiff opposition from Cora Bickel. Evidently, Cora never liked Ellis, feeling her very self-centered and engrossed with herself, not a warm friendly person and not Cora's type of person at all. Why, she even was a divorced woman. Ellis's more "worldly" personality and sometimes tactless remarks offended Cora, who was more used to the gentle shyness and beauty of Aline. Aline and Ellis were so diametrically opposite that Mrs. Bickel questioned her son's infatuation with, to her mind, a common showgirl. Fred's hometown friends were also surprised. Ellis did not seem at *all* like the kind of girls Fred had dated seriously. All were astonished to hear he had married without his parents' consent, and in front of a judge rather than a minister. This was not like the Fred they remembered. Cora did manage to hastily arrange a tea for Ellis, but that was the extent of her kindness. Sensing his parents' disapproval, Fred gathered some of his boyhood articles that he wanted in New York and shepherded Ellis back to Chicago.

Ellis managed to alienate Fred's relatives, too. Mary Bickel, wife to his older brother Jack, described her as an excessively "ladylike" creature in spiked heels who raved at length about the Bickels' dog but completely ignored Mary's new baby. Fred, however, could bear no criticism of his lady of the moment. According to Mary, when this languid damsel felt kind enough to stroll with the Bickel family on one Sunday morning, she tried running around the block on her high heels with Fred smiling fatuously, "You wouldn't know she was such an outdoor girl!" What really enraged Mary, though, as she got to know Ellis, was Ellis's bitter professional jealousy of Fred's success (unpublished article by Mary Bickel, "March-To-The-Altar," c. 1932, March Papers).

In Chicago, Fred enacted the juvenile lead of young attorney Emmett Carr in the John Cromwell production of *Tarnish* by Gilbert Emery (*Tarnish* had been one of the successes of 1923 in New York with Tom Powers as Emmett Carr). This play was to tour throughout the Midwest August 1924 through January 1925, opening in Chicago August 16, 1924, at the Oliver Theater. *Tarnish* was a great success for Fred. O. L. Hall reviewed the play: "Mr. March as Emmett Carr, brings you forward in your seat. Yesterday, at the Oliver, he did a rare piece of work. It would be hard to imagine anyone more convincing or genuine. He went straight under the skin of his part, into the flesh, bone and marrow. He made us live with him the emotions of a not extraordinary youth in an extraordinary situation" (March Papers).

The troupe closed in Chicago on September 25, 1924, moving on to Kansas City and opening at the Shubert Theater on September 27. Traveling next to

Peoria to present *Tarnish* at the Orpheum Theater the month of October, they ended up in Indianapolis at the Murat Theater by November 7. Walter Wittworth, the Indianapolis theater reviewer, reported that there was a player in *Tarnish* who was more important than the play: "This Fredric March, who is the blemished hero of the piece, is honest, sincere, straightforward and unaffected in his work. He bears watching, for he has talent and a proficient knowledge of his craft. It is a rare sight to find a juvenile lead free from the stagy mannerisms and affectations so soon acquired, and Mr. March has no taint of these iniquities" (March Papers). After Indianapolis, *Tarnish* went to Detroit at the Garrick, November 10; Cleveland, at the Hanna, November 17; and Pittsburgh on November 25. The *Pittsburgh Post* prophetically compared March's skill to that of the great John Barrymore (little did Fred realize just how much Barrymore was to influence him in the near future). The play moved to Cincinnati, December 1; Toronto, December 30; finally closing the run in Baltimore on January 6, 1925.

Almost immediately Fred was cast as Bruno Monte in *The Knife in the Wall*, a melodrama about the members of a circus puppeteer troupe by Frances Lightner, to open at the Providence Opera House February 2, 1925. The Providence paper accounted: "Few actors, and Mr. March is a young and apparently most promising actor, have given us the impression they are not acting at all, that there is no audience, that they are the character being played" (March Papers). *The Knife in the Wall* moved to New Haven on February 17 and premiered in New York at the Selwyn Theater, March 9. In New Haven, Miriam Hopkins was brought in to replace Berta Donn in the lead role of Angela Smith. Years later Fred remarked to *Screenland*, "Little did Miriam know I would one day choke her to death in front of a camera in *Dr. Jekyll and Mr. Hyde*" (March Papers). It was in New York that the name of the play was changed to *Puppets*. Changing locations on April 26, and the name back to *The Knife in the Wall*, the play closed in Chicago.

Fred and Ellis next toured Europe during an infrequent hiatus. Arguments ensued, for Ellis was forever trying to manage every aspect of Fred's life, primarily his career. Fred, by now, however, felt he was managing fairly well *without* her! Fortunately, he was called back to New York in answer to a cable from John Cromwell requesting that he play Richard Knight in John's production of *Harvest*, opening September 19 at the Belmont in New York. Naturally, Ellis disagreed with Fred's choice, presumably chanting "I told you so" when *Harvest* was generally panned by its reviewers, with criticisms such as "six or seven generally dull and uninteresting people sit around a Michigan farm house boring themselves and all within earshot" (March Papers). After *Harvest*, Fred was cast as Anthony Harrison Converse in a three act comedy, *The Balcony Walkers*, that ran November 13 in New York, November 17 in Bridgeport, closing in New Haven, November 20—another bomb. The kindest review said "The cast is better than the play" (March Papers).

Proceedings were not going at all well in the March household. The continual separations, both performing in different tours and cities, arguments plus the slow realization that Ellis was close to a textbook description of an alcoholic, began to wear on Fred. Even so, Ellis was unaware of her affect on him, fondly remembering in the *Picture Play* article "He had the most extraordinary quality of endearing himself to people so much that immediately they would feel a deep personal interest in his well-being and his future" (March Papers). Ellis recalled that Fred often scolded her for not putting herself out more to be nice to people who might help him or further his career. Apparently, even before he became a great success, Fred had mastered the technique of endearing himself to everyone up and down the line, from office boy to producer. Fredric March would soon outgrow his need of Ellis Baker.

He appeared next in *The Half Caste*, March 29, 1926, at the National Theater in New York as a weak-willed, spoiled, drunk young man named Dick Chester. Fred impersonated the unlucky debauchee as well as possible, likely drawing from his home experiences with Ellis. It was while Fred was performing in *The Half Caste* that Melville Burke, current director of the Elitch's Gardens summer stock theater in Denver, Colorado, recognized his talent. Burke was so impressed with Fred's potential that he recommended him as leading man for the following 1926 summer season to John Mulvihill, the manager of the Gardens. As Fred remembered it "I felt exceedingly fortunate to be selected as leading man in 1926. It was the tradition of the place. At that time it was known all over the East and it was considered a feather in the cap of an actor to have played a season at Elitch's. Anyone who was successful there had an excellent chance of getting better parts when he returned to New York" (Levy 1960, 260).

Ellis urged him to go to Denver even though it would mean another three month separation. She could not be expected to comprehend what the summer of 1926 would cost her as she waved good-bye to her husband at Grand Central.

6

Florence

Fredric March met Florence Eldridge on a cross country train to Denver, Colorado, in May of 1926, reportedly in the dining car. The usually vociferous Fred felt his throat constrict when he realized the attractive young lady who sat opposite him was none other than Florence Eldridge, star of Broadway's *The Great Gatsby*. He had just seen the play and felt she did a marvelous job as Daisy. Fred at this time must have appeared to Florence as an extremely handsome man of about age twenty-seven or twenty-eight. After light conversation, both realized they were to play the male and female leads at this season's Elitch's Gardens Theater. She would call him Freddie, feeling Fredric too formal. Their attraction was immediate and Fred could only wish that he was not married to Ellis at that moment, but he was. Nevertheless, this was not to stop him once he decided that Florence rather than Ellis would be of greater benefit to his career.

The Summer Theater at Elitch's Gardens, Denver, Colorado, was the oldest summer theater in the United States, founded by John Elitch, Jr. May 1, 1890. At the time Fred was employed, Elitch's was managed by John M. Mulvihill with Melville Burke acting director. The number of performances given in the theater during the Mulvihill management and Fred's tenure as leading man comprised nine performances, each play opening on Sunday evening and performed every evening of the week, together with two matinees (Wednesday and Saturday). To ready themselves for each play, the actors were allowed the limited rehearsal period of one week. Typically, on Monday morning the company gathered at 11:00 a.m. for the first rehearsal and went through the entire play mapping out entrances, exits, groupings, and the mood Burke wished to develop for each character and for the play. On Tuesday, rehearsal began at 10:30 a.m. with the actors repeating the directions of the preceding day. On Wednesday morning, rehearsals began at 10:00 a.m. continuing until noon, with a matinee performance of the current week's play.

Thursday was a rest day with no rehearsal before the evening performance. On Friday the cast must have their lines memorized for the rehearsal, which began at 10:00 a.m. and continued until late in the afternoon. Another shorter rehearsal followed on Saturday (before the usual matinee), and on Sunday rehearsal began at 11:00 a.m. This run-through was a combination dress and technical rehearsal, which included setting of lights, first use of costumes, and setting all technical cues. Often, this difficult rehearsal continued until 7:00 p.m., just ninety minutes before the performance began.

The Mulvihill management selected actors from a wealth of talent available in the New York theater and in eastern stock companies. Since Elitch's was one of the few summer theaters in operation during the Twenties, it was particularly attractive to actors such as Fredric March, who knew Broadway would be unavailable during the summer months. He recalled, "I remember the first thing I did when I arrived in Denver, even before I unpacked my luggage, was to drive out to the Gardens and look around the place. I stood in the lobby and looked at the array of photographs. There were some great old actors represented there, and it was inspiring" (Levy 1960, 260). Fred inevitably became the most popular actor at Elitch's, working for three seasons, 1926 through 1928, and appearing in thirty-four plays.

Fredric March was to play leading man to Florence Eldridge's leading woman, an enviable part to his mind. Florence Eldridge was born Florence McKechnie in Brooklyn on September 5, 1901, daughter of a Brooklyn editor and graduate of the Institute Players of Brooklyn. Her debut was in a musical comedy but she was soon appearing as an actress in stock, her first dramatic role as Kitty Sharrow, the parson's daughter in *Seven Days Leave*. Her New York debut was as a chorus girl in Jerome Kern's musical comedy *Rock-a-Bye-Baby* (1918). Brief engagements in *Pretty Soft* and *The Short Cut* broke the monotony of stock experience in Rochester and Syracuse and led to another New York appearance in support of Marguerite Silva in *The Song Bird*. On the strength of her performances in a few minor roles thereafter, she was engaged by the Theater Guild for an important role in *Ambush*. This was followed by a series of leading parts in *The Cat and the Canary*, *Six Characters in Search of an Author*, *The Dancers*, and *Young Blood*. She, too, had encountered John Cromwell, who cast her in *Bewitched* at the same time that he engaged Frederick Bickel for the lead in the touring company of *Tarnish*. She was the Elitch's Gardens female lead the summer of 1925 and was asked to come back for 1926. In between, her next important role was that of Daisy Fay in F. Scott Fitzgerald's *The Great Gatsby* (1926). Hence, by the summer of 1926, she was already a leading woman on Broadway.

As far as Fred was concerned, heaven had descended right onto that stage. In one fell swoop all his nerve, all that colossal cheek with which he had pounced on D. W. Griffith and a number of others, deserted him. He watched other men hovering around her, trailing devotedly at her heels, and loathed them, giving the appearance, when she was around, of being not quite right in the head. In short, Florence upset Fred enough for him to forget, momentarily, Ellis. And what better atmosphere for the couple to fall in love. The whole setting and circumstances of their lives in Denver were made for love. To play the leading man and woman in Denver was to belong socially. It meant being wined and dined by Denver's elite. It meant being followed in and out of stores by admiring wide-eyed kids. An aura of glamour surrounded them wherever they went. Even an enterprising automobile agency, alive to the value of publicity, turned over one of its best and newest models to Fred for his use during that summer. They were young, they were beautiful, they were, for the moment, picked to be the darlings of the gods. They read the same books, they admired the same people, they scorned the same weaknesses and best of all, they laughed at the same jokes. They gravitated to each other as a matter of course.

Although infatuated with Florence, Fred continued his policy of writing daily letters to Ellis, telling her how trying it was to be apart from her. Ellis recalled, "Then, as if the tides stood still, the letters stopped! For a week none came; I became alarmed. When a letter finally arrived, Fred said *nothing* of how he missed me, only how great a success he was" (*Picture Play* 1937, March Papers). As usual, Ellis feared that this was all going to Fred's head and that his overestimation of the value of the success he was scoring in Denver might hurt his career. At her mother's urging, and through her own fears, whether about his theater future or most likely about *their* future, Ellis boarded a train to Denver.

Fred may have been nervous offstage with Florence; however, on stage, it was a different story entirely. The first offering of the 1926 season was Ferenc Molnar's comedy about court life, *The Swan*, the week of June 12. Fred portrayed tutor Dr. Nicholas Agi to Florence's Alexandra. The *Denver Post* wrote, "Fredric March, the new leading man, is destined to become one of the most popular members of the company." The offering the week of June 20 was a comedy, *Love 'Em and Leave 'Em*, a stage presentation of John V. A. Weaver's poems converted into three acts by Weaver and actor George Abbott. Again the *Post*:

> You would never know Fredric March to be the same young man who played in *The Swan*. His voice, his movements, are changed to suit the role of the philandering youth who swerves between two sisters. Mr. March does not over play anything and the quality so very desirable and not found nearly often enough, that of restraint, distinguished his performance last evening. (March Papers)

In *Dancing Mothers*, Elitch's third presentation of the 1926 season for the week of June 27, Fred was again cast as the lead, portraying Gerald Naughton, a notorious bachelor. His characterization was even better than in his two previous plays. With his exceptionally fine speaking voice and his ability to act convincingly, Fred was rapidly becoming one of the Elitch favorites. It was in the fourth play of the season, *The Music Master*, written by David Belasco, that Fred finally got a rest, playing the "second business" part of the young German musician, while Moffat Johnson played the Music Master. Director Burke believed that characters should be assigned according to the individual qualities of the actors, rather than by company status, making it no longer a necessity for two actors to carry the major burden throughout an entire season. For instance, in the fifth play of the 1926 season, George Kelly's *Craig's Wife*, Burke believed that Cora Witherspoon ("second woman") was better qualified than Florence Eldridge ("leading woman") to portray the title role, and that Douglas Dumbrille ("second business") would be a better choice than Fredric March ("leading man") for the leading male role. Nevertheless, Burke thought highly of Fred, for he was cast as the lead in eight of the 1926 season's twelve plays.

Ellis had arrived by now and surely must have noticed the rapport between Fred and his leading lady, Florence. Unfortunately, rather than praising and building up Fred's success, which was well warranted, she minimized the importance of Denver. After yet another argument, she left for New York in a huff—fully expecting Fred to apologize, still secure that he loved her. However, no more letters from Denver were forthcoming as Fred basked in the attentions his leading lady bestowed upon him, for Miss Eldridge had seen the same potentialities for success in the young actor that Ellis had seen—save that her tactics for bringing them to the fore were different. Florence praised him!

The entire Elitch experience helped Fred fine tune his acting technique, his distinctive "not acting" but "actually being" each of his roles. He impressed one as having the rare faculty of really living the role he portrayed. The *Denver Post* wrote often about Fred, describing him as a refreshing type of modest thespian, a thoroughly wholesome young man, unaffected in manner, clothing or speech. Unlike the traditional matinee idol, the most noticeable impression Fredric March gave was a lack of egotism—the sparse use of the pronoun "I." For that very reason he was not so easy to interview; too interested in all phases of life that self-interest was largely submerged.

The week of July 18, Fred was back in the lead for a play about college life, *The Poor Nut*, by J. C. and Elliott Nugent. As John Miller, "the poor nut," Fred's characterization of the dreaming, self-conscious lad with an inferiority complex was so thorough and sincere that he did not seem to be acting the role, but was actually "the poor nut." Next, the week of July 25, came *Icebound* by Owen Davis, a drama of cheerless New England life. Fred was Ben Jordan, the wayward youth, the black sheep of the family, to

Florence Eldridge's Jan Crosby. He dramatized his role as though he really were living it—living it and enjoying it. Every detail of his performance was carefully worked out: sincere, fiery and convincing. The week of August 1 found Fred enacting, surprisingly, a Jekyll/Hyde character in the mystery comedy *Not Herbert*, by Irving Young. Fred, of course, was Herbert, a mooning poet by day and a high-class jewel thief at night. As the poetic souled thief who stole jewels just for the thrill it gave him, Fred made the very most of every opportunity the role afforded him. It was now the week of August 8 and Fred was still in top form as Liliom in *Liliom*, by Ferenc Molnar. The *Denver Post* was fast beginning to run out of celebratory adjectives to say about him, but tried once again: "Every week we marshal adjectives to herald his fine work, so we will just say that a regiment or two could tell of his eloquent interpretation of this roughneck ashamed of his own fine emotions" (March Papers).

Fred was given a break, finally, the week of August 15 by playing a very minor role in Owen Davis's *Easy Come, Easy Go*, but was back in the lead again as Rufe Pryor, a holier-than-thou charlatan of the Blue Ridge Mountains, in *Hell Bent fer Heaven* by Hatcher Hughes, the week of August 22. The manner in which he handled the part not only delighted the audience with his villainy, but proved his versatility. Katharine Ommanney, from her *The Stage and the School*, was an eyewitness to Fred's technique of "getting into character" in advance of each entrance: "He would begin, ten minutes before his entrance, walking backstage in the sanctimonious, hypocritical, slinking manner of Rufe Pryor; when he made an unobtrusive entrance at the top of a flight of stairs far upstage he was so much in character that the malign influence of the role reached the consciousness of the audience long before he spoke" (Levy 1960, 262). This particular role was important background for Fred's future characterization of Mr. Hyde.

The final play of the season, *These Charming People* by Michael Arlen, offered Fred blessed relief from the strenuous burden of the previous weeks by filling a considerably lesser role. Even so, by the conclusion of the Elitch season two most definite events had transpired. Fred had perfected his technique of acting—that is, he did not make the character he played fit his own personality, but made himself the vehicle for the projection of his role. Second, Fred had resolved to make Florence Eldridge his wife. Therefore, his primary purpose upon his arrival in New York was to dissolve his marriage to Ellis as fast as possible.

Upon his return he remained with Ellis only two days, then disappeared for a week. She was frantic, recalling, "When he returned he was grave, explaining a genius must live alone" (*Picture Play* 1937, March Papers). Fred then told her he intended to take up separate residence because he felt marriage and his ambitions were not compatible. Well, Ellis was stunned. She asked him whether he was in love with anyone else, although she didn't believe he could be. She was naively reassured, though, when he told her he was not. Fred left for another apartment after only two days.

Later that fall, Fred's brother Jack visited Ellis and asked that she give her absent husband a divorce. Feeling that Fred still might come to his senses and regret his hasty actions, she refused. But Fred remained steadfast in his purpose, obtaining a Mexican divorce and thereby forcing Ellis to bring divorce proceedings in the United States. She settled for $50 alimony a week based on his salary in 1926, and at the time of the *Picture Play* article (1937), she was still receiving the $50. As she felt it was enough, she never reopened the case to sue for more on the basis of his new status as a rich and successful movie star. In the early 1940s, Florence was instrumental in stopping any further alimony payments, thus cutting all ties to Fred's "sordid" first marriage.

Once he became a popular movie star, neither he nor Florence mentioned Ellis, so the majority of their friends and his public believed Florence to be his one and only wife. It appears that the rest of their lives together was spent erasing the memory of Ellis as if she had never existed. They pretended to all that Florence was his first, and therefore, *only* wife. Studio publicity, in fact, harped on this. When interviewed in 1990, Rose Hobart, who portrayed Dr. Jekyll's love interest in the 1931 picture, was aghast that Fredric March had been married before, stating that she wondered how the Marches' managed to keep it a secret. The *Picture Play* article was the only occasion that Ellis was brought up, and by Ellis herself.

By 1926 Frederick Bickel had changed more than his name. The Fred of 1926 *had* changed (even though he promised his parents he would not) from an idealistic college graduate totally in love with young Aline to another person: outwardly, the same affable chap from Racine, but inwardly, a man with a driving ambition, a rage almost, to be an actor, not just any actor, but the "best" actor.

There is certainly nothing wrong with ambition, and how could Fred not fall into the trap of all singular individuals held up for public viewing—the total adulation of their public, and in Fred's case, audiences and in particular, women. Fred was not immune to advances and attentions showered upon him as he worked his way up the acting ladder, for he was an extremely handsome and talented young man. He was subject to the same character flaws that affect all human beings. However, fortunately, when he gained that fame, he remained to friends and family "just an old shoe," not taking advantage of it.

Fred began rehearsals mid-November for the part of Jimmie Chard in Tom Cushing's *The Devil and the Cheese*, to open December 29 and continue through the winter. Fred had to acquire a midwinter tan for his part, so he underwent violet ray treatment to look the tanned playboy hero part. Dwight Frye and Bela Lugosi, soon to gain fame and fortune in Bram Stoker's *Dracula* for Universal, were also in the cast. However, it was a bust, with reviews containing such adjectives as "inept," "awkward," and "boring."

By December Fred had convinced Florence to marry him and so began their engagement with rehearsals for a play they were to do together at the Selwyn. Years later, in an interview with Ed Sullivan for his "Take the Stand" column (1938), Fred recalled this specific play:

Q. What would you say had been your most bitterly disappointing moment in your career?

A. I suppose it would be the winter before I married Florence. We had been playing stock in Denver, and we'd gone on to Broadway for Edgar Selwyn to play the leads in *The Proud Woman*. This was to be my first honest-to-goodness lead on Broadway, and naturally I wanted to show off in front of the girl who was my fiancée. We rehearsed for six days at the Selwyn Theater, and at that time each contract carried a seven-day provisional clause. The seventh day of the probationary period fell on Sunday, and I kept thinking to myself that if I could get through that last rehearsal, I was in. The rehearsal ended and I started edging toward the stage door. Just as I got to the door, the company manager called me—told me they'd decided to use another actor, that I wasn't sufficiently sophisticated. I guess that was the toughest blow that ever hit me.

Q. I can imagine.

A. I felt awful. She and I walked home together through Central Park. I was trying to be nonchalant; she was attempting to be consoling. I was convinced that she'd stop loving me immediately because I was a flop—I said to her "Perhaps it's all for the best. Now I can have that operation for hemorrhoids." She's never stopped teasing me about that speech. (March Papers)

This would also be Florence's second marriage. During a 1929 interview, she remarked, "The first time I married (to an alcoholic dentist considerably older than she), it was for what is commonly known as love. Actually it was—well, shall we call it the animal spirits of youth." It took her five dreadful years to learn what one should really marry for: companionship. "You should marry the person whom it's more fun to be with than anyone else in the world. Someone who thinks as you do about all the people you know and the things you do. That's really being in love and really being happy. That's why I married Freddie March, and that's the only reason anyone should ever marry" (March Papers). Florence and Fred ran off to Mexico on May 30, 1927, tying the knot for what was to be a forty-seven-year marriage. It was at this time of his life, through Florence's nickname for him, that Fred became known by the moniker "Freddie." Florence was to provide Fred a stabilizing influence throughout the rest of their lives. She initially and consciously took a back seat. From that moment, her primary goal was to act with Fred, not dart off on a competitive path. Later, however, her inability to impress Hollywood did lead to her nagging Fred to return to Broadway.

The newly married couple had signed on as leading man and leading woman for the 1927 Elitch's season and were anxious to start. However, when manager Mulvihill found out that his two leads for the Elitch's 1927 season were married, Miss Eldridge was asked to step down in favor of her more popular husband because he felt that audiences would not be interested in seeing a leading man play love scenes with his own wife. In a *Los Angeles Times* interview by Ray Loynd just before the September 21, 1987, Fredric March Hollywood Tribute, Florence, in an attempt to prove that she was the talent in the March family, remarked, "When we got married, I didn't want to start my marriage making more money than Freddie, so I asked our management at the Elitch's Gardens stock company in Denver to combine our two salaries and divide the check in half." As history and actual Elitch's Garden records show, the couple never acted together at the Gardens once they married, so there never was *any* combining of salaries. Regardless, Fred's 1927 summer season was as popular and as busy as in 1926, with the common review "Fredric March is the dashing Captain Brown (in *Quality Street*), thoroughly at home in the role, and a very satisfying character. His first appearance on stage started an outburst of applause that indicated his fine work last season has not been forgotten" (March Papers).

Once the second season was over and because they wanted to act opposite each other, the Marches accepted an assignment with the New York Theater Guild's first traveling repertoire tour. They thought of their future together as a sort of Alfred Lunt/Lynne Fontanne combination. Certainly, they started out determined to play together and to work for and toward the more intelligent "Art of the Drama." The tour involved four plays, *Arms and the Man*, *Mr. Pim Passes By*, *The Guardsman*, and *The Silver Chord*, to start September 1927 in Hanover, Massachusetts, ending February 1928 in Montreal and lasting some thirty weeks. Fred recalled, "The plays themselves were fun, but the tour was badly managed. So very badly arranged that finally we were making train connections at four in the morning or arriving in a town two hours before curtain time. It was miserable. We played everywhere but in theaters" (*Screenland* 1932, March Papers). This irritated him, for, before the Theater Guild tour commenced, he had been asked to portray Anthony Cavendish in the new Ferber/Kaufman play on Broadway *The Royal Family* but could not accept because of the Guild tour commitment.

The scenery of these four plays could be used in theaters, schoolhouses, auditoriums or what have you; therefore, this first traveling company played in 132 cities. They even managed to breeze into Fred's hometown of Racine on December 15, 1927, to present *Arms and the Man* at the Orpheum, where Fred had graduated from high school. Their next stop was Madison at Fred's alma mater, the University of Wisconsin, to present the same play Fred enacting Major Sergius Saranoff. Lawrence Langer, who arranged the tour, remembered the greeting Florence and Fred gave him in his 1951 autobiography; "We visited them to congratulate the actors on their tour, and I have seldom met such a group of indignant, overworked people. The verbal chastisement which I have received from time to time at the hands of these two artists has taught me a lesson I will always remember" (Langer 1951, 222-223).

At the conclusion of the tour, Fred and Florence bought their first automobile and visited their families. Cora loved Florence, for even though an actress she was not the "showgirl" Ellis had been. Why, with her large dark eyes, she even resembled Aline, the daughter-in-law Cora had always wanted. With the Bickel family blessing, they were next off to Fred's third Denver Elitch's Gardens season as the leading man. Typical reviews again extolled his talent; "Fredric March, popular enough to be commencing his third season as leading man, makes his bow as Joseph Meadows (in *The Baby Cyclone*) and the welcoming hand he received threatened to impede the movement of the first act" (March Papers). And so went the summer of 1928.

7

Barrymore

During August of 1928 Fred discussed leaving Elitch's before the last play in the season with Melville Burke, director of the Gardens Theater troupe. He explained to Melville that he had previously been given a chance to do the Tony Cavendish role for *The Royal Family* on Broadway and lost out because of signing with the Theater Guild tour, which by most standards was a disaster. Now he was being asked to do the same part in Los Angeles. Plus, he felt Florence and he needed to get some stability in their lives. Besides, *The Royal Family* might be a very long run. As Burke would not let married performers work together, that virtually left Florence out in the cold. At least in Los Angeles, she could work, possibly in the fledgling movie industry.

George S. Kaufman and Edna Ferber spent eight months writing *The Royal Family*, one of six plays they co-authored from 1924 to 1948 and one of their most successful. This comedy about a theatrical dynasty named Cavendish actually implied a take-off on the famous Barrymore family's claim to be the ruling clan of American theater. Any impression that the Cavendishes were not caricatures of the Barrymores was dismissed when Ethel Barrymore sought legal action against the authors. Her lawyer determined that only John Barrymore had been slightly slandered, but John couldn't have cared less. Ferber did admit Tony Cavendish had *some* resemblance to John, but in reality, the character was an exact duplicate to the Great Profile.

The Royal Family opened originally at Broadway's Selwyn Theater on December 28, 1927. When it was sent on the road to the West Coast, the producers found their original Broadway choice for "Tony"—Fredric March, free. March bore a striking resemblance to John Barrymore, especially when comparing their distinctive profiles. The March ability at mimicry, leaping over banisters, and generally behaving in the fashion of a harmless lunatic also helped the producers in their decision. After Burke's reluctant approval, the Marches' were set to arrive in Los Angeles by August 31 for rehearsals, coincidentally Fred's thirty-first birthday. He started rehearsals that same day for *The Royal Family* in preparation for the premier at the Lobero Theater, Santa Barbara, September 13 and 14. The company would then move on to San Francisco September 16 through the month of October at the Geary Theater, with the Los Angeles opening scheduled at the Belasco Theater, October 29.

All Hollywood, relishing the antics of the real John Barrymore, flocked to see his reincarnation on the stage. Fred did not disappoint the Los Angeles theater crowd. He deliberately imitated Barrymore's gestures, profile acting and quick, darting mannerisms. It was not surprising that his well thought out mimicry in the role soon brought him to the attention of "the" John Barrymore. Interviewed soon after the Los Angeles premier Barrymore commented:

> Fredric March played the fellow who was supposed to be me. He made me an utterly worthless, conceited hound, and he had my mannerisms, exaggerated but true to life. After I saw the performance, I went around to congratulate Freddie March. I was red-faced from laughing, my hair was tousled. Freddie jumped up, stared at me, and sprang into an attitude of defense. He thought I had come to attack him. If you saw Freddie March in that show, you saw a great deal more of John Barrymore as a youth than I like to confess.

"That's the greatest and funniest performance I ever saw," Barrymore told the cringing Fred, who stood as if frozen to the very floor.

"Oh," Fred gasped, relief flooding his face. "Oh!" Fred sank into a chair, "Thank God! I'm glad, John. I'm very, very glad. Thank you. They told me you'd be so sore that you probably would kill me" (*American Magazine* 1933, March Papers).

Fred remarked in an interview about *The Royal Family*, "The experience was a tremendous one for me, and the effect on me of the character I played was very powerful. For a while, it was hard to break away from it. While I was in the play, my wife used to tell me I was being John Barrymore around the house" (Ross and Ross 1962, 361). For example, one night, as Fred was slinking up to Florence in typical Barrymore fashion, she retorted, "Please be yourself, or I'll think I'm committing adultery" (March Papers).

The coveted role of impersonating John Barrymore garnered Fred excellent reviews. *San Francisco Chronicle*: "Fredric March plays Tony, the son of old Fanny; a stormy, more than half-mad youngster; enraged easily; and as suddenly quiet; always in trouble; fascinating so that women are crazy about him and keep him in hot water all the time. And March puts these qualities into his impersonation and makes an enormous hit" (March Papers). *Los Angeles Times*: "A riproaring performance is that of Fredric March as

Anthony. It is perhaps one of the most dynamic roles ever written" (March Papers). In fact, it benefited Fred more than if he had played it in New York, for his Barrymore characterization brought him to the immediate notice of the Hollywood motion picture producers, in particular, Paramount Studios.

The motion picture, current lord of the entertainment world, was a relative newcomer. During the Twenties, the young medium grew from a scattering of nickelodeon shows and occasional full-length features to a systematized $2 billion industry with a steady flow of films and a dazzling array of stars. Before Fred arrived in Los Angeles, sound had just come into motion pictures, and the industry had discovered to its horror that many of their handsome young male stars could not talk, at least not well enough for the infant microphones. A few companies held out, producing "silents," but by the spring of 1928, in any given community, the worst sound film could outdraw the best silent picture. Gradually, the serious fact dawned that the silent motion picture medium was doomed. Chaos and panic swept Hollywood as the companies moved to convert to sound. Recording problems now obsessed producers and directors who formerly focused on doing without sound. A static, stage-like technique developed because the microphone was at first immovable and all action had to be geared to its location, and because the cameras in soundproof booths could not move about freely. For more than three years, until these mechanical difficulties could be overcome, the microphone was king. This new king proved toughest on the silent players for most had not spoken in public since high school, generating a need for good looking actors and actresses with the trained "stage voice" or "pear-shaped" tones of Broadway.

Fredric March's deep-throated delivery was the answer to Paramount Studio prayers for not only did he have a handsome profile that could accommodate the most rigorous requirements for camera close-ups, he also possessed a stage actor's well-trained voice. At first, Fred thought "talkies" were a fad, but when asked to test for Paramount Studios, he jumped at the chance. Of course, there was no question that Paramount would offer him a contract, as they did, for five years. After all, how could he refuse the hefty $1,000 salary a week! "When Paramount offered me a picture job, I grabbed it. The idea of a house and garden, living simply and quietly in one place for a while, was too much to pass up" (*Screenplay* 1932, March Papers). He signed the Paramount contract December 7, 1928. And now, come what might, Fredric March was in the movies.

Paramount's films were produced on both coasts. In New York, there was a studio on West Fifty-sixth Street; in Hollywood, they expanded the Vine Street studio. Their gigantic Astoria studio on Long Island opened in 1921. By 1926, Paramount Pictures Corporation had consolidated its operations when they took over Famous Players-Lasky and added to the already existing facilities on Melrose and Marathon Avenues. When Fred joined Paramount,

B. P. Schulberg had just been made General Manager of the company's West Coast production. Schulberg supervised Hollywood's least regimented production style, giving a director full autonomy. Actors and actresses, too, were accorded considerably more respect, their shooting schedules measuring into months rather than weeks. Most of the "new order" Paramount players came from the New York stage: Claudette Colbert, Nancy Carroll, Kay Francis, Maurice Chevalier, and, of course, their newest all-purpose leading man, Fredric March. Those who survived the dreaded "mike" included William Powell, Gary Cooper, Buddy Rogers, Fay Wray and Jean Arthur. Fred was to be kept exceptionally busy by Schulberg, appearing in no fewer than eighteen feature length movies between March 1929 and December 1930.

Fred's first picture for Paramount was *The Dummy* enacting the role of Trumbell Meredith opposite Ruth Chatterton's Agnes Meredith. He remarked, "Not that I have a large part. It's very small, only allowing me a few scenes. It's what you might term my 'break in' part. The studio gave me this role to get me used to working before a camera and also to get an idea as to how I look on the screen" (March Papers). Actually, the part of Meredith was hardly more than a bit, but it was a start, for despite the poor early talkie restrictions, Fred proved photogenic and his speaking voice pleased audiences. Fred's good friend, John Cromwell, also appeared in this rather poor imitation of the stage comedy by Harvey O'Higgins and Harriet Ford, released March 3, 1929. Robert Landry in *Variety*: "Ruth Chatterton, number one in the billing, has what amounts simply to a bit. Fredric March is among the three names billed on the main title, although he has even less to do than Miss Chatterton" (Quirk 1971, 40).

Next on Fred's schedule was a chance at leading man opposite the "IT" girl of the silents, Clara Bow, in *The Wild Party* released March 30, 1929. The movie posters proclaimed "The It Girl Talks!" as Clara made her sound-movie debut, with Fred portraying a new anthropology professor in a girl's college. Dorothy Arzner was director, one of the first women directors in Hollywood. Said Dorothy, "Freddie March said to me, during the filming of *The Wild Party*, 'I always know when I'm doing a scene right by looking out at your face. Your face is my barometer" (Leyda 1977, 13). Although it was only March's second film, his force of character shone through, even when the script forced him to mouth pretty awful tripe, for instance, when Professor March had just saved student Bow from certain rape by a drunk:

Bow catches his arm. He turns to face her. She asks, "Why do you hate me so?"

Incredulously, he responds, "Hate you?! Why, how could I hate you when I would have killed for you!" They clinch.

Or, later in his house after an altercation during class (he had embarrassed Bow during his anthropology lecture, she stormed out) they reconcile, sitting on the floor in front of his fireplace.

As the suave professor March adds kindling to the fire, sexy Bow asks, "You certainly know how to kindle a fire." She smiles up at him wickedly, "Did you learn that in the jungle, too?"

He stares down at her seriously. "Had to come North for that." He descends toward her saying, "You little *savage*!" Kissing her, he bends her back to the floor before the fireplace as the camera focuses on his Barrymore-like profile.

Nevertheless, *The Wild Party* was not well received although March's voice was proclaimed excellent. Opposite Bow's Bronx accent, how could it have been otherwise! College moviegoers, indifferent to the histrionic tactics of Bow, were surprised and pleased to see the handsome earnest actor whom Miss Bow's directors had cast opposite her. For the first time they saw a movie college professor move through the sets as if he had once endured the four-year experience of watching the classroom manner of members of the professorial ranks.

Unfortunately, Fred's third film involved another bit part, that of Richard Hardell, a philandering actor who is murdered ten minutes into the film in an aptly titled *The Studio Murder Mystery*. Released June 9, 1929 *The Studio Murder Mystery* was adapted from a *Photoplay* magazine serial and a typical whodunit and featured Florence as Fred's jealous wife. Tedious and strained, with emphasis on stiff humor, *The Studio Murder Mystery* had all the faults of the early mike-dominated talkies. And, for the most part, Fred was not mentioned in the film's reviews.

Studio was Florence's first film venture. She next appeared in *Charming Sinners*, *The Greene Murder Case*, *Thirteen Women*, with Myrna Loy, and as Richard Dix's wife in *The Great Jasper*, although she was unable to command the attention in Hollywood that she could on Broadway. She was clearly less obvious film material than her husband, her career practically coming to a standstill. She contented herself with appearing on the local stage with Edward Everett Horton's stock company in such plays as *Her Cardboard Lover*. Florence's reputation of being waspish, too hard and too metallic for any but the most disagreeable roles caused directors to shy away from her because they had heard she was difficult to manage, albeit a fine actress. In fact, Miss Eldridge was extremely opinionated; was jealous of anyone with a college education, including her husband, and alienated many of his Hollywood friends. In a 1990 interview, Ralph Bellamy remarked, "Florence didn't hit it here (Hollywood), ever. Nowhere near the rank that he was. She and I, I guess, never hit it off. I wrote her a long letter after Freddie died, which was from the heart—never got an acknowledgement. I always felt she didn't care too much about me, just accepted me because of Freddie. She was a strange gal, very strange" (Interview, Ralph Bellamy, 9 August 1990). Florence felt Hollywood society superficial, grandiose, and full of phony people with their endless conversations about the movies. She felt Fred's popularity in the early 1930s was bad for their relationship. Consequently, not many people cared for Florence, while she cultivated non-actor type friends. She also managed to swerve Fred away from his Presbyterian upbringing and membership in the Republican Party (during the Depression, most of America had switched from Republican to Democrat already!).

Fred had a break between films and decided to take Mother Cora up on an invitation to Racine for Florence to meet some of the old gang. They arrived August 6, 1929, having a general tea affair in the afternoon to meet some of the neighbors and then going out to supper with some of Fred's old high school friends who still could not believe his current employment was as an actor. Fred commented on the astonished attitude of Wisconsinites:

> Friends drop in to see me, josh about a bit, ask me when I am going to get to work. They simply cannot believe that I am doing anything more significant, anything more permanent than larking about. It's a swell racket, they think, but, of course, it isn't one's job. Men just do not do this sort of thing. But I do. I do it and I do it seriously. Too seriously, if anything. (March Papers)

Back in Hollywood, and regardless of bad, or worse yet, *no* reviews, Fred found he was in demand by some of Hollywood's leading ladies. Jeanne Eagels, the sensational star of *Rain*, asked for him to star opposite her in *Jealousy*. The picture had been completed with Anthony Bushell, however, the temperamental star demanded that it be reshot with Fredric March. Miss Eagels had a promising career and was well on her way to becoming one of the screen's leading personalities, but she was actually near death from drugs when the film was reshot with Fred. She was dead before it was released, September 13, 1929. That was probably for the best, for the reviews were indifferent. Eagels was criticized for affecting a British accent and March was criticized for *not* affecting a British accent.

Luckily, Fred was loaned to Pathe for his fifth picture, cast as Jim Hutton opposite Anne Harding in her screen debut in the sophisticated comedy *Paris Bound*, released September 20, 1929. It was in *Paris Bound* that March finally got his film career off the ground by portraying an unfaithful husband in what was termed an "open" marriage (during the twenties, Paris was the popular location to receive a divorce). It all ends happily, however, with the young couple reconciling. Lawrence Quirk stated in *The Films of Fredric March*, "Director Edward H. Griffith succeeded in moving the film away from the talky, static deadliness so common to films of the period, and the piece came across on film as bright, smart and well-paced. The film did much to showcase March as one of the more accomplished and striking leading men of the screen" (Quirk 1971, 45).

Colleen Moore, a star from the silent era who had continued into talkies somewhat precariously, asked that Fredric March star opposite her in her next picture, *Footlights and Fools* by First National. Once again, Fred was loaned out to portray Gregory Pyne, a wealthy admirer of Miss Moore's character, a Broadway musical comedy star. The role was not the best, and the reviews proved it. It was released November 8, 1929. *Variety* reported, "Two male leads, Raymond Hackett as the gambling kid and Fredric March as the millionaire, have rather difficult assignments but both pull through neatly" (Quirk 1971, 50).

It was during this period, despite the poor talkies he had been cast in, that the women of America started to take notice of Fredric March's handsome face and pleasing mannerisms. He was even beginning to appear in featured articles of the popular fan magazines, most generally compared to silent favorite John Gilbert. Gilbert eminently represented the good old sure-fire movie idol in his most absolute form: The flashing eye . . . the flamboyant sex appeal . . . the gleam of sword and teeth . . . the heave of chest. A passionate figure, sure enough . . . voice as yet unjudged. On the other hand, March represented with equal eminence the new order of leading man: The man from the stage . . . the man with the appeal to the more delicate nerves. His appeal was perhaps slower, but it was deadlier, much more devastating. However, Fred did not enjoy being likened to John Gilbert, observing, "I think it's silly to say that I, or anyone else, can take the place of John Gilbert. If the stage people had not come to Hollywood, I have an idea things would have gone on just the same. The screen people would have done what the stage people are doing and they probably will anyway" (March Papers).

Fred's last picture for 1929, *The Marriage Playground*, based on the Edith Wharton's novel *The Children*, was thoroughly enjoyed by Depression-ridden audiences. It had romance, a handsome leading man, children, and, above all, a happy ending, something everyone needed after the Great Crash of October 1929. When it was released December 13, 1929, Mordaunt Hall of the *New York Times* wrote; "It is quite an intelligent production with well-woven strands of humor and sympathy, pathos and an appealing romance. The brunt of the acting falls on Fredric March and Mary Brian, who are thoroughly believable in their roles" (Quirk 1971, 52). Years later, in an interview for *The Player* in 1962, Fred recalled, "I learned about the importance of relaxation when I started making pictures. The director of *The Marriage Playground* (1929), Lothar Mendes, was the first person to mention it to me. He said, 'Freddie, when I say 'Camera,' all it means is—relax'" (Ross and Ross 1962, 299).

At the end of his first year as a movie personage, March remarked to one movie magazine that he felt too new to Hollywood to have much idea what it was all about. He didn't act as a movie actor should and was green about fans and publicity angles and being recognized and not at all accustomed to such universal staring. "I imagine I have not gone Hollywood, whatever that may mean. If, by going Hollywood, orgies are implied, I know I haven't. Florence and I have been hunting down an orgy ever since we arrived. So far, no good. We have come to the conclusion that they must start going after we leave places" (March Papers).

Fred's first few pictures of 1930 were bombs, the first casting him as a handsome lawyer in love with Sarah of *Sarah and Son*. Ruth Chatterton (Sarah) was opposite him once again, although, this time, both were in leading parts, rather than the bits they suffered during *The Dummy*. Chatterton portrays a bereft mother and successful opera singer fighting for custody of her son and aided by lawyer March, when love blossoms. Released March 14, 1930, the film produced mixed reactions, with March supporting Chatterton in a "trifle stiff" role of an attorney. March's appearance in *Paramount on Parade* (Apri 19, 1930), was negligible: he appeared in a doughboy sequence for this revue extravaganza. His next picture, with the unlikely name *Ladies Love Brutes* (May 15, 1930), however, was even worse. For unknown reasons, he was cast in a minor role with George Bancroft as the star, but tackled the lesser role with his usual unfailing skill. Actually, Fred was delighted *not* to be the lead in *Ladies Love Brutes*. By this time, he felt pretty discouraged about the various vehicles Paramount was placing him in, and it got worse, with the part of "Bull's Eye" McCoy in *True to the Navy* (May 23, 1930). The suave debonair Fredric March was badly miscast, playing a gum chewing sailor with an eye for target shooting the massive guns on the battleship *Mississippi*, cast opposite a fast declining Clara Bow, Lawrence Quirk quipped, "It's an ill wind that blows nobody good; doubtless some feminine members of the nationwide Paramount audience thought March fetching in a sailor suit [he was] . . . but *True to the Navy* will never go down in March's, or anybody else's book as one of his ten best films" (Quirk 1971, 61).

Between films, Fred was called home to Racine. His mother had died April 28. Cora Bickel was on public view at 1635 College Avenue, as was popular in those times. An old high school friend who wanted to pay her respects joined the seemingly endless line of mourners, until she realized that the line she was in was for receiving an autograph from Fredric March, the movie star. Fred was on the front porch signing autographs as all of Racine turned out for his mother's funeral, but more importantly, a view of a real live movie star. Spying his friend, Fred motioned for her to come to the porch. Giving her a big hug, he confessed that if he hadn't come out on the porch, his father was afraid the adoring Racine fans might break in, so Fred was promptly ushered to the front porch to fend off his multitudinous hometown admirers. After this somber event, Fred and Florence moved to New York in May to fulfill future contract commitments with Paramount. Prior to May they had moved six times between Hollywood and New York. When in New York they rented an apartment to occupy while Fred worked in the Astoria Studio. They also purchased a beach house in California that they rented out.

In *Manslaughter*, a novel by Alice Duer Miller, filmed in Astoria and released July 23, 1930, Fred portrays yet another district attorney, in love with a spoiled rich girl (Claudette Colbert) who has accidentally (through her careless speeding) caused the death of a motorcycle policeman. It is up to March's district attorney to convict and place her behind bars. She inevitably reforms and the DA naturally falls in love with her. This was March's first of four films with Colbert, and he was soon infatuated with her. During an interview in 1970, Lawrence Quirk asked March whether he had responded emotionally and physically to Claudette's attractiveness. "What male co-star of hers didn't!" March laughed. "I don't deny I was as human in my responses as any of them" (Quirk 1986, 32).

Fred's sister-in-law, Mary Bickel, wrote of the Marches' relationship at this time.

> If you think, wives the world over, that it is not a full-time, man-size job
> to remain successfully married to a handsome, romantic idolized screen
> star, you're just crazy, that's all. It requires a technique that the
> ordinary woman is never called upon to know. We who are married to
> the Jack Bickels, the Tom Browns and the Bill Joneses of this world,
> may not be *safe* in our husbands' affections (who is, alas?) but at least
> we know that our men are not going to be waylaid every hour of every
> day by beautiful young girls who are only too obviously on the make.
> (*March-to-the-Altar*, c. 1932, March Papers)

March was next cast in what was to be among his favorite films, *Laughter*, with Nancy Carroll. *Laughter*, by Donald Ogden Stewart, was fashioned especially for Nancy and Fred with Frank Morgan making his talkie debut as Nancy's millionaire husband and Fred portraying the amorous composer yearning for the married Carroll. Carroll portrays a former chorus girl married to a super rich ticker-tape Wall Streeter (Morgan) and coping with the return from Europe of an old boyfriend (March), a dashing but penniless young composer determined to win her back. Carroll's character lives day by day knowing she has made the wrong choice by marrying rich. There is no laughter in her life, which March promises to change. In *Laughter*, one can view the outlines of later popular 1930 movie comedies, with Carroll's and March's escapades and jokes anticipating the screwball style of later romantic comedy. One silly scene involved the illicit lovers crawling around on the floor of a house they had broken into to escape a thunderstorm. Crawling around on the floor might not appear silly until you realize they are covered in two large bearskin rugs and imitating the roars of a white and a black bear (this is really a rather embarrassing scene to view).

Regardless, *Laughter* emerged a brilliant, witty film, possibly the best early talkie conceived especially for the screen (November 14, 1930). The *New*

York Times said, "Mr. March is splendid as the impertinent, lighthearted and unruffled Paul" (March Papers). Good reviews, however, did not guarantee popularity. It flopped with the public (the bear scene may have had something to do with this). Producer Herman Mankiewicz explained later that it proved unpopular because they had made a mistake: "Our heroine had a husband who made 84 million dollars every day, had a Rolls-Royce to take her from bedroom to bath when she was finally exhausted from trying on dresses and jewelry all day. The elemental trouble with our plot was that we started off with the assumption that all this was no good because—she didn't have *laughter!*" (Lorentz 1975, 62).

Still, Fredric March was fast becoming a popular and "handsome leading man." He also had a reputation of being utterly unconscious of the camera and himself. On the screen he became lawyer, composer, bear, or whatever character he was playing. Many recognized his talent for completely losing his own personality in the part he played, while some hailed him as a second Barrymore. Of course, he enjoyed the comparison to Barrymore, and was most eager to start his next film, a film that reprised his role as Tony Cavendish, proved to be the start of a fast rising career, earned him his first nomination by the Academy for Best Actor, a film that, even today, presents a most wonderful and colorful portrayal of character. That film, of course, is *The Royal Family of Broadway* retitled from the stage play *The Royal Family* to accommodate British subjects' concern over confusion with "the" Royal Family.

After so many roles that represented basically staid characters laced with great integrity, March surprised moviegoers by giving his temperament its head in *The Royal Family of Broadway*. Re-creating the role that brought him to the attention of Paramount in the first place, he pulled out all stops to portray Tony Cavendish, the character patterned on John Barrymore, an outrageously flamboyant matinee idol who had sold out to Hollywood. He plays Cavendish as a combination of rake and clown, tolerated by an amused and affectionate theater family, thrust back into their lives from Hollywood through a breach of promise suit. While awaiting a passport to hide in Europe, Tony practices fencing up and down stairs reciting lines appropriate to the moment. After a whirlwind tour of Europe, Tony descends on the family again, informing them that he has bought a musical play to star in. While rummaging through his suitcase to find the script, he comes upon the flimsy undergarment of his last affair and holds it up to view, trying to remember its wearer, failing, he carelessly tosses it to the side. After he finds the script, it turns out that he has bought the musical version of the *Passion Play*. When asked what part he intends to play, Tony, affronted, responds, "Why, the *lead*, of course!"

March sketches Cavendish (Barrymore) as the perpetual actor onstage and offstage. His impersonation of Barrymore was done with such skill and conviction that it was hard at times to believe it was March and not Barrymore on the screen. His portrayal was not limited to just a superficial similarity but showcased the Barrymore whirlwind personality, his flamboyance, his unconscious humor, and his spoiled, impatient demands on his family and friends. Also, an occasional glimpse of family loyalty and genuine affection beneath the flamboyant nature was superbly executed by March, who received the lion's share of all reviews when it was released December 22, 1930. The *New York Mirror*: "Fredric March gives the performance of the year as the mad matinee idol, Tony, in this hilariously amusing movie about the private life of stage aristocrats. He completely dominates the picture, and five minutes of his comedy are worth the whole price of admission" (March Papers). The role netted him his first Oscar nomination.

One could surmise that, after such a success, Fredric March would go Hollywood. This was not to be, for he was his own closest critic. The screen gave him an opportunity to study his stage mannerisms and eliminate them, and he had done an excellent job. March's popularity soared, and that concerned him, for he did not want to be a star, a matinee idol, nor a great lover. He maintained; "Stardom is just an uneasy seat on the top of a tricky toboggan. Being a star is merely perching at the head of the downgrade. A competent featured player can last a lifetime. A star, a year or two. There's all that agony of finding suitable stories, keeping in character, maintaining illusion. Then the undignified position of hanging on while your popularity is declining" (March Papers). An interviewer could talk to Mr. March for an hour without hanging a single tag on him, without observing the slightest bit of theatricalism in gesture or voice. And without having learned a great deal about the inner mind of Fredric March, although he had answered every question put to him. Offstage he lacked the assertiveness which marked his roles, divesting himself totally of the drama, revealing no trace of temperament. March revealed only that he was a well mannered, handsome young man, well poised, without the slightest indication that he felt he was under observation and compelled to give a show. In fact, he was really distressed to find himself endowed with a romantic appeal for the movie fans, for all were screaming for more of him!

The *Film Mercury Magazine* in 1931 held great hopes for Fredric March—"If Paramount casts March properly in his next two or three vehicles, he will sweep the country before the year is out and be one of the five biggest drawing cards on the screen. The performances March has given so far are nothing to what this truly remarkable actor will deliver if presented the opportunity" (March Papers). Moviedom felt Fredric March, at thirty-three years old, to be the biggest star possibility on the screen horizon and continually compared him to John Barrymore in all-around talent. Yet he still acted normal, as if he were just arriving from Wisconsin. Everybody at the studio liked him. He was "Freddie" to the electricians and to the grips and to the others who worked with him daily on the lot. Some of the stars were chill as ice. It's "Here comes so-and-so and get out of the way if you know what's good for you." Not so with Fred, who would say to an electrician, "Howdy, Jake, how's the baby getting on?" He was cheery, a good scout, never off his head. From executive to gateman they said after him, "Now there goes a swell fellow." In fact, the gateman on the Paramount lot had learned much about college students since Fred came on the set. He had been overrun with "classmates" of Fred's, and commented, "It would be absolutely impossible to have a university as large as the one that could be made up with Fredric March's gate crashers" (March Papers).

March was next reunited with his secret "heartthrob," Claudette Colbert, in *Honor among Lovers*, filmed at the Astoria Studios and directed by Dorothy Arzner. He recalled, "Dorothy had a lot of masculine force. She could raise as much hell as Wyler or any of them. I never felt I was dealing with a woman—she was one of the guys. How Claudette felt about her I could never determine; my guess is that she made Claudette a little nervous" (Quirk 1985, 34). Unfortunately, *Honor among Lovers* was a poor follow-up to *The Royal Family of Broadway*. Presumably, the only memorable item about this film, for March, was his close proximity to Colbert as he enacted the role of sexual harasser of secretary Colbert. "Mr. March makes his part as believable as it is humanly possible," described the *New York Times*, upon its release, February 17, 1931 (March Papers).

Things went from bad to worse to unbelievable, when Paramount cast March once more as an attorney in one of the worst films of his career, *The Night Angel*, with Nancy Carroll. March endeavored to do what he could with his role of Berkem, but when it was released June 10, 1931, *Photoplay* intoned, "Fredric March is the hero and struggles with the stupid story" (March Papers). Disheartened, Fred took Florence on a well deserved three-week vacation cruise to the West Indies. On their return, he was hopeful that *My Sin* with Tallulah Bankhead would bring him out of his depression. Such was not to be, for March found himself in yet another failure, playing a degenerate *and* alcoholic attorney, reformed by his successful murder defense of Bankhead. On the wagon, he becomes successful helping Bankhead to start fresh in New York. After a bit he realizes his love for her, and she for him, etc. Actually, his character becomes quite uninteresting once he changes his ways. He turns into a dull and much too nice young man, winning Bankhead in the end, but not by putting up a fight. He rather hangs around in the wings until she is ready to admit that she loves him. When it was released for public viewing September 11, 1931, March made sure he was not available for comment.

By now, Fredric March questioned this five-year hold Paramount had on him. Sure, it was steady money but, to Fred, it was degrading and not even of the level of bad theater. And what did he have to look forward to? His next film would probably force him into the rank of supporting actor. After all, it was a period piece, something he never felt comfortable with. There were possibilities, although, as he would be performing two separate and distinct personalities. He had enjoyed the various dual roles he had enacted during his early theater days, and he had gotten rave reviews. Possibly—could this total reversal of all he had done in pictures up to now actually be a hidden opportunity? And he did admire Rouben Mamoulian; it was Mamoulian who convinced him to accept the dual role in January of 1931.

8

Jekyll and Hyde

It took most of January 1931 for Rouben Mamoulian, Paramount's most recent import from Broadway (it was Mamoulian's growing reputation as an inventive Broadway director that caused Paramount to recruit him to direct, first, the hit *Applause*, and then *City Streets*), to convince Fredric March to play the dual part of Dr. Jekyll and Mr. Hyde in Hollywood's first talkie version of the Robert Louis Stevenson novel. Fred argued that Shulberg had hand picked character actor Irving Pichel for the part and was not so sure he wanted to portray a monster. Jekyll, yes. But, Hyde?

Mamoulian convinced him, however, by stressing, "Can't you imagine what a great chance this is, playing these two? They are entirely different characters, total opposites." He induced Shulberg to give March the role. Fred must have muttered to himself after this realization, "I can't believe I committed myself to play a monster. Well, I guess no Oscar nomination *this* year!"

In an interview conducted by John A. Gallagher in 1978, Mamoulian was asked to comment on his choice of Fredric March for the difficult lead in Robert Louis Stevenson's story of repressed emotion in Victorian society. Mamoulian replied that Paramount had asked him whether he would be interested in doing *Dr. Jekyll and Mr. Hyde*. Of course, he said yes for the story was very exciting. Then Paramount told him they had an actor for it, Irving Pichel, a very fine character actor, but Mamoulian was not interested in Pichel because he wanted to see a young handsome man as Dr. Jekyll.

Paramount countered, "But Irving Pichel is perfect for Hyde."
Mamoulian said, "Mr. Hyde is not a problem. Any actor can play Mr. Hyde, but not any actor can play Jekyll *and* Hyde."
Paramount stormed, "This is ridiculous. Who would you like to have for it?"

Mamoulian said calmly, "Fredric March."
Paramount complained, "He's a light comedian."
Mamoulian said, "Fine. He can do it."
Paramount dissented, "This is crazy. Forget it."
So Mamoulian forgot it.
A week later they called him back and said, "Do you still insist on that crazy idea?"
Mamoulian replied, "Yes. Otherwise I'm not interested."
Reluctant, Paramount agreed, "All right, it's on your head." (March Papers)

However, despite Mamoulian's confidence, all of Hollywood was aghast at the casting of Fredric March in the title role. Until this time he had been considered a matinee idol, but Mamoulian's judgment would eventually prove correct.

Mamoulian was not merely going to crank out a horror story geared to stimulating audiences and drumming up box office receipts. He took decided liberties with Stevenson's original story, especially in pioneering the idea of introducing two women, one sexy and promiscuous, Ivy Pierson (Miriam Hopkins), the other Victorian and pure, Muriel Carew (Rose Hobart). These two opposing characters paralleled the two sides of Dr. Henry Jekyll's nature. Mamoulian wanted to capture the struggle between the Jekyll and Hyde personalities precisely and he also wanted his audience to identify with the very real plight of the handsome and noble physician and scientist. Jekyll, by exploring the dual nature of man, succeeded in unleashing a separate bestial figure, the dark side of Jekyll's civilized but repressed character. Therefore, Jekyll is made not only the center of the film's narrative but the primary vehicle for the development of the action. Viewers are invited to identify with Jekyll as he first articulates his theory of the separation of the good and evil within men, then experiment with the drugs that eventually effect the separation, and finally live out the consequences of his work. Because of the close audience identification, they then forgive Jekyll for the apparent lack of foresight and judgment of his theory.

One of Mamoulian's surprising tricks to enhance his theme, especially for a very early talkie, was his use of a subjective camera: that is, the audience views the action from Jekyll's point of view in several sequences. For example, the film opens with a shot of Jekyll's pipe organ (which he is playing), pans to the keyboard to see Jekyll's hands, sheet music, then his butler entering the room to remind Jekyll of his lecture. Next, the audience follows the butler through the main hall, and only then views Jekyll's handsome reflection in a mirror as he adjusts his cape and top hat. We do not actually see Jekyll until he enters the lecture room, when the camera pans the lecture audience left to right, then back to Jekyll on the first word of his lecture, "Gentlemen . . . London is so full of fog . . . that it has penetrated our minds, set boundaries for our vision."

Scripted by Samuel Hoffenstein and Percy Heath, Mamoulian's *Jekyll and Hyde* has an unequivocal sexual basis, slipping in under the Production Code net before the new powers of sanction made the going tougher in 1933. It openly traces the cause of Jekyll's troubles to the frustration by society of his own perfectly natural desires. Thus, Mamoulian's Hyde indulges in the unmentionable lusts that Jekyll only dreams about. For a long period the only available print of the 1931 *Dr. Jekyll and Mr. Hyde* was the Production Code cut version. This print, although enjoyable, does not do justice and it is hard to discern Jekyll's very real cause of Hyde: namely, sexual frustration. The restored version (1992) points directly at Jekyll's sexual futility and inability to hasten his marriage to fiancée Muriel, then plays up his unholy relationship with the prostitute, Ivy.

For example, there is a poignant scene toward the end of the restored version between Jekyll and Muriel. Jekyll, under Hyde's influence, has just murdered Ivy Pierson, and realizes he can no longer control his transformation (March was always at his best as the tortured soul with a bleak future). Much of the scene was cut because the lovers spend most of their time on the floor. This version leaves nothing to the imagination and employs heightened emotions, particularly in the scene where Jekyll feels he must give up Muriel by first asking her forgiveness. Of course, she does not understand what she needs to forgive and feels he has fallen ill. Jekyll, however, is visibly upset, desperate in his need for Muriel's forgiveness.

He is so upset when she asks him to tell her what is wrong that he shakes uncontrollably, proclaiming, "I've come to set you free." He then grasps his quaking hands together as if to stop their tremors. Muriel panics and asks again what is wrong. In a closeup on Jekyll's face—the terror and hopelessness is evident as he stammers, "Ev . . . everything's wrong!" In the manner of a broken man, he tries not to cry. "I no longer have any claim on you!"

She then sits down on the piano bench facing him as he watches her. "Whatever it is, I know you've never done anything base or mean!" Jekyll interrupts her in desperation, "Oh, please, my dear." Leaning down on his knees in front of her, he buries his head in her lap, his hands playing nervously with the folds of her dress. Muriel asks Jekyll if he no longer wants her. Quickly, he looks up at her, "*Want* you!? I want you. So that I can envy the damned . . ." Staring at her, he gasps, "I am damned," then looks down once more. After she proclaims that she will love him and help him, he stares at her, love on his features momentarily replacing his prior despair, and says, "Oh, my love. My darling. My beautiful. If I could take you in my arms; if I could only touch you. Oh, think of it." He leans back away from her, horror now on his face as he realizes what he has said, "I daren't even touch you. Ever again. In this world or the next."

She grips his shoulders, shaking him hard, as if by her actions she can bring back the old Jekyll, and drops down on her knees, too, to face him. She brings him forward to her and reaches around his neck as his arms involuntarily encircle her waist. "Oh. Trust me, believe in me, I'll help you!" Now it gets really interesting as Jekyll, who can no longer stand his proximity to her, pulls away, sinks to the floor with his back to her, and beats the ground with his balled fist, claiming he is *beyond* help and in Hell and he *must* give her up. Naturally, she joins him on the floor in an attempt to convince him of her love. He refuses to give in but instead says, "If I . . . if I could only have you, I . . . I'd give my soul, but I . . . I have no soul. I'm beyond the pale." In hopelessness, "I'm one of the living dead!" She forces him back onto her lap, his head cradled in her arms. "Oh, I won't let you go!"

She soothes him, rocking him gently. His eyes close and he is seemingly at peace as she croons to him. Remembering his dilemma, he becomes alarmed. He then takes her arms from around him, getting up fast, but she stands up to follow, forcing him into a tight embrace that he succumbs to, holding her close. "I love you," she rains kisses upon him, "I love you." He finally takes her by her upper arms and *forces* her away from him, breathing fast, hard and tense, "No . . . no . . ." She waits for him to speak. "I give you up, because I love you, so. This is my proof. This is my penance." Placing his hands in fists he looks heavenward, asking, "Do you hear, oh *God*?! This is my penance!" He walks quickly away with a brokenhearted Muriel sobbing at the piano.

Mamoulian's inventions for the scenes showing March changing from Jekyll to Hyde would alone have made this film memorable. Specially toned makeup, colored lights and colored filters were used to change the look of March's face, first to obscure then reveal portions of makeup. The actual process of making-up by famous Paramount artist Wally Westmore in itself was tedious, taking three hours for the full blown affect of Hyde. At the beginning of the transformation scene, Westmore would line Fred's face with red, which, when the transformation began, would make it seem as if the lines were gradually appearing in his face. In order not to have them show before this, they put a red filter in the camera, thus eliminating the red lines in Fred's face from registering on the film. Then, when the right moment came, a green filter was placed into the camera and the red lines on Fred's face could be seen (in this way—when the film is viewed—it seems as if mysterious lines suddenly appear). Then Fred held his pose. A still Graflex camera was placed beside the regular camera and, instead of taking a still picture of him, an artist sketched the outline of Fred's body on the frosted glass of the Graflex. Fred proceeded to his dressing room for some more of the gruesome Mr. Hyde makeup. Back on the set, he took the pose he had held before—guided exactly by the sketch on the frosted glass of the Graflex. After a few moments of grimacing and twisting—changing from Dr. Jekyll to Mr. Hyde—Fred again retired to his dressing room to put on a little more of the Mr. Hyde makeup. There were four additions of makeup to be put on before the transformation was complete.

In preparing for Mr. Hyde it was necessary for March to wear exaggerated false teeth. There were four different sizes of teeth to be inserted into his mouth to show his tusks growing longer. His nose was built up with putty, a little more added each time the camera stopped. Hands, too—to begin with, Fred's own hands were painted a neutral gray on top with red hair glued on. With each change, longer hair was glued on and more makeup added to give them a more horrible appearance. He even seemed to grow taller, accomplished by placing lifts into his shoes. His increased girth and stature were achieved by means of especially built leather jackets, heavily padded. He endured some discomfort because of them, though. They shut out the air; the padding made him sweat like a mule. When he transformed himself from Mr. Hyde back to Dr. Jekyll, the same process was employed, except that he took off makeup when the camera stopped.

In a 1990 interview, Rose Hobart (Muriel) remarked, "I loved working with Freddie and Mamoulian. Freddie was a very generous actor to work with and Mamoulian knew exactly what he wanted in every scene. I didn't always agree with him as I felt he was crossing his T's and dotting his I's a little too much and not leaving enough to the audience's imagination, only to realize now that it was that technique for which he is famous." Hobart also remembered a scene between Fred and costar, Miriam Hopkins:

> I was on the set one day when they were shooting the first scene in the cabaret where Freddie and Miriam Hopkins were in the raised box and Mamoulian had set up a camera out on the floor. They were facing each other and as the scene started Miriam managed to edge up so that she was facing the camera and Freddie almost had his back to it. When the scene was finished the word "Cut" came from behind the curtain at the back of the box and Miriam whirled around and said, "Is *that* where the camera was?" and Mamoulian answered, "Yes, that's where the camera was. Print!" (Interview, Rose Hobart, 9 August 1990)

For March, there were some painful memories about the making of this film, remembering makeup difficulties, during an interview in 1938 with Ed Sullivan for his "Take the Stand" column. Sullivan asked March what was the most unpleasant role he had ever played in pictures? March replied,

> *Jekyll and Hyde*, purely because of the makeup problems involved. In the first place, I had to get up every morning at five o'clock to be at the studio at six. Wally Westmore would start work immediately on my

eyes. First he'd put collodion under my eyes, so that no perspiration would come through. Then he'd weight the under part of the eye with pieces of surgical cotton to force open the eyeball. The idea was that every time I talked, the eyes would open in an unnatural leer. To accomplish this, he'd attach threads from the cotton down the cheeks and tie them under my chin. As a result, every time I opened my mouth, the lower eyelid would be dragged down an inch. It was horrible at the time, but interesting to look back at." (Hollywood Citizen News, 14 June 1938, March Papers)

Sometimes, March found being made-up as Hyde highly effective. As the making of *Jekyll and Hyde* was tiresome, with its many changes of makeup, makeup that was, at the very least, uncomfortable, long days were the norm for this film, running past 10:00 p.m. each night. March soon decided it was high time that he got off work at least by 8:00 p.m. so he confronted Schulberg, wearing full makeup as the gruesome Mr. Hyde, and demanded that he be permitted to go home earlier in the evening. It worked. Another episode involved Wally Westmore driving March to a location spot, after, of course, putting him in full Hyde makeup. It never occurred to Westmore that March looked unusual. That is, until Westmore wheeled into a gasoline station to ask directions about how to find the location site. The attendant came up smiling, took one look at March, gasped, screamed and ran off. "Let's scram!" shouted Mr. Hyde (*Hollywood Studio Magazine* 1973, ss-2).

March remarked on his Mr. Hyde characterization in an interview January 1932. He conceived Mr. Hyde as more than just Dr. Jekyll's inhibited evil nature, seeing the beast as a separate entity—one who could, and almost did, little by little, overpower and annihilate Dr. Jekyll. "I tried to show the devastating results in Dr. Jekyll as well. To me, those repeated appearances of the beast within him were more than just a mental strain on Jekyll—they crushed him physically as well. In the last scenes, he looked as though he already had one foot in the grave. Hyde was killing Jekyll physically as well as mentally" (March Papers).

Fredric March's characterization for this exceedingly difficult role was made more difficult by the fact that such classic actors as John Barrymore and Richard Mansfield had done it before him, on the screen and on the stage, setting an almost unattainable standard. Nonetheless, March relished his dual role. When he emerges as Hyde there is no confusion that this is a new character, the complete opposite of the cultured and celebrated Dr. Jekyll. He succeeds in portraying Jekyll and Hyde as fully developed and separate characters. In the first place, as Jekyll, he is warm, vibrant and impulsive, the very typification of all that is best and noble in man. What is more remarkable, he even makes a living understandable being of the usually uninteresting Dr. Jekyll. At all times, he suggests the turbulence that exists beneath the well-controlled exterior of Stevenson's hero. Then, under that astonishing Hyde makeup, he becomes an unrecognizable animal, fashioned after an ape-like monster, capering and romping, swinging from chandeliers, vaulting balconies, and leaping from trees and walls in the pure joy of liberated evil. Released New Year's Eve, December 31, 1931, March's version of *Dr. Jekyll and Mr. Hyde* has remained the finest of the many film interpretations of Stevenson's novel. Ralph Bellamy and his wife attended the Chinese Theater opening of the film with Fred and Florence. Bellamy recalled, "During a repeated transformation of Jekyll to Hyde for the second or third time, well into the picture, which had the audience spellbound, a young man seated near us said to himself, but quite audibly, 'Jeez the guy's goin' sc-a-rewy again.' Almost the entire house heard it and bust into laughter" (Interview, Ralph Bellamy, 9 August 1990).

New York Times reviewer Mordaunt Hall wrote, "Mr. March's portrayal is something to arouse admiration, even taking into consideration the camera wizardry" (Quirk 1971, 81). *The Mirror*: "March establishes himself with *Dr. Jekyll and Mr. Hyde*. He gives an impressive, intelligent, touching performance" (March Papers). *New York Evening Post*: "Mr. March's performance is inexpressibly good. . . . There can be no doubt that Mr. March is an actor of high intelligence and of hitherto unsuspected power" (March Papers).

In 1941, Metro-Goldwyn-Mayer decided to film another version of the Stevenson novel starring Spencer Tracy. Wanting no competition for Tracy, chiefly since March had been awarded an Academy Award for his portrayal, MGM purchased the Mamoulian version from Paramount, condemning it to almost total obscurity in its vaults. Tracy was not happy about the part, especially when he overheard Somerset Maugham, who visited the set during shooting, and was told that Tracy differentiated the roles without any changes in makeup, ask, "Which is he playing now?" (Halliwell 1982, 69). MGM thought the picture splendid, but they had not counted on the critics' going after Tracy. The trouble was March's success as Hyde in the earlier version. He portrayed a far more inhuman monster than Tracy, and at the same time, since March was a very handsome fellow, he made a much more debonair Dr. Harry Jekyll. Some people felt the critics didn't review the picture at all, but merely compared Tracy with March, and Tracy lost.

"I thought Spence did a fine job, as he always does," Fred commented. "His Jekyll and Hyde weren't anything like mine, but why should they be? After all, we're two different actors, aren't we? I'm sure Spence would never look at a performance and try to copy it. "When Fred telephoned Tracy to tell him what he thought, Tracy laughed and said, "Why, Fred, you son of a bitch, I've just done you the biggest professional favor you'll ever have!" (Swindell 1969, 173)

After the success of *Dr. Jekyll and Mr. Hyde*, Fredric March was now, unquestionably, a major star with immeasurable creative skill. Unfortunately, he was still under contract to Paramount, who selected roles that were not always in his best interest. Paramount placed March in another dual role (and why not, *Jekyll* worked!) in *Strangers in Love* (originally called *Intimate*, for whatever unknown reason) with Kay Francis as costar and released March 5, 1932. Fred portrayed twin brothers, one good and one bad, and he did his normal admirable best, but *Strangers in Love* ranked as one of his less memorable films. *The Sun* reviewed the picture: "Mr. March is in a dual role . . . he again is cast in a role that takes more than average ability. He is handicapped by a banal story, obviates underscored dialogue and extremely clumsy plotting" (March Papers). After this picture, March started to worry that he did not have any real existence in the public mind except as an impersonator and imposter, feeling he occupied a niche in the gallery of film celebrities, not as Fredric March, but as "the man who played Barrymore," or "the man who leads a double life."

March's reviews for his next picture, *Merrily We Go to Hell* released June 10, 1932, were good, but the story was typical of the early 1930s happy endings and is a rarely mentioned effort. In *Merrily*, March portrays an alcoholic newspaper columnist and part-time cad, yearning to make it big as a Broadway playwright. He is fortunate enough to meet a naive young rich socialite, Sylvia Sidney; marries her; goes on the wagon and proceeds to write a successful play. The star of the play, however, is his former girlfriend, who happens to be responsible for his initial alcoholism. Things deteriorate rapidly when he begins an open affair with her, drinking profusely once again. Meanwhile, Sidney discovers she is with child. After she loses the baby, March rushes to her side proclaiming his undying love. The end.

Obviously, the part represented a many-sided personality and March made the most of it. Lawrence Quirk described March's character as "the temperamental writer that seems a very self-centered and prickly and unreliable fellow for any girl to romance —let alone marry." Or, "He rushes to her (Sidney) despite papa's opposition and there is the requisite stuff about repentance, forgiveness and a fresh marital start. Though considering the character's record up to that point, any wife would be a fool to bet on it" (Quirk 1971, 85). Viewing the playwright character through late twentieth century eyes, however, March's portrayal makes him most attractive and it is not at all surprising that Sidney or anyone else falls for him. Still, most of the reviews sounded the usual note of regret that March could not get better vehicles from Paramount. The *Post* reported, "Sylvia Sydney and Fredric March as the chief protagonists, with their intelligence, their arresting personalities, their high individual skill and their adroit teamwork, almost bring the picture up to the level of an original creation" (March Papers).

Make Me a Star, released July 1, 1932, only deserves mention here for

March's small bit in the film, playing himself on a sample movie set for Stuart Erwin to visit in hopes of learning how to become a movie star.

During the summer of 1932 the Marches' decided to adopt a child to start a family. Apparently, Florence was unable to have children. According to Ellis Baker, Florence never told Fred that she could not have children before he asked her to marry him. One can only guess at his reaction to that bit of news. Fortunately, at the time, Fred had yet to be discovered and evidently forgave a wife that never let her own career overshadow his. Proceedings were started through a well known Evanston, Illinois, orphanage and adoption agency called The Cradle, an organization used by all the Hollywood folk. Meanwhile, production started on March's next picture, a loan-out to MGM and an opportunity to star with Norma Shearer in *Smilin' Through*. Based on a 1919 play by Jane Cowl and Jane Murfin, *Smilin' Through* was one of Norma Talmadge's biggest silent hits ten years earlier. Fred was to portray dual roles, again, but *Smilin' Through* became a 1932 record-breaker, netting an Academy Award nomination for best picture.

9

Popularity

Smilin' Through involved another dual role for March. In what can be described as the costumed episode, Fred portrays a love-maddened man, Jeremy Wayne, who attempts to shoot his rival (Leslie Howard) and accidentally kills the woman he loves (Norma Shearer). Then, in the modern scenes, he portrays Kenneth Wayne, the son of the murderer, who finds romance with the niece, Kathleen (also, Shearer), imperiled by his heritage. Released October 14, 1932, *Smilin' Through* was Fredric March's first MGM appearance, showcasing him in important MGM theaters and winning him much praise. *The Herald-Tribune*: "Fredric March, always one of the best actors in the cinema, manages his double role with the skill that might have been anticipated" (March Papers).

Fred commented to his first cousin, Kathryn Davis, about working with Norma Shearer, that, yes, she was a great actress, professional, etc., but could be difficult, because she constantly expected perfection. When Kathryn asked what that specifically meant, Fred replied, "She was never satisfied, kept having us do take after take." Pausing, he continued, unabashed, "Especially our love scenes. She always wanted to redo *all* the love scenes, several times!" Kathryn wanted to ask why he supposed Shearer always wanted to retake the love scenes in particular, but thought better of it and kept silent (Interview, Kathryn Davis, 24 September 1990).

As *Smilin' Through* swept the country it was nominated to *Family Circle*'s Hall of Cinema Fame as the best romance film of 1932, whereas the best individual male performance went to Fredric March for *Dr. Jekyll and Mr. Hyde*. March also received his Academy Award nomination for Best Actor (for *Jekyll/Hyde*) and notification that there was a baby girl waiting for adoption. Penelope March, born August 20, 1932, was formally adopted by Fred and Florence in September. Fred was an honest-to-goodness family man. Interviewed about what he considered love to be, Fred answered,

Love, to my way of thinking, is friendship plus sex. We Americans go at love the way we would a business problem. BANG! BANG! BANG! No time for subtleties. Sell the girl the idea of marriage, rush her into signing a contract, draw a nice long sigh of relief when it's all over, and settle down to raise a family. Our big deal with life is completed. Or is it? Usually when we arrive at that "settled" state, it's time to watch our step or we'll find ourselves facing a judge! (March Papers)

With great anticipation, Fred and Florence attended the Academy Awards ceremony at the Fiesta Room of the Ambassador Hotel in Los Angeles, hosted by Conrad Nagel, on November 18, 1932. Columnist Jimmy Starr predicted Wallace Beery the winner for *The Champ* over Fredric March in *Dr. Jekyll and Mr. Hyde* and Alfred Lunt in *The Guardsman*. However, when Norma Shearer presented the Best Actor award, she did not read the name of the winner. The Academy flashed Fredric March's photograph on a wall while his voice was heard from the sound track. Thus, the Academy proclaimed Fredric March the victor for *Dr. Jekyll and Mr. Hyde*. Fred received the statuette, remarking, "I must thank Wally Westmore, who made my task an easy one" (March Papers).

B. P. Schulberg, who was overseeing the voting committee, discovered that Wallace Beery was only one vote short of March in the Best Actor race, which, under Academy rules, meant Beery had tied with March. Therefore, Beery was also awarded the famous statuette. March laughed over the whole outcome, as well as over the coincidence that he and Beery both had just adopted children. The papers recorded March as stating, "I never met Mr. Beery, although I believe we do have something in common. Both Mr. Beery and I have adopted baby girls this year, which makes me question the advisability of awarding us prizes for the best performances." According to the notes left by March to the University of Wisconsin Film and Theater Research Archives, this quote was fictitious for, scribbled next to it, Fred wrote, "What I said was 'It seems to me the height of incongruity.' FM" (March Papers).

Wisconsin's favorite son had been boosted to the loftiest notch of its glittering star-laden ladder. Screen stars had never seemed like real people to Wisconsinites. Even after the Oscar, when Wisconsin folk mentioned actors and Fredric March in the same breath, they inadvertently added, "Oh, well, he's different . . . I know his Dad." Or they said, "I knew him in college." At this time March was also elected president (shades of his college days) of the Mayfair Club in November 1932. The Mayfair Club was one of the most exclusive social clubs in all California and all the biggest stars were members; Fredric March was the first *actor* elected to the presidency.

Following on the heels of the popular *Smilin' Through*, Paramount starred March in the prestigious Cecil B. DeMille production of the costume epic *The*

Sign of the Cross, based on an old play by Wilson Barrett. The storyline covers a few days shortly after the Great Fire of 64 A. D. involving the persecution of Christians under the reign of Emperor Nero, portrayed in grandiloquent style by Charles Laughton. March is cast as a prefect of Rome, Marcus Superbus, who desires Christian Mercia (Elissa Landi), with Claudette Colbert as the extremely seductive Poppaea, wife to Nero and trying in vain to catch Marcus's attention. It must have been especially hard on March to feign indifference in the sexy Colbert.

March is impressive in his opening scene. Commanding a three horse chariot, he thrashes his way through the Roman crowds, driving them from his chariot wheels with a whip. He saves Mercia from the crowd, then proceeds to try to seduce her. Of course, her Christian ideals prevent her from succumbing, even though she, too, loves Marcus. In frustration, he saves her once again during a Christian meeting that his archrival has disrupted. Spiriting her away to his home, he professes love for her during a typical Roman orgy, however, she struggles against him, realizing he wants her only as his mistress. Disgusted, Marcus sends his guests away, planning to take Mercia against her will. With the captured Christians singing ominously in the background, he attempts to carry out his intentions, but she tries desperately to convince him otherwise.

"Marcus! Listen to me. I don't want to live like this. I want to die with them." Mercia backs quickly away from him.

Not understanding, Marcus asks, "You mean, you'd give up life with me, and would rather die for a belief for some vague . . ."

"It isn't vague! It's certain! One man proved it, he changed men with it." Conviction is plain on Mercia's face.

He scoffs at her, "An illusion! It's madness, I tell you! Rome and mankind will go on as they are forever. Your Christianity will be stamped out and dead within a year!" He moves closer, facing her.

"I know better!" Mercia exclaims.

Marcus quickly embraces her, "Oh, Mercia. Don't you see what this thing has done to you? It hasn't let you live. It's deformed you! It's made love impossible to you."

Mercia struggles futilely in Marcus' arms, "As you look at love, yes. Not as I look at it. I've no use for your kind of happiness. Send me back to them." She pushes away from him backing toward a nearby divan.

Following, Marcus forces her to the edge of the divan, "No! You're not going to die with them. You're going to live with me!" He bends Mercia backward on the divan, his intent clear. "Mercia, be honest. You want to be with me. You love me!"

She cries, "I want to be with them!"

As she falls backward onto the divan, Marcus on top of her, he lowers his voice, "Ah, but with me, first."

"Marcus! Let me go!"

Mercia is about to meet the inevitable, but is saved by Nero's troops bursting in upon their cozy scene with plans to arrest. Marcus uses his influence to try to save Mercia while she awaits her turn in the Roman Colosseum, but realizes her conviction to her Christ is too strong. Unable to convince her, and understanding now that he cannot continue to live without her, Marcus joins her as they both walk up the stairs leading to the arena. As the door closes on them, the sign of the cross is reflected in the door's outline.

The Sign of the Cross was premiered November 30, 1932, but did not go into general release until February 1933. There was not a worse time in the history of the film industry to launch such an extravagant and expensive film, primarily because the country was economically at the deepest part of the Great Depression. Yet *The Sign of the Cross* did exceptionally well. Mordaunt Hall of the New York Times; "Marcus, acted admirably by Fredric March, who, if his diction constantly reminds one of his impersonation of Dr. Jekyll and other roles, wears his Roman uniform as if to the manor born" (March Papers). This was an important role for March, for virtually everyone in 1933 America saw *The Sign of the Cross*. With this portrayal, March became Hollywood's foremost "historic" actor, the Charlton Heston of the 1930s.

Unfortunately, March was to find no relief from Colbert. He was again cast opposite her, in *Tonight Is Ours*, based on Noel Coward's play *The Queen Was in the Parlour*. But, *Tonight Is Ours*, released January 21, 1933, bombed at the box office. Once again he found himself in close contact with Claudette Colbert, a happenstance that was to become exceedingly difficult. Insiders claimed that Colbert was, on screen and off, resisting Fredric March's continual passes. It was obvious enough that Mitchell Leisen, associate director on this film, commented:

> He was so taken with her that it was hard to tell when he was acting his role and when he was being himself. On the set between scenes he walked around in a kind of daze—one could never figure out whether he was working himself into the mood for his role or just walking off the effects of closeness to Claudette in front of the camera. And everyone hoped and prayed his wife wouldn't come visiting on the set. (Quirk 1985, 54)

One can only speculate about the so-called attraction Fred and/or Claudette felt for each other. Years later, during his fiftieth class reunion at the University of Wisconsin in Madison, Fred and Florence were asked to a private dinner party of former 1920 Wisconsin University graduates. In the course of the evening, one of Fred's college buddies brought up Colbert, wondering what it had been like to act opposite her. Fred promptly kicked him under the table, confessing later that Florence did not like to hear about Colbert, for Claudette almost broke up their marriage in the early thirties. Lawrence Quirk interviewed Fred for his book on Colbert. March's words to him were "I'm just sorry as hell that I didn't get more of a chance with Claudette —that is, er—to make more, and better, films with her. A pity" (Quirk 1985, 55).

A more satisfactory film arrived in the guise of the World War I aviation drama *The Eagle and the Hawk*. More dramatic than romantic lead, the role of Jerry Young provided March another chance to continue developing his versatile acting style. The part was a complex one by 1933 standards and allowed March to cover a wide range of emotions. He plays with sensitivity and great pathos the role of an American ace pilot with a British World War I flying squadron who loses his nerve, sickened by the necessity to send out to their death the young men under his command. His superior officer, noticing his emotional disintegration, gives Jerry ten days' leave in London, where he becomes appalled by all the lighthearted chatter of London natives about the war as great adventure. He returns in time to witness the death of his best friend (Jack Oakie), and then the death of his observer, or copilot. Jerry can no longer stand the strain and commits suicide. The scene is shot from below the bare springs of a stripped bed—that of his observer, killed that morning during an air battle. His former gunner (Cary Grant), the "hawk" who can take death in stride, smuggles Jerry aboard his plane and riddles it with bullets, crashing it, so that Jerry is remembered as a hero.

When it was released May 12, 1933, the *Hollywood Reporter*, reviewed *The Eagle and the Hawk* with "Fredric March shows what we have frequently suspected in watching his more stereotyped characterizations —that he is capable of getting under the skin of a part when there is skin to get under" (March Papers). *The Eagle and the Hawk* displayed March most credibly, proving that his style had always been a timeless and universal one.

March obtained Carole Lombard's services for this film, although her part was quite small. She played a passing fancy or one night stand during his London leave. March remembered the strict Production Code rules concerning the filming of their scenes together: "It was one of those 'regiment leaves at dawn' things and naturally, I was supposed to sleep with Carole. So, the next morning, I left a gardenia on her pillow. When the censors got a look at the scene, they said, 'You can't do that!' They made us re-shoot the scene, with me leaving the gardenia on Carole's bedside table" (*New York Times*, 27 May 1973, 3, March Papers).

During the filming of *The Eagle and the Hawk*, March's roaming eyes and hands got him in trouble with the soon to be popular Carole Lombard, who repelled his advances in her own inimitable way. Hoping to discourage March she feigned interest, inviting him to her dressing room for a drink and other unknown delights. Mad for a chance with the seductive Carole, Fred arrived eager to get the show on the road. When he found her waiting on her couch dressed in a sultry negligee, he promptly dropped down beside her, raining kisses wherever bare skin appeared. Meanwhile, in the manner of all men, he deftly moved his hand up under her ensemble, along her ankle, her leg and knee, then her thigh, when he felt something no woman, none that he had known, anyway, should have as part of her anatomy. Quickly, Fred disengaged himself, with her laughing uproariously, and backed out of the room, *never* to bother Carole Lombard again. Before his arrival, Carole had strapped on a dildo, an item guaranteed to dismay and disarm the most ardent of male admirers.

March gained a needed break from his busy picture schedule and headed East to Chicago for a June 22, 1933, appearance at the Chicago World's Fair, representing Wisconsin. On June 23, he and Florence arrived in Racine for a family reunion. Fred consented to appear at the State Theater in Racine that evening to narrate the evening's showing of trailers of his big successes of the year. However, they hastened back to California to oversee the building of their three-story Normandy-style house in Beverly Hills on Ridgedale Drive. They wanted a comfortable residence, with the feel of an English country house and containing enough guest rooms for their many East Coast friends as well as a dining room that could accommodate ten for dinner. The master suite overlooked a swimming pool and large flagstone terrace. Inside, a spacious Normandy kitchen served as the family room. Dominated by a large fireplace, the room had walls of whitewashed brick, a beamed ceiling, rows of bookcases and an oak table.

On September 18, 1933, *Screenplay* released its Box Office Champions. Fredric March clicked about even in all sections of the United States and in any and all types of households. In fact, his was the most balanced count. Following is the list with point scores:

Fredric March—74	Gary Cooper—23
Leslie Howard—52	James Dunn—18
Ramon Novarro—37	Ronald Colman—15
Clark Gable—30	Richard Dix—15
Clive Brook—28	George Brent—13
Warner Baxter—28	Joel McCrea—11
James Cagney—28	Nils Asther—11

The following received ten votes or fewer; Robert Montgomery, John Barrymore, Paul Lukas, Johnny Weissmuller, Phillips Holmes, George Raft, Buddy Rogers, Ben Lyon, Franchot Tone, Doug Fairbanks, Jr., Lee Tracy,

Richard Arlen, Richard Barthelmess, Maurice Chevalier, Warren Williams, and Chester Morris (March Papers). March also won acclaim, from *New Movie Magazine*, when the People's Academy selected Gold Players of the Year for 1933. He won Best Performance All Around for maintaining a high quality of work in all 1933 films, but was thought best in *The Sign of the Cross*. March was also elected second vice president to the fledgling Screen Actors Guild, formed October 4, 1933, as a response to the Motion Picture Committee's new regulatory code. This producer created code placed a ceiling on the salaries of writers, actors and directors, declaring that actors could not accept bids from other studios when contract time rolled around until the original studio decided not to rehire them. Consequently, the actors resigned from the Academy, forming the Screen Actors Guild.

March's next picture, *Design for Living*, involved a challenging moral idea to 1933 America—two men (Fredric March, Gary Cooper) sharing one woman (Miriam Hopkins). This menage à trois was considered quite daring in 1933, at least in pictures. March, Hopkins and Cooper were cast in the parts originally played by Alfred Lunt, Lynn Fontanne and Noel Coward. In this watered down version of the Noel Coward stage comedy, March was to receive good reviews; the film would not. Ben Hecht's screenplay did not recapture the wit and style of the Noel Coward play, although Ernst Lubitsch's touch as director added some entertainment value to the film.

Fred recalled mentioning to Schulberg that he wanted the chance to work under the direction of Ernst Lubitsch. His request was granted when he was given his choice of the two chief roles in *Design for Living*. Unable to make up his mind whether he wanted to play the Alfred Lunt part or the Noel Coward part, he put himself entirely in the hands of director Lubitsch, who promptly cast March in the dramatist role, Cooper as the artist. March felt that working under Lubitsch was a most interesting experience, entirely different from anything he had ever known before in motion pictures. Fred also felt Lubitsch's style was richly inventive, primarily because he worked out every detail himself and required the players to follow his instructions minutely. When it was released November 22, 1933, Mordaunt Hall wrote, "Fredric March is excellent as Thomas Chambers. He gives an amusing conception of a dramatist at work and later he makes the most of the author in a theater listening to laughter at his own lines" (March Papers). Actually, the movie was not so popular with American audiences. So, it was with great anticipation that March awaited the start of his next film, for the character he was to portray was indeed unusual, that of Death.

10

Romantic Leading Man

Fred was under pressure from Paramount to renew his contract: two years for $200,000, a goodly sum in the Depression era. He was reluctant because of some of the bad films they had forced on him. As a matter of fact, Paramount *was* placing Fred in some bombs lately. They did not give him any freedom to choose roles he wanted, and lately, they seemed to think superficial, silly romantic leads were his cup of tea. March's contract with Paramount would end in November of 1933, but he worked on a day to day basis to complete his final three picture commitment. The three pictures, *All of Me*, *Death Takes a Holiday* and *Good Dame*, would be completed by the end of December.

He yearned for the independence to choose roles more suited to showcase his talent. After all, he was not getting any younger, having just turned thirty-six, and felt he must guarantee a future beyond matinee idol status. Hence, March cast about for a more flexible contract with another studio, preferably one that would allow an option to loan himself out if need be. Once the word got around to the various Hollywood studios, offers inundated March. He decided on Darryl Zanuck's new company, Twentieth Century Pictures, because Zanuck offered him a salary running into a million dollars in two years, one of the largest salaries ever paid a screen star at that time. In return, March *must* complete two pictures picked by Twentieth, though not in sequence (the first was to be *The Affairs of Cellini*, the second, *Les Miserables*).

After finishing the last scenes on *Good Dame*, relieved, Fred and Florence went on a January visit to New York City before the start of his new contract with Twentieth on February 1. Renewing their acquaintance with college friend Chuck Carpenter and family they joined in the christening ceremony of Chuck's daughter and Fred's goddaughter, Jane. While in New York, March commented about why he was leaving Paramount in an interview granted to

Film Weekly, January 26, 1934: "I have two reasons: I want more money than Paramount apparently thinks I am worth, and which Mr. Darryl Zanuck is ready to pay me and I want a contract that stipulates for not more than forty weeks worth annually" (March Papers). One cannot blame him, for the Marches' had not enjoyed very many vacations for the entire duration of the Paramount contract. In fact, he had made twenty-nine pictures in that five year period! By the end of his contract with Paramount, March had worked continuously on his last four films, without a day off, from July 1, 1933, through New Year's Eve, working, more often than not, until 10:00 p.m. each night.

March's first picture for Twentieth was to start production by mid-February, Edwin Justus Mayer's 1928 Broadway hit *The Firebrand* (eventually renamed *The Affairs of Cellini*), a witty boudoir romp inspired by Cellini's self-proclaimed reputation as a lover and swordsman, costarring Constance Bennett. Darryl Zanuck wired March in New York that Benvenuto Cellini was to be his next part and *please, above all*, "do not cut your hair!" March wired back assuring Zanuck that his hair would be much longer by the fifteenth of February. He then started to read Cellini's autobiography and visited the New York Public Library to start familiarizing himself with both the period and the man.

Meanwhile, *All of Me* was released to theaters February 4, 1934. And a horrible little film it is! For this picture, March drew more notice of his wavy hair style likely affected by him in rebellion against Paramount. *All of Me* is based on the play *Chrysalis* by Rose Albert Porter, with Miriam Hopkins portraying the main character, a rich society girl with wayward inclinations. Fred portrays her enthusiastic young college professor boyfriend who has secured a job in the Boulder Dam construction project. She is unwilling to move West until inspired by the noble example of a crook (George Raft) and his pregnant girlfriend (Helen Mack), who jump out a window rather than be parted (what a plot!). At one point during the filming, Fred was endeavoring to show Miriam just how he would go about conquering the mighty river. After erecting imaginary dam walls and mountains with living room furniture, he got down on his hands and knees to imitate the rush of the river. The scene required three rehearsals and several retakes, and by the time director James Flood was happy, Fred had worn two neat ovals in the knees of his trousers. Naturally, with such an inferior story, the reviews were poor. *The Hollywood Reporter*; "March is handicapped by very unbecoming waved hair and quite a group of mannerisms. However at moments, he is splendid" (March Papers). Or, "The worst (acting), incredible as it may seem, comes from the usually reliable Fredric March. Either he was weighed down by his part or depressed by that extraordinary hair-cut" (March Papers). Many felt Paramount was punishing March for not renewing his contract and forced him into this particular role.

After the horror of the *All of Me* release, March left New York for a stop in his hometown, Racine, on his way back to Hollywood to start *The Affairs of Cellini*. After taking his father to the Chicago auto show, where Mr. Bickel admired a maroon-colored Oldsmobile sedan, Fred left the next day with a plan developing in his mind, a plan to surprise his father on Valentine's Day. Through secret negotiations with a Racine auto dealer, Fred had a shiny new 1934 model maroon-colored sedan delivered to Mr. Bickel in the middle of the night on February 14. The delivery man drove the car into the Bickel garage, placed a Valentine on the hood, closed the garage door, and sneaked away. What a commotion this caused with the College Avenue neighbors when Mr. Bickel went careening down the street in the gift Fred had bought him, for Mr. Bickel had always been a horrible driver, never quite getting the hang of it.

Mitchell Leison was the director for *Death Takes a Holiday*, Fred's next picture and most likely a mistake in casting on the part of Paramount. Adapted by Walter Ferris from Alberto Cassella's 1929 play *La Morte in Vacanze*, *Death Takes a Holiday* is one of Fredric March's *best* and a personal favorite of his. He portrays the physical incarnation of Death, disguised as the extraordinarily handsome Prince Sirki. Bored with his eternally lonely mission, Sirki spends three days on earth at an Italian villa to discover why humans cling to life and shrink from death. Unexpectedly, he falls in love with the beautiful Grazia (Evelyn Venable). When he must leave, Grazia begs to go with him, and Death complies. (While making this film, Fred had a girl's bicycle (Florence's) placed strategically near his dressing room door. He had borrowed it to use between *All of Me* on stage four and *Death* on stage one and had to take quite a bit of ribbing from fellow thespians.)

March is perfectly cast. His masterful presence and commanding voice give just the right feeling of all-knowing wisdom to Death's speeches, and his theatrical technique of overplaying some scenes is just right for the imposing aura of the inhuman Prince Sirki. He is in his element, playing the role with a combination of arrogance and childish delight. One scene, involving the placing of a live flower in Sirki's buttonhole by Grazia, captures this delight. His response is priceless as he continuously glances at or touches the flower, delighted that it does not die because of its close proximity to Death. March adopts a cultured accent and haughty speech, but also manages, with his attire, to cut a very attractive figure.

At the film's start, March appears to Sir Guy Standing (portraying Duke Lambert) as Death shrouded in black. The effect of Death's transparency was very difficult to create because director Mitchell Leisen wanted it done with the camera rather than having the lab put it in. Plus, they had to keep March within two or three feet of Standing, who had to remain solid. Duplicating certain pieces of the set in black velvet, they placed a mirror in front of March that was only 30 percent silvered so that the crew could shoot through it.

They then lit up certain portions of the black set, which reflected in the mirror superimposed over Fred, giving the appearance that he was transparent. Death's costume was many layers of chiffon from charcoal gray to black; Fred's face was made up like a skull with tiny lights under the hood to light up at appropriate moments. The shadows hovering over the ears were printed in by the Special Effects Department.

The character of Prince Sirki wears a monocle so March had to be taught to wear one. After he had spent a bad half-day trying to manipulate it, Sir Guy Standing, who knew all about single eyeglasses, rescued him. Standing told him to rub a bit of resin on the edges. It worked, to the delight of director Leisen, the cameramen and the harried property man. Another vexing problem occurred on the set, or at least it was thought vexing by March. It seems that the contract of Evelyn Venable provided for no kissing in her movie love scenes, causing awkward moments. After March, in character as the cavalier of the film, had contented himself with a brotherly kiss on the lady's shoulder, he frowned at Evelyn good-humoredly.

"Well, I can't help it," said Evelyn. "My father had the clause written into the contract."

"But what would my father say," retorted Fred, "if he saw me sitting here with you on this luxurious divan, midst music, low lights and sundry, if I DIDN'T kiss you?" (*Death Takes a Holiday* Press Book, 1934). Despite adamant protests on his part, Fred was not allowed to kiss Evelyn, on screen or off.

When it was released February 23, 1934, *Death Takes a Holiday* had extraordinary reviews. The *Sun*: "Death is played by Fredric March in one of that star's most striking performances. Mr. March, even when disguised as the gaunt unhappy Prince Sirki in glittering uniform and a foreign accent, is careful to underplay rather than emphasize the fantastic note" (March Papers). *Chicago Daily Tribune*: "Fredric March's inspirational performance will prevent my thinking of him as Fredric March for a long time to come. The man is completely submerged in, probably the greatest role he has ever played" (March Papers).

After this triumph, the *New York World Telegram* carried the results of the Executive Committee of the Atlantic League for the Rehabilitation of Speech; they picked Fredric March as Hollywood's best speaker. Following these commendations, March premiered in his final film of the Paramount contract, a misnamed caricature of a movie, *Good Dame*, released March 16. Picture the suave, sometimes described as "drawing room" Fredric March depicting an underworld tough guy redeemed by his love for Sylvia Sidney. Edward G. Robinson must have cringed when he saw *Good Dame*, if, indeed, he bothered. Miss Sidney and Mr. March did what they could to make their roles seem less trite than they were, but they were so handicapped by poorly written and characterized parts that their efforts failed. Reviewers were disappointed that such a picture had to follow the success of *Death Takes a Holiday*. *New York Times*: "Fredric March, using a quasi-underworld accent that varies from one scene to another, is so far beneath his usual standard that his performance must be attributed to the part he is forced to play" (March Papers). Lawrence Quirk summed up expertly: "The Paramount contract finally limped to a close with a film so mediocre that March and everyone connected with it must have despaired. . . . possibly the worst film of his career" (Quirk 1971, 26).

Miss Sydney had her own memories: "Fredric March had the reputation of being a ladies' man. We made two pictures together, *Merrily We Go to Hell* and *Good Dame*. But he never laid a hand on me, never made a pass at me! Freddie was happily married. He'd tease me by saying, 'Look at those boobs!' or 'Look at that toosh!' But it was all in fun" (*Hollywood Then and Now* 1991, 11). Perhaps Miss Sydney was just not Mr. March's type.

March was ecstatic over his new contract with Twentieth Century Pictures, especially with the proviso that he had control over his material (he thought) and could do outside parts. Hollywood was embarking on its Costume Epics period. Over the next several years, March was to appear primarily in costume films, emerging as the premier male lead over Errol Flynn and Ronald Colman, but, in reality, he never felt comfortable with historical role playing. March's first costume picture for Twentieth was to be *The Affairs of Cellini*, a seriocomedy, performing the part of Benvenuto Cellini, the talented Italian rogue whose private escapades almost overshadowed his artistic achievements. Once March knew definitely that he was to play Cellini, he gathered all available material on the subject, reading the autobiography of Cellini and all the historical data he could find that related to the character and that period of history. During an interview, March remarked about his character research procedure, feeling it was important to a film. "In some cases little attention is paid to the actual appearance of a character, although we try to preserve as much resemblance as possible. Cellini wore a pointed beard, so I tried to conform to his physical appearance to that extent" (March Papers). If, on the other hand, the character was not a historical one, but purely fictional, March tried to visualize the author's idea of the man he was to portray. As Cellini had been a masterful fencer, March practiced with the studio's fencing instructor for two hours a day, six weeks straight. In this, too, for realism purposes, March refused to use a mask or protective vest because he did not want his practice experience to feel different from the real thing. Despite this, he never was to be in the same class as Stewart Granger or Basil Rathbone in the fencing discipline.

Unfortunately, most of that in depth character study went for naught, for although March made a passionate and dashing Cellini clad in Renaissance tights, vaulting over walls to make mad love to various ladies on one hand, sword fighting palace guards on the other, he had the show stolen from him by Frank Morgan's Oscar nominated duke of Florence. Most of the film revolves around various misunderstandings, some silly, some dangerous, between Cellini, his model (Fay Wray) and the duke and duchess of Florence (Frank Morgan, Constance Bennett). Of course, Cellini is after any pretty young thing, especially his model, but so is Morgan. So, Cellini inveigles his way out of trouble with Morgan and into the duchess's bed. March exaggerates his way from one scene into the next, while Bennett mouths one innuendo after another. An extremely senseless script, as March felt later, admitting in a 1937 interview, "I shouldn't have played Cellini. It was a silly farce and the characters were silly. When they (Twentieth) first approached me about the role I was keen about the idea until I saw the script, then it was too late" (March Papers). *Cellini* opened September 5 to lukewarm reviews. Herald Tribune: "Mr. March, an admirable actor who is at his best in florid romantic roles with a suggestion of comedy, should have been not far from perfect as the Great Cellini, but for some reason he seems curiously restrained and retiring and, although he is pleasant and engaging in the part he is far from the brilliant success that I, for one, had anticipated" (March Papers).

Subsequently, March accepted an offered part from MGM, and another chance to star with Norma Shearer. Back in costume, he was to portray Robert Browning opposite Norma's Elizabeth Barrett in *The Barretts of Wimpole Street*. For this part he pursued the same diligent study of character. This time it was photographs of Robert Browning, revealing a youth wearing a beard that extended from one temple around under his chin to the other temple, the type of beard one associates with old sea captains. Naturally, March could not use this style of makeup or he might be mistaken for the heavily bearded vaudevillian comedy team of Weber and Fields. Necessarily, the part of the beard that extended under the chin was eliminated, keeping the long sideburns that gave the character a more youthful appearance. These sideburns were not counterfeit, but March's, a fact he was most proud of at the time for some unknown reason. However, March despaired about the Browning role, thinking director Sidney Franklin paid more attention to Norma, allowing him to get out of hand. He remarked later:

Let's face it, Robert Browning was a rather flighty, artificial-bonhomie type of guy, bouncing in and out of Elizabeth's room, applying the moral adrenaline; bouncing up and down and sashaying around with Victorian style flourishes that, to me, bordered on the fey and effeminate. I realized that the character was frantically trying to get Elizabeth off that couch, and I tried to get into his psyche, but he brought out the worst ham elements in me, and I feel I failed in the role." (Quirk 1988, 165)

March always admitted that he needed direction, often telling his directors,

"Please let me know if I am *overacting*!" Sometimes they did, sometimes they didn't. Perhaps the directors had trouble focusing on March. According to Shearer's biographer, Lawrence Quirk, March always wore his Robert Browning costume pants without underwear and rather tight around the crotch to "entice females." This is extremely noticeable in the film, especially when Robert first meets Elizabeth, in reality so conspicuous, one is hard pressed *not* to notice and to concentrate on what Mr. March is saying!

Released September 28 to good reviews, *Barretts* benefited March primarily because he was acting in an MGM prestige film opposite two other Academy Award winners, Norma Shearer and Charles Laughton (who ably portrayed Edward Barrett). March's personal reviews really were not all that bad, either. *Liberty*: "Fredric March, as Browning, shows a keen blend of comedy and romance, his robust energetic mannerisms being especially distinctive, contrasted as they are with the stuffy repression of the Barrett household" (March Papers). However, March felt he should not have played Robert Browning, because "I am essentially too American a type. I brought to that role the enthusiasm and vim, but I don't think much else. . . . I was fearfully tired when I started 'Barretts.' Again my own exuberance at tackling a new type of characterization overpowered me and I made a false step" (March Papers). During a 1964 radio broadcast, March remembered one of his lines from *Barretts*: "When he's (Robert Browning) reading his poems to Elizabeth and she says, 'What does that particular line mean, Mr. Browning?' And he said, 'Well, Miss Barrett, when that passage was written only God and Robert Browning understood it. Now, only God understands it.' What a lovely line" (*Yale Reports* 1964, 8)."

Interviewed by *Film Weekly* during the *Barretts* production phase for his opinion on the acting profession, March responded, "I have earnestly endeavored to perform my own share without fuss or temperament. An actor has no more right to be temperamental than a bank clerk. Possibly a very sane bringing up as a child has helped me to retain my sense of proportion in these matters" (*Film Weekly* 1934, March Papers). Incidentally, during the filming of *Barretts* the Marches' brought home a baby boy, born January 19, 1934, later adopting him in August 1935 through a superior court proceeding. They christened him Anthony for Fred's role of Anthony Cavendish in *The Royal Family of Broadway*. Unfortunately, Anthony was to prove a most difficult child, causing the Marches' heartache throughout his teen years and beyond. He got kicked out of every school they enrolled him in. Apparently, Anthony was not blessed with the agile mind of his adoptive father, continually disrupting the March family. Anthony eventually found happiness beyond life with Father, no real estrangement, but the Marches' rarely saw him. He ended up in Texas driving semitrailers and fatally crashing one in Oklahoma March 21, 1982.

The Marches' were next in the midst of planning their first actual vacation, a cruise to Tahiti. They would leave August 29 not to return until October, in time for filming his second commitment to Twentieth, *Les Miserables*, another costume vehicle. Before vacation March had agreed, somewhat apprehensively, to star opposite Anna Sten in the Samuel Goldwyn production of Leo Tolstoy's *Resurrection*, retitled *We Live Again*. Anna Sten was a Ukrainian actress discovered by Goldwyn. Convinced that he had unearthed a major star, Goldwyn first placed her opposite Gary Cooper in *Nana*, where she bombed with the American public.

After reading the script, March at first turned down the part of Prince Dmitri, claiming it was small and indifferent, but more likely because he was reluctant to appear second-billed opposite possible "box-office poison." Nonetheless, Goldwyn wanted Fredric March, so he delivered a blow to his Achilles heel by offering him twice his usual salary for a few weeks' work ($100,000), thus immediately changing March's previous opinion of Prince Dmitri. And, after all, it would reunite him with a favorite director, Rouben Mamoulian. So March started on yet another costume drama.

11

Romantic Leading Man, Part II

We Live Again, retitled from the *Resurrection* of Leo Tolstoy, relates the idyllic courtship of an aristocratic young cadet and an apple-cheeked peasant girl. A grim struggle develops through misery and despair toward happiness and peace in the screenplay by Preston Sturges, Maxwell Anderson and Leonard Praskins. This beloved Russian story has the countryside in the days of the czars as its early setting. Colorful religious festivals, Gypsy songs, intricate cavalry maneuvers, Moscow and her debauched gaiety, prisons, and trial scenes are the details in the patchwork panorama that director Rouben Mamoulian has taken out of Tolstoy's great humanitarian novel as a setting for the screen version.

March was still concerned about playing opposite Anna Sten, for she had not received good reviews in her first movie. However, Sten was not unattractive, and their few previous scenes together revealed an on-screen electric spark that looked promising. One can imagine Fred taking advantage of fledgling Sten during filming. And, during one of the their scenes together, he seemed to take full advantage. In the days of Movie Code it is surprising this scene made it through the strict censors. The scenario involved Sten as the hapless servant girl, Katusha Maslova, and costar March as her boyhood sweetheart, Prince Dmitri Nekhilyudov. Dmitri has returned home for Easter from the service after a two-year absence. The two attend church services where he eyes Katusha with *more* than mild interest.

Both were preparing to retire for the evening when Dmitri, an obviously jaded soldier, simply decides he wants Katusha and walks determinedly to his bedroom door, down the dark stairway, across the foyer and out the front door. Noticing Katusha's open window, he walks toward it and finds her combing out her abundantly long hair at the dressing table. Pausing, staring at her, his desire for her apparent on his face, he flips the cigarette over his shoulder casually then walks toward her window and leans against it, drawing her curtain aside so she can see him. After convincing her to take a short walk in the moonlight, he lifts her out of the window as she silently consents to go with him. He carefully places her upon the ground, then hand-in-hand they walk away from the window. He guides her strategically toward the greenhouse; the music swells ominously. Once inside, he shuts the door silently after them then walks toward her, smiling (leering) eagerly.

She leans down and picks some violets, holding them up to Dmitri, asking, "Remember?" At first he is quizzical, then a memory of two years ago, the last day they saw each other, comes back to him. "Violets?" . . . Oh, yes . . . (he takes them out of her hand, placing his arms around her) . . . violets." He tries to kiss her, but she ducks away walking further from him. He follows closely. She turns to face him, exclaiming that they shouldn't do this, but he places his arms about her waist, drawing her close to him, asking, "Why not? When two people love each other?" His intent is clear, as he tries to kiss her again. Again he is rebuffed by her reminder that he has not seen her for two summers.

Dmitri takes his arms from around her waist but quickly catches both her hands in his. Leaning into her, drawing her close, he speaks softly, gradually moving his mouth ever closer to hers, "Is everyone going to scold me tonight? Very well, then. I should have come back or I should have written. I didn't. Now tell me that because of that you don't love me any longer and I'll go away." Repeatedly he tries to kiss her, with better success, until she reluctantly turns her head away. In agony, she says, "No, No, Dmitri Ivanovich . . . please, no!" But he has her trapped, enfolded in his embrace, his mouth hovers a bare inch above her, as he implores, "Katusha, army maneuvers aren't child's play . . . I may be hurt, perhaps even killed!" His head descends, but she places the palm of her hand against his mouth to prevent it. A little exasperated, he still holds her close, determined to have her, "It's *you* who have changed, not I. I'm just as I was. Every bit as much in love with you as before I left. It's you who have forgotten me."

She is panicky now, "Oh, don't say that!" Dmitri *must* know she loves him! Surrendering, she allows the kiss—they part for an instant, then kiss again, deeply (too deeply for the moral code of that day). Her arms come up around his shoulders as he gently forces her down, presumably upon some form of a bed. The camera pans discreetly toward the ceiling of the greenhouse, leaving the conclusion of the scene to the imagination of audiences. She winds up pregnant, however, loses the child at birth, and is ostracized from her community (Preston Sturges, Maxwell Anderson, Leonard Praskins, 1934).

Most of the Russian players in the cast were members of the Dukhobor Colonies in California and Canada. Their migration to America was financed out of the money realized by Tolstoy from the sale of *Resurrection*. The 42,000 rubles he received for the work was the only money he ever made from his writings. And forty years after he turned it over to people who believed as he did and sought escape from tyranny and oppression, the children of those people took part in the filming of Tolstoy's greatest story in the land in which they had taken refuge.

Some non-romantic incidents that transpired on the set included one in which March, who had a knack for picking up languages, decided to surprise the Russian-speaking Mamoulian by reciting a carefully rehearsed anecdote in the foreign tongue, which he did with flying colors. When Mamoulian wanted to film a cavalry drill as a detail of Dmitri's wild and reckless life as a cadet, March refused a double for the maneuvers. He said there was nothing the professional riders—many of them former Cossack officers—could do that he couldn't do. And, in the picture, he proved it, displaying the skill he had learned as a 2nd Lieutenant of Cavalry and Instructor in Riding at Camp Zachary Taylor, Kentucky, during World War I.

As the Russian Prince Dmitri, who loves a peasant, leaves to become an officer (with all the wine, women and song he can handle), returns to seduce the ill-fated Katusha, leaves again, etc., March, proving his ability to overcome a part he was not totally comfortable with, is splendid. His dashing and gallant lieutenant is naively buoyant at the picture's beginning, but then, he gradually sinks into lighthearted army life and "ruins" Katusha, promptly forgetting her for the livelier life in the city and an engagement to a judge's daughter. While appearing as a juror, he discovers the defendant to be his childhood love, Katusha, now forced to use her body to support herself. Confusingly convicted of murdering a client (she didn't), Katusha is destined for Siberia. March is moving and emotionally touching as the bearded and conscience-stricken aristocrat, who somberly contemplates the ruthless oppression of the czarist regime. To March fell some of the most interesting scenes in the drama as he strove to convince the wretched Katusha of his sincerity and to free her from the imperial machine intent on sending her to Siberia. One scene involved intense soul searching in the privacy of his apartment. With peasants singing in the background, tears (not artificial) slowly drip from his eyes, eyes that do not blink, as the stricken look on his face mirrors the realization of his responsibility for ruining Katusha's life.

March was interviewed on the set of *We Live Again* in July for *The Evening News* by Andrea Angel. She found him friendly and unaffected and admired the unselfish way he praised other actors, seemingly having that rather rare gift of being able to appreciate other men's work without comparing it with his own. Miss Angel watched him in action during the *We Live Again* "turkey" scene. Prince Dmitri had just arrived home and all the peasants were giving him gifts. One gift was a live turkey that had an extraordinary way of screeching and whirling around in the air everytime poor Fredric March tried to take it. This scene was done over and over again; and over and over again the turkey screeched and whirled. And so Miss Angel left him still taking the bird with the utmost patience and good temper, discovering it would take a great deal more than a turkey to upset Fredric March.

March personally felt he did a poor job as Dmitri, but viewing the movie today reveals the kernels of the future March characterization of Count Vronsky in *Anna Karenina*. In fact, he looked and acted so right as Prince Dmitri, especially in the seduction scene, that he was the obvious choice to star opposite Garbo in *Anna Karenina* in 1935. Released November 1, 1934, *We Live Again*, despite the casting of Anna Sten, who actually did an excellent job, received good notices but did not attract large audiences and was a disappointment to Goldwyn financially. *Variety*: "Fredric March turns in probably the best job of his career, a compelling performance" (March Papers). *Herald Tribune*: "There is a good portrayal of the amorous prince by Fredric March, who is at his best in this type of costume character" (March Papers).

After the filming of *We Live Again* completed, Fred and Florence carried out their vacation plans for their two month trip to Tahiti. Fred kept a diary of this vacation published in an article for *Photoplay*, March 1935. Some notable excerpts are included herein:

Wednesday, August 29—

We sailed from San Francisco, today at 4:00 p.m. Ten more days, then Tahiti. There was the usual gaiety at sailing time and we'd had telegrams, flowers, and books sent us, but the fact that we'd be two months away from Tony and Penny sort of took the edge off things. They're swell kids and it'll be the first time we've ever left them for so long. Florence insists that they won't even remember us when we get home. Of course Tony won't, but Penny's two, now and she should.

When I saw the loot we'd collected for going away, I wanted to take up leaving-for-Tahiti as a profession. How gratifying it is to have friends.

September 8—

Up at five to see the sun rise over Tahiti. It was beautiful as nothing else shall ever be.

Tonight our hosts, Mr. and Mrs. Cook, brought us leis of beautiful and fragrant flowers, hibiscus, tiara tahiti, bougainvillea. If a Tahitian wears a flower behind the left ear it means, "I have a lover;" behind the right, "I want a lover;" flowers behind both ears mean, "I have a lover of whom I'm tired, and want another."

I've known all along that ears couldn't be just for hearing with.

September 14—

This afternoon we drove eleven miles the other side of Papeete to the leper colony. Jack and Phil [Jack and Phyllis Morgan] and I went in, but

Florence refused to budge from the car. We who did go were badly shaken by what we saw. I was scared pink when the whole French hospital staff insisted on shaking hands!

Evidently the disease isn't as contagious as we imagine it to be . . . But the period of incubation of the disease can extend up to six years, so for that long I'll be inspecting myself for spots at least three times daily.

September 20—

The Morgans and the Marches' and all the children on Moorea spent the morning hunting scorpions. We found two and Jack insisted that if ringed with fire they'd commit suicide. They were; and they didn't. So we popped them into a jar of alcohol to take home to the kids.

September 30—

We went to the local Market. By now the market was showing signs of life and we made our tour. The thing I remember best is the deposed native queen's cook. He is, believe it or not, what my father calls a sissy-boy. I almost died watching him mince from stall to stall, pinching the vegetables and paying for his purchases out of a woman's handbag, which he carried with his arm extended in much the same way I might tote an overripe piece of cheese. So they have 'em even in Tahiti!

October 8—

We sailed at six. In the early sun the island was even more beautiful today than on the day of our arrival.

Good-bye, Tahiti. (Photoplay 1935, 56–57, 98–99, 100–101)

From his comment about an obviously gay man, Fredric March's dislike for such individuals can be surmised. As a young and handsome actor in New York, March was approached often by gay actors. He was approached by Charles Laughton (a known homosexual) during their first film together, *The Sign of the Cross*. March recalled to Lawrence Quirk that Laughton always made him very nervous and uncomfortable, especially when Laughton used to try to look up his toga in *Sign of the Cross*.

Upon their arrival home, March started filming his second commitment to Twentieth, *Les Miserables*. As the forever pursued Jean Valjean pitted against Charles Laughton's Inspector Javert, March gave one of his strongest and most admired performances. *Les Miserables* spanned thirty years in the life of a poor man, Jean Valjean, beginning with his sentencing to the galleys for stealing a loaf of bread to feed his sister's starving family; following him upon his release, his slow and painful rise to respectability and eventual shadowing and pursuit by Javert. March handled the thirty year interval with ease, relishing the various characterizations he was allowed to portray: the young idealistic man, the hardened criminal, the respectable shop owner, the adoptive father, the look-alike idiot about to be convicted, the hunted persecuted hero, and, finally, the older but wiser Jean Valjean ready to accept his fate, his lot in life, when Javert commits suicide, freeing Valjean forever.

Nominated for Best Picture, *Les Miserables* was destined to become one of Twentieth Century's most popular and best remembered movies, largely because of the inspired casting of Fredric March and Charles Laughton, and the extremely fine direction of Richard Boleslavsky. Running 108 minutes, it was the longest Zanuck film to date with enough plot twists for two films. March and Laughton staged the greatest acting dual in cinema history up to that time, with some critics believing it a dead heat for first honors, but the majority felt *Les Miserables* placed Fredric March among the immortals of the screen. *Daily News*: "Fredric March again reveals himself as Hollywood's finest actor" (March Papers). *Los Angeles Examiner*: "This out-Jekylls Jekyll and out-Hydes Hyde as the high point in Fredric March's colorful career" (March Papers). *New York Times*: "Mr. March's Valjean is a flawless thing, strong and heartbreaking" (March Papers). *New York American*: "Fredric March storms the histrionic heights . . . never once does the actor falter . . . always his portrayal is such that the audience may follow his every thought through all exigencies of the part" (March Papers). Such praises echoed through the country April 21, 1935, the day after its premier.

During the filming of *Les Miserables*, early in 1935, March toyed with the idea of trying Broadway once again. In this quest, Florence was not far in the background. She influenced him because her own Hollywood picture career had not taken off; one excuse was that she was not "photogenic." She was most anxious to act again on the familiar turf of Broadway and if she could lure audiences with a headliner such as her husband, all the better. The idea of playing no more costume parts influenced him, too, for March felt the American public had forgotten what he looked like in modern tweeds. Until Robert Donat as the Count of Monte Cristo came along, it was generally conceded that Fredric March had the costume field pretty much to himself, for no actor so effectually combined a brisk, modern youthfulness and a sense of humor with the classic features and resonant if slightly Sixth Avenue voice of the traditional thespian. But he had been letting his hair grow long for many months now and was fast growing tired of it. *Death Takes a Holiday*, *Affairs of Cellini*, *The Barretts*, *We Live Again*, and *Les Miserables*, were all more or less in the hairy line. "Look at this scraggly thing," he would mourn on the set of *Les Miserables*, pointing to the Svengali-like beard which rather doubtfully adorned his chin (March Papers). The *Los Angeles Times* reported February 2, 1935, "Freddie (and how many actors do you know who specialize in heroics and still let you call them Freddie?) wants to take a flyer in the theater" (March Papers).

Still reeling from *Les Miserables*, March was precisely *told* his next role would be opposite the Great Garbo in the MGM production of *Anna Karenina*. March, who had not liked *We Live Again* and was adamantly against taking another costume role, balked. He told Twentieth that he would only portray Vronsky if they insisted. They did, so he did. So much for choosing one's own films. In reality, March's curiosity about Garbo plus the prestige of starring opposite her swayed him more in accepting a role that was, to him, superficial, and not really his kind of part. Garbo had starred with John Gilbert in a 1927 silent version of Tolstoy's novel and could not be talked out of this lavish talkie remake despite the warnings of producer David O. Selznick that heavy Russian tragedies were then box-office poison. It turns out that Garbo knew exactly what she was doing. The story line is familiar. Anna Karenina (Garbo), unhappily married to a Russian aristocrat and politician (Basil Rathbone) in nineteenth century Russia, falls in love with a handsome and dashing cavalry officer, Count Vronsky (March). Once Vronsky realizes Anna is cramping his style, he manufactures with help from his old regiment a need to go to war. Through various misunderstandings the affair ends in tragedy, as Anna steps in front of a train to end her miserable existence.

March described working with Garbo as fun but he did not really get to know her very well. As the saying went at the time, costarring with Garbo hardly constituted an introduction. During the making of *Anna Karenina* he maintained that she was very friendly, not always reserved. For instance, they would bounce a medicine ball back and forth during breaks. One day she stripped to the waist to take the sun, then she caught herself and asked whether it embarrassed Fred. He claimed it did not. On another occasion, he told her how wonderful she had been with the boy in the silent version of *Anna Karenina* (opposite John Gilbert), letting him really take over their scenes together. Fred suggested maybe she should adopt a child. "A little late in the picture for you to make such a proposition to me," the ever mysterious Garbo answered (Zierold 1969, 90).

March told reporters, "Actually, I was not overwhelmed by Garbo's beauty. I think at the time women were more attracted to her than men" (March Papers). This last statement is a curious one for him, especially considering that Clarence Brown, the director on *Anna Karenina*, commented of March and Garbo, "She had a droll sense of humor and she could be clever. While working with her in *Anna Karenina*, Fredric March showed signs of wanting to get romantic. Before each love scene Garbo put a small piece of garlic in her mouth. It worked" (Zierold 1969, 95).

Despite the garlic, March managed to portray the dashing Russian officer, Count Vronsky, as he surely must or should have been. Garbed handsomely in military uniform for the first part of the film, March was able to portray the enthusiasm and shallowness of a man much younger than his thirty-seven years, especially Vronsky's selfishness in romantic entanglements. Still, March again felt he did a poor job. Regardless of his personal feeling, *Anna Karenina* was released August 30, 1935, and was a resounding success at the box office. Of course, Garbo was whom the picture was built around; therefore the majority of the reviews exulted her talents, but March received good notices, too: "Mr. March, as befits an eager soldier-lover, impetuous in his amours as in the wars is more physical in his acting and expresses himself by words and deeds. He fits excellently into the role of Vronsky—one of the best he's done" (March Papers). In fact, both *Anna Karenina* and *Les Miserables* were voted two of the ten best pictures of 1935 by the critics of the nation in the Film Daily Annual Poll.

While filming *Anna Karenina*, March attended a Hollywood gala given by L. B. Mayer. Eleanor Powell, new to MGM, was in attendance and was shocked enough to recount the following story years later: Suddenly, while she was dancing with Mayer, a gentleman dancing nearby with a young lady stopped very dramatically and said, "L.B., I *must* dance with this fascinating, charming creature!" So Mayer introduced Eleanor to Fredric March.

Exchanging partners, Fred held Eleanor close, pulling her toward him. She had on a dress that had a low back, where he placed his hand. Moving his hand a little lower and a little lower, he stopped and said, "Miss Powell, may I ask you a personal question?"

Eleanor replied, "Well, that depends."

"Are you wearing a girdle?"

Eleanor was a little shocked at this last question. She thought he was going to ask her how old she was. Looking directly at Fred, she said, "No, I'm not wearing no girdle."

Fred continued, "You want me *just* to dance?"

After looking at him questioningly, it dawned on her what he wanted. Quickly, she replied, "Just dance." It became a joke between the two. Whenever they saw each other passing on the set, he would yell at her, "Hey Ellie! Just Dance! Just Dance!" (Kobal 1985, 235).

March's popularity in costume films was beginning to wear on him, for he was becoming restless, longing to appear in modern dress. He voiced his opinion about this typecasting throughout 1935, even threatening to leave Hollywood because of too many costume pictures. *Tattle Tales* reported; "It is painful to contemplate a screen devoid of the amazing Mr. March, but if it takes that to awaken producers to the fact that he can act just as effectively without a beard as with one, then his fans should be willing to stand loyally by while the lesson is being taught" (March Papers). March did manage to duck out of costarring with Norma Shearer for a third time in her updated version and pet project, *Romeo and Juliet*. He refused to read the script or even discuss the project when informed he was Norma's first choice for Romeo. "I would have looked like a damn fool in tights climbing balconies and making pretty speeches. My God, I was 38 years old at the time. I would have totally lost my audiences bouncing around like a sixteen-year-old kid!" (Quirk 1988, 171–172). Leslie Howard later accepted the role.

September of 1935 found Fred and Florence bound for London on holiday, where a London newspaper reported that Mr. March revealed a total absence of the sort of patronage or self-assumption that marked some of the stars who visited London. While they were away, March's latest picture, *The Dark Angel*, was released September 5, 1935. He was proud of his work with Merle Oberon in the semimodern *Dark Angel*, remarking, "I honestly believe I turned in a good performance" (March Papers). A Samuel Goldwyn picture, *The Dark Angel* also met with nationwide approval. Guy Bolton's play had been filmed in 1925 with Vilma Banky and Ronald Colman, also for Goldwyn, but this time out it was scripted by Lillian Hellman and Mordaunt Shairp and directed by Sidney Franklin. March portrays a man who is blinded in World War I but pretends to have been killed in order not to be a burden to his girlfriend (Merle Oberon). March made the most of his opportunities, particularly in the scene when he, having been discovered alive, acts as if he can see by carefully arranging everything in the room before Miss Oberon's visit. March played scenes of his blindness with considerable skill and he continued to bring to his love scenes that passionate romanticism with which his work had generally been associated.

Somewhat humorously, Andre Sennwald's review in the *New York Times* remarked, "Fredric March in his new film continues to be lacking in common sense in his relationships with his screen loves. At the Capitol, you will remember, he is deserting Miss Greta Garbo five times a day in his passion to go to war. Now in *The Dark Angel* he pretends that he is dead in order to escape marrying the lyric Miss Merle Oberon" (March Papers). The *London Times*: "March, especially, unburdened with costumes, is at his best in the juiciest role he has ever had" (March Papers). The *Evening News*: "Fredric March gives the best performance of his career as the man who is blinded. Every touch of the part is firm and understanding" (March Papers).

As much as March enjoyed the chance at a modern film, RKO wanted him to portray the earl of Bothwell opposite Katharine Hepburn's Mary in *Mary of Scotland*, a carefully calculated picture undertaken by producer Pandro Berman to undo the *Sylvia Scarlett* damage and bring Hepburn back to public favor. Using Maxwell Anderson's drama as a basis, Berman employed a prestigious and huge cast, making it the second most expensive production of the year (behind *Swing Time*). *Mary of Scotland* concerns the chronicle of the life-and-death struggle for supremacy between two iron-willed women, Mary Stuart and Elizabeth I of England portrayed excellently by Florence Eldridge. *Mary of Scotland* was the only film in which March was directed by John Ford. He commented, "I liked working with Jack. I still remember asking him how he saw my character of Bothwell. 'It's a comedy,' he said about the tragedy. 'Play him for comedy!'" (Sinclair 1979, 69).

Costar Katharine Hepburn from the start of shooting (winter 1935) fought and bickered with Ford. In fact, she never encouraged camaraderie during filming with her directors; or for that matter with any of her leading men. When contacted for this biography in 1990, Miss Hepburn reported that she did not know Mr. March well, as they only acted together in one picture, but he was a sweet man and a good actor. Before Florence began work on the picture, director Ford told Fred, "Tell your wife not to come in here with preconceived ideas about Elizabeth."

"Well," Fred said, "How do *you* see the character of Elizabeth, Jack?"

He chewed on that old handkerchief of his for a minute and finally said, "Elizabeth's a comic."

"Jesus!" Fred replied. "There sure are a lot of comics in this movie" (Sinclair 1979, 69).

Bette Davis had wanted the part of Elizabeth and in her memoirs mentioned that she did not get it because Florence Eldridge was the wife of the star. When asked his opinion of this during a 1990 interview, Ralph Bellamy nodded emphatically, replying that March was definitely a big enough star to have forced RKO into casting Florence as Elizabeth. That may well have been the case, for, after Davis's subsequent portrayals of the balding queen, it is hard to imagine anyone other than Bette Davis as Elizabeth (with the possible exception of Flora Robson) although Florence fared quite well in the reviews.

March's character, the earl of Bothwell, is an interesting historical figure, a romantic individual born to power in a time when might was right and only the unscrupulous survived. He alone had the audacity to fight the powerful lords of Scotland and Mary's scheming half-brother, the earl of Moray. Fearing neither man nor the Devil, Bothwell scorns the lords; makes reckless love to Mary, abducting her in a plot of which she was secretly a part; and marries her in defiance of Scotland. Mary's passion for Bothwell costs her the throne of Scotland and eventually her life. Whether it was passion or ambition, or a combination of both, Bothwell pays dearly in the end for his recklessness, driven from Scotland to die in a Danish prison. March is always in character as the impetuous, dauntless, romantic earl of Bothwell. His portrait of the man who is unable to remain away from Mary, even after she flaunts his love by marrying another (before him), is indeed a fine, most eloquent performance. He creates a duplicate of the Bothwell historians describe: arrogant, sardonic, full of impetuousness, fire and, above all, *bravery*. In the face of such a man, Mary never had a chance. In the role of Mary's lover and third husband, the earl of Bothwell, March had to wear a skirt. How fortunate for us that he had good legs. What a resplendent Bothwell he made, Scottish brogue, legs and all.

When it was released to theaters July 30, 1936, audiences witnessed a guarded and somewhat stiff portrayal of Mary by Hepburn. Though the final product received respectful praise from the critics, it flopped with the public. Not all the reasons for failure fell on Hepburn, however. For *Mary of Scotland* was long, ponderous, episodic, in other words, an utter bore. March commented, "It would have been a still stronger film had the devastating passion of Mary for Bothwell been brought out in the plot, had another scene or two to show emotional feeling between them been added. I suggested the one sequence which did show their dramatic love, but there should have been more" (March Papers). March's personal reviews, however, were excellent. *New York Times*: "His is a first-rate portrayal of the bold, roistering, devil-may-care border Scot history shows him to have been" (March Papers). William Boehnel of the *New York World Telegram*: "As the rough, tender and noble Bothwell, Fredric March does his best screen work, contributing a performance that is clear and forceful in every respect" (March Papers).

By the end of *Mary* March had had his fill of history. But this distaste for costume roles was temporarily subdued when he realized what he was slated to do next.

12

The Road to Glory and Free-Lancing

Early January 1936. Twentieth Century-Fox lot, the far corner of a spacious outdoor set much larger than the usual handmade set, easily 300 feet wide, 100 feet deep. High above the entire set is stretched sheeting to diffuse the brilliant California sunlight. Around three sides rising from the ground to the cloth ceiling are bleached canvases painted with faint ripples of gray to simulate a smoke-clouded horizon. Raised off the ground about six feet, a "no-man's-land" had been constructed on a foundation of wooden platforms, crisscrossed with a labyrinth of trenches and barbed wire entanglements. Here and there stood a scarred and barren tree, bullet-shattered. And underfoot, everywhere, there is earth—earth so thick that a heavy wetting had converted it into soggy mud.

The trenches do not look as if they had been manufactured by studio carpenters and plasterers, but look exactly like a "registered area" just behind the Western Front, late 1916. Only one small section of the set was devoted to the area across which the troops had to run. This particular section was devoid of any trench but pockmarked with imitation shell holes. It was not easy ground to run across, even though the distance was only a few feet. A bevy of activity started at the signal of "Action!"

There was a dull explosion in the distance, as if a shell had found its mark. Then, two more explosions in quick succession—nearer. In front of the weary men in mud-covered, faded, blue French uniforms, the ground ripped apart. Instinctively, they ducked, shielding themselves from the shower of earth and rock and shrapnel. A moment later, they were tensely peering ahead once more, into the low-lying, agitated battle haze, trying to see the shell-torn area across which they soon would be running. As soon as Lieutenant Denet gave the order.

Day and night, night and day, the Germans were raining shells on this narrow strip of land, this "registered area" behind the Western Front—at ten-second intervals. Replacements for the front-line trenches could not reach the front lines without crossing this particular segment of Hell. They could not cross except between the bursting of shells. And shells, with clocklike precision, fell every ten seconds. *Seconds*, not minutes.

The whole platoon could not cross all at the same time. They had to cross in sections, timing their breaks for the other side so perfectly that there would be explosions just ahead of them, then just behind them. The soldiers showed no terror of this race with Death. Young and old, they were battle-hardened, grim, and too well-disciplined to do anything but carry out orders.

The first section started running. On their heels raced the second. Then the third. Into an inferno of acrid, sulphurous smoke, sharp explosions, volcanic earth. The Lieutenant straining his eyes, saw the third section vanish; where they had been, there was only a crater-like shell hole. The Germans had mistimed one of their shots, had blown them to bits. But the Lieutenant had no time to think about it. He and the fourth section had to take their own chances. They, too, started running . . .

A moment later, the explosions stopped. The smoke began to clear. Simultaneously, a sharp voice called out: "CUT!" The scene was ended. The Lieutenant and his platoon, including the recently destroyed third section, slogged back through the heavy mud. (*Movie Classic* 1936, 30)

The Lieutenant pulled off his trench helmet and sank into a canvas chair labeled "Mr. March" to contemplate his next scene in the Twentieth-Century-Fox film *The Road to Glory*. After *Mary of Scotland*, March had the good fortune to be cast in this film that qualifies as great tragedy. Based on the French film *Wooden Crosses*, *The Road to Glory* utilized the talents of director Howard Hawks and producer Darryl Zanuck plus the scripting of Joel Sayre and William Faulkner. *The Road to Glory* is a tribute to French patriotism, heroism and gallantry under fire where the rightness of the Allied cause is never even momentarily questioned.

Although it was a World War I period piece, March savored his role as a lieutenant recently assigned to the 39th regiment of the French Army headed by Captain Paul LaRoche (Warner Baxter).

March recalled:

Of course, sometimes a costume picture comes along which is a positive relief, such as the role I played in *Road to Glory*. I was covered with mud and dust throughout most of the picture. My face was streaked with it. My boots and uniform were caked with it. I was happy—for I could forget personal appearance for the camera's sake. I was free to concentrate entirely on the job of acting. (March Papers)

However, there had to be a romantic interest, supplied herein by a beautiful young nurse, Monique (June Lang), friend and companion to Captain Paul LaRoche (Baxter), who loves her, but Monique only admires the Captain.

March's Lieutenant Michael Denet, flippant, daring, new to trench warfare, joins LaRoche's outfit just before it moves back into the front lines. Denet meets Monique before he encounters LaRoche during an air raid over the town where the troops are quartered. Monique has to take shelter in the doorway of a house in whose cellar Denet has found a battered old piano on which he is pounding out an improvised symphony when he spies her pretty ankles. He persuades her to come inside and attempts, naturally, to seduce her in the fast military manner, but she refuses him, leaving without telling him her name. Romance develops but against their wills. Inexorably, they are drawn together, their guilt finally overwhelming them, for they feel they have betrayed their friend LaRoche. Because of this, especially after the death of LaRoche, the relationship can go no further. Love is all very well, but duty comes first. Denet takes command of the platoon, repeating the same speech to new recruits that his predecessor always used, including the same inflections and quick swallowing of aspirin from his pocket as he turns to retreat into the office (Baxter's Captain is addicted to aspirin).

Interviewed in 1990, June Lang felt she was too young (nineteen) to be cast opposite thirty-eight-year-old Fredric March and forty-five-year-old Warner Baxter. "It was a very quiet set and serious because of the war theme. No joking or laughing as is the usual situation during other types of films. Mr. March was always polite and of course very handsome. He did not seem to have a flamboyant personality that would allow one to know too much about his personal being." Then, hesitantly, "The scuttle butt around the set inferred he was interested and making a play for or whatever, to my hairdresser" (Interview, June Lang, 11 August 1990). Apparently, Mr. March was not serious and quiet throughout all the film. Fred once confided to his sister-in-law about enticement. She later wrote, "Naturally, there are temptations (Freddie's only human). And, as he says himself, it's not the stars, not the women he makes love to on the screen, who constitute the chief menace: it's the extra girls, the girls who do bits, or are only looking for a job, that are the hardest to resist. They have so much to gain and sometimes so little to lose, poor dears ... And they are, there is no question about it, seductive" (March-to-the-Altar, c. 1932, March Papers).

When it was released August 5, 1936, reviews for *The Road to Glory* were admirable. The picture rates as one of the most moving and accurate of all antiwar films about World War I; the strain of trench warfare is never better conveyed than in the sequence where a terrified platoon lay quivering in the dark listening to German "sappers" placing explosives under their position, eventually blowing the whole area apart including the platoon. The *London Times*: "Mr. March and Mr. Baxter act as though they believe in it all" (Quirk

1971, 142). *New York American*: "Fredric March is the debonair hero, who grows in depth and stature under fire" (March Papers). *New York World-Telegram*: "The acting reveals an admirable integrity. Fredric March and Warner Baxter bring a force and validity to their characterizations" (March Papers).

During the production phase of *The Road to Glory*, March was called to testify for James Cagney in Cagney's lawsuit against Warner Brothers during February 1936. Cagney alleged that he had an oral agreement with Jack Warner four years prior (during the Motion Picture Academy arbitration, during which Fredric March was on the Panel). Evidently, in 1932 outside the panel meeting room, Jack Warner promised that Cagney would not be overburdened with work, implying that he would not have to act in more than four pictures annually. March arrived to testify straight from the set, so was militarily attired as the dashing Lieutenant Michael Denet. When he took the stand to affirm that he was privy to remarks made by Jack Warner in 1932 to the effect that Cagney would only be obliged to make four pictures a year, March's testimony in an army uniform must have lent credence. Cagney won the suit.

March hardly had time to get out of khaki from *The Road to Glory* before he had to squeeze back into tight pants for yet another costume picture for Warner Brothers, *Anthony Adverse*. Adapting Hervey Allen's sprawling best-selling novel about Anthony Adverse, that globe-trotting adventurer of nineteenth century Napoleonic Europe to 140 minutes of screen time was one of Warner Brothers more ambitious productions and Mervyn LeRoy's last directing effort for Warner's. Allen's massive novel with its long narrative of romance and intrigue in Napoleonic times was difficult for Warner's to compress for the screen, but the results were nonetheless entertaining and profitable. *Anthony Adverse* was their biggest hit of 1936, garnering four Academy Awards plus a nomination for Best Picture, Best Supporting Actress (Gale Sondergaard), Best Camerawork (Tony Gaudio), Best Editing (Ralph Dawson), and Best Music (Erich Wolfgang Korngold).

Translating this epic to the screen involved some 2,500 players, ninety-eight speaking parts and thirty-six principals led by Fredric March in the title role, who was then at his height as Hollywood's favorite costume hero. Anthony Adverse is the orphaned "love child" adopted and raised by a wealthy merchant sent abroad to tend to his stepfather's interests. Before embarking, Anthony marries his childhood sweetheart (Olivia De Havilland) but through various complications leaves her behind. After several years as a degenerate slave trader in Africa, Anthony has a soul wrenching experience with the death of his friend, a priest, who asks Anthony to return home. Adverse complies and is eventually caught up in the various Napoleonic court intrigues. After finding his beloved and discovering he has a son, all his happiness is crushed when he finds out that his wife is the mistress of the French emperor.

He sails to America with his son, proving the truth of his last name. LeRoy insisted that the character of Anthony Adverse (named for adversity) be changed from a passive person to a man of action so that his presence would hold together the varied and many plot directions.

LeRoy considered Fredric March a brilliant actor, but believed he needed a firm hand. He realized that right away on the first day during the first scene. In an African hut, March was emoting with an African woman, played by Steffi Duna, and overacting terribly. With a man of March's reputation, it was a ticklish situation to get him to stop. LeRoy felt that a director had to be a working psychologist. There must be an instinctive ability to tell actors what you want in ways that are best suited to the particular situation and the individuals concerned. In March's case, he knew he could not come out flatly and say, "You're overacting," feeling that March would respond more readily if the suggestion were couched in humorous terms.

So LeRoy turned to his first assistant director, Bill Cannon, and said, loud enough for everybody to hear, "Bill, get the Shredded Wheat set ready."

March gave him a funny look, asking, "What's a Shredded Wheat set?"

"Well, Freddie, if you're going to eat the scenery, we'll have to make it out of Shredded Wheat" (Leroy 1974, 128–129).

March got the message, laughed, and from then on his performance was controlled and disciplined and a joy to watch. Billy Mauch portrayed the young Anthony and has many fine memories of *Anthony Adverse*.

> I was never personally involved in any scenes with Mr. March; he did, however, visit the set often. We had some memorable conversations concerning the arts and the acting profession in particular. He was a fascinating man and I admired him not only as a fine man and gentleman, but as one of the finest actors I have ever met. Believe me, the memories of Mr. March as Anthony Adverse linger on and will for the rest of my life. (Letter, Billy Mauch, 30 May 1990)

Olivia De Havilland, then nineteen and fresh from her triumph with Errol Flynn in *Captain Blood*, was enchanting as the love interest for Anthony. Reportedly, she, still fascinated by Flynn, felt Fredric March had less romantic appeal than Flynn. According to her, March was stiff, giving nothing in love scenes, seemingly too conscious of the presence on the set of his wife, Florence. Odd, for it was rumored that Jimmy Stewart, director Anatole Litvak, *and* Fredric March had been linked romantically with De Havilland when she first arrived at Warner's in 1935.

Anthony Adverse premiered at the Strand in New York and the Carthay Circle in Hollywood, August 26, 1936, to 50,000 movie fans jammed outside on the sidewalks. The arrival of Fredric March at the Carthay Circle premier and his guests, the Prince and Princess Hubertus Zu Lowenstein, was the signal for an uproar from the crowd. Newspapers recounted that March was like a fencer sidestepping many opponents, dodging the enthusiasts fighting to shake his hand. While everyone was impressed with the grand scale of the production, *Anthony Adverse* left no emotional impact, only an impression of a great many costumed actors and varied scenes. The reviews were a mixed bag: Frank Nugent, *New York Times*: "We found it a bulky, rambling and indecisive photoplay which has not merely taken liberties with the letter of the original but with its spirit . . . Fredric March is a thoroughly spiritless Anthony" (March Papers). However, the *Hollywood Spectator* said; "Freddie at times has given us a lot of acting. Here he gives us none. He is not pretending he is Anthony Adverse, not showing us what March would have done if he were Adverse. He IS Anthony Adverse" (March Papers). According to Lawrence Quirk, "March was quite fine in the role of Anthony, underplaying gracefully so as to keep the characterization moving forward easily through the numerous episodes of the film (not an easy feat in pageant-style epics like this) and although his approach was misunderstood by the 1936 critics and got a mixed reaction, as seen in 1971 the star's skill and restraint can be more fittingly respected and appreciated" (Quirk 1971, 145).

March at this time made a major decision, a daring choice that would place responsibility for the future in his own hands. At the peak of his career, he refused to sign another contract with Zanuck. He wanted to pick his own movies, in other words, to work free-lance. "I'm not going to work as regularly as I have during the past year or two. I'm planning from now on to do no more than three films a year, if I can have my way" (March Papers). He was still hesitant, for in his efforts to find what he wanted he was hypercritical. He did not want studios to think he was a high-hat, but only ambitious to find the thing he knew he could do well. He had too great a respect for the art of acting to turn in a bad job. "Then, too, I am sometimes overcome by doubts—do I know, absolutely know, the type of stuff I'm suited for, or is it just my idea and not practical?" (March Papers).

March, fortunately, made the correct choice, for at a price of a whopping $125,000 per picture, studios were clambering for his talent. By 1937 with the help of his new agent, Myron Selznick, March became the highest paid free-lance star in pictures with every important studio still begging him to sign a long-term contract at his own figure. March would often turn down three parts a week in his quest for the perfect part. The role he was after was *modern*, even comedy if he could find it. He also expressed an interest in a return to Broadway with Florence, possibly for the 1937 winter season, although he confessed a feeling of apprehension. It had been eight years since he had appeared in a stage play and he had grown used to working before a camera with an audience of only a handful of people whom he knew, all of them coworkers, busy with their own jobs. "After these eight years, it will be quite an ordeal for me to appear before an actual audience, with its critical attitude of, 'All right, let's see what you can do'" (March Papers). But a play was not forthcoming so March's first free-lance assignment was in a two picture deal Myron Selznick negotiated for him with his brother, David O. Selznick (Selznick had recently left MGM, creating his own company, Selznick International). The first picture was inspired by a 1932 film, *What Price Hollywood*, and dealt with life in Hollywood among the stars. William Wellman was slated to direct and suggested filming in Technicolor. *It Happened in Hollywood* was to be a film about Hollywood, more precisely about a young woman who rises to greatness as a Hollywood actress, while married to a rapidly declining matinee idol. The husband is an alcoholic who eventually drowns himself at the film's end. The sad character of the husband had its basis in at least four real life actors: Mary Pickford's first husband, Owen Moore; silent star John Gilbert; the alcoholic, self-destructive John Barrymore; and another failed silent star, John Bowers, husband of Marguerite de la Motte.

To play the leading roles Selznick chose two stars whose circumstances were almost the opposite of the characters they were to play. He chose Janet Gaynor, then thirty years old and regarded in the industry as a star in decline, for the part of the young girl who makes good in Hollywood, Esther Blodgett—renamed Vicki Lester. To portray the self-destructive Norman Maine, her husband, the has-been matinee idol, Selznick chose Fredric March, a man whose own career bore no similarity to the character's, who in 1937 surely looked more like a matinee idol than did James Mason in the 1954 remake. The film these two starred in is by far the finest of the three versions, the first in the trilogy renamed *A Star Is Born*. Rose Pelswick's column in the *New York Evening Journal* proclaimed, "No little boy looking forward to his first pair of long trousers could have been more pleased than Fredric March when he learned that his role in *A Star Is Born* would let him wear an up-to-date business suit" (March Papers).

Before the start of filming, late October, the Marches' headed east to New York City for some business and a holiday because Florence was being considered for a role on Broadway to start that winter. She signed on to do the Lillian Hellman drama *Days to Come*, scheduled to open December 15, 1936 at the Vanderbilt Theater. After clinching the deal, March was expected back in Hollywood to start on *A Star Is Born* by October 28. Filming took eight weeks of actual camera work. For the first time, streets, buildings and places of amusement which had made the name of Hollywood world-famous were filmed in color: the Santa Anita racetrack, the Tracadero, Grauman's Chinese Theater, the Hollywood Bowl, Hollywood Legion Stadium, and the Brown Derby. Two of the most famous of Hollywood scenes, the Academy banquet and a typical Hollywood premier, were recreated. Re-enactment of the annual banquet of the Academy of Motion Picture Arts and Sciences took two days to film but the spectacle was more than two weeks in preparation.

Early in the picture March's character, Norman Maine, is still popular but alcoholic. March's performance at all times runs true to character. At first, as the lionized screen hero, he is dashing, daring, nonchalant and full of conceit. When his star dipped into obscurity, becoming the "man who used to be," he slumps into a beaten, frightened and dazed individual who cannot comprehend the fates which have treated him so rottenly. His constant companionship with Demon Rum turns him into a hated, ignored derelict. Realizing his effect on his wife, he nobly ends his life as a drowning suicide.

The scene in which Maine retreats to a sanitarium to cure himself, and is seen in the company of a male nurse and his employer/friend Oliver Niles, is entirely Barrymore-inspired. This is exactly what Barrymore did in 1936 in order to be able to play Mercutio in MGM's *Romeo and Juliet*. Among his visitors was George Cukor, who directed James Mason in that same scene eighteen years later in the second *A Star Is Born*. March told Lawrence Quirk that playing that particular scene made him very sad. "I had been called the best John Barrymore imitator around at the time of the film *The Royal Family of Broadway*, but imitating or even recalling him in that sanitarium scene was no laughing matter—his decline was very tragic" (Quirk 1988, 173).

Lionel Stander, who enacted the role of Libby, the studio promotion manager, remembered, "I did not know Fredric March before this film, but admired him as an actor and a person. And then, watching him on the set! Very professional, a much better actor than Cooper, splendid, technically brilliant, etc. You could tell he had been on Broadway, you know, stage-trained" (Telephone interview, Lionel Stander, 17 May 1990). Upon completion of filming, in late December just before Christmas, David Selznick presented Fred with a gold embossed personal movie script of *A Star Is Born* signed, "For Freddy, Who won my own private award. Gratefully, David" (March Papers).

Right after the filming of *A Star Is Born*, Sheila Graham was granted an interview. She found that even if March weren't practically the handsomest person alive, he would still be the best looking because he was six feet tall, with dark eyes and brown hair and a straight nose and a cleft in his chin. He had wide shoulders and almost no hips and a swell, sudden smile. Besides this, he had the added virtue of looking intelligent. He almost always frowned when he talked, except when he laughed, and then he looked suddenly boyish and his eyebrows would go up and he would throw his head back while his shoulders would shake. Graham questioned March about his yearning to return to the stage. He again mentioned wanting to act opposite Florence, stating that the best part of acting with ones wife was the enforced lovemaking. "You can put so much more abandon into the scenes—and practice at home. I'm much more scared of stage acting than my wife is. Eight years is a long time to be away from the theater. And the public will expect so much more from me now than it did then" (Graham interview, 24

December 1936, March Papers).

A Star Is Born's California premier at Grauman's Chinese Theater, April 22, 1937, featured Fredric March receiving his Walk of Fame award: having his hands, feet and signature in cement on the sidewalk outside the theater. Critics applauded. *Herald Tribune*: "Mr. March has the difficult assignment of acting an actor whose acting days are ended, but does it with flair and versatility. It is a cruel, authoritative and perfectly modulated portrait that he draws" (Quirk 1971, 149). *A Star Is Born* earned March his third Oscar nomination. It was also Oscar nominated for Best Production (David O. Selznick), Best Director (William Wellman), Best Actress (Janet Gaynor) and Best Screenplay (Dorothy Parker, Alan Campbell, and Robert Carson), but actually won awards for Best Color Cinematography (William Howard Greene) and Best Original Story (Wellman and Carson).

The second film for Selznick, *Nothing Sacred* with Carole Lombard, earned March quite a bit of money before actual filming began. Myron Selznick had negotiated a deal for Fred's services, literally selling him to brother David for an eight week period at $15,000 a week, totaling $125,000. This worked fine for *A Star Is Born*, but, unfortunately, the script for *Nothing Sacred* was not ready by January 1937 so extensions on the starting date were requested. Myron said no; therefore, March received $35,000 for sitting around his pool before the brothers came to a compromise.

Since the Wellman/March collaborative effort for *A Star Is Born* went so well, Selznick obtained Wellman again to direct *Nothing Sacred*, scripted by Ben Hecht and written expressly for Carole Lombard. Lombard portrays Hazel Flagg, the small town girl supposedly dying from radium poisoning who is taken to New York by a fast talking newspaper reporter (March). She is then entertained by the New York citizens who turn her final days on earth into a royal gala, only to find that the diagnosis is wrong. It ends happily with Hazel and the reporter falling in love. Another early technicolor production, *Nothing Sacred*'s has a brisk pace and cutting dialogue. Even though it was a Carole Lombard film, March more than held his own.

Remember, Lombard did not like March. She claimed he had tried to seduce her during their contract days at Paramount, the famous dressing room fiasco during the production of *The Eagle and the Hawk*. However, it appears they managed to amuse each other during the production phase of *Nothing Sacred*. The set was as dizzy and laugh-filled as the movie itself. Director Wellman, coaching Lombard for the great slugging brawl with Fred, taught Carole how to tackle and work a straitjacket on an opponent, so Carole and Fred bought a straitjacket as a present for Wellman. At other times Lombard and March could be seen tearing around Selznick's lot on a fire engine, sirens blaring. Even during the shooting, Wellman used humor to break Lombard or March from a dry spell in motivation, or to comfort a concerned actor who had dropped his lines. At least once he told his leading lady, "Miss Lombard,

I know it must be tough for a woman to look into Freddie March's frozen puss and pretend to be in love with him. But close your eyes or something and let's do it just once more" (Thomas 1970, 83).

One of the most famous scenes from this picture involved March's slugging Lombard, something he undoubtedly enjoyed immensely. Apparently, this scene had many retakes, with both stars ending up in the local hospital for minor cuts and bruises. Whatever the costars' personal feelings were, *Nothing Sacred* turned out to be a most entertaining newspaper comedy, and remains fresh even today. Released November 25, 1937, it had excellent reviews: *Hollywood Reporter*: "Fredric March, as the reporter, gives a performance comparable with his drunken actor in *A Star Is Born*. He delivers a dashing and adroitly farced portrayal, matching point for point the rollicking spontaneity of his co-star" (March Papers). Jean Spaulding: "His modern work is as rich as his own personality, his light humor is a delight, and his sincerity dominates every scene" (March Papers).

March's venture into free-lancing was more than just successful, for his popularity soared. By the end of 1937 Fredric March reported a compensation of $484,687 for that year; Selznick International paid him $334,687 and Paramount Pictures paying him $150,000 for *The Buccaneer* (he had raised his fee from $125,000 to $150,000). He was the fifth highest paid individual on the national list for 1937, following William Randolph Hearst's $500,000!

While March began studying a French accent for the character of Jean Lafitte, conflict had been brewing in Europe that contributed to the eventual involvement of the United States in a the Second World War. American eyes had been watching Spain after General Francisco Franco raised the flag of revolt July 18, 1936, not to mention the activities of an Austrian named Hitler in Germany. Many Hollywood folk joined in making speeches denouncing the Nazi activities in Europe and the neutral position of the United States in international affairs. Among these were Lillian Hellman, Ring Lardner, James Cagney, *and* Fredric March. This was a dangerous stand because if there was one principle upon which the vast majority of the American people agreed in 1937, it was that what was happening in Europe was no concern of theirs; and that if Europe were so stupid as to get into another war, America would stay out of it.

One such speech was held Sunday, March 29, 1937, sponsored by the Contemporary Theater in Hollywood. It involved a public reading and audience discussion of the antiwar play *Bury the Dead* by Irwin Shaw. Read by Fred, Florence, and John Cromwell and followed by open discussions with James Cagney, Groucho Marx, Basil Rathbone, and Lionel Stander, the play was bitterly satiric in content, involving six soldiers in "the next war" who refused to stay buried. Nor could all the forces of army, government, church or woman shake them in their determination to live the lives of which war had deprived them.   Unfortunately for the Hollywood denouncers of war, their audiences at these various speeches included those who were compiling lists of names that later would be made available to studio management and, much later, to the House Un-American Activities Committee (HUAC), that was to be formed in Spring 1938 under the chairmanship of Texas Democrat Martin Dies.   HUAC eventually became a forum for right-wing attacks against the Roosevelt administration, eventually leading to the McCarthyism of the late 1940s.

The very moment March finished work on his second present-day role in several years, he signed on with Cecil B. DeMille for the Paramount production of *The Buccaneer* to portray that romantic figure from history, the vigorous privateer Jean LaFitte. Back to costume!

13

Back to Broadway

March was once asked to comment about "Women Whom Men Don't Leave":

I admit that women who are both vivid and good don't grow all over the landscape like California poppies; but at least one such exists, for I married her. Florence Eldridge and I have been married for 13 years and it's only the beginning. That's what I mean by the kind of woman a man never tires of. I'm lucky in being married to a fine actress whose opinion is of real value and help. But she's had personal experience in similar work, which means that she knows too much to butt in while I'm in the midst of a job. (March Papers).

Then, in the next breath, March tries to seduce Evelyn Keyes, DeMille's new find for *The Buccaneer*. Keyes remembered the rather scandalous Mr. March in her autobiography *Scarlett O'Hara's Younger Sister*. Her big moment with March was after DeMille yelled at her for paying too much attention to her makeup. Upset, she began to cry, so March came to her rescue. In her words:

Afterwards Mr. DeMille patted me on the shoulder and said it was fine. No apology. Fredric March, though, thought I needed further soothing. He invited me into his trailer dressing room parked just outside the stage. He was so handsome in his elegant, tight white trousers, black boots, and short red jacket. His hair was dark and curly. About forty then, March was in his prime. The complete Movie Star.

He told me to sit beside him, and asked where I was from, where I lived, told me I mustn't let DeMille get me down, the old boy could be a bastard sometimes.

And then, in the gentlest way, he took my hand and placed it over the bulge in the front of those tight white pants. My first movie star erection, in person.

I was taken so off-guard that I didn't snatch my hand away. It rested there, a lifeless object, belonging to somebody else.

There was a knock at the door. "Ready when you are, Mr. March," said the voice of the assistant director.

Mr. March picked up my hand and gave it back to me, polite as could be. "Please," he said in a courtly fashion, gesturing around his dressing room, "feel free to rest here." And he left for the set.

I got out, fast. (Keyes 1977, 22)

The interesting relationship between Fred and Florence, balanced against his reputation as an extreme libertine and womanizer, alone would have lent grist for many a journalist's mill. And this was one characteristic March felt obligated to live up to, repeatedly. His predilection for the as yet unknown screen personalities might be explained, in some cases, by the "extra" or "bit" girls on the make in order to boost their own career. March often allowed himself to be seduced, much to Florence's chagrin. Bradford Dillman mentioned in a 1990 interview, "Freddie liked ladies—to a very distressing extent as far as Florence was concerned. But she put up with him. Freddie knew she was a dynamite lady so that every time he got caught with his hand in the cookie jar he went running back for forgiveness" (Interview, Bradford Dillman, 11 August 1990).

If only the couch in Fredric March's dressing room could talk, or type, for it would surely have made a sizzling best-seller. Evidently, he was the original Love Machine, long before Jacqueline Susann thought of the title. One has to wonder at Florence's steadfast loyalty. After all, though, she was married to an extremely handsome and celebrated star and if she left him where would *she* be? Plus, she knew Fred loved their adopted children. To her credit, Florence provided a stable home and family. To atone for his philandering, March would always try to convince producers to hire Florence when they were interested only in signing him. So, out of guilt, as in the case of *Mary of Scotland*, Fred continued to use his movie star clout in order to allow Florence a chance to act. Florence denied his infidelities, or put up with them, for, in reality, she was a millstone around his neck, and if his career was hurt in any way, it was because of her.

It was July 1937 at Baldwin Oaks (adjoining the Santa Anita racetrack) during the filming of the Battle of New Orleans for *The Buccaneer*, that Florence convinced Fred to try Broadway. DeMille was now in his fourth week of filming. Tempers were running high since local youths had put scrap iron and BB shot in some of the prop guns, resulting in a smashed reflector when the soldiers were ordered to fire, but fortunately, no human fatalities. Fred, dressed as the buccaneer Jean Lafitte, was resting in his studio chair during a break when Florence broached the subject of Broadway. Florence felt that after all, they could finally act together again. She felt she had found the perfect return play: *Yr. Obedient Husband* by Horace Jackson. They had certainly been talking about it enough this past year. John (Cromwell) would be available to direct.

This "Back to Broadway" exercise was a very courageous step to take considering there was a regular Mason-Dixon line between Hollywood and Broadway in 1937. Anyone who tried to cross it found himself in danger of being disowned by *both* coasts. In spite of this, Fred committed to *Yr. Obedient Husband*, the comedy about Richard Steele, an early eighteenth-century essayist and playwright who had edited the *Tatler* and the *Spectator*. March was to play the rakish Steele, Florence his tormented wife, Prue. The play was scheduled to hit Broadway December 1937, after a tour in key cities during November. When asked about his Broadway attempt, March replied, "I believe that a flyer behind the 'foots' will do one a lot of good. I need the change. Heaven knows, I've been howling about the idea for several years. So now it looks as if it were really going to happen. Florence had her baptism earlier this year when she starred in Lillian Hellman's drama in New York, which, incidently, proved a flop" (March Papers). John Cromwell had unearthed the play which would serve the Marches as the vehicle for reentry into the theater and would also fulfill his ambition to direct again over footlights rather than the camera.

Before undertaking *Yr. Obedient Husband*, March had to complete Cecil B. DeMille's epic, *The Buccaneer*, another "grossly tight-panted film," according to Lawrence Quirk (Quirk 1988, 165). DeMille once again used history as his backdrop by telling the story of Jean Lafitte, that French privateer who helped General Andrew Jackson whip the British army January of 1815—the only major battle of the otherwise confusing War of 1812, a battle fought, ironically, two days after the war was ended by the Treaty of Ghent. Byron wrote of Lafitte: "He left a corsair's name to other times. Linked with one virtue and a thousand crimes" (March Papers). That one virtue was Lafitte's teaming with Jackson to save New Orleans; the many crimes were not touched on by DeMille.

DeMille had been thinking of producing a picture about buccaneers for quite some time when a former theater chain owner based in New Orleans and a good friend directed his attention to Lafitte as a subject for a motion picture. Yet, who would and could play Lafitte? It was not until he went on a fishing trip that took him past Lafitte's stronghold of Barataria and in and out of the moss-hung, mysterious bayous of lower Louisiana that DeMille found *the* buccaneer, a man who deserved America's gratitude, yet also merited Byron's description. In his biography, DeMille wrote, "Fredric March made a dashing and completely believable Lafitte, a man of curiously mingled ruthlessness and honor, a vagabond of the high seas who wanted desperately to be rooted somewhere" (Hayne 1959, 357).

The Buccaneer was DeMille's Twenty-Fifth Anniversary production, marking a quarter century of activity and progress during which he had produced and directed sixty-four pictures, usually of epic proportions. As was standard with a DeMille production, action and swashbuckling abounded. March portrays a vibrant Jean Lafitte, leader of the horde of criminals and misfits rejected from polite society that prey upon all nature of ships, other than those of the United States, the country Lafitte wanted to call his own. Franciska Gaal portrays Gretchen, the Dutch girl he rescues from an American ship sunk by one of his own captains, whom he punishes by execution. (Gaal came to DeMille's notice when he viewed eight of her European films. Born in Budapest, Hungary, she was taken to America late in 1936 under contract to Paramount, taught English and cast opposite Fredric March for her American film debut. She only appeared in two more American films, returning to Budapest in 1940. Her portrayal is a little irritating to view, partially because of her accent, but mostly because her character is glaringly out of place.) Gretchen falls for Lafitte, but he loves a New Orleans society girl and is always striving for "ray-speck-taa-bi-lity!" When war breaks out, he and his men (plus Gretchen as a totally useless powder monkey) assist General Jackson. For his efforts pirate Lafitte is honored at a celebration ball, but when it is learned of the sinking of the American ship, he leaves his fiancée (whose sister died on board) and takes to the sea, Gretchen in tow, with piracy and Gretchen his only future.

The Buccaneer required more than four months location work at New Iberia, Los Angeles, Catalina Island, and Baldwin Oaks. The New Orleans Cabildo, Jean Lafitte's home, and the American first presidential home all had to be constructed at Paramount Studios, where the unit shot for an additional ninety days. Employing more than 6,000 people, DeMille revived such historical incidents as the Battle of New Orleans, and the attack on Lafitte's pirates by the U.S. Navy. Fifty-six men worked four weeks to construct the seven acre settlement representing Barataria at White's Landing, Catalina Island. The settlement, an affair of thatch-roofed, fortified homes, duplicated the island stronghold Lafitte maintained at the entrance to Barataria Bay off the Gulf of Mexico. The casting of 600 extras was no easy task, either, requiring weeks, with producer/director DeMille, his associate producer, William Pine, and the casting staff interviewing hundreds of applicants daily. There was one insistent rule that appeared on all casting sheets: "Men without stomachs and women without red fingernails" (March Papers). The bigger the men, the better their chance of acceptance; the more exotic in type, the surer of a place as an extra. More than thirty different nationalities were represented by the extras finally chosen for the sequences depicting the siege of Barataria by American warships. At the conclusion of shooting the set was burned and bombed as warships fired on it from the bay.

For the scenes of the Battle of New Orleans an entire regiment of men who would not look miscast as Scottish Highlanders had to be hired. (More than 1100 Highlanders advanced and only 134 survived, as DeMille duplicated impressively in the filming.) Set dressers had covered close to four acres of the Baldwin Oaks region neighboring the Santa Anita racetrack with parapets of cotton bales and sandbags. Actual filming of the battle was done in sections, using the pirate line one day, the British line another, and spending a week on the tragic charge of the Highlanders. Congreve rockets used in the battle repeatedly set fire to the trees, hung with spanish moss, snuffed out by a fire company kept on duty throughout shooting.

Wally Westmore, head of the Paramount makeup department, supervised makeup of this vast company that toiled on *The Buccaneer*, including the curling of March's hair in order to portray Lafitte. Though head of a large staff handling makeup on eleven other productions, Westmore was on the set of the DeMille picture personally every morning at 7:00 a.m. to make up the principals. He enlisted all of Hollywood's available makeup talent, sending them to Catalina, where makeup work on the 600 extras began at 5:30 a.m. and was conducted under canvas the size of a sideshow tent. In fact, the four-week location at Catalina Island produced one of the greatest mass movements of motion picture equipment: eighteen barges and eighteen tugs carried over trucks, automobiles, cameras, lights, wardrobe, properties plus March's dressing-room trailer.

Premiered in New Orleans, February 16, 1938, March's performance in *The Buccaneer* received mixed reviews. Frank Nugent of the *New York Times*; "Fredric March's Lafitte is hamstrung. Akim Tamiroff's Dominique You, cannoneer to Napoleon, is so superior to it, so far the more full-bodied characterization, that Mr. March should have asked for a restraining order" (March Papers). Nugent was also responsible for the quote that referred to the picture as "run of DeMille" dismissing March in a widely quoted phrase, "March comes in like a lion and goes out like a ham" (March Papers). (One criticism was even hurled at his "affected" French accent. This outraged March for he had to study weeks in advance of production with a native born Frenchman in order to have the accent letter-perfect. Therefore, he felt the critics did not know the facts of the case, or they would not have referred to the accent as an affectation.)

Other reports were at the opposite end of the reviewing scale. *Los Angeles Examiner*'s Harrison Carroll: "Fredric March, with his hair curled, and speaking in a broad accent, may not meet your conception of Lafitte, but he gives a vigorous performance and one that probably will be popular" (March Papers). *Washington Post*'s Nelson Bell: "Never has Fredric March brought to the screen so dynamic a performance as he gives here. His Jean Lafitte is a polished rascal and noble criminal whose personal charm was such that even those who had placed the price on his head were willing to strike a bargain"

(March Papers). Lawrence Quirk claimed March was experimenting with new approaches in his Lafitte characterization, which apparently baffled reviewers who expected a more typical "March" approach (Quirk blamed this in part on the resident director). Regardless, March demonstrated his multipurpose acting style, as the engaging free-booter after his own heart, in battle, making love or thwarting foes. If Lafitte was really as March portrayed him, he was a gallant and irresistible gentleman. Even DeMille thought highly of the March portrayal and when interviewed January 1938, complimented Fred for his great performance in the part of Lafitte. "It is the most difficult part in the picture to play carrying the weight of the entire story upon its back and sweeping into prominence with it three fine character performances, but it is Freddie's great characterization from which the picture derives its power" (March Papers).

Anthony Quinn, one of Lafitte's right-hand men, gave a glowing reference when asked to comment on the making of *The Buccaneer*. Quinn's was a rather small part, but during one of their dialogues together, March was supposed to turn to Quinn and give him an order. Quinn's answer was very simple, but March responded with a strange look. As his back was to the camera, the camera did not capture this look. After the shot, March sat next to Quinn and said, "You know, in pictures, I seldom hear a ring of truth from my fellow actors, and that's why I looked at you so peculiarly, because you sounded real and truthful in your answer. You're either going to become one of the lousiest actors in the world, or one of the best." Quinn wrote,

> I often think of that remark and I think of Fredric March with great affection. He came to see me in a play I did in New York (*Becket*). He and his wife came backstage, and he hadn't forgotten the statement he had made to me and he said, "Well, I was right, you are going to be one of the best." Unfortunately, and this is purely personal, I thank him constantly for his belief in me, but I don't think I became the worst, or the best. But I must say, I spend my life trying to justify his prophecy. (letter, Anthony Quinn, 27 November, 1990)

It was soon necessary for the Marches' to start rehearsals for *Yr. Obedient Husband* in order to open on the road in Columbus, Ohio, by November 26, 1937. March, however, let it be known to all the powers that be that he was *definitely not* forsaking the screen for the stage, explaining the joint appearance in the historical comedy by Horace Jackson as a realization of an ambition both he and Florence had nourished for ten years—to play together before a New York audience. He was bucking a rumor that had been circulating for some time concerning handsome Fredric March's return to the stage in *Yr. Obedient Husband* was but a gallant gesture to permit his wife to emerge from the comparative obscurity that had claimed her since the talkies took Fredric to their heart and made him one of the top-ranking favorites of the film fans. The tale went that March chucked $300,000 in offered contracts to indulge the little woman in this whim and the insinuation was that for all his he-man roles in the movies, March wasn't exactly the master in his own household. Consequently, he was persuaded to make the stage try by Florence, who had grown tired of Hollywood's lack of interest in her acting ability. Therefore, she it was, the gossips declared, who managed to get her famous husband to adventure behind the footlights. And she it was who played the leading feminine role opposite her cinematically celebrated husband. When asked his opinion of March's return to the stage, Ralph Bellamy remembered, "Florence wanted to go back. He was happy doing films. Florence never really made it or hit it big. She thought if she could get back on the stage, but he still dominated her there, too. He had a great presence . . . My God . . . the minute he walked on stage, you were in the presence of something great" (Interview, Ralph Bellamy, 9 August 1990).

Fred denied the rumors that Florence had forced his hand—"I wanted to do this play every bit as much as she did. It's been common knowledge among our friends for several years that we were on the lookout for a play in which we could co-star and when Horace Jackson's *Yr. Obedient Husband* fell into our hands, we knew we had just what we wanted" (March Papers). To prove the gossips wrong, March invested his own money in the venture and, unlike so many luminaries of the film world who returned to the stage as exhibition pieces for the delight of their movie-mad fans, March had the avowed intention of adding a Broadway reputation to his Hollywood successes.

On the road, *Yr. Obedient Husband* played to full houses and good reviews. Of course, the presence of Fredric March in the cast doubtless attracted vast numbers of devoted admirers he had accumulated in his screen career. The world premier was set for the Hartman Theater in Columbus, November 26; Cincinnati, November 30; and St. Louis, December 7. The *Cincinnati Times Star* reported: "Fredric March and Florence Eldridge with a brilliant supporting cast, delighted a full house at the Cox Theater on Monday evening. Thunderous applause attested to the success of this play" (March Papers).

After St. Louis it was on to Pittsburgh where Fred received disturbing news from home, news that was eventually to result in a skirmish with the soon to be active Martin Dies House Un-American Activities Committee (HUAC). Movie stars, government officials, waterfront labor leaders, several attorneys and scores of others were named in a sensational $5,100,000 damage suit in San Francisco as conspirators in a vast Communist plot to bring the entire West Coast under Red control and filed by Ivan F. Cox, former treasurer and suspended trustee of the International Longshoremen's Association Local. Fredric March, motion picture star, was one of those named. Fortunately, in September of 1938, Fred was absolved of this charge. It turned out that the $5 million dollar suit against more than 5,000 people charged with being

Communists (including James Cagney and Franchot Tone) was only a publicity stunt. Ivan Cox admitted that he knew none of the persons named in the suit, declaring that the suit had been prepared by one Stanley Doyle, a self proclaimed "roving Pacific-Coast investigator." Cox said that he had received only $400 for making the perjured charges, although he had been promised much more. In a retaliatory effort, many of the defendants mentioned (March included) became associated with the Hollywood Anti-Nazi League, and, eventually, Films for Democracy. Actors, writers and others planned pictures to combat the wave of bigotry and intolerance that was sweeping the nation, fanned by individuals such as Martin Dies. ("Red" and "Pinko" charges were continually to haunt the Marches' through the 1940s, culminating in their lawsuit against *Counterattack* magazine.)

Nevertheless, the show must go on, and on it went, reaching Detroit by December 20 where Herbert Monk reviewed it.

Long, black curls dangling about his shoulders and clad in a tan velvet suit, Fredric March stepped out of the movies through the window of a charming 18th century English sitting room on the stage at the American Theater last night to demonstrate that his talents and personality are not as ethereal as the medium which gave him fame, and to provide the theater here-abouts with one of its more glamorous evenings. (March Papers)

Interviewed locally, Fred commented, "I want to mix up my roles. *A Star Is Born* and *Buccaneer* are perfect examples of what I call mixing them up. Then include a stage play along with a couple of movies a year and you have my idea of the ideal life" (March Papers). With this in mind, both Marches' eagerly looked forward to opening night at the Broadhurst Theater in New York, January 10, 1938. This date had been delayed one week by a form of arthritis that had prevented Fred from opening Christmas week.

The play opened and closed within seven days. The reviews were, in a word, *horrible*! George Jean Nathan in *Theater Week*:

In *Yr. Obedient* we had renewed evidence of the gulf that separates the theater and Hollywood. Written by an illustrious movie scenario writer, staged by an illustrious movie director (John Cromwell), acted by an illustrious movie actor, and produced with illustrious movie money, it got no nearer to the heart and soul of quality theater than the greatest movie ever made gets to even the better grade second-rate drama. (March Papers)

Another critic voiced that he supposed Mr. March was partially attracted to the play by the fact that it enabled him to make his first entrance vaulting

picturesquely through a window, which was the proper manner for a film hero
to make his appearance.   The majority of the reviews felt it proved
conclusively that what was ability in Hollywood was only pretty poor side-
street talent when it came to the theater.   The Marches' felt the critics were
against movie actors, regarding them as brash intruders; therefore, the
prejudiced reviewers could not be objective. This may have been true, for *Yr.
Obedient Husband* only served to reenforce their opinion that movie stars
should stay in Hollywood, where *Yr. Obedient*'s premier should have been on
Sid Grauman's Hollywood screen, with ten thousand dazzling searchlights
illuminating the heavens outside and with twenty thousand Hollywood fans
tumbling all over each other to get the great Mr. March's autograph.   The
whole experience caused a temporary setback in March's Hollywood movie
career.

According to Louella Parsons, March, realizing that the play was a flop and
rather than have people pay their good money into the box office because they
wanted to see a movie star, closed the show after a week, losing $65,000 in
the process (although the play did net him $500,000 in the Midwest before
Broadway). With characteristic good sportsmanship, and to conceal their hurt,
the Marches' and director John Cromwell placed an ad in each of the New
York papers apologizing via a cartoon picture of two trapeze artists missing
each other in midair, captioned, "Oop—Sorry!" and signed by all three (Maney
1957, 14–15). John Houseman during the Fredric March Tribute in 1987
remarked, "I well remember when that ad came out in the *New York Times*.
It created a tremendous impression.   Nobody had ever kidded about a
disaster.   Very impressive.   But very typical of those two people" (Fredric
March Tribute Movie, 21 September 1987, Jean Bickel Owen). Fredric March
responded with the characteristic tenaciousness that enabled him to wage war
in the Wisconsin oratorical contestants in 1913 and win: "I want to make
pictures in the summer and play Broadway winters. I *will* do another play
next November, and will keep it up until I get knocked down three times!"
(March Papers).

March was interviewed by Bosley Crowther during his hiatus from
Hollywood and Crowther found a relaxed Mr. March. Dressed simply but
well groomed, March wore a dark blue suit, white shirt and dark tie and
looked more like a bond broker than a Hollywood hero. His deep set eyes
were serious and his generous eyebrows were occasionally drawn together as
he talked. Crowther found March more handsome offstage than on and
without that semi scowl that had become so familiar to film fans, March was
apparently unconscious of the fact that he was the object of worship of
idolatrous millions. He left his acting to the stage and in everyday life his
manners were those of everyday folk. Hollywood had left him unaffected.
Fred commented, "Swashbuckling parts bother me. I'm inclined to ham them
too much." With a wry smile, he continued, "And they were beginning to put

the finger on me for it" (March Papers).

When asked about autograph hounds, fame, etc., he replied, "To tell the truth, I don't think I'm the type they get particularly excited about. Oh yes, I sign my share of autograph books when in crowds, but somehow I never take that sort of fame—if you can call it fame—seriously. In this business, you soon realize—providing you use your head—that popularity doesn't last forever and that someday—well, who knows?" (March Papers).

After the debacle of *Yr. Obedient Husband*, could it possibly get any worse? An emphatic yes, for March next signed on with the king of slapstick, Hal Roach, in a comedy with Virginia Bruce called *There Goes My Heart*, for half his normal salary but with a percentage of the profits. He was also offered a part by Jack Warner in *The Sisters* but turned down the chance to portray a drunken, self-pitying reporter who marries a Montana girl and drags her down to a life of poverty in San Francisco with "It is not a particularly interesting character, principally because he is so frightfully weak and sorry for himself throughout" (March Papers). In order to support a $1,000 a weekend hobby of boating, Errol Flynn later accepted the part. Roland Mader, who handled the Marches' finances in 1946, was working for Leland Hayward, Fred's agent after Myron Selznick, at this time. Mader remembered, "Fred was not interested in being a star. He just wanted good roles. Whenever an offer came in he had three rules: (a) I want to read the script. (b) Who is going to direct? (c) Who was the leading lady?" (Telephone interview, Roland Mader, 27 August 1990). Apparently, March could not get past (a) for *The Sisters*.

Before filming on *There Goes My Heart* started, Fred consented to play the lead free of charge at Baltimore City College in their production of *Death Takes a Holiday*, May 21 and 22, 1938. Then it was on to the Hollywood Roach studios to film what became a carbon copy of *It Happened One Night*, but Fred and Virginia were by no means equal to the task of following such a hard act as the Clark Gable and Claudette Colbert characterizations. When it was released October 13, 1938, Fred thought so little of this film that he did not keep copies of the various reviews. Fortunately, Lawrence Quirk did: "March was not at his best here, not that he had that much to work with. Recent viewings reveal the film as far below March's previous standards in its production, direction and general mounting, and as eminently forgettable in 1971 as it was in 1938—more so, in fact" (Quirk 1971, 158). Frank Nugent in the *New York Times*, commented, "At its worst it has Mr. March and Miss Bruce being chased by a drunk on an ice-skating rink" (Quirk 1971, 159).

Nineteen thirty-eight was the year of that famous gentleman from Margaret Mitchell's novel *Gone with the Wind*—Rhett Butler. Eighty-thousand moviegoers (and the producers) chose Clark Gable to play Rhett Butler. March came in second with the public but was not even considered by Selznick (feeling March too old), much to the dismay of March fans everywhere. On August 11 of that year, Joseph Hoar wrote in his "Hollywood under Observation" column: "In 1932 March was Gable's only rival and today he exceeds Clark in both acting and billing status, having topped Charles Laughton on the marquee three times, while Gable was Laughton's subordinate in their one screen appearance together." As he was writing before the release of the horrific *There Goes My Heart*, Hoar continued, "For a steady dependable favorite who isn't good one week and fair the next, but who can be seen in screen hit after screen hit, eternally satisfying with really fine performances in big pictures, you can always rely on Fredric March" (March Papers). In truth, this reliability held, for it was primarily in pictures of inferior quality and scripting that March "hammed" it up dreadfully. In fact, when Selznick had cast Fredric March as the fading actor in *A Star Is Born*, this unintended audition showed him to good advantage—a charming, adroit actor and a possible Rhett. But suddenly allegations began to appear in the public press that Fredric March was a member of the Communist party.

Gable went on to do Rhett, while March signed with director and creator Tay Garnett for the Walter Wanger production of *Trade Winds*. It seemed Garnett had recently returned from an eighteen month photographic expedition to the Orient, bringing with him 150,000 feet of film negative and an equal amount of positive printed film plus a dog-eared script. Garnett had to make a picture immediately to replenish the treasury his cruise drew heavily upon; therefore, he convinced Walter Wanger to produce. They got together and selected only 4,000 of the original 150,000 feet for use as atmospheric background. Art director Alexander Toluboff created seventy-nine sets for the picture ranging from a piece of dock at Bombay to a Japanese geisha house in Tokyo.

Wanger felt, "March's salary is too high. If he'll cut it in half and take a percentage, I'll do it" (March Papers). *Trade Winds* was a "spec picture," that is, a film made on percentage. Small salary, but if it clicked one collected. March portrayed a ladykiller gumshoe named Sam Wye in pursuit of Joan Bennett, who is trying to flee from the San Francisco police after she thinks she has shot Sidney Blackmer's character. Ralph Bellamy joined the cast as Blodgett, a member of the regular police force, a self-righteous fellow who takes his ninety days training too seriously and frequently becomes more amusing than he intends. March remarked, "It was fun to make, different from anything else. I never really got over being fascinated by those process shots. They just didn't seem possible. We'd make a scene up in front of a screen. Then we'd look at the rushes, and swear we must have been in China" (March Papers).

Trade Winds, released January 12, 1939, did moderately well at the box office. Frank Nugent, *New York Times*: "Tay Garnett earned the distinction yesterday of being probably the first man in history with the temerity to invite 80,000,000 persons to pay to see the movies he took on a world cruise. At least, it has been glibly written and has the services of a well-mannered cast. Mr. March has a good line to toss for every toss of the Bennett shoulder" (March Papers). William Broehnel of the *New York World Telegram*: "My chief criticism of the film is that it is a shame to place such a good director, expert actors and fine writers in competition with scenery, although, if the truth must be told, the competition isn't very stiff, since most of the backgrounds look alike, whether they be Bombay, Colombo, Singapore or Saigon" (March Papers).

It was while making *Trade Winds* that Fred and Florence signed on to do the George S. Kaufman/Moss Hart play *The American Way*. This was to be their second comeback play set to open January 1939. The Marches' wanted to prove to the theater world that they were willing to give Broadway a try once again and they could not have picked a better play to appear in, considering the temper of the country in 1939. Regarding his most recent accusation by Ivan Cox, that of being a Communist, Fred was extremely proud to be appearing in *The American Way*, a cavalcade of a German immigrant's life from the day he lands at Ellis Island (age thirty-five) until he grows old and mellows in a typical American town in Ohio. Two hundred fifty men, women and children in 3,000 different costumes depicted the passing of four decades. In two acts and eighteen scenes, Martin Gunther (Fred) the German immigrant landing in America in 1896 with his wife, Trina (Florence), grows deeply American, consciously indebted to the land that gives them freedom, opportunity and success. They lose their son in the First World War, endure the Depression, and live to see their grandson about to join a Nazi organization. Old Martin tries to persuade his grandson not to join and is killed for his efforts.

Opening January 27, 1939, *The American Way* was the initial play presented at the Center Theater in New York and was a tremendous success, averaging $40,000 a week for twelve weeks. At that time it could rightfully claim to be the largest average gross ever coined by any play on Broadway up to 1939. Burns Mantle, *Daily News* expressed that the play was especially fortunate in having enlisted the services of Fredric March, who had come back from Hollywood determined, apparently, to recover such prestige as he sacrificed in playing *Yr. Obedient Husband* a year ago. "Well, Fredric may look in his mirror and indulge a smile of satisfaction this morning. He gave as finely sustained a characterization as the simple hero of *The American Way* Saturday night as any actor has given in any drama this season, and there have been a lot of fine performances here-abouts the last few months" (March Papers). *Variety*: "That March, carrying a dialect throughout, wholly wins audience sympathy seems a sterling test of his acting ability. He makes the character lovable" (March Papers). In short, March gave of his skill as an actor and his sincerity as an American, a pride in character that pulled the whole play together. However, he did have one trying moment during one performance of *The American Way*. He was working in his carpenter shop, in character, on stage, and the absent-minded stage manager started to lower one of the elevator platforms that made up the stage floor. To his horror, Fred suddenly found himself playing with one foot two feet higher than the other. Said Fred, "It was the perfect example of the right foot never knowing what the left foot was doing!" (March Papers).

Meanwhile, on the European front, Hitler gobbled up most of Czechoslovakia, even though he had promised not to back in September of 1937. Hitler had, in a single stroke, destroyed any pretext that his ambitions were restricted to the desire to reunite Germans, rendering general war all but inevitable. President Roosevelt did all that he could, short of war, such as asking Congress for larger appropriations to rebuild the American army and gaining approval for a Naval Expansion Act. On April 14, Roosevelt sent a personal message to Hitler asking him to promise not to attack some twenty small countries in Europe. Hitler made an insulting reply and then bullied some of the countries (which he was about to swallow) into assuring Roosevelt that they had no cause to fear good neighbor Germany.

March remembered the impact of Germany's advance, spring of 1939:

We couldn't have Nazi flags in the last scene of *The American Way*, because we thought it would be dotting the "i" twice and because we weren't supposed to name the Fascists. We weren't at war and we couldn't affront the Nazis. Just about that time Dorothy Thompson was thrown out of the Bond rally at Madison Square Garden and we noticed the applause at the anti-fascist wind-up at our play was a lot stronger than it had been. (March Papers)

Even if the nation still did not feel that its own security was at stake in Europe, Fred and Florence continued to raise their voices against what they felt *was* a threat. Fred was just one of the growing number of film players who were actively supporting democratic and liberal movements and was quick to emphasize that the new concern with social responsibility in Hollywood was absolutely genuine. Florence was on the board of the Hollywood Anti-Nazi League and both of them worked for the lifting of the Spanish embargo earlier in the year. On May 27, Fred and Florence were awarded the Badge of Tolerance by the National Conference of Jews and Christians. They were selected for this honor for their service in spreading the principles of democracy and tolerance both in the play *The American Way* and in several radio broadcasts. In addition, Fred narrated *The 400,000,000*, a film about the ragged Chinese army defending itself from the Japanese. March continued these efforts, narrating on April 15, 1940, *Lights Out in Europe* and the *Call to America Pledge*, July 4, 1940.

While Fred was on hiatus from *The American Way* (to do the narration for

The   400,000,000 in Hollywood), Florence went farm shopping in New Milford, Connecticut, eventually buying a 200-year-old farmhouse on forty acres. "Last month I bought what Mr. March calls 'half of Connecticut'—a forty-acre farm in New Milford with a house so tiny there isn't room for a maid" (March Papers). This was by design for she wanted Penny and Tony to do things for themselves to compensate for the overprotection of Hollywood, where she felt their "fiber" was in danger of being weakened. The Marches' added a kitchen/family room that recalled the one in their Beverly Hills Ridgedale home. They installed new plumbing, built a "mud bottom" swimming pool and a tennis court, and moved an old barn onto the property in order to convert it into a guest cottage and study. Christened Firefly Farm, it was to become Fred and Florence's much-loved retreat. At this time, too, they sold the Beverly Hills Ridgedale home, buying a smallish ranch on Mandeville Canyon Road to remove them further the Hollywood life Florence found so distasteful.

In 1939, Fred expressed his feeling for Firefly during an August interview. "So you want to talk," March began from the depths of a hammock slung between two stately elms on a spacious lawn. "Having a farm is a thrill. What I'm trying to say is that in one way or other most of us try to get back to or recapture some of the beautiful irresponsibility and charm of our childhood, and that's what this place represents to me. I've wanted to have a place like this way back when" (March Folder). On free weekends in New Milford, Fred could be found driving around town oblivious to the rest of the world, reading a script on the steering wheel, in an old jacket with a slouch hat pulled down low over his eyes. As he grew older, his big deal in New Milford was to go to town and get the paper. Actually, according to Ralph Bellamy, although he loved Firefly, Fred was ambivalent about where he lived and could never be described as a country gentleman. Servants mowed the lawn and tended the spacious grounds while Florence reveled in her various gardens. While Fred was swinging in his hammock, Germany attacked Poland (September 1, 1939), resulting in war with England and France. Yet, Americans still did not want to become involved, did not feel threatened. Not even Russia's attack on Finland in November shook this determination. Since the war seemed so unreal, there was little to shake the conviction that Hitler would be defeated in a war of attrition. But storm clouds could not be ignored forever.

Fred continually tried to make it back for the ten year reunions (without Florence because she did not want to attend) of his university graduating class, and some fraternity reunions of the Alpha Delts. During November, he traveled to his alma mater, the University of Wisconsin in Madison to attend the 1939 Homecoming game between Wisconsin and Purdue. With him were college buddy Chuck Carpenter and his two brothers, Harold and Jack. Fred stole the afternoon away from the players as he led the Wisconsin band in a rather unique treatment of "On Wisconsin."

Virginia Hall, newly wed to Fred's college roommate during the football road trips, Laurence Hall, met Fred at this game for the first time. "All I could remember were those beautiful brown piercing eyes of his" (Interview, Virginia Hall, 18 March 1990). By 1939, Fredric March could be described as a handsome man six feet tall, weighing 170 pounds. His right shoulder was much lower than his left, requiring the right shoulder pads of his suits to be raised so the shoulders would appear on the same level. He was fond of eating, practically any dish his favorite, and he had to watch his weight. He was fond of keeping accounts, and for a while he used to list the household expenses. He had an elaborate bookkeeping system and could tell you what he was worth to the penny (which was considerable). He was generally chewing gum, a moderate smoker, emptying a pack of cigarettes a day; allowed himself one cigar a day after dinner, and was a mild drinker. He was an avid letter writer, and he kept up a large correspondence. Whenever he was asked by a newspaper or magazine for an article, he did not allow any publicity man to ghost it for him, but wrote it himself. He also liked to do a little rewriting on his scripts.

After the Homecoming game, March was due in Hollywood to fulfill a picture commitment he had signed to make between theater engagements. He had now been away one and one half years from the picture making business and managed to astonish the trade by collecting $100,000 for his return movie after his second appearance on Broadway. No more than half a dozen bona fide stars were then functioning exclusively as freelancers without at least a partial studio tie-in, and not even a Cary Grant commanded a per-picture fee in six figures. At the same time, MGM paid Fredric March $100,000 to hold Joan Crawford's coat in *Susan and God*. This was to be his first and only appearance with Joan Crawford.

Crawford was billed over March in this melodrama. March commented, "She was a nice person, but a real movie star. She even brought her own music to the set—a whole entourage, a violinist and a pianist, to play her favorite songs, to get her into the proper mood for the scene" (March Papers). In a patchy version of the Gertrude Lawrence stage hit, Joan Crawford is the thirty-fivish socialite using a newfound religious movement as a way to meddle in the private affairs of her friends. March is unlucky enough to be her neglected alcoholic husband (naturally, Fred was always at his best when portraying such parts). He turned in one of his most impressive enactments as the bewildered husband, a victim of liquor. He makes a bargain with his wife, that he will give her her freedom if only she will spend a summer with him and their equally neglected daughter. Per usual, it all ends happily: the couple stays together.

When it was released July 11, 1940, said William Boehnel, *New York Telegram*, "Fredric March is flawlessly brilliant. So much so that he almost annexes the honors from Miss Crawford" (March Papers). Even though the reviews were good, Fred's own brother, Jack, was disappointed, as we can witness from a letter Fred wrote to him.

Monday am July 1, 1940.
Dear Jack
  Sorry you didn't like 'S & God' better. Most critics have indicated it was Crawford's best to date and my best since "Star is Born."
  We love our new little house & are having a swell summer.
  Our best love to you all—
Ever—
          Fred
(Jane Morris, Jack's daughter, copy of this letter to author, 3 November 1990)

14

Communist!

August 15, 1940, the *Los Angeles Examiner*:

GRAND JURY WITNESS ACCUSES SCORE IN FILMS AS REDS
More than a score of Hollywood leading film luminaries have been
named by the Los Angeles County grand jury as outright members or
active sympathizers of the Communist party. Heavy financial
contributions of these directors, actors and writers served to finance 65%
of the Communist activities in Southern California for a two-year period.

Through the luminaries, and through Communist infiltration into studio
labor unions, the Red Party sought to gain control of the vast motion
picture industry, both to use it as a means of Communist propaganda and
to prevent it from being used for capitalistic propaganda.

Allegations were made by John L. Leech, former Communist organizer
and member of the state executive committee of the Communist Party,
who testified. Leech told the Grand Jurors that the following had been
members of the Communist Party during the years 1931 to 1936. Herbert
Biberman, director, Jean Muir, actress, and Fredric March, actor.
(March Papers).

Fred knew what such an accusation meant in the Red-hunting atmosphere that
Martin Dies's House Un-American Activities Committee had started. He
responded:

That man Leech is an unmitigated LIAR! None of the charges of this
man—who by his own admission is an ex-Communist and one-time
advocate of our Government's overthrow by force and violence, is true in
the slightest degree. I do not even know the man. I have *never* knowingly
contributed a single penny to the Communists or any other un-American

cause. In fact, if I have been duped by anyone, including Mr. Leech, at any time during the past, I want to be the first to know it.

Fred continued, "My record and conscience as an American and as a man are clear . . . I will welcome the opportunity to meet Mr. Leech face to face and *call* him a liar" (*Los Angeles Evening Herald and Express*, 17 August 1940, March Papers).

Fred got his opportunity on Saturday, August 17, when he met with the Dies subcommittee at the Biltmore Hotel. Behind closed doors for more than two hours, Leech repeatedly made his allegations and Fred steadfastly denied them. Dramatically coming face to face with his accuser, he called Leech a liar. Florence reported that her husband wanted to "Sock Mr. Leech," but held himself back with difficulty. Four days later, Representative Martin Dies, who was known as a man with political ambitions, demanded that Fredric March, James Cagney, and Franchot Tone appear before the House Un-American Activities Committee (he was now chairman).   After hearing Cagney's, March's, and Tone's statements, he dismissed all the charges. Mr. Dies cautioned that numerous screen people had, through kindness, made contributions to, and let their names be used by, certain organizations which the Committee had found unanimously to be organized under Communist leadership. Before a Los Angeles grand jury, John Leech named forty-two actors, actresses, writers, producers, and directors as Communist party members, sympathizers, or contributors. Released to the press, it turned out to be a mixed bag, containing both flaming devotees of the party and persons who had merely lent their names or their money to some apparently worthy cause in which the Communist party had a hand.   Leech was known for making strong charges against well-known individuals and then backing down when pressed for evidence or confronted by the accused. Most of his testimony dribbled away like sand. The kind of attack at which Martin Dies was expert would be exhibited on a wider screen in 1947.

As the war in Europe escalated (Hitler occupied half of France) the Nazi blitzkrieg soon shattered America's illusions about the outcome of the European war and its own impregnability. If France capitulated, Britain might soon go under. In 1940, Fred and Florence donated an ambulance to Great Britain to help the cause; it was placed in service in the West Kensington section of London. That same year March played two completely different movie roles. The first was as a moustached beachcomber in the adaptation of Joseph Conrad's *Victory* for Paramount opposite Betty Field. *Victory*, directed by John Cromwell, involves a loner who discovers the hard way that no man is an island, and, once again, proves the difficulty of adapting Joseph Conrad novels to the screen.   March plays the role of a recluse, Hendrik Heyst, with controlled emotion, as he battles with wit against a murderous trio that has come to ransack the secret and lonely island to which Heyst has taken a girl for protection. Released December 21, 1940, some critics liked his interpretation: "Fredric March gives his usual polished performance and is more than satisfactory" (March Papers). And some didn't: "Fredric March, looking somewhat like Robert Louis Stevenson, plays the hero in a studied and oddly detached manner, as though he was never quite sure about the role" (March Papers).

The second picture effort found March as a German expatriate in the adaptation of Erich Maria Remarque's *Flotsam* under the title of *So Ends Our Night*. Of the two performances, *So Ends Our Night* is the more polished effort. One of the forgotten near-greats of early World War II—before the United States was directly involved in the war—*So Ends Our Night* relates the story of refugees from Nazi Germany trying to keep one jump ahead of Nazi expansionism throughout Europe. Again directed by John Cromwell but for Universal, some of it was slow-moving and episodic but the performances by Fredric March, Margaret Sullavan, and Glenn Ford were all exceptionally good.

March portrays Captain Steiner, a former German officer who has been run out of his country because of his anti-Nazi political activity. He gave a very honest and simple portrayal that more than any other single factor gave *So Ends Our Night* authenticity. However, released February 27, 1941, it was not considered a box office success, but did receive good reviews. William Boehnel: "Fredric March emphasizes his performance by his contempt for the Nazis and his tough courage as in the face of their persecution. As Steiner, Mr. March gives one of his finest performances" (March Papers). *New York Post*: "Fredric March, utilizing the command of German accent he had in *The American Way* is at the top of his form as Josef Steiner" (March Papers).

The Marches' had next committed themselves to a Theater Guild Production to open on the road in Boston's Colonial Theater April 7, 1941. They were to play the leading parts in a play that dealt with the consequences of putting too much effort into machinery, and too little into building human character to handle the machinery. *Hope for Harvest*, by Sophie Treadwell, describes a disquieting social situation in America, that of the decadence of the American spirit in the farm and fruit lands of California. The play did well on the road, receiving good notices: "Mr. March, portraying a dispossessed rancher, gives a vigorous and compelling portrait of a beaten man, shamed into renewed pride in his inheritance" (March Papers). The troupe played the National Theater in Washington, D.C. on April 22, then Baltimore and Pittsburgh. As Fred had a picture commitment to start filming in Hollywood in June, the play closed in early May, to be reopened in Philadelphia November 17, then on to Broadway by December.

March's new picture obligation was based on Hartzell Spence's novel *One Foot in Heaven* about his father, Reverend William Spence, a Methodist minister, and was to be filmed by Warner Brothers. This biographical drama centered on a turn of the century minister, Reverend Will Spence, and his family coming to terms with the changing face of America, through one small parsonage after another across the United States. When Hartzell Spence was informed that his father's life story was to be filmed by Warner Brothers, he wrote to his mother that the only man he could see in the role of the devout but very human minister was Fredric March. Mrs. Spence agreed and was all set to request March when Warners cast March. Irving Rapper, who directed *One Foot in Heaven*, invited Mrs. Spence to visit California as a guest of the studio. When introduced to Fredric March, she gasped, "Why, he's almost as good looking as Will" ("Cinematters," *Los Angeles Daily News*, 6 October 1941, March Papers).

Technical adviser was Dr. Norman Vincent Peale, and having him on the set every day produced a certain strain, especially when everybody had to be careful about his language. Martha Scott, new from the theater, portrayed the reverend's wife, and did not know how to play for the camera.   She remembered how Fred helped her through their close-up scenes. He told her not to move her shoulders. She did anyway, so Fred placed his hands on her elbow, out of camera range, in order to stop movement.

A much more amusing incident happened in August, when Penny and cousin John Bickel, then nine and eight, respectively, visited the set. Penny was bored but John, during a break, went up to Fred and pulled at his coat, questioning, "Why do you have to make that scene over so many times?"

Fred answered, "I wasn't good enough the first time and have to do it over again."

Worried, the boy went over to director Irving Rapper and asked, "It isn't true what Uncle Fred said, is it? He's really all right as an actor, isn't he?" (March Papers).

The story starts out in 1904 in Canada, where Mr. Spence receives "the Methodist Call" and switches from medical to religious studies. He marries his sweetheart, and they arrive in muddy Fort Dodge, Iowa, to begin his preaching. For the next twenty years, he and his soon to be burgeoning family trek from parish to parish with many side episodes and anecdotes, some funny, some not. Many revolve around the various run-down parish houses the good minister and his family are forced to live in. For example, one scene takes place on a rainy Saturday afternoon when Reverend Spence is diligently writing his Sunday sermon, when water dares to drip onto his pages. Exasperated, he stomps around the house, getting more and more agitated as he steps in and stumbles out of their total bucket supply and cooking utensils, all filled with water from the leaky parish roof.   Through much hard persuasion, he is able to convince the parishioners (now in Denver, Colorado) to build a new church *and* a new house for the reverend's family. Once all is done and the much older Spence family move into their first real house, the reverend receives the call to help another small church in Iowa. All realize what Reverend Spence will do.

After March read the book, he was convinced that Reverend Spence was a flamboyant fellow full of dash and good manners, and that was the way he wanted to play him. Mrs. Spence concurred, becoming a valuable ally during production. Fred succeeded in humanizing the character and revealing the reverend's inherent strength and the courage of a small man with a mission. He also played him as a gracious charming man whose personal appeal in no way lessened his spiritual qualities. His performance, in fact, was so pleasing to Mrs. Spence that on her return home she sent Fred the leather bound hymnal her husband had always used. At the time of Fredric March's death in 1975, Larry Swindell mentioned his performance in *One Foot in Heaven*:

> The preacher has worked hard, building a church from scratch. Now he has an imposing edifice, and the belated promise of comfort for his large, often-deprived family. Except now the bishop is asking him to take over another struggling parish—to begin the work all over again. The man is visibly tortured by disappointment. Alone with his agony, he enters the empty sanctuary and regards the long-promised, expensive new pipe organ. He sits; he begins to play. As his jaw tightens, the sacred music transforms him. He is almost smiling now, but tears are welling. As the camera pulls closer, we see a face of commitment. Never has an actor imparted more subtly or so triumphantly the conviction of a real man of God. But in that moment and for all time, Fredric March is also conveying to us what it can mean truly to be an Actor. (Swindell, *Inquirer* Book Editor, March Folder)

Released November 13, 1941, *One Foot in Heaven* was a great success, nominated for an Academy Award for Best Picture. *New York Herald Tribune*: "Fredric March has always struck me as an actor more suited to costume melodramatics than the solid stuff of actual human experience. He refutes that judgment triumphantly. His portrayal of Spence is so sensitive and assured that you cannot fail to know a Methodist minister and, through him, all of mankind infinitely better after leaving the picture" (March Papers). *New York World Telegram*: "That so much of the man Spence, as well as the inspired preacher, comes through is due to Fredric March's brilliant acting in the part. March tempers his severity with drollness, his religious convictions with worldly wisdom. In short, he makes William Spence a breathing, vital person" (Quirk 1971, 174).

March kept most of the fan mail received for this portrayal, answering as much as he could personally. Many were from actual Methodist ministers predicting a huge success and allotting space in their church bulletins urging their respective flock members to see *One Foot in Heaven*. In fact, one minister almost addressed Fred as the Reverend Fredric March. "Reverend"

March then moved within a week from the touching portrait of a minister to the mood of a broad marriage farce at Columbia, in a picture titled, suggestively, *Bedtime Story*, costarring Loretta Young. March demonstrated to America and its movie critics his all-purpose abilities, once again, first by playing the minister so clerically and effectively in *One Foot in Heaven* and then as an insincere, conniving, conceited, resourceful male in *Bedtime Story*.

Director Alexander Hall felt the only actor he could see in the role of the wild, eccentric playwright was Fredric March. *Bedtime Story* is an engaging romantic comedy, with March portraying the theatrical impresario and Loretta Young his actress wife. They both want to retire from the theater —at least, March says he does. She wants to quit show business in favor of a more domestic life, much to the chagrin of her husband, who rather wants her to star in his new play. Miss Young's efforts to escape into domesticity are constantly thwarted, however, and she finally embarks for Reno and remarriage. These legal formalities over with, she discovers her "ex" is carrying his creative tendencies a little too far. He even writes and stages her honeymoon night, so that her romance ends in a riot.

In one scene, Loretta Young avenged all her screen sisters who received slaps in the face and well-aimed blows in the name of art; she caught March bent over with laughter during a scene and launched a kick which not only deposited him in the gutter, but also left him with his face in a mud puddle. Fortunately for March, director Alexander Hall okayed the first take, saving him from further indignity. Usually, that would have been the cue for the star's double to take over. Not so for March, who remarked, "I'll take my own bootings and mud baths, thank you." Surprised, the studio managers asked why. "Because I enjoy making comedy and I'm willing to do anything it demands," responded March, winking at Loretta (March Papers).

During March's tenure as a motion picture star, he had received an assortment of oddments from admiring film fans. Among the presents were patented devices for quelling rebellious hair, recipes for unorthodox dishes; a half-dozen alarm clocks, a memory course, a superb trout fishing outfit, two dozen pipes from as many different admirers, bedroom slippers, tips for married men and a crate of lemons. On the eve of the release of *Bedtime Story*, he was somewhat fearful of what the morning's mail might bring. He explained, "They always select their gifts from the title of the picture, so it all depends upon how they take this title" (March Papers).

Released March 19, 1942, *Bedtime Story* did a moderately successful amount of business at the box office. *Daily News*: "Loretta Young and Fredric March respond to Al Hall's persuasive direction with an engaging awareness of the pictures comedy values in pretending to be the outstanding actress and playwright-manager of the stage" (March Papers). *New York World Telegram*: "If Fredric March seems a little on the synthetic side early in the film, unwillingly or with intention, the men who made the film scored a direct hit in pointing up the character of the principle involved. For, as matters progress, he blossoms out as a thoroughly devoted husband who loves only two things in life—his work and Miss Young" (March Papers).

After finishing the filming of *Bedtime Story*, the Marches' visited his sister's home in Centralia, Washington, during September of 1941, where Fred's father Mr. Bickel had moved because of failing health. In fact, things were not well with the elder Bickel. In a letter to brother Jack, Fred disclosed, "Trip worth it but we hoped H. L. [brother Harold] could stop by there, as father slowly declining, tho Bess would not admit it" (Jane Morris letters, 3 November 1990). Fred had no more time to visit his father or sister Bess, for the Theater Guild production of *Hope for Harvest* was booked to reopen in Philadelphia November 17, 1941, moving on to Broadway by November 26. Then, if current considerations in the Jesse Lasky unit at Warner's matured, he would travel back to Hollywood to play the title role in *Mark Twain*.

While in Philadelphia, *Hope for Harvest* received magnificent critical notices and acclaim, applauding Fredric March as natural, unaffected, and completely believable. However, when *Hope* opened on Broadway, the New York critics came to the play, heard something discussed about agriculture, and promptly decided that it could not be of the slightest interest to New York audiences. *Newark News*: "The acting for *Hope for Harvest* is vastly superior to the scattered story at hand" (March Papers). *Wall Street Journal*: "Mr. March pleased this reviewer considerably as the discouraged but finally reenergized peach grower. If only he had more of a play to work with" (March Papers). As the play was so well liked outside New York, the contrasting reactions, divided as they were along geographical lines, surprised the Guild so much that it went to the trouble of taking a large advertisement in the drama pages of the local newspapers, quoting from the rave notices of the critics in other towns. Why, the advertisement seemed to imply, should the critics of New York differ so widely in their estimate of Miss Treadwell's serious work from the verdict set down in Washington and Philadelphia?

To add insult to injury, on the third night of *Hope*, November 28, 1941, Fred's father died quietly in his sleep at age eighty-two years at the home of his daughter Bess in Centralia, Washington. The funeral was scheduled in Racine, Wisconsin for Sunday, December 7, and the Marches' were to attend. After the Saturday evening performance, Fred and Florence caught the overnight plane to Chicago, arriving in Racine in time for the 10:00 a.m. funeral. Spending the rest of the day with friends and relatives, they caught a train back to New York by 7:30 p.m. that same night. Fred was not to see Racine again until twenty-five years later in 1968.

The Marches' continued in *Hope for Harvest* but had a short run. Fred was disappointed that *Hope* was not a hit, especially because it prevented him from accepting leads in several screen productions. "I think it was a fine play. But maybe it's not the kind of play I would have picked to see just at this time. Now that I think about it, I realize that I want either to see an out and out play about the war or something very light. Perhaps it was the wrong time to show it" (March Papers).   It turned out he was right.   While the Marches were en route to Racine to witness a funeral, the Japanese carried out their attack on Pearl Harbor with devastating effect. At the end of this sad and bloody day, 2,403 American sailors, soldiers, marines, and civilians had been killed; 1,178 more wounded, 149 planes had been destroyed on the ground or in the water; the battleship *Arizona* was sunk beyond repair; the *Oklahoma* shattered and capsized; the *Tennessee*, *West Virginia* and *California* resting on the bottom; the *Nevada* run aground to prevent sinking. Next day, Congress declared a state of war with Japan—then Germany and Italy, faithful to their tripartite pact with Japan, declared war on the United States. Pacifism and isolationism had been strong enough to keep America at peace for more than two years after the invasion of Poland in September 1939, but in the end the United States, too, was embroiled in the Second World War.

Once *Hope* closed, March still insisted that his allegiances were about half-and-half divided between films and the legitimate stage. He felt that what an actor learned in making movies helped on the stage and vice versa, citing that in Hollywood you always had to bear in mind exactly where the cameraman's chalkmarks were and make a blind landing on them while seeming to do other business. Everything was figured out by camera angles and the field of action was small because cameras were always thrust close. He complained, "You get your lines one day and the next you are before the camera and every working day from then on is like a kind of opening night. Working for the theater, you have more chance of concentrating on the burden of the lines, and on the acting. It is harder to fit into movie-making after play-making than the other way around" (March Papers). Admittedly, both had for him their compensations and their inconveniences, professional and personal. "Sometimes I think that, if it weren't for the necessity of paying taxes, Florence and I would just go and hole up on our farm in Connecticut for the duration" (March Papers). Fred's daughter, Penny, remembered her father during her growing up years of the early 1940s as fun, charming and very kind, writing in 1990, "I remember very well how handsome he looked back in the days when people really dressed up in the evening, and he'd have on tails and an evening cape to go out and I got to pop up his beautiful top hat" (Letter, Penelope March Fantacci, 12 September 1990).

Initially for *The Adventures of Mark Twain*, Warner's had debated the matter of having an actor undertake the role who, because of a mustache and other facial and physical attributes, might be more like the famous American humorist. However, it was felt that the impersonation could just as well be feigned, providing the actor could simulate the mental qualities of the subject of the interpretation. Therefore, by April 1942, the role of Mark Twain was cinched for Fredric March with Irving Rapper set to direct the Warner epic.

March was interviewed after netting this plum role; he claimed his success was because he had never acted; that is, whatever success he'd had in pictures and on the stage was due to the fact that he did not know how to act. There was no false modesty about this surprising statement, for March had a very realistic manner of looking at life and his work. He maintained that simplicity and sincerity in a story, its direction and its acting could not fail to make a good picture.   He pointed out that love, hate, anger, happiness, the fundamental emotions, do not require a bag of acting tricks to express them. "I feel parts that are simple and sincere and play them just as I react to them. It's as easy as that" (March Papers).   March declared that most important roles hit an actor right between the eyes and consequently there would be little difficulty interpreting them.   With this in mind, his next role before starting *Mark Twain* would test his theories to the breaking point, hitting him not between the eyes, but in a much more tender area of his anatomy.

Fredric March and Florence Eldridge shortly after their May 30, 1927 marriage. Photo courtesy of Kathryn Davis.

Fredric March on the set of *Anna Karenina* (1935). Photo courtesy of The State Historical Society of Wisconsin.

Fredric March posing for a publicity still during the early 1940s. Photo courtesy of The State Historical Society of Wisconsin.

Fredric March, Florence Eldridge, Bradford Dillman, and Jason Robards performing in Eugene O'Neill's *Long Day's Journey into Night* (1957–1958) on Broadway.

15

The War Years

March was set next to act in the adaptation of Thorne Smith's *The Passionate Witch*, retitled *I Married a Witch*. The film was one of three made by the short-lived Cinema Guild. During the war studio space was at a premium, so United Artists had *I Married a Witch* filmed at and by Paramount, which had more production facilities than its distribution outlets could cope with. This is a delightful story involving a witch (Veronica Lake) and her father (Robert Benchley) returning to earth to plague a New England stuffy gubernatorial candidate named Wallace Wooly (March). Wooly's ancestor, it seems, burned them at the stake during the seventeenth century. Through devilish tricks and magical hijinks the witch manages to break up the politician's engagement and eventually falls for him herself, thus the title.

During production Veronica Lake, the sultry, provocative glamour star of the 1940s, would test March's rarely seen temper daily. So much so that it appeared the production had a hex on it, with the two stars battling it out loud and clear. March *did* patronize Lake, primarily because she was not professionally trained. She had heard that March called her "a brainless little blond sexpot, void of any acting ability" (Lenburg 1983, 104). Therefore, Lake, already noted for being hot-tempered on the set, found working with March a chore. His opinion of her plus her newness to movie making caused her insecurity. She rarely made a good take after the first one, while March, as an oldtimer, invariably got better and better. René Claire, the director of *I Married a Witch*, commented, "The discrepancy between the two actors' best takes on any given shot led me to devise all sorts of tricks, including actually shooting Veronica when she thought we were still rehearsing" (Dale 1986, 313).

Another conflict between the two stars developed immediately upon their first meeting and led to the practical jokes Lake inflicted on March during production. As March had established himself as quite a womanizer, he was not initially immune to Veronica Lake and thought her breathtaking. Since he tried making advances on her and the other women working in the film, his reputation of being on the make all the time caused Veronica to be constantly on guard. His flirtatious manner did not set well with her, adding to if not creating the ongoing feud between them. She railed into him about being a "horny old guy" (Lenburg 1983, 104). As the shooting went on, her acute dislike for him intensified and the inherent hostility between the pair deepened. She played as many pranks on him she could devise.

For example, in several scenes Fred had to pick Veronica up and carry her offstage. He carried her through a hotel fire, up stairs, down stairs, to beds, and finally from an automobile crash in the final scene. Six-foot-tall March generally had no trouble carrying ninety-eight-pound Lake. However, as part of her offensive strategy and with help from a cameraman, Veronica placed a forty-pound weight under her dress for the final carrying scene. Because of her purposefully inept acting, the scene was shot three times, with an unsuspecting March breathing heavily and gradually losing his strength. After the final take, he asked Veronica why she seemed so heavy. "Big bones" was her reply (Lenburg 1983, 105). When March learned the truth, it irritated him to such an extent that he never spoke to her offstage thereafter.

Another incident is described by Lake in her autobiography, *Veronica*. After her character had been knocked out by a falling picture of the very ancestor who had condemned her to burn, the present-day descendant (March) had to lean over her (she was in a sofa chair), patting her hands with characteristic worry. The shot reveals only the two of them from the waist up. Lake said,

> He was standing directly in front of the chair. I carefully brought my foot up between his legs. And I moved my foot up and down, each upward movement pushing it ever so slightly into his groin. Pro that he is, he never showed his predicament during the scene. But it wasn't easy for him, and I delighted in knowing what was going through his mind. Naturally, when the scene was over, he laced into me. I just smiled. (Beck 1978, 170–171)

Censorship troubles also plagued the set. At an interview, René Clair responded to a question about the troublesome shooting of the hotel fire scene, a scene that necessitated a nude Veronica Lake. "The censors protested because when the witch comes through the smoke, she is nude. I told them that the audience would see no more of Veronica Lake than if she were wearing an evening gown. We see only her shoulder; the rest of her is in smoke. They replied that the audience might not see her, but March would!"

"You mean to tell me that they were protecting the morals of movie stars?" the interviewer asked.

Clair replied, "Isn't that preposterous? If you start protecting the virtue of Fredric March, you'll find yourself very busy!" (Samuels 1972, 94–95).

Another time, Veronica was excessively late for a portrait setting and when she did arrive, Fred was ready to slit her throat. She remembered,

> The crazy part of the whole affair was that we had to take love scenes, and, when I saw the finished results, I roared with laughter. Such pure loathing you've never seen on any two faces, particularly when they were lying so alluringly cheek-to-jowl. So I went to Freddie and apologized. He agreed to make the sitting over, and that time the results were slick. (Lenburg 1983, 105)

In the end, whether the two principals got along or not, Clair managed a curious contrasting rapport between the stars: a girl with a sultry look but no acting experience, turned by a great director into appearing the equal of a serious actor who throughout his twenty-two years of increasing distinction had been prepared to take on the occasional light comic role. Released November 19, 1942, *I Married a Witch* was a hit, March receiving his usual good reviews. Bosley Crowther, *New York Times*: "Mr. March is amusingly sozzled by her (Lake) baffling bedevilment" (March Papers). Alton Cook, *New York World-Telegram and Sun*: "Fredric March is present with one of the stalwart and good performances standard with him" (March Papers).

When March was questioned about the film, he remarked, "It was just another picture." But he was still stinging from Lake's shenanigans two years later when he made a guest appearance on the radio talk show "Information Please" (April 10, 1944). March was asked to name three films in which he caused the death of the heroine. He got through two-thirds of the answer and dried up. Racking his brain to think of a third instance, "*I Married a Witch*," he suddenly exclaimed. "No, I didn't," he added hastily (March Papers).

Fortunately, March's next picture would not witness so many uncharacteristic mishaps. Jesse Lasky's previous hope of producing a picture about America's favorite humorist, Mark Twain, finally came together summer of 1942. March's casting as Twain was helped by Twain's only living daughter, Clara Clemens Gabrilowitsch. It was she who agreed emphatically with producer Lasky's first choice of Fredric March for her father's screen shadow, and it was she who gave March the most hints about imitating the way her father moved and talked. She was so determined that Warner's pick Fredric March that she refused to work with anyone else. She felt March was the only artist capable of impersonating the many sides of her father's nature. To her it required a special kind of art to represent faithfully the deeply serious, even tragic strains of her father's disposition that alternated with his light, more humorous impulses. Her conversations with Lasky were recorded in a letter she wrote to March detailing how he was chosen for the role;

Lasky asked, "Would you be willing to be photographed with Mr. March, and state in print that he is your choice?"

Clara replied, "Most certainly."

Lasky continued, "Would you consent, then, to come to the studio and give us suggestions—work with us?"

Clara complied, "Gladly, if you decide on Mr. March. But, to be quite frank, if you select any other actor, I shall be unable to cooperate with the studio in any way. I should not even wish to step inside the theater to see the production" (Letter to Fredric March, 26 February 1942, Clara Clemens Gabrilowitsch, March Papers).

Accordingly, Warner's had the good fortune to be able to hand the title role to Fredric March, who above all things was a conscientious player and in an instance such as portraying Mark Twain would do nothing short of moving heaven and earth to ensure authenticity. However, neither Lasky nor the director, Irving Rapper, could convince March to believe himself suited for the part until the makeup department made him up like Twain at age sixty-five. Fred remarked about this during an interview, looking at a picture of himself, as Twain, with two others, relaxing at a table in the studio commissary. "Mrs. Ossip Grabilowitsch—she is Clara Clemens, you know, Twain's daughter—told me that when she saw this picture in a newspaper, she just thought it a good picture of her father. It wasn't until she read the caption that she realized it was just me sitting at a table with Irving Rapper and Jesse Lasky" (March Papers).

This was to be the most difficult role March had handled, primarily because this assignment to bring to the screen such a generally revered personage as Mark Twain was one filled with perils and pitfalls. Millions had admired, even worshiped, the great humorist. Every facet of his personality, every detail of his career, had been the subject of exhaustive study, and any unwitting deviation from a faithful characterization would inevitably set up the actor as a target for the wrath of the multitude. The published announcement by Warner's that Fredric March would portray Twain started a deluge of letters pouring into the Warner studio by the hundreds. All types of comment were included but a great many were convinced in advance that justice would not be done to their literary hero.

Mark Twain or Samuel Clemens died in 1910, leaving only enough published work to fill about two dozen books. However, by the time Warner Brothers' research department prepared for the filming of Twain's life, at least 305 volumes had been published solely about him, and 1,750 books and periodicals contained references to him. It took a period of fourteen months, a seventy-two-page bibliography, 2,345 photographs and 148 individuals who had known Twain to build up the portrait of him for *The Adventures of Mark Twain*. The photographs included originals or copies of every available portrait of Twain, along with pictures of hundreds of articles to be used as film properties from

Mississippi steamboats to jumping frogs.

Once March had decided to accept the part, he proceeded to go in for a bit of research himself. He studied at length the one brief (100 feet) film movie of Twain taken in his later years. Photographed long ago, it used a different speed from the films of the forties; the newsreel showed Mark Twain walking in a peculiarly fast, jerky way. That worried March enough to run the newsreel off on a hand machine. Still Twain's walk was fast and jerky, difficult to reconcile with some of the mannerisms he had heard and read about the popular writer. Some people said Twain took a minute between each word, that he drawled out his sentences, and some said he talked fast and jerkily, rather like the newsreel. Fred remarked, "At last I managed to reconcile the two descriptions, after talking to everyone I could find who knew him. It seems that both descriptions were right. He used to start off slowly, making sure you were following his meaning. Then, when he was sure, he would run right through to the end. Anyway, I tried to pick up all the Twain mannerisms I could" (March Papers).

In fact, March later commented on the one affectation of Twain's he failed to imitate. The one thing he missed completely in Twain, and he just loved it when he saw Hal Holbrook do Twain later, was the way Twain fooled with his hand and caught the bottom of his sleeve on and on. That was one thing March forgot and it broke his heart that he had not captured this small mannerism.

Starting late June 1942, for twelve weeks straight, March secluded himself in the makeup department. Averaging ninety minutes daily, there were ten different makeups and thirty-two wardrobe changes. The makeup department had the many pictures of Twain showing the changes in his appearance as he aged, from his early twenties until his passing at seventy-five. Because Twain's nose seemed to broaden as he grew older, three noses had to be built for the screen Twain. All in all, seen side by side, photographs of the real and the movie Twain exhibited a startling likeness. Warner's was ready to begin production on *The Adventures of Mark Twain*. The film follows Twain's picturesque career as a steamboat navigator on the Mississippi, editor in the Wild West, and world famous lecturer, showing some of the inspirations for many of Twain's best stories. The picture also displays his brief courtship but lengthy marriage to his wife, portrayed too fetchingly by Alexis Smith. March may have made himself up to look like Twain and succeeded, but in no way does Alexis Smith even come close to the homely Mrs. Clemens.

One of the worthwhile effects of the film, according to producer Lasky, was the effective introduction of well-known characters other than the central figures of the film. Such notables as Ulysses S. Grant, Henry Wadsworth Longfellow, Oliver Wendell Holmes, Ralph Waldo Emerson, John Greenleaf Whittier, Bret Harte, and William Dean Howell, and some others are exposed, at least briefly, to the camera. Part of the story plot hinged upon

Twain's meeting with some of these luminaries at the famous Whittier birthday party. Another effect that made this biographical film valuable, the producer believed, was the possibility offered by using actual historical backgrounds in the filming. The picture was in production sixty-nine camera days and was filmed on eighty-five different studio settings and nine locations, among them being Hannibal, Missouri, Twain's boyhood home; the Twain Quarry Farm study at Elmira, New York, and the still preserved home in Hartford, Connecticut. Special effects, too, played a part. The Mississippi in the background for the film was really a studio river. A miniature stream created inside the studio was photographed by a camera crew in all its moods from twilight peace to muddy eddies. Rotting stumps lining the shores were miniature, as were the model of Mark Twain's craft and the paddle-wheeler, which was wrecked in a final blaze of glory during the Civil War period. Yet, the finished product looked as if it all took place on the Mississippi.

Once production finished, the release date for *Mark Twain* was indefinite. Films dealing with the war were being produced and released while they were topical. Pictures that had nothing to do with the war, such as the biographical story of Mark Twain, were good at any time. Eventually, upon March's return from a USO tour he made in late 1943, and at his suggestion, the film was released almost two years after actual production (March of 1944) to America's men in uniform with general release to the public coming later, May 3, 1944.

Upon viewing one is left with an impression of an extremely complicated man, but not a clear understanding of the Twain mind-set, possibly because of the lavishness of the production, the necessity to compete with the various personages and sceneries paraded by Warner's before the public. What made the man great was hard to capture on film, though March's portrayal stood up well with a war weary American people. It is one of his better remembered roles and his reviews are noteworthy. *New York Sun*: "Mr. March, in his finest screen performance, captures Clemens's essential eagerness, the gift of seeing the world still afresh through youthful eyes. The picture is, as it must be, Mark Twain's and Fredric March's" (March Papers). *Cleveland News*: "March has so far sublimated his own personality that one is never conscious of Fredric March—only Mark Twain" (March Papers).

March dominates all the action, as he should. With intelligence and superior make-believe, he reconstructs Mark Twain in utterly believable shape, narrating famous anecdotes, or riding rough-shod over conventions with extraordinary skill. His makeup is perfect, but so are his gestures and his ability to communicate the essential spirit and surface foibles of a famous writer. (*New York Herald Tribune*, March Papers)

The Marches' next theater project was to be the Thornton Wilder comedic play *The Skin of Our Teeth*, produced by Michael Myerberg and directed by Elia Kazan. The Marches were to portray Mr. and Mrs. George Antrobus, with Tallulah Bankhead cast as their general utility maid, Lily Sabina, all of Excelsior, New Jersey. The Antrobuses have survived fire, flood, pestilence, the seven-year locusts, the Ice Age, the black pox and the double feature, a dozen wars and as many depressions. George Antrobus represents John Doe, the average American, at grips with destiny, sometimes sour, sometimes sweet. He alone invents the wheel, discovers the multiplication table, separates *M* from *N*, sails in the Ark from Atlantic City and sires Cain, all in the course of this play. The family has survived a thousand calamities "by the skin of their teeth," and Mr. Wilder's play is a tribute to their indestructibility.

Part of the Marches' contract stipulated that they approve the director; so Elia Kazan visited them with Michael Myerberg at their New York apartment to undergo a baptism by fire. Florence, as always, dominated the conversation, not about the impending play, but about current social topics. Here is the first open occurrence of the somewhat odd relationship that existed between the "dominant" Florence and the "passive" Fred. Kazan felt that March was an overgrown boy in a pin-striped blue suit and a banker's tie. Kazan was to soon find, as he came to know Fred, that one of his pleasures was to be "naughty and have Florence—his surrogate mother—chide him. 'Now Freddie,' she'd say, 'now Freddie.'" (Kazan 1988, 196). Apparently, Fred was one person when he was around his wife and quite another when she was out of his vicinity. Kazan made it through the audition, but came away with a negative feeling for the female half of the March family. He did feel her "to be a decent, honest, sincere, reliable woman, but how tedious those virtues can become when they're not leavened by doubt, self-depreciation, and openheartedness" (Kazan 1988, 197).

Bradford Dillman, who portrayed the Eugene O'Neill role opposite the Marches' in 1957 in O'Neill's *Long Day's Journey into Night*, tempered this opinion: "Florence had so much to do with Fred's career—and certainly a lot to do with his outside interests. He needed her—she brought to him an element of class—he himself had class—but it was enhanced by her presence" (Interview, Bradford Dillman, 11 August 1990).

Phil Gersh, Fred's agent asserted,

It is not my impression that Freddie was "henpecked." As I recall, I would submit a sreenplay to Freddie, and if he liked it, he would call me immediately to move forward on it and make a deal. Regarding Florence's input, I would say that it was a collaborative effort. Fred would always have Florence read the material ... but I believe Fred made the final decision. (Letter, Phil Gersh, 28 June 1991)

When Kazan directed Florence in *Skin of Our Teeth*, he found her a conscientious professional, but he never heard her utter a sentence that surprised him. According to Kazan, Florence thought in a straight line and brought Freddie along with her.   Fortunately, if Florence did exert such influences on Fred, her choice of *Skin* was auspicious. For, even though the play started off bad, it ended up with a Pulitzer Prize. One difficulty arose between Florence and Tallulah. Kazan wrote, "I'd anticipated that Mrs. March, with her rather artificial manners, 'society' laugh, and inflated big-star posture, would be an irresistible target for Tallulah." She was, for when rehearsals started, tensions ran high, with Kazan trying to keep the two from major battles. "The prospect of having to play scenes with Tallulah terrified Florence March . . . she scorned Florence March for being so controlled and goody-good" (Kazan 1988, 205–206). Fred caused Kazan the least problems, supporting him in his direction of *Skin*.

The play opened at the Shubert Theater in early November 1942 in Thornton Wilder's hometown of New Haven, Connecticut. The first dress rehearsal was a nightmare of hysteria. Kazan remembered that Bankhead was never quiet offstage, never on time for her entrances, never anything but hateful to the other actors. "Florence March was wretched and, it seemed to me, frightened; Freddie furious, and Monty Clift awed by the minefields of temperament exploding around him" (Kazan 1988, 210). Regardless, it was a success in New Haven but wavered in Baltimore, where the audience hooted at the actors and actresses, one member bellowing, "Give us our money back!" (March Papers). On top of that, the word-of-mouth was so bad that people who had ordered tickets in advance cancelled their reservations. Then they reached Philadelphia just in time to run smack into the opposition of the touring *This Is the Army*. They weathered Philly, played Washington successfully and headed for New York.

By now all the actors had come into New York comfortable with the play, certain they were in a hit. This attitude worried producer Myerberg, who had booked the play's first performance as a benefit before the actual Wednesday night opening November 18. He felt that if the benefit performance went too well, his company might be too indifferent for the real opening. Hence, he sabotaged the benefit performance by hiding the opening act, or rather their clothes (the costumed marching band's uniforms), in order to delay the curtain more than half an hour. The actors were thus forced to play to a hostile audience and made a poor showing.

The Wednesday opening was to be a happier occasion because this would be the first time Thornton Wilder had seen it; his military commitments had prevented him previously. So with Wilder in the theater, and with a Broadway audience occupying every seat in the house, the show played its preview performance. Reviews were generally good. Howard Barnes, *New York Herald Tribune*: "March plays the poor fool who goes on trying to make something of the wreckage of the world with immense power and Miss

Eldridge is right behind him in giving a parallel human sympathy and warmth"
(March Papers). *Christian Science Monitor*, John Beaufort:

> Mr. March creates for each act a new aspect. At first, the exuberant
> discoverer of the wheel, the alphabet, the multiplication table; next the
> paunchy disagreeable, fez-decked president of a secret order, and, finally,
> the weary, war-torn individual gathering his strength to begin again. His
> is a playing of strength, eloquence, and variety. (March Papers)

However, not everyone liked *Skin*. March remarked, "Our play either
makes people so mad they want to throw bricks or they love it. There isn't
any middle point of view" (March Papers). Some disliked it so heartily that
they walked out during the intermission, fuming and groaning. In one case,
March left the theater one night after a performance. After he hailed a cab,
the cabbie recognized him asking, "How's business, Mr. March?"

"Fine," Fred answered, "We've got a smash hit."

"I dunno," said the cabbie. "I been hackin' on Broadway 20 years but I ain't
never caught so many fares after the first act of any hit I can remember"
(March Papers).

After the play had been selling out for three weeks, producer Michael
Myerberg decided that it needed a poster to reflect the play's timeless quality,
Toulouse-Lautrec style. The ensuing poster or sketch showed Tallulah
Bankhead in a bathing suit, with Fredric March in muffler and fur hat,
romping over the tundra with a dinosaur. Florence Eldridge was missing and
would have regarded her omission from the drawing as a personal insult and
a breach of contract, but Meyerberg thought sure he could convince her to
accept the poster. As one might guess, she refused and a new poster with her
romping near the dinosaur with Fred was produced. Remember that billing
is the be-all and end-all of the theater's children. To achieve it they will
sacrifice their young, slash their salaries, forage for food and sleep in the
subway. To maintain or enhance it they'll stop at nothing short of murder.

Skin made smash hit status by the skin of it's teeth, running until late May
of 1943. On May 15, 1943, in its twenty-fifth week at the Plymouth it won the
Pulitzer Prize despite being the center of a hot literary controversy. *Reader's
Digest* editor Henry M. Robinson and Professor Joseph Campbell of Sarah
Lawrence College had accused playwright Thornton Wilder of literary grave-
robbing from James Joyce's *Finnegans Wake*. Wilder declined to dignify the
charges with a reply. Fred remembered, "Before the Pulitzer was awarded,
people used to come to the show as though they were visiting the zoo. Now
they come in on tip toe, hat in hand, as though entering a cathedral" (March
Papers).

The play was not without its memorable behind-the-scenes moments. As
Mrs. Antrobus, Florence spoke a long, difficult marriage speech in Act II,

after which the curtain dropped.   On several occasions, Florence was perturbed by Tallulah's scene stealing presence on stage during the speech, for Tallulah was generally throwing her head back over a railing, letting her hair fall free in order to comb it out slowly, and thereby distracting the audience.

"Would you mind not moving during my speech?   It's very difficult for me to concentrate," Florence requested of Tallulah.

"I haven't moved a goddamned eye!" was the reply.

"Now, Tallulah," Florence replied, rather patronizingly, "be a good girl."

"I'm sick of being a good girl, and I'm sick of your fucking frustrations!" Tallulah countered to a white-faced Miss Eldridge. (Israel 1972, 216).

According to Kazan, it took action on Fred's part to cause Tallulah to stop these antics.   After Fred's exit, Tallulah had a favorite speech in the act following Florence's. Fred walked into the wings to his dresser waiting with a small enamel bowl along with a glass containing a medicinal solution (Fred had a severe sore throat at the time).   He then lifted the glass to his lips, tilted his head back (he was standing just offstage, where some of the audience could see him) and he gargled.   Then he emptied his mouth into the enamel bowl and, as Bankhead spoke, gargled again.   His gargles were timed to coincide with Bankhead's lines. After that, Bankhead did not comb out her hair during Florence's speech. Bankhead thought she'd get back at him for such a trick, but he was ready for her. In their kissing scene, "she thrust her tongue deep into his mouth." He bit it. (Kazan 1988, 221).

During *Skin*'s run March managed several other activities, such as a Red Cross Benefit at Madison Square Garden April 5, 1943, for the Red Cross War Fund. The act he was in proved the hit of the evening. It was a strip-tease number performed by Fred with Alfred Lunt, Bobby Clarke, Howard Lindsay, Allan Mowbray, Allen Jenkins, John Emery and Arthur Treacher, called the Million Dollar Strip Tease, with Ethel Merman singing "Take It Off." He then made a radio appearance April 12, on Cavalcade of America's radio play, *The Lengthening Shadow*, a dramatization of Thomas Jefferson's life. However, he struggled with his material and finally went down in defeat. No actor could have tossed off the passages from the Jefferson state papers and public utterances as if they were the ordinary speech of a living man. On April 13, marking the opening of the second war loan drive, the Treasury Star Parade presented March and an all star supporting cast in a special half-hour radio adaptation of the book *This Is America* by Eleanor Roosevelt and Frances Cook MacGregor.   May 22 found him giving a dramatic reading for the opening broadcast of the New York Philharmonic Symphony's fifty-two-week series.   At the intermission, March recited Abraham Lincoln's memorable farewell speech to his townsmen in Springfield, Illinois, made as Lincoln left for Washington to assume his duties as president in 1861.

By May, both Fred and Florence wanted out of *Skin*. Their contract held them until June 1, but management permitted them to leave after the May 29 performance. They announced that they wished to work on their Connecticut farm, which came as a shock to people who thought actors never went out of doors in the daytime, and never off the pavements. They planned a summer away from Hollywood and New York, working on a large scale Victory garden. Fred commented, "It's impossible to get help to cultivate the farm. It's a shame to let the land lie idle in times like these . . . seems much more important to produce crops this summer than continue acting" (March Papers). He and Florence plus the two children planned on doing all the work. At the time he had no film prospects and had not the slightest idea when he would return to Hollywood.

Fred did not stay completely down on the farm that summer for he helped to create a national conference board to coordinate the theatrical profession's part in the war effort. Show people wanted to share the dangers and work of war just the same as everyone else. The board's goal was to bring more entertainment to the armed forces. The ensuing conference set up a national pool of available theatrical talent, including not only actors and actresses, but also stagehands, electricians, writers and all other professionals in the allied fields. They would be paid by the existing war-entertainment agencies according to standards mutually established by the agencies and the trade unions. During June, Fred narrated the first documentary of naval operations to be released by the Soviet Union, *Black Sea Fighters*, with commentary written by Clifford Odets. The film was photographed by official cameramen and told the full story of the Black Sea Fleet's role, on land and sea, in the epic 250 day defense of Sevastopol, the naval base Hitler expected to seize in two weeks. On July 4 Fred narrated a dramatic section for a radio broadcast entitled *One World* in the afternoon, and again spoke Lincoln's farewell to Springfield on the "American Scriptures Program" that evening. He was one of the most popular and high-paid radio personalities, receiving $2,500 per broadcast because of his excellent radio personality, appealing delivery, resonant voice and ease at rehearsals.

By August, Fred started wondering what the Manpower Act might do to him if Chairman McNutt ever got too technical. For, technically speaking, he was still employed by the National City Bank, the bank he obtained a six month leave from back in 1920 to pursue an acting career. He could be drafted back to work, but hoped that the bank either wouldn't look up their old employment records, or else would give him up as beyond redemption as a banker. Obligingly, they gave up.

With no play arranged for fall 1943, Fred started planning a USO tour of his own to entertain the boys overseas. In a letter to brother Jack in September, 1943, he quipped, "When I changed into my *uniform*, I drove over here and surprised all hell out of the family! I look like a cross between a street-car conductor and a West Point plebe—but Boy! do I feel good!" (Letter to Jack Bickel care of daughter Jane Morris, 1 September 1943).

The USO trip was to involve a 33,000 mile tour of American military camps on five continents, during which 160 performances were scheduled. Fred had another man and two women traveling with him: Sammy Walsh, a veteran cafe entertainer; Jeanne Darrell, a singer; and Evelyn Hamilton, accordion player (yes, an accordion player). Embarking from New York September 13, they would not see home again for fourteen weeks.

16

USO and Victor Joppolo

Early December 1943 found March and his entertainment troupe at Allied Headquarters in Algiers. Since Fred played mostly to noncombat troops in isolated areas, he did some morale building by telling them that their jobs were as necessary and contributory as anybody elses. Then, impromptu changing from Dr. Jekyll to Mr. Hyde broke up the audience several times. On one occasion, Sammy Walsh, acting as Master of Ceremonies, had just introduced Fredric March to close their USO Tour. Approximately 2,500 soldiers fell silent as March walked toward the center of the makeshift stage. Bareheaded, dressed in army khakis with sleeves rolled up, March stepped up to the microphone with head down. With his hands clasped behind him, he slowly looked up, turning his head left to right, his gaze scanning the military audience, then smiled warmly and began:

"You know, when I began this trip, I had a lot of humorous stuff, kidding news commentators and radio in general. Good stuff, especially written for me by George Kauffman." Some applause was heard from the soldiers, then it died down quickly as they waited for Mr. March to continue.

"But I found out from your letters home that it was not what you wanted from me. Yes, I found out that you expected something more serious, something better than jokes from Mr. March."

Fred shifted his weight, addressing the soldiers. "I first want to thank you all for being such a grand audience and laughing at the few jokes I managed to pull off." The soldiers began to clap once again, but Fred held up his hands to quiet them.

"I now wish to close with a quote from President Roosevelt's 'No Compromise' speech." The audience grew quieter, many taking their hats off. In a silence broken only by occasional bursts of ack-ack in the distance or an airplane ranging overhead, the soldiers listened eagerly.

Standing simply, hand in pocket on the bare stage, Fredric March spoke

Roosevelt's words into the microphone: "We are fighting, as our fathers have fought, to uphold the doctrine that all men are equal in the sight of God. Those on the other side are striving to destroy this deep belief and to create a world in their own image—a world of tyranny and cruelty and serfdom." Dead silence from the soldiers.

Fred continued in the voice that helped make him famous, with patriotic conviction written on his handsome features. "That is the conflict that day and night now pervades our lives. No compromise can end that conflict. There never has been—there never can be—successful compromise between good and evil. Only total victory can reward the champions of tolerance and decency, and freedom and faith."

The soldiers and stage crew jumped to their feet, awarding March a standing ovation (March Papers).

The trip was not without hardship, however. Both March and Walsh suffered the "GI trots" (dysentery) plus Fred had to have a tooth pulled at one station. Another incident happened in Khartoum. On his way to the open air theater in the darkness, Fred walked smack into a thornbush, damaging an eyeball slightly. He traveled so many miles sitting on bucket seats in cargo planes that he threatened to write a book entitled *Sideways across Africa*. His advice to the wives and sweethearts back home was to "WRITE YOUR MAN!" March was quoted, "If there's to be any estrangement when he gets home from overseas, it'll be the woman's fault. Her letters are the only things that can bridge the gap of these years apart" (March Papers).

Once home, March and Walsh were interviewed at a press conference. Fred was asked, "In your discussions with the soldiers, did any of them mention the strike situation here in the States?" (Despite the no-strike pledges of the major unions, there were nearly 15,000 work stoppages during the war, involving the loss of more than 36 million man-days.)

Fred answered, "The men aren't in a mood to discuss anything unless you sit down and draw them out." He began to talk further but was interrupted by the officer stationed at the Press Conference, Captain Fred Driver, who acted as censor for the army. "That will have to be stricken. It is a political matter" (March Papers).

On several other occasions when interviewed about his trip, March was stopped from making statements described as dangerous to the safety of Allied troops. Later, the Public Relations Office of the War Department ruled that this interference was legitimate. Mr. March, it was said, had signed the usual pledge to submit to that office any interview concerning what he saw or heard; the purpose of the pledge was to prevent publication of information that would disclose matters regarded as military secrets. Now, this would have been silly if it were not so disturbing. As far as military secrecy was concerned, it was no secret that many soldiers and their parents felt that strikes crippled or tended to cripple the war effort.

Once March had returned from his USO trip, he was in demand by various radio programs for interview purposes, appearing January 13, March 7, and for Ed Sullivan, March 13. He tried to explain to the war time audiences how homesick the American boys were. They could not understand why the movies they received, they had already seen two years prior to the war. As already mentioned, Fred was instrumental in obtaining the release of *The Adventures of Mark Twain* to the troops abroad. He remarked,

They go every night if there is a movie. I couldn't tell people at home that it lowers the venereal disease—but it does—in direct proportion. Many told me, if we have no movies, the rate would go up. We can't tell them that at home. . . . They are naturally hungry for women . . . the towns are nearby . . . just as diseased as hell. . . . I had no idea how important movies were in the soldier's life until I got over there. I don't think most people at home realize it. When you are up at five in the morning, and not a darned thing to do in the evening—you can't go back to your bunk with 500 others and write letters home every night. (Radio script fragment, 7 March 1944, March Papers)

Beyond radio interviews about his adventures overseas, March appeared on the Gertrude Lawrence Theater once to substitute for an ill Brian Aherne in the play *Michael and Mary* (January 3, 1944), once to recreate his Oscar nominated role in *A Star Is Born* (January 16, 1944) and once for the play *Dark Victory* (February 5, 1944). He also participated February 13, 1944, in the "Philco Radio Hall of Fame" from the Academy of Music in Philadelphia, where 3,500 seats were sold for war bonds. During the broadcast he was presented with a citation: "For his moving and superb portrayals, his honesty and vitality of characterization, he has earned his place in the Hall of Fame among American Actors of the stage and screen" (March Papers). The citation was a result of a weekly radio review of the best in the world of entertainment as judged and selected by *Variety*.

Busy with the war effort, Fred could not be persuaded to do a movie until spring or summer. He turned down *Mrs. Parkington* with Greer Garson explaining that the overseas trip had taken a lot out of him. He did manage to narrate *Salute to Freedom* (March 17, 1944), a dedication to the black men and women in the armed services. He also headed the dramatic presentation at the Hollywood Bowl for Treasury Secretary Henry Morgenthau, Jr.'s, Fifth War Loan drive in March and was the treasurer of the Independent Voters Committee of the Arts and Sciences for Roosevelt. In April, Fred guested again on radio to play the leading role in Norman Corwin's drama *Untitled* for Columbia Presents the dramatic case history of an average American soldier who died in battle. Fred was asked to re-create this role again May 28 for a special Memorial Day program.

One other notable event that spring occurred at a war benefit fashion show where Fred had donated his time draping furs on the models. Florence was seated in the audience when a young lady sitting next to her became extremely agitated. Turning to Florence, the young woman stated, "Would you look at how he's putting his hands on that model; would you look at what he's doing to her?"

Florence asked, "Why should that upset you?"

The woman responded, "Why should it upset me? I've given him three of the best years of my life and look what he does out in public!" Questioned later by Florence, Fred responded, "The woman was lying!" (Interview, Bradford Dillman, 11 August 1990).

Regardless, typical newspaper column gossip concentrated on what they deemed a successful marriage for the Marches : "Married in 1927 it's been a romance ever since—one of those amazingly complete things encompassing successful careers; children; three homes—a New York apartment, California house and a Connecticut farm where they enjoy summers" (March Papers).

When Warner Brothers offered March the Will Rogers role in a film producer Mark Hellinger wanted to produce around the life of the late comedian, he turned it down, expressing doubt about the part. Actually, he was hopeful that the rumors about producing a movie based on Gene Fowler's best-selling biography of John Barrymore (Barrymore died in 1942), *Good Night Sweet Prince*, would come to fruition. The rumors started November 1943, citing Paramount's closing a deal to buy Barrymore's life story and star Fredric March, naturally, as the Great Profile. The picture was slated to start as soon as a script could be finished, ideally the latter part of January 1944, which coincided with March's availability. When interviewed February 1944, Fred revealed: "At least it seems as likely a possibility as any that lies ahead of me. All I know, really, is I have got to get busy by next summer and make some money" (March Papers).

At the time, March was still under a doctor's care for a case of exhaustion and did not appear, to the interviewer, the quietly dynamic person he used to know. There were hollows in Fred's cheeks and deep blue patches under his eyes, his whole manner revealing an uncharacteristic lassitude.

I am all right, though. Merely a case of exhaustion, which, though not serious, is nonetheless annoying and generally unpleasant for a normally energetic man. I have been asked to read *Good Night, Sweet Prince*, and if it reaches the screen, they seem to think I'm a logical candidate for the role of John Barrymore. I'd like to do it, too—though I think I'm a little too old (forty-six), perhaps, to do the Great Profile in his prime. (*Sunday Mirror Magazine*, 16 April 1944, March Papers)

Unfortunately, this project never came about; later Errol Flynn portrayed

Barrymore in *Too Much Too Soon* in 1957.

Once recovered, March had to get down to the business of doing a movie, or, more importantly, making money. He had not starred in a movie since *Mark Twain* and started casting about for the proper vehicle. Now that Franchot Tone's option on the movie rights of Howard Fast's *Citizen Tom Paine* had expired, March was interested in playing the role of Paine in the screen version. He also was sent the script for *Tomorrow Is Forever*, based on the book by Gwen Bristow, made into a highly dramatic story by Lenore Coffee. With its message from a survivor of the last war to those affected by the present war, it sounded as if it might be what March would enjoy doing. Late in April he was approached by James Cassidy to portray Abel, the leading character in W. H. Hudson's famous novel about South America, *Green Mansions*. By May, Fred finally announced that he would do only one picture for 1944. He had seen the play *Tomorrow the World* with Ralph Bellamy, liked it and signed on for the role of a Midwestern college professor and scientist who wrestles with the job of reforming a twelve-year-old Nazi boy left in his care. The Marches' left Firefly for their Mandeville Canyon ranch home near Hollywood in order for him to start *Tomorrow* by June 15.

Tomorrow is the story of a young Nazi-indoctrinated refugee wreaking havoc on a small American town. The boy's behavior as a self-appointed fifth columnist was portrayed ably by Skippy Homeier, who also did the role on Broadway. March plays the topflight scientist engaged in secret war work whose home is invaded by this youthful Nazi, the son of the scientist's sister, killed in a Nazi concentration camp. The impact of this lad's Nazi ideals and convictions upon a typical American home and upon his schoolmates is diabolically chaotic. Betty Field portrays a lovely young Jewish schoolteacher, the widowed scientist's prospective second bride. This was a motion picture that commanded complete attention from an audience, smashing hard at its emotions, leaving it pondering the question of the day: what to do with Nazi indoctrinated postwar Germany. When it was released December 21, 1944, Skippy Homeier garnered most of the reviews. *Variety*: "Skips performance stands high among the most memorable in juvenile acting history, potency of part overshadowing even the seasoned trouping of Fredric March and Betty Field, at their dramatic best" (March Papers). *New York Telegram*: "The expansive glow of one of Fredric March's most sincere and ingratiating performances provides the proper contrast in the conflict" (March Papers).

During production on *Tomorrow*, March became interested in playing the lead in Crane Haussamen's theater production of *Return to Eden*, recently acquired by Guthrie McClintic, but turned it down since it had no part for his wife. A play with a part for Florence was not in the cards, however, for Fred next announced that he would star in Leland Hayward's production of *A Bell for Adano*, adapted from John Hersey's novel by Paul Osborn and scheduled to open in Boston November 14, 1944. *A Bell for Adano* was the first play which discussed seriously and intelligently one of the major postwar problems: the restoration of something approaching normalcy in the huge areas of Europe occupied and eventually evacuated by the Nazis. March was to portray Major Victor Joppolo, a Bronx native of the U.S. Army of Occupation in Italy. Fred revealed how he came to understand Victor Joppolo:

> I knew the minute I read it that it was what I wanted to do . . . By August I came east and began to work on it at our farm. Upstairs in the barn, away from everybody, I broke the back of this part. I kept reading the script and comparing it with the book. Then I marked the book for character. My copy is full of those marks, in every place where some little thing sheds light on the kind of man Victor Joppolo is. Before rehearsals started I knew him well. That's what I call breaking the back of a part. (March Papers)

March considered Joppolo a fascinating guy—a man who really came up the hard way, who really and sincerely loved and understood America. Joppolo's role is essentially that of a crusading torch-bearer whose principal task involves education for democracy behind the lines. This Joppolo—this man of goodwill—has a fundamental feeling for what the country is and what it could become. He has a lot of rough edges but, above everything, he is overjoyed to do a good job back where his ancestors had come from. March commented, "I've been on five continents entertaining our troops. I've had a chance to get some idea of what the war is all about. That's part of why I wanted to do this play. Life's pretty short for all of us and we have to stand up and be counted. We have to contribute whenever we can" (March Papers).

March was just right for his role, but the danger in playing Joppolo was that it could be a very corny part. Because March *believed* everything he said and did as Joppolo, with genuine political conviction, he brought to the role a brilliance rarely seen. He played it with such conviction and sincerity that the audience was inclined to overlook the fact that Joppolo was too sweet a character. "I have played dozens of characters over the years, many of them outstanding historic figures . . . but never have I had the opportunity to create so humble and human a man as Joppolo. Above all else, he typifies hope, the hope of mankind that through right teaching, wars will end and peace with dignity will come for all" (March Papers). Joppolo's tragic defeat, when he is kicked out of his post just as he is making Adano a place to live in, is an extraordinary blend of writing and acting.

The play, without exception, was a hit. It moved on to New Haven before opening on Broadway at the Cort Theater December 16. March held nothing but admiration for Hayward for producing it because the movie rights had already been sold, and only a courageous man would invest so much money in a play knowing there would be no Hollywood money if it failed. It did not fail, running throughout the next spring with a six-week summer hiatus and reopening August, 12, 1945. The reviews were outstanding. Howard Barnes, *New York Herald Tribune*: "Fredric March, who has frequently seemed to me to be a rather wooden actor, is magnificent in the part of Major Joppolo. He does not bring an extended variety of make-believe to the portrayal, but it has the sharp intensity of a carefully thought out and brilliantly executed characterization. Here is one of the great performances of the season." In the Fredric March Papers collection, March wrote beside the John Mason Brown *Saturday Night Review*, "Don't *lose this* one! (And it's by our *best* critic!)." Brown's review: "As Joppolo, Fredric March gives the best performance of his career. If visually he is handsomer than the Joppolo we saw in Mr. Hersey's pages, if vocally the Bronx is scarcely more to him than a point of reference, the fact remains that spiritually he is to the full the novel's Major. That is all that counts" (March Papers).

When *Bell* reopened at the Cort Theater August 12, it had as competition the movie version by Twentieth-Century-Fox starring John Hodiak. March viewed this as neither an asset nor a liability to the progress of the legitimate production. In the course of its transfer from the stage to the screen, much was lost, which is all the more regrettable, for Twentieth made a sincere, expensive and credible effort to duplicate the success of the Pulitzer Prize winning play. It is not that it was a poor picture; on the contrary, it is superior to most. It is just that it did not live up to the drama. For once, the screen, by extending scenes to the outdoors and widening the range of a play, weakened the general effect. Therefore, where in some circumstances a screen attraction could undersell a stage show, in the case of *Bell*, the celluloid version received such a universal criticism for its approach to the controversial issue involved, that entertainment seekers with any taste for realistic fare necessarily visited the Cort Theater for the evening, to view the *authentic* Major Joppolo. In fact, the greatest point of difference lay in the performances of Fredric March and John Hodiak. Here again, Hodiak was attractive, capable and likable; but he was in competition with one of the finest actors alive, and he was not equal to it.

Fred commented, "Many come backstage to tell me not only how much they like the play, but also that they intend using Joppolo as a stencil in their jobs. The play gives them this exalted feeling, and it is one of the most gratifying experiences of my life to know we are setting a pattern which in actual practice will do so much for the advancement of democracy" (March Papers). Coincidentally, during his run as Joppolo on Broadway, Fredric March was awarded the Eisenhower Medal as the actor who had done the most for democracy.

17

The Best Years of Our Lives?

The Best Years of Our Lives was the first big movie of the postwar era really to sink its teeth into current American problems. It was a powerful, provocative film dealing with one of the major problems at that time, problems that involved three widely different war veterans returning from World War II to a small American town facing the difficulties of adjusting to civilian life. Each faces a crisis upon his arrival, mirroring the experiences of many American soldiers who found an alien world awaiting them when they came marching home. The film went from one end of the spectrum to the other, from laughs to tears, compassion to romance, and was emotional dynamite for American postwar audiences. The film weighed in at a hefty two hours and fifty minutes. It was expertly written by Robert E. Sherwood, based on a novel by MacKinlay Kantor, and skillfully directed by William Wyler.

During the spring of 1946, many World War II veterans were finally returning home to their families after three- and four-year absences. Al Stephenson, as portrayed by Fredric March, was one of those "lucky" soldiers returning without any obvious injuries. The scene in which Al first meets his wife, Millie, is filled with tension and poignancy.

Al advances slowly down the hallway toward the apartment and family he has not seen in four years. He is burdened with army gear, so he stops in front of the door and drops it to the ground. Hesitating, he stares at the door, then haltingly lifts his left arm to ring the doorbell. Rob, Al's son, opens the door. His father immediately rushes in and places his left hand over his son's mouth to prevent any exclamation, asking where Millie is. Beaming at the sight of his father, Rob gestures behind him toward the dining room down the hall. Al enters further into the apartment with the intention of heading toward the dining room, but his daughter Peggy, carrying a tray of food, appears from the kitchen. Spying her father, she smiles, opens her mouth to yell 'Dad,' but is choked off by Al placing his hand over her mouth, too. Understanding, she falls silent.

From the dining room Millie begins to speculate as to who might be at the door and questions her daughter. When there is no answer, Millie slowly turns around toward the kitchen, realization dawning on her. Placing the remaining plates she is holding in her hands on the table in a pile, she walks toward the hallway, toward her husband, surprise and hesitancy etched on her features. Al starts toward her slowly, then picks up speed, arms out to enfold his wife. She rushes into his arms, throwing her own about him. They hold their pose as if never wanting to part again. After long minutes, they separate, just a little. (Robert E. Sherwood) The rest of the family gathers around to greet the returning war hero, a scene repeated in millions of households throughout America.

It is odd how destiny played a part in March's acceptance of the Al Stephenson role. He took the part of the middle-aged sergeant-banker only because William Powell had been chosen over him for *Life with Father*. But he did accept, commenting, "I liked the book from the beginning and I had the feeling it would make a good picture, but I reckoned, in my naive way that most veteran's problems would be solved by 1947 and that the public would have lost interest in the subject" (March Papers).

March liked the part of Al Stephenson because his was the most complex homecoming. Al's son and daughter have grown up during his years overseas and, adoring though they are, he finds it hard to resume the rhythm of the family life with these strangers. His new job at the bank places him in charge of GI loans causing him a constant struggle between his training in banking practice and his new judgment of men, picked up in the stress of army life and battle. His experiences as an enlisted combat infantryman have given him more than the conventional banker's appreciation of the needs and problems of returning soldiers. To help overcome his feelings, he drinks. March admitted to interviewers that some film goers might object to the considerable emphasis on Mr. Stephenson's drinking, but he felt that this aspect had not been overplayed but was incidental to the main theme.

Production began April 15, 1946, and ended August 9. Teresa Wright, who portrayed Al's daughter remembered especially the scenes between Al and Millie (Myrna Loy):

To me their scenes still stand as the epitome of married love on the screen. You can take all the erotic pictures of the world and they won't compare with that bedroom scene the morning after. She brings that breakfast tray in and he looks at her and sets it aside. It's a marvelous moment because you've seen them the evening before dancing and coming together with the beautiful subtle things that both of them did. What's being felt and played underneath is exciting. (Katsibilbas and Loy 1987, 199)

This scene follows:

> It is morning.   Al, nursing a hangover, stumbles out of bed,
> ceremoniously throwing his army shoes out the window while squinting at
> the sun.   He then makes his way to the dresser and studies a younger
> photograph of himself, finding he currently does not compare favorably.
> He somehow finds the shower, starts the water, begins to sing, then
> suddenly tears the shower curtain aside as he realizes he is still in his
> pajamas.
> Millie has prepared Al's breakfast, planning to give it to him in bed. As
> she walks toward their bedroom with a breakfast tray, Al admires his
> cavalier reflection after donning a robe with cravat. Millie, also in robe,
> enters the bedroom.   Al moves to greet her.   Their conversation is
> strained.   After she sets the tray down on a nearby chair he follows her
> around the bedroom as she tidies up, doing anything to keep her mind
> and hands busy.
> As she makes the bed, he recalls, somewhat shyly, "I seem to have a
> vague recollection that we had a couple of children; is that right?"
> "That's right." She continues to make the bed, talking about the children
> with Al unconsciously getting in her way, hands in the pockets of his robe.
> She then takes the breakfast tray to the bed with Al following her every
> move, saying, "Alright," nervously setting the tray on the bed, "Here's
> your breakfast." The tension between them is palpable. As she moves to
> walk away, Al catches her right wrist, moving quickly to embrace her in
> a long needed kiss. She responds accordingly. (Robert E. Sherwood)

Many times during the production unexpected acting occurrences, normally
reshot, were kept in. Teresa Wright commented, "When Fred asks Myrna to
dance in the bar scene, they begin to kid and ad-lib, contributing texture that
wasn't written in the script. But Willy liked it, so that's what you see in the
film" (Katsilibas and Loy 1987, 199). Harold Russell, too, commented in his
autobiography about production on *Best*: "Wyler caught an unexpected but
delightful piece of action. March entered his living room swaying from side
to side and immediately went for a glass of Alka Seltzer. While talking with
his wife, Millie, he gulped down the fizzing liquid and suddenly hiccupped.
Wyler liked the belch and kept it in the film" (Russell 1981, 40). Harold also
remarked on Mr. March's help: "This classically, tall, dark-haired and
handsome actor made it a point to help me with my role whenever he could,
usually by observing my performance in a scene and offering tips of technique
that would improve my acting" (Russell 1981, 42). During a beer hall scene,
Harold had to manipulate a beer bottle with his hooks (Harold had no
hands).   After the scene was shot, March chided Harold good-naturedly,
"When I say my lines, keep those goddamned hooks down! Don't lift that

bottle of beer, because I want people listening to what I'm saying, not watching you drink beer!" (Russell 1981, 43).

When all was said and done Fredric March's faultless portrayal of Al Stephenson ranged from the devil-may-care warrior, determined to get plastered his first night home, to the dignified bank executive with a fine sense of duty. March managed to make Al the salt of the earth, a splendid American, without being stuffy, a touching portrayal of a businessman who has learned that making money is not all there is to life. Released November 21, 1946, *The Best Years of Our Lives* met with overwhelming nationwide approval. *New York Times*, Bosley Crowther: "Fredric March is magnificent as the sergeant who breaks the ice with his family by taking his wife and daughter on a titanic binge. His humor is sweeping yet subtle, his irony is as keen as a knife and he is altogether genuine. This is the best acting job he has ever done" (March Papers). *New Republic*:

> Fredric March does a superb job in mixing the rebellion and feeling for humanity that he achieved as a sergeant in the Army with the qualities of the solid citizen-banker that he was before the war—reactionary and close-mouthed, conforming, respected in the community, a model for the kiddies. Every touch seems exactly right for the hard-bitten successful executive—his knifelike movements, the tight self-control, the ferocity and self-hatred of his type of alcoholic. (March Papers)

For his portrayal as the middle-aged war veteran in *The Best Years of Our Lives*, Fredric March was nominated for a fourth Academy Award, reasserting his position as one of the finest actors in American cinema. On March 13, 1947, he snagged the Best Acting Oscar for 1946 from contending candidates, Laurence Olivier (*Henry V*), Gregory Peck (*The Yearling*), James Stewart (*It's a Wonderful Life*), and Larry Parks (*The Jolson Story*). The film won nine Oscars overall, including two for real-life amputee Harold Russell (one for Best Supporting Actor and a special Oscar for inspiring other veterans), Best Picture, Direction, Screenplay, Editing, Score, and Sound Recording. This Samuel Goldwyn picture became the most honored release in RKO history. March was in New York in his latest Broadway play, *Years Ago*, so Cathy O'Donnell, who played Harold Russell's girlfriend, accepted the Oscar for him. He and the rest of the *Years Ago* cast listened via radio after the play ended for the night. March remarked later, "That was really an embarrassing experience. The way those Oscars rolled in—one after the other. It reached the point where my collar got tighter and tighter and all I wanted was to run out of the room and stay away. I would have to apologize if I *didn't* get the best performance" (March Papers). He felt that by all the standards with which Academy Awards generally were determined, his part wasn't of that stature, or the usual stellar role with hundreds of facets and the camera constantly centered on one character. He felt the picture had more to it than the display of a single actor, commenting, "Frankly, I was surprised and at the same time relieved. It honestly was not so much a case of personal satisfaction but a feeling that to lose out in the final tabulation would be to let the picture down" (March Papers).

Best was to signal more than one milestone in the career of Fredric March. Apart from the second Oscar for his sensitive delineation of a returning disoriented war veteran, it also marked the demise of Fredric March, the matinee idol. March was still one of the best-looking men around, but he was also forty-nine years old and knowledgeable enough to know that the time had come to turn away from the handsome leading man image to the character type of role. March made the transition with such good grace that he never lost his hold on his public. Some of his finest films were yet to be made, plus an engagement on Broadway that was to garner him his first of two Antoinette Perry awards for Best Actor.

Years Ago, a bio comedy by Ruth Gordon, involved her reminiscing about her early life in the year 1910, when she left her home in Wollaston, Massachusetts, to go on the stage in New York. From her diary and a good memory, Miss Gordon had written a bittersweet drama of a spirited youngster's battle to break away from a humdrum existence on the respectable edge of poverty to live in a world of dreams. The story traces Ruth Gordon Jones's girlish high hopes to become an actress and her determination to reach for her star during her senior year in high school. She and her husband, Garson Kanin, coproduced the play while he directed it. Originally titled *Miss Jones*, the autobiographical comedy was withdrawn in 1945 after trial runs in Wilmington, Washington and Philadelphia. Revised over the summer months, it was completely recast with Fredric March as her father, Clinton Jones, Florence Eldridge as her mother, Annie Jones, and Patricia Kirkland playing Ruth Gordon Jones.

Clinton Jones, a man who followed the sea from the age of eight until he married, had great respect for education. He could be tough, rough, and formidable about little things like the cat sleeping on the register making him sneeze, but he was also gentle, sympathetic and sacrificing over big things. Clinton Jones became the symbol of the worried wage earner of the early twentieth century, a man whose quick temper expressed not paternal tyranny but the tensions of inner conflict—particularly the frustrations of a man of independent mind in the position of a factory foreman, of a generous man forced into the inclinations of a miser. When he sacrificed his one precious possession, an old spyglass, that his daughter might have her chance for stardom, it was Clinton Jones who claimed the audience's wholehearted acclaim and admiration.

March fully realized the father as a character role of great emotional range. Comparing himself and Florence to Miss Gordon's actual parents, he remarked, "You might think this would make Ruth Gordon hard to suit, but on the contrary she's been extremely patient with our version of the Jones'. Just once, she gave me a suggestion. It was about chilblains, a subject I talk about in the play. She said, 'Father always took chilblains seriously.' After that I took them seriously, too" (March Papers). To understand the role of Clinton Jones better, March visited Sailors Snug Harbor in Staten Island, the place to find old sea captains. "That is just the usual way I work, whether it's a picture or a stage production. I guess I do it because I like it. I go around watching people who are like the part I'm going to have" (March Papers). Florence once explained that she and her husband had very different ways of approaching their individual parts. Fred's method was twenty-four-hours-a-day and worry-every-minute, mulling it over at home. Florence preferred to learn her part at the theater. Fred liked to point out that Florence and he never tried to influence or criticize each other in their roles, beyond making a few suggestions. "It's a rule with us. She might be down in the theater rehearsing her lines, and I might be pacing the floor right here, learning mine. That part of our life is separate" (March Papers).

The on the road tryout in Boston, November 3, 1946, met with success. *Boston Herald*: "Without Fredric March's virtuoso portrayal of Clinton Jones, bitter, worried, yet full of kindness and common sense, with the actor's personality and voice submerged in the character, *Years Ago* would be negligible" (March Papers). It was obvious to all that an actor less skilled and restrained than Fredric March could have overplayed, thereby caricaturizing the role of Clinton Jones.

The play opened at the Mansfield Theater in New York December 3, 1946, and again had most favorable reviews. "Play by Play," Irving Hoffman:

Right now I want to say something about Fredric March because for my money, he's the whole show . . . He takes a familiar dramatic daguerreotype —you know, the one of the cantankerous, similar to a Clarence Day character —adds a dash of salt and plenty of pepper and out comes an enchanting, entertaining etching. . . . I've read too many dull books about Sir Henry Irving and Edmund Booth to try to describe the remarkable development of Mr. March on stage and screen. Catch his act when you come to town." (March Papers)

Roland Mader, Fred's friend and business agent had sent the Hoffman review to Fred along with a note proclaiming that this was the first time Hoffman had ever given anyone a decent review and to make him write one like this, Fred really must have been "super-colossal wonderful " (March Papers).

And since Fredric March is playing the part, Miss Gordon's father will now have to be added to the gallery of stage worthies to be remembered and respected. For Fredric March, acting in very high fettle indeed, has created a vigorous, colorful character out of many simple details. . . . In Fredric March's playing, Mr. Jones is a marvelously entertaining person. For this is character-acting of great distinction by a master of the craft who has not lost his respect for unrenowned people. (*New York Times*, Brooks Atkinson, March Papers).

March's performance as the blustery and endearing Clinton Jones was rewarded April 6, 1947, with presentation of the Antoinette Perry Award for best actor in the American Theater during the 1946–47 season. This marked the inauguration of the new stage award, the Tony, established by the American Theater Wing in memory of Miss Antoinette Perry, veteran Broadway actress and director. Hence, for the first time in the history of the stage and screen, the highest awards for giving the best performances of the year in two distinct mediums of entertainment, and, of course, in two separate and distinct plays, went to the same actor—Fredric March. What added to the stature of his unusual accomplishment was the fact that few actors in the prior two decades had managed to leap so frequently and successfully from Hollywood to Broadway and back again. In the space of one month, Fredric March was awarded the Oscar, the Tony, and finally the One World Award, a citation and silver plaque given in the field of motion pictures for international-mindedness and public-spirited attitude.

The balance of 1947 was spent making two successive pictures to be released in 1948 for Universal-International. The first, *Another Part of the Forest*, was a prequel to Lillian Hellman's *The Little Foxes* (Goldwyn, 1941) about the hateful Hubbard family. In *Forest*, Miss Hellman takes the bad sister and brothers of her earlier play back twenty years, to 1880, to show how they got that way. It seems life with Father (Fred) and Mother (Florence) did it. The elder Hubbard, Marcus (March), is a self-made Alabama merchant-thief who loves only money, music, Greek classics and his willful daughter (Ann Blyth). He dominates his children (sons played by Dan Duryea and Edmond O'Brien), thwarting their romances and ambitions, but, with him as example, they take naturally to treachery. The body of the film deals heavily with his tyranny over the three children, his calculated cruelty to their compassionate mother (Florence), the secret incident in the Civil War which estranged the family from the entire community, and the final defeat of the father by both wife and children.

Released May 18, 1948, *Forest* received fine reviews, even though it had little in it to ingratiate itself with audiences, being a relentless catalogue of family in-fighting and avarice. *Daily Mirror*: "March is in one of his finest roles as the cantankerous Southerner, afraid that some day the townsfolk will rise against him" (March Papers). *New York Times*: "Miss Hellman showed no compassion toward Marcus and propelled him toward a staggering retribution. She should be grateful that Fredric March brings this tyrannical soulless man to full life" (March Papers).

The next film, *An Act of Murder* (also know as *Live Today for Tomorrow*), deals with the controversial subject of murder for mercy, euthanasia. The central character of the picture is a judge (Fred) in a suburban Pennsylvanian town, his wife portrayed by Florence. The judge is unaware that his years on the bench have produced a callous indifference to human beings, seeing none but the legal side of issues. This unconscious metamorphosis in his former nature of a basically understanding and tolerant man becomes more inexplicable when compared to the happiness of his home life, and complete devotion to his wife. When he learns that she is the victim of an incurable and progressively painful disease, his agony is unbearable to the point that he tries to take both their lives by driving over a cliff. Unfortunately, he survives, his legalistic mind forcing him to confess and take the consequences; charges against him are dropped because of the circumstances surrounding the act of murder.

Released December 5, 1948, to excellent reviews, *An Act of Murder* was hailed as head and shoulders above the average film. *Los Angeles Examiner*: "Fredric March is splendid as the husband who is called upon to make the too-great decision—again proving himself one of our best actors. . . . But perhaps Florence Eldridge holds the spotlight as the woman who falls under the sentence of death. Miss Eldridge is by turn strong, pitiful and chilling in a demanding role" (March Papers). Bosley Crowther, *New York Times*:

> Especially qualified to play these characters by the fact that they are actually husband and wife, Mr. March and Miss Eldridge give to them a scope and sensitivity that are superb. In scenes of uncommon revelation of a married couple's mutual tenderness —an attachment which all too often appears synthetic on the screen—Fredric March and Florence Eldridge manage to build a plausible situation into a personal drama that is genuine, moving and profound. (March Papers)

While on the set of *An Act of Murder*, Florence was subpoenaed by California Senator Jack Tenney. Tenney asked her why, in 1945, she had attended the International Women's Conference in Europe, a postwar conference (considered leftist) with representatives from forty-two countries who came together to set up a program of aid for the children of war areas. Florence stated, "I am not, have never been, and do not intend to become a Communist. I am not a member of any Fascist group and I oppose totalitarianism, be it Communism or Fascism." That appeased them for a while. Fred admired Florence for her stand, commenting, "I like the way her mind functions and the way she cuts through sham and hypocrisy. I like her kindness to all people everywhere and I like her principles and what she stands for in this muddle-thinking world" (March Papers).

The schedule on *An Act of Murder* was rushed because of the Marches' previous commitment to make a Technicolor production of *Christopher Columbus* for Sidney Box in England, slated to start April 1948. However, before sailing for England, the Marches' had some legal business that needed immediate attention. In the fall of 1947 an event occurred that eventually caused their inability to find work late 1948 through 1950, with a general slowdown in Fred's career until 1954. Even though they were employed currently for *Columbus*, after production was over and they landed back home, work was nowhere to be found. This occurrence was wrapped up in the late forties Red Scare, culminating in the phenomenon known to historians as McCarthyism, named after the unfortunate senator from Wisconsin, Joe McCarthy.

Several events in 1948 provided the background for McCarthyism: the Communist takeover in China, detonation of an atomic bomb, the Cold War with the Soviet Union, the Korean War. To many it was unthinkable that Communism could win on its own and incredible that Soviet scientists were as clever as American—the answer had to lie in subversion and treachery, perhaps by intellectuals and "one-worlders." Anxiety over such subversion caused President Truman to issue Executive Order 9835 in March 1947. Though this order to investigate the loyalty of civil servants set up procedural safeguards, it also embraced the doctrines of guilt by intention and by association. Potentially the most ominous feature of the executive order was the authorizing of the attorney general to prepare lists of subversive organizations, giving these lists a quasi-legal character.

The Marches' particular incident involved a Red-hunting weekly newsletter called *Counterattack* (mailed to all studio heads, incidentally). *Counterattack* was operated by former Federal Bureau of Investigation agents with the announced purpose of keeping labor and management informed on Communist infiltration. The newsletter branded the Marches' as Communist sympathizers on eight separate occasions, starting October 17, 1947, and continuing to pound at them until March 5, 1948. Apparently, their names appeared on membership lists of organizations which were branded "pinko" by the U.S. attorney general. The couple had spent considerable money and effort, out of patriotic and humanitarian instincts, helping some of the organizations on the Attorney-General's list, but they had at the same time performed equal service for anti-Soviet groups. Elia Kazan mentioned in his biography about this period in the Marches' life together: "Florence was the intellectual leader of that household. Poor, blacklisted Freddie was no more a Communist than my cat, while Florence was a rather rigid liberal who believed it her duty to straighten out whoever wasn't thinking right and supported organizations she thought deserved the family name on their letterhead" (Kazan 1988, 479).

Fredric March could not, however, remain silent for long. He stated to newspapers that an "informer" reported that his wife and he were members of a Hollywood Motion Picture Committee that collaborated with the Medical Bureau to aid Spanish democracy. This was true, but the informer might have gone further and said that they also sent an ambulance to the Spanish Republicans. They also contributed an ambulance to Finland when that little country was attacked by Russia and another ambulance, given to France in May 1940. They joined with Herbert Agar and Wendell Willkie to form a group that became Fight for Freedom, which worked for all-out support of Great Britain during the time that Germany attacked that country. As was frequent during the Red Scare years, the truth never quite caught up to the lie and the Marches suffered considerably. Until the *Counterattack* accusation, they had worked steadily for years; but in 1948, their tax return showed a net income of a mere $2.58.

A number of producers, in both Hollywood and New York, who were personally friendly to them told them frankly that they had no doubt that the Marches' were not Communists. They, however, were fearful of employing them while the stigma was attached to their names. They advised them to clear themselves of the charges and jobs would be open to them, especially to Fred, since he acknowledgedly ranked among the top handful of American performers. Consequently, legal action had to be taken to clear the March name. A libel suit was filed against *Counterattack* March 15, 1948. Each brought a suit of $500,000 but they were not to see it settled (out of court) until December 1949. The Marches' suits charged that the newsletter had falsely referred to the couple as Communists, that large numbers of people had been caused to believe that they were Communists, and that his standing, in particular, in the movies, on the radio, and on the stage, had been destroyed. The suit was placed on the trial calendar of the New York State Supreme Court.

Before embarking to London, Fred was the presenter for Best Picture and Best Actress at the Academy Awards Ceremony March 20, 1948, at the Shrine Auditorium, Los Angeles. Fredric March said that Oscar was a character with a heart. He invited the audience to listen to one statuette's heartbeat and the throng heard someone beat a kettle drum. He then announced that *Gentleman's Agreement* had been voted Best Picture. Everyone thought that Rosalind Russell would win Best Actress, so some of the audience started to leave as this category was the last to be bestowed. When March opened the envelope, he started to say "Rosalind," then did a double take, for the winner was Loretta Young for *The Farmer's Daughter*. Young was in a state of shock, making Mr. March show her the name in the envelope when she got up on stage, then accepting the Oscar gracefully.

The Marches' sailed under a dark cloud on the Cunard White Star Ship RMS *Queen Elizabeth* for London during April in order to start production on possibly the most boring historical epic ever made, with March uncharacteristically portraying himself rather than Columbus. First, they were under attack for their political beliefs, and second, Fred was not in the best of health. From letters in the March Papers, the best one can surmise is that he suffered from transurethral resection (TUR), or frequency of "bladder emptying." He ended up having surgery in London with the doctors inventing a contrivance for him to wear in the tights that were a necessity when one portrayed Christopher Columbus. Florence commented, "Just in case of emergency so at least he can dismiss the fear of letting America down in public" (March Papers). On the trip over, Universal released one copy of *Another Part of the Forest* to the cruise line. Fred suggested they run it the last night so they would not have so far to swim should it fail to please.

18

Columbus versus *Counterattack*

Christopher Columbus chronicles the adventures of the most famous of all explorers from his arrival in Spain to his declining years; his travails as he reaches the Spanish court to beg Ferdinand and Isabella (portrayed by Florence) for ships; his frail caravan sailing ever westward through uncharted seas and undercurrents of mutiny; and his triumph as he first sights a glimmer of light in the New World and plants the Spanish flag in this new land. Florence told American reporters, "I don't want to be tied down to a large part. We will have the children with us in England, and I want to be free to do some sightseeing with them." She must have done more sight seeing than in depth character study, prompting Bosley Crowther's comment, "Queen Isabella, as played by Florence Eldridge, is a rigid representation of the legendary queen" (March Papers).

Once filming started March wrote brother Jack from Claridge's Hotel in London, where the main cast members were housed. This letter revealed some of his personal concerns about the *Columbus* film. "I'm working without make-up in most of the picture and this is quite revolutionary in Technicolor. (The bags under my eyes bother *me* but everyone else thinks they are fine!—but I try to stop worrying.) Over here the so-called Star is very top-dog (different from home) and helps much with directing. So I'm having fun at this, too. (Say a prayer)" (Letter to Jack Bickel, 1949, March Papers). March must have had a premonition the production would be a flop.

Judging from the grand scope and history of events, *Columbus* was not done without problems and was beset with more catastrophes than any production had a right to expect. First, while studio scenes were shot in Shepherd's Bush studios in London, exact seagoing replicas of two of Columbus's ships, the *Santa Maria* and the *Niña*, were being constructed in the West Indies on the beach at Holetown, Barbados. By summer of 1948, after a full year, the vessels neared completion with hidden equipment that would make

Columbus's pioneering easier—telephones, electricity, stoves, fans. The cast arrived for filming, meeting the 400 remaining descendants of the original Carib Indians who had been hauled from their native reserve in Dominica for crowd scenes. The wife of the governor of Barbados was on hand, too, to witness the launching ritual. Unceremoniously, the *Santa Maria* got stuck in the sand; it took ten days to get her seaborne. Then, the yacht responsible for close-up shots, maneuvered too close, rammed her amidships, and she limped back to port for repairs. Later, the *Santa Maria* accidentally caught fire and was burned to the water line. So it was decided to carry on with the *Niña* alone. Unfortunately, during a squall, the *Niña* ran away with her crew, vanishing over the Caribbean horizon. Emergency searchers eventually found her, still dragging her anchors on the shores of St. Vincent 100 miles from Barbados.

To make matters worse, the temperature all this time was very high. March, in a hundred pound suit of armor (chain mail shirt, long woolen stockings and suede thigh-high boots), nearly joined the real Columbus. And the final disaster—while on location at Barbados, Elia Kazan sent March the script to Arthur Miller's *Death of a Salesman* for the Broadway stage version, asking him to portray Willy Loman. Because the leading actor was expected to assist with suggestions on the direction and other matters, March found himself in a day and night job. When the script arrived, Kermit Bloomgarden the producer and Kazan the director wanted an early decision. March kept putting off reading the play until he could do it thoughtfully, without interruption from the demands of *Columbus*. His only communication with Florence had been by cable and letter, as she had already left for home, her part, as Isabella completed. "Florence had said that she thought the play would be wonderful for me, and in the back of my mind was the surmise that she was eager about it because of my role rather than hers. So while she kept urging, I kept thinking of her as a very sacrificial person. Then I had to give a decision. Literally between film takes I had to appraise the play. So I said no" (March Papers). Another explanation of March's not doing *Death* on Broadway was that when the producers came to him for the part of Willy Loman, he couldn't see it, so he turned it down. It seems earlier the producers had offered the role of Willy Loman's wife to Florence Eldridge. And she, not understanding the lead was to be offered to her husband, had decided not to do it. But when it was presented to them as a drama that they might do as a team, she told her husband, "We must do this play." "But I," said Fred, "thought she was just being noble, and still didn't want to do it" (March Papers).

Bloomgarden remembered, "We sent it (the script) to Freddy March, who was making a picture in London. Freddy turned it down because he believed we were really only interested in getting Florence Eldridge, his wife—or some such nonsense. Much later after seeing the play, he told us he ought to kick himself around the block for turning it down" (Kermit Bloomgarden Papers). So, Lee J. Cobb said yes and went on to portray Willy Loman while March read the horrific reviews on *Columbus*, released first in England June 16, 1949. Under the circumstances, hampered as he was by both screenplay and direction, it was unfair to expect much from March in the title role. He did convey the man's single-minded drive, his impertinence in the face of royal temporizing, but his performance lacked color, continually hitting a brusque tone, rather than a dominant and persuasive one. The *Daily Mail* intoned:

An epic in sheep's clothing, Fredric March, looking very handsome with bobbed hair takes an unconscionable long time to discover America. It would have been better if America had in this case discovered Christopher Columbus. Hollywood might have fiddled the history, but it would at least have jollied things up a little with battles with pirates and perhaps an earthquake or two. (March Papers)

In America, *Columbus* was appropriately launched on Columbus Day, October 12, 1949. This did not prevent reviewers from bashing *Columbus* unmercifully. *New York Journal American*: "The British film was made on a large scale. Its sets and costumes are impressive, its Technicolor photography is lush, and its intent is admirable. But director and scripters were apparently so concerned with pretentious trappings and historical research that they overlooked the importance to a movie—movement" (March Papers). At least Fredric March made an impression on Nora Swinburne, who portrayed the love interest, Joanna de Torres (even Columbus had a love interest). "Fredric March was a big star when stars were stars, and very grand. I remember Mr. March came to the first rehearsal with his script in a beautiful leather folder with his name embossed in gold letters which made us laugh" (Letter, Nora Swinburne, 21 May 1990).

March left for America on the *Queen Elizabeth* November 4, 1948, after a grueling production, arriving in an environment unwilling to hire a suspected Communist. Nineteen forty-nine was to be one of the Marches' roughest years. On front pages all over America they were called Communists, starting in June 8 with typical newspaper offerings such as "In Washington today a secret FBI report read to the jury in the Judith Coplon espionage trial identified 'Fredric March,' the actor as a Communist party member in 1947. His wife, Florence Eldridge, was also named" (*The Mirror*, 8 June 1949, March Papers). Other public figures branded as Communist included singer Paul Robeson and writers Dorothy Parker, Donald Ogden Stewart, Ruth McKenney, and Dalton Trumbo. Those branded as Communist sympathizers included Boston University president Daniel Marsh, radio writer Norman Corwin and actors Edward G. Robinson, Sylvia Sidney, Paul Muni, John Garfield and Melvyn Douglas. Evidently, the Washington reports were being read before a federal court jury hearing a spy charge against Judith Coplon, arrested in New York on March 4, 1948. She was a former employee of the Justice Department charged with stealing state documents for transmission to Russia. The whole furor arose out of Miss Coplon's trial. The FBI documents consisted of reports from confidential informants who identified themselves with numeric symbols—Fred's informant was #402. Much of the information was obviously gossip and hearsay for there was no assessment of the informant's reliability and their varied statements were unrelated and fragmentary:

On April 25, 1947, we were advised that March was a member of the Communist Party and has been cooperating for many years. The informer #402 stated that on one occasion a few years ago March was criticized in the *Daily Worker* [Communist paper] for his acting. March was upset about this and through someone sent word to the *Daily Worker* that he did not mind criticism generally, but he did not like criticism when it came from the world in which he believed. According to #402, the individual who conveyed March's message advised that the subject (March) had tears in his eyes when he sent the message. (*Los Angeles Daily News*, 9 June 1949, March Papers)

Government prosecutor John M. Kelley, Jr., protested in vain against reading such testimony, presented by defense attorney Archibald Palmer for Miss Coplon. March was quoted as saying the same thing he said in 1939, when confronted by Martin Dies: "It's an unmitigated lie! My record and conscience as an American and as a man are clear" (*Los Angeles Daily News*, 9 June 1949, March Papers). Regarding testimony of secret informers March responded, "Isn't it high time for us to reaffirm that the American way is for a man to stand forth in full light and make his accusations where the accused may defend himself?" (March Papers).

On June 30, March gained his chance to blast the Red smear during a banquet speech at the Carpenter Hotel in Manchester, New Hampshire. The banquet marked the opening of a drive for $500,000 toward $1,000,000 for erection of a restoration hospital on Crotchet Mountain, Greenfield, by the New Hampshire Society for Crippled and Handicapped Persons. Fred, accompanied by Florence, stated emphatically (again) that he and Mrs. March were not Communists, never had been and never intended to be. His speech, for he also wrote it, was impressive and is worth quoting in its entirety;

Let me make clear that false accusations and opprobrious labels do not deter either of us from doing those things which we consider our prerogative and duty as good citizens . . . the freedom that Americans enjoy is threatened. First, I believe it is threatened by the spreading of poison of the nondemocratic theory of "guilt by association." Each American citizen has the right to be judged by his words and deeds and by the issues for which he stood up to be counted.

The second threat to American citizens today is the acceptance and encouragement of the testimony of secret information. [Thunderous applause]

One informer reports that I received an acting award from the magazine New Masses for my acting performance in the play _A Bell for Adano_—but the informer omits the fact that I happened to receive seven or eight other awards that year, including the Eisenhower Medal for—now, don't laugh—that actor who contributed most to democracy in 1945. (_Boston Globe_, 1 July 1949, March Papers)

The Judith Coplon case was taken for a big ride in the headlines. The sensation quickly petered out, but most of the damage was done without denials and retractions, and explanations never quite caught up to the original story.

One of the Marches' few enjoyments that fall was the acquisition of a television set. They were so fascinated by the newfangled contraption they sat through the most "awful tripe." March gave the new medium a try October 7 of 1949 on Ford Theater's first live telecast portraying the John Barrymore role in _Twentieth Century_ opposite Lilli Palmer. He considered live television, a more intense medium by far, the hardest acting to do and remarked, "You don't dare to blow a line. I missed one in a production with Lilli Palmer. Subconsciously I was waiting for the 'Cut!' of movies or for a stage manager's assist. I didn't get it. Lilli finally pulled me out of it but it was an uncomfortable moment" (_Minneapolis Star_, 18 December 1951, March Papers). He was never to feel comfortable with live television.

In late October, the Marches considered and eventually accepted an offer from Hume Cronyn to act in his production of _Now I Lay Me Down to Sleep_. Rehearsals were to start December 15 preparatory to a warm-up whirl on the road. With something tangible in the future they concentrated on their lawsuit against _Counterattack_. Faced with the necessity of proving the truth of its charges in court, the publication sent their attorneys to seek a settlement when the case approached the trial calendar. Counsel for _Counterattack_ and the Marches agreed on wording of a retraction statement to be printed December 23. Headline on the retraction story was "Fredric March and His Wife, Florence Eldridge, Condemn Communist Despotism in Stalinist Russia" (March Papers). The publication then pointed out that the Marches had contributed to an ambulance for Finland during its war with Russia in 1939 and that March had traveled over 33,000 miles to entertain troops during the war. The Marches were quoted by the publication as affirming, once again, their non-Communist ideals; the litany "We are not Communist, Fascist," etc., plus "we believe in the system of free enterprise," etc. The retraction was buried on back pages inside the same papers that previously plastered the charges against them on the front page. The lawsuit eventually cost March $50,700 in legal fees to obtain the retraction that most did not read, for they could not find it in the papers *to* read.

Elia Kazan commented in his autobiography on this period:

We had Mr. and Mrs. Fredric March to dinner one night, and drink loosened Florence's tongue. . . . She spoke of how she'd constantly been forced to hold Freddie up politically. "How hard it is," she said, "to be a mother to someone your own age!" Freddie said not a word. They'd both been under assault by a watchdog newsletter, *Counterattack*. . . . For six months, she told us, the calls for Freddie's services could be "counted on the fingers of one hand, with a finger or two left over." Finally they sued *Counterattack*. Her husband, Florence maintained, had not been staunch in the crisis. "He was ready to take anything he could get and run."

Kazan recalled, "Despite the clearance, the smudge remained, and it was a while before Freddie worked again. It was a demeaning time and put a bitter barrier between the couple" (Kazan 1988, 441).

The couple was interviewed on "Radio Reports" by Tex McCrary December 29. Fred stated, "There has grown up an entirely false idea about actors. Actors are people, too. And most actors are good Americans, just like anyone else. As for Mrs. March and myself, we don't intend to stand for such libels, such gross accusations and intimidation." When questioned about the retraction, Fred responded, "The retraction of the unwarranted charges against us naturally gives us great personal satisfaction. We are glad that we, and our children, can again walk in honor and that we are now free to work in our chosen profession without the limitations which these unjust aspersions have imposed on our careers" (March Papers).

After their decisive victory against *Counterattack*, Fred had to build up his career stone by stone since America in the McCarthy era (ironically, a senator from Fred's home state of Wisconsin) did not forget nor forgive easily those who were felt to be even the slightest "pink" in their politics. Consequently, Fred chose his parts carefully during the 1950s, for example, *The Bridges at Toko-Ri* to prove his patriotism and that he was, indeed, employable. Despite the clearance, it would be a long time before Fredric March would be back on top of the character acting heap, especially once Senator Joseph McCarthy captured the minds of the American populace. Although Fred was never summoned to testify before the McCarthy run HUAC in Washington, memories of the *Counterattack* accusation were still fresh in the minds of the American public. A December article from *Film in Review* about his life mentioned, "He was summoned to testify before the House Un-American

Activities Committee in Washington." March circled this part and wrote "*Never* F. M." (March Papers.)

The Marches' first major job after the retraction was the staged version of *Now I Lay Me Down to Sleep* with Hume Cronyn directing. A comedy in three acts by Elaine Ryan based on the novel by Ludwig Bemelmans, this play is the story of celebrated General Leonidas Erosa (Fred) and his spinster governess, Miss Graves (Florence). The general is a man who is all appetite and ego. The governess is a prim Englishwoman who has loved the general for twenty years but has recoiled at the idea of doing anything about it. When war begins in his country he hires a Greek freighter, taking his whole staff to a fantastic villa in his native Ecuador. This odd, fascinating, sometimes funny, sometimes sad and invariable provocative affair is described on the program as a comedy, probably because someone flipped a coin and decided that such a description was as good as any other if not strictly accurate: a play full of nonsense. The road premier was in Philadelphia January 30, 1950. *Variety*: "The presence in the two leads of Fredric March and his wife gives this difficult and moody play just the stability and also the spirit it needs. Without their presence there wouldn't be a lot of use in figuring on a stage future for *Sleep* after the obviously necessary cutting and all-around editing are completed. *Sleep* needs plenty of work before it can risk Broadway" (March Papers). Fred wrote beside this review, "It's *getting* it! (F)." (March Papers). After Philadelphia, *Sleep* appeared in Boston February 13. The reviews were still not great.

They decided to try Broadway, and opened at the Broadhurst March 2. If it was successful after their Broadhurst premier they hoped to take it on the road. It wasn't, so they didn't. *Now I Lay Me Down to Sleep* was exactly what one wanted to do while seeing it. *Daily Worker*: "Fredric March is forced to ham atrociously in the attempt to make the repulsively-conceived general likeable" (March Papers). *Hollywood Reporter*, Irving Hoffman: "I hate to predict it, but they have another bust on their hands. Truth to tell, Mr. March is not in full command of the role of the general" (March Papers). *Time*: "A gaudy extravaganza, the show is sometimes fair fun, and Fredric March and wife squeeze some good burlesque moments out of their roles. But there is not much human warmth to the laughter, and there are none of the suddenly touching moments there should be" (March Papers).

After *Sleep*'s failure, 1950 was to be another meager work year. *The Titan—The Story of Michelangelo* was a documentary released the end of January, with narration by Fredric March. He also appeared on the Salvation Army broadcast in March during their annual drive and introduced Mrs. Roosevelt on "The Talking Magazine" radio program in April. Fred did have his University of Wisconsin thirty-year reunion to look forward to on June 16, an event he nearly always managed to attend every five or ten years because he had been the president of the 1920 class. Florence rarely, if ever, went with him, and such was the case for this thirty-year reunion, too.   Fred reacquainted himself with college buddies Jack Ramsey, Chuck Carpenter, Larry Hall and others (he kept up a considerable correspondence with most of them throughout his life).

At the 1950 reunion Larry Hall's wife, Virginia, had to pick Fred up at the hotel and chauffeur him around the lake to meet at a fraternity brother's house. She described, "So I drove Fredric March around the lake and I was driving fast, I will admit that . . . [long pause, blush] . . . he was quite a rascal . . . an interesting drive around the lake, and I thought what if I had an accident? All alone with Fredric March" (Interview, Virginia Hall, 18 May 1990). Well, she got through the drive only to have to break up all the women who swooned over him at the reunion. "Really, it was all in fun. You know, I never felt comfortable with Florence, but Fred was charming. She did not like the Midwest, so rarely visited. Which was alright with us, because he was not the Freddie that we knew when she was around. He was under wraps—he was not the fun Freddie March. Very reserved" (Interview, Virginia Hall, 18 May 1990).

At the height of the McCarthy hysteria, the Marches appeared in Arthur Miller's bold adaptation of Henrik Ibsen's stinging indictment of corrupt society, *An Enemy of the People*, about a teacher's stand against small-minded, small town people. The leading character, Dr. Stockman, whose idea it is to construct baths using the beneficent water of his native town, discovers that the water, badly polluted by refuse from the tanneries, is spreading typhoid fever. In his fight to remedy the situation that will cost the taxpayers many thousands of dollars, the mayor, the newspaper publishers, together with the majority of the townspeople turn against him and denounce him as an enemy of the people. Opening at the Broadhurst Theater December 28, 1950, it closed shortly thereafter for it was too controversial a subject for the American public to accept. The play was picketed by a group known as the "Wage Earners," and, of course, affected attendance. Florence remarked later, "We took the idea to Arthur Miller in the first place. It seemed to us that a lot of people were being tarred and feathered, when the only crime they were guilty of was trying to clean up the sewers. But the play didn't have the effect we thought it would. It was quickly taken up by the people in the audience, both left and right, and on closing night there were police lines out front" (March Papers).

The reviews, however, were good. *New York Times*, Brooks Atkinson: "An enormously rousing performance.   The breadth and volume that are overwhelming" (March Papers). *Enemy* was entirely pertinent, dramatizing the spectacle of one man standing against the mob, the only honorable stance. The production lasted only thirty-six performances.   Broadway was never much interested in controversy, but it provided an occasion when a number of actors of integrity could stand up and be counted.   At year end, Fredric

March received the Cusade for Freedom certificate for his unselfish effort to help free minds and souls under Communist tyranny. He also received a citation from the National Collegiate Players for his work on *An Enemy of the People*.

The Marches' next Broadway adventure was another comedy, Lillian Hellman's *The Autumn Garden*, produced by Kermit Bloomgarden, opening on Broadway at the Coronet Theater, March 7, 1951, closing June 1st. The Marches' chose this play because they liked producer Kermit Bloomgarden, because Lillian Hellman's plays were always distinguished and worthy of an actor's best efforts and because it gave them a chance at roles utterly different from their recent depictions.

Autumn Garden takes place in a shabby southern mansion turned into a summer resort by a surviving member of its once prosperous family. Most of the people vacationing there are, like the house, in the decaying autumn of their lives still clinging to old dreams. Before they depart, all have learned to face a number of truths, especially that everything is "too late" to change. Fred portrayed an attractive painter who cannot paint and fancies himself as both a lothario and a counselor to less gifted people. Actually, he is a weak drunk pompous failure. Florence portrayed a silly, nagging wife whose husband, a retired general, is sick of her. Basically, the play revolved around long conversations by characters who really had very little worthwhile to say. However, Fred's personal reviews were quite good. William Hawkins, *New York World-Telegram and Sun*; "March is the painter, vain and petty, noisy and shallow. It is a magnificent job of an actor exposing a character" (March Papers). Jane Wyatt, who portrayed Nina Denery, liked him very much indeed and enjoyed enormously working with him. She felt he was one of those actors who are like the Rock of Gibraltar as far as the play went. His performance never varied and was consistently full of energy night after night.

Fred had a free summer to star in two pictures: the first, the movie version of *Death of a Salesman*; the second, a guest spot on *It's a Big Country*. March remembered, "I was offered the part of Willy in the London production and again in the road company in this country. Somehow, having muffed the chance to open on Broadway, I found that neither of these other offers appealed to me. Playing Willy in film is different. Pictures have a great untapped audience even after the play has had a good run and there are other advantages of a technical nature—the closeup, for instance, and the care with detail" (March Papers).

March was not going to blow his chance to portray Willy Loman in Arthur Miller's *Death of a Salesman*; he grabbed the part once it was offered to him by the producer, Stanley Kramer. Willy, a Jewish traveling salesman, always believed that back-slapping and perseverance were the keys to success in business as well as in life. At sixty-three he has reached a dead end, and the long drives on the road making him dizzy. He talks to himself and has hallucinations in which the present is intermingled with episodes of long ago. Willy appears to himself the perfect American, the ideal father and husband—an image shattered for his son, Biff, when the boy comes upon his father in a hotel being unfaithful to his wife with another woman. And Willy is tired when he asks his young indifferent boss for an in-town job but is fired instead. Willy Loman is through. His insurance is all paid up; if he dies in an accident he will be worth more than he is alive. Loman, the beaten, pitiful human being, attains stature through the devotion of his wife, Linda, who loves him for what he is and who foresees the catastrophe but can do nothing to prevent it. Kramer remarked in a 1990 interview, "Fred was Willy Loman. I felt very deeply about him. He rarely made a wrong move. Very intense. I picked him. He wanted to do it. He always asked me, 'Am I approaching this as a Jewish salesman would?'" (Interview, Stanley Kramer, 10 August 1990).

In the movie March showed, in the opinion of most observers, as the greatest Willy Loman of them all. Willy, to Fred, was typical of the many men who went through life with a set of false values and false slogans, and it was because of this confusion and reliance on false concepts of success, that made Willy Loman so completely understood not only in this country but throughout the world. Of course, the goal of *Death* was to project Willy Loman to movie audiences so well that they would empathize with the unhappy salesman and his false dreams and ideals, as painfully personal to the viewer as his own frustrations. March observed, "I understand that every actor who plays the part makes a completely different character of Willy. He's such a universal character. I guess the part is actor-proof. Willy on the verge of insanity is always there. I worked hard to find some normal moments and to make the most of them" (*Minneapolis Morning Tribune*, 19 December 1951, March Papers). It was a physically and mentally exhausting part that demanded his presence in almost every scene, made worse because March accidentally fell, twisting his knee the second day of shooting, and thereafter had to superimpose a limp on Willy all the way through the picture.

In *Death*, Kramer used a technique that was to be followed more and more in Hollywood during the fifties, that of rehearsing the entire picture for ten to twelve days before shooting began. As a result of the rehearsals, they were able to bring the picture in with a shooting schedule of twenty-six working days compared with many shooting schedules that would run as long as ten to twelve weeks. Laslo Benedek directed and felt himself very fortunate to have Fredric March play Willy. It was also a great advantage for him to have some of the players from the original production: Cameron Mitchell, Howard Smith, Don Keefer and Kevin McCarthy, who had played the son, Biff, with Paul Muni in the London Company. And, of course, Mildred Dunnock, as Willy's wife. One of the actors, Don Keefer, who portrayed Bernard on stage and in the movie, was surprised *Death* was made into a movie during the

McCarthy era, with anything considered "left" not being a good prospect for a box office bonanza.

Once the physical production was over, the producers were rushing *Death* through its finishing up stages to qualify Fredric March and *Death* for the Oscar derby. It had to open before the end of the year to be entered in the 1951 race. Released December 20, just under the line, *Death of a Salesman* was not what you might deem a box office smash, although generally the reviews were good. March's performance was prized at the Venice Film Festival (gaining him the Lion of Venice Award) but was unfavorably compared with those given by Lee J. Cobb in New York and Paul Muni in London. Among the better reviews: Bosley Crowther, *New York Times*: "Now that Arthur Miller's *Death of a Salesman* has been brought by Stanley Kramer to the screen and Fredric March has been given the opportunity to play its difficult leading role, a great many more million people, not only in this country but in the world, will have a chance to see this shattering drama at what is probably its artistic best" (March Papers). *New York Post*, Archer Winsten: "In the matter of the several who played Willy on the stage and Fredric March who has the picture role, it must be said that March's version is that of a man who is physically near the end of his run. His truncated gestures, the stiffly bent back and his fitful changes of expression from worry to happy memory and back to worry are marks of the old human engine when it begins to race out of control towards doom" (March Papers).

March was feeling pretty good about these reviews, as well he should: "I remember I was very happy about the New York notices, they were very good and they were good for me personally. I was glowing until *Life* came out and whoever was reviewing it had hated everything about it, including me, and he said I played it (and this is the only one I remember of all the good and the bad ones) 'March played Willy Loman like a documentary for Alcoholics Anonymous.' I took it to heart" (Yale Reports, 17 May 1964, 6, March Papers).

With the closing of the Broadway version, the Marches signed on to do *Autumn Garden* as their first road tour since the disastrous Theater Guild tour in 1927/28 to start in October at the New Nixon Theater in Pittsburgh and end in February in Toronto, Canada. *Autumn Garden* provided Fred's old high school and college friend, Jack Ramsey, an opportunity to introduce his daughter, Jackie, to the Marches when the play was scheduled to show in Milwaukee. Jack, wife Helen, and daughter Jackie were treated to dinner by the Marches after the play. Jackie remembered that Fred and her father drank profusely. Fred was unpleasant and too loud in a voice that reminded Jackie of the obnoxious character he portrayed in *Autumn Garden*.

Jackie remembers it vividly: "Fred embarrassed me. Father and Fred drank a lot—Fred was loud-voiced and made fun of me, which I did not appreciate. It seemed he was too much like the character in the play. Too obnoxious, as he was in the play. I had remembered a nice Fred so this was surprising to me" (Interview, Jackie Ramsey Macaulay, 24 February 1990). Later, when he was receiving his honorary degree in 1960 from Ripon, Wisconsin, Jackie met Fred and Florence once again over dinner. Her father, Jack, wanted Fred to meet his law professor son-in-law, Stewart Macaulay. Fred had just returned from Southeast Asia and proceeded to imitate Chiang K'ai-shek (this apparently involved spitting) and Madame Chiang. "Fred thought they were sleaze and had captured them to a tee. She was a greedy bitch and he a bumbling idiot," Stewart commented (Interview, Stewart Macaulay, 24 February 1990).

Both felt that the current cast capitalized on the play's dramatic potentialities to the fullest. It was while in Milwaukee during an interview that Florence announced plans to retire. "I have a feeling that this is going to be my swan song on the stage. Oh, I know, everybody says there will always be another play I'll want to do. But it becomes increasingly difficult, for a woman, to keep her home going and to follow a career at the same time" (Toronto, 14 January 1952, March Papers). When asked if marriage to the idol of thousands of women presented some problems, she admitted that when out in public together, she had the feeling that people would look at her and think to themselves "I wonder what he sees in her?" (Toronto, 14 January 1952, March Papers). In answer Fred chuckled the contented chuckle of a man who had been able to keep his wife just a little bit worried for twenty-five years (in reality, probably a *lot* worried).

While they were playing Minneapolis, interviewers asked the Marches' about the rumors that Fred was about to get another Oscar nomination for *Death of a Salesman*. As the charges of Communist still lingered in the memories of a number of people, Florence replied, "Of course, after what we've been through the past few years, it would mean so much to us if Fredric could get the award because it would indicate a favorable state of mind in the industry" (March Papers). On March 5, 1952, and for the first time in the history of the Academy of Motion Picture Arts and Sciences, Fredric March received his fifth nomination for an Oscar. March, unlike other actors who had been Oscar contenders, received his five nominations over a range of years encompassing a diversity of screen delineations unexcelled in the annals of motion-picture production. A third Oscar was not in the cards, however; Humphrey Bogart won for *The African Queen*.

The second film March did in 1951 for a January 8, 1952 release was *It's a Big Country*, an ambitious project that was in production most of 1950 and 1951. MGM's Dore Schary had marshaled an army of writers to celebrate the American way of life in nine separate episodes. By the time the film was released, seven had survived but the movie itself died at the box office. March's particular episode, portraying an Italian-American, was negligible. Lawrence Quirk:

Poorly written, inadequately, indeed obscurely motivated, the vignette is an outstanding example of a much-ado-about-nothing situation, and in what perhaps rates as the most forgettable of his screen appearances, March was no more than adequate; indeed he must have been fully aware (too late) of what he had let himself in for, as his performance radiates (if that is the word) a half-hearted, half-baked quality that is distinctly not March. (Quirk 1971, 205)

Summer of 1952 was spent quietly at Firefly Farm with Penny and Tony home from school. In fact, the remainder of 1952 was pretty quiet all the way around until Fred had to pack his bags for the movie *Man on a Tightrope*, directed by Elia Kazan and to be filmed on location in Bavaria. Scripted by Robert E. Sherwood, *Man* is about the highwire artist who walks across the thin borderline separating Iron Curtain domination from freedom in Western Europe. Based on the Brumbach Circus' 1950 flight from Soviet domination, it was renamed the Cirkus Cernik for the movie. March portrays Karel Cernik, the clown-manager of an over-the-hill circus in Czechoslovakia, where he plans his escape into the West. For Sherwood and March it was a reunion of two of the wizards of *The Best Years of Our Lives*. For Kazan, it was an initial opportunity to direct an entire film in Europe with all the American know-how and skills at his disposal.

Dressed as the clown tightrope walker, March was called on to hang by heel hooks from a fifteen-foot wire. Although the actual wire walking was, naturally, done by a double, March insisted on doing the "hang by his heels" sequence himself. Mr. March also engaged in other activities, as described in Elia Kazan's biography. Reportedly, he got himself into trouble with a chambermaid and her threatening husband. Kazan interceded on his star's behalf at the local police station. Kazan explained that, when Florence came to visit, Fred became another person. "One of the damned fool women in our group warned Florence March that she'd arrived just in time. But Mrs. March was used to Mr. March being 'naughty.' She didn't like it, but she wasn't unaccustomed to it. . . . He altered miraculously when she left to return to the states. (Kazan 1988, 478)"

When it was released June 4, 1953, March received his normal excellent reviews. *Saturday Review*: "As Cernik, Fredric March gives another of his beautifully turned performances, a man seemingly broken by events yet with the ultimate spiritual strength to defy authority" (Quirk 1971, 208). *Los Angeles Daily Mirror*: "Adds another exceptional performance to his already long list of fine roles. It is his show, actor-wise not withstanding" (March Papers). *New York Times*: "His portrayal of the clown-manager who loves his calling and his colleagues no less than freedom is sensitive and moving. He is truly a steadfast rock to which his frightened flock can cling" (March Papers). When interviewed after the picture had played for a bit, March admitted that he felt *Man on a Tightrope* was sold as a sex opus. "We made an anti-Communist picture, a true story, with the original real-life circus, and the ads came out, 'Love in Pink Tights.' The minute the studio found out they had, what did they call it—an 'intellectual' picture—they cut it, cut a lot of it. And they angled the ads towards sex" (March Papers).

After filming ended the Marches' spent another quiet summer on Firefly before Fred reported to Hollywood by September in order to participate in Robert Wise's production of *Executive Suite*. Cameron Hawley's *Executive Suite* boasted a big-name cast with effective performances (besides March, William Holden, June Allyson, Barbara Stanwyck, Walter Pidgeon) and describes wheeling and dealing in the boardroom of a large furniture manufacturing firm. When the president dies, the various vice presidents vie for control with mounting tension. March portrays the sly, scheming, typical "finance-oriented" controller who takes the lead in the race for the top spot by quietly arranging a lot of those little behind-the-scenes deals that place him in solid with the right people. Except for March's character, Loren Shaw, disciple of the decimal point and net return on all dividends, the rest of the board is likable but pretty poor when it comes to management. However, in the end, it is the vice president of manufacturing (William Holden) who wins the coveted title, through his feverish speech about quality and pride in workmanship rather than shapely fiscal figures.

John Houseman (producer) and Robert Wise (director) both agreed that March would be ideal for the Loren Shaw role. Wise remarked that he had heard March's "Willy Loman" had been much too "rich" a performance, and not having worked with Mr. March before, he was worried that he might overact. Upon meeting March, his fears were, at first, realized: "You know, Bob," commented March, "I've been thinking about this part; the first time I read this part, I thought about all the marvelous wonderful things I could do with this character." Wise's heart sank. Then March said, "I read it again and thought that the less I do, the better. If I go overboard, just let me know—and I'll bring it down" (Interview, Robert Wise, 10 August 1990). Wise was overjoyed, for when all was said and done, the small touches March lent to the character of Loren Shaw, such as his constant use of a handkerchief to wipe his sweaty palms or forehead, or his constant furtive, telling glances, helped to build the absolutely scheming nature of the company controller.

Shelly Winters, also part of the cast, was a devoted Fredric March fan, so much so that she blew her lines. Miss Winters, invariably letter-perfect in her lines before reporting to the set, found herself watching March in their scene during rehearsal, commenting, "I simply forgot I was in the scene." Many years later, during the Fredric March tribute in 1987, she remarked, "I can't remember shooting the film. I think I just stared at Freddie March the whole time. . . . I have no memory almost, of doing it" (*March Tribute Movie*, Jean Bickel Owen, 21 September 1987). March helped her to make her decision to do *Hatful of Rain* in New York telling her always to be aware of the audience, that they were the best teacher, better than any director, because the audience taught the actor, not only by their applause, but by their silence, or their shifting around, or even their coughing. She delightfully recalled one of her scenes with Mr. March where tears were rolling down his face, "and then I felt someone pinching me on my right buttock and it was Fredric March . . . while he was weeping . . . and suddenly I had a whole different concept of acting!" (*March Tribute Movie*, Jean Bickel Owen, 21 September 1987).

Executive Suite was released May 6, 1954 with March receiving good personal reviews. *New York Herald Tribune*:

> Ranking first among the personal symbols is Fredric March as Loren P. Shaw, the company's controller. He represents the figure-minded man who places dividends first in importance and is fiercely and cunningly ambitious for the presidency. He is something of a villain because he ignores ideals while staring fixedly at the mathematical results. He is supremely well played by March as a nervous, furtive master of the small tactic. (March Papers)

New York Times, Bosley Crowther:

> The nervy controller, whom Mr. March so adroitly plays, is a vivid personification of the type of bird that catches the worms. He is the on-the-job, sly, quick-witted schemer, presumptious in reaching for command and ruthless in putting his associates under obligation to him. This moist-handed, lip-licking toady has no hesitation at all in blackmailing. It is a not pretty but very lucid portrait of a rodent that Mr. March draws. (March Papers)

At age fifty-six, Fredric March announced formally in September that he would do no more theater and would do only one picture a year because he wanted to taper off a bit. In conjunction with this, the Marches' sold their Beverly Hills home on Mandeville Canyon Road. They refused to read any new plays because they were not looking for any. March commented, "There's the glamour of opening night, but you kind of get wise to yourself after a while. That business of night after night can get kind of boring. I'd rather travel and settle down on the farm for a rest" (March Papers).

He liked movie work, for he felt that the films had grown up. They were more adult in their themes; the people making them were more efficient, wasting less time, effort and money. March rejoined, "You can learn your script, go out to Hollywood and make a picture in eighteen to twenty days and earn as much money as you would in forty weeks on Broadway." He explained further that there was so much else to do in life besides earning money, such as golf and gardening and reading and travel. March lamented, "Trouble is, all this takes money, and that's why I work. I'd retire completely if my wife had her way about it, but I still want to do enough to keep my hand in it. It's the ham in me, I guess" (March Papers).

While he was making *Executive Suite* in Hollywood, Fred's oldest brother, Harold died in Pasadena, October 26, of cancer at the age of sixty-six. Fred and Florence attended the funeral and became second parents to Harold's daughter Jean, then just sixteen years old. Back to the small screen on March 25, 1954, at the NBC Century Theater in New York, he cohosted the Academy Awards ceremony with Donald O'Connor, the Hollywood representative. The event was televised with March and O'Connor bantering back and forth between coasts. Another happy event occurred that summer of 1954 on Firefly Farm when daughter Penny, just graduated from Vasser in May, married Umberto (Bert) Fantacci August 14. It was a beautiful wedding under summer skies, and the couple settled far away in Florence, Italy. This signaled an every-other-year summer visit by the Marches to Italy, and on off years the Fantaccis would fly to Firefly for a two-month summer visit.

Live television still annoyed March, but he was convinced to give it another try in late 1954, first in a revival of his Tony Cavendish role and second as the miserly Ebenezer Scrooge in *A Christmas Carol*. In the fall of 1954 the television networks introduced a new programming concept: lavish drama specials, scheduled monthly, with big-name stars in sixty or ninety-minute productions, usually adaptations of twentieth-century stage plays. One such series of specials, *The Best of Broadway*, opened September 17, 1954, on CBS with the Kaufman-Ferber comedy *The Royal Family* with Fredric March as Tony, Helen Hayes as the mother, and old love interest Claudette Colbert as his thespian sister. Unfortunately, the comedy play lost some of its original impact in the sixty-minute television version, for cutting the drama to less than an hour's playing time and still preserving all its hilarity was virtually an impossible job. Into this framework CBS squeezed an unusually large number of big-name stars, possibly a mistake. There were fine individual performances, but overall the play did not come off well. If one role stood out above all others it was the one filled by Fredric March, who played a flamboyant Tony with his sharp opinions of Hollywood movie making, his antics in fleeing to Europe to escape a process server and his zest for a new play he had discovered in a little theater abroad. He captured the audience totally as he had in 1929, on stage, and in the 1930 movie.

Another television production was done for *Shower of Stars*, which presented a musical version of Dickens's *A Christmas Carol* with March as Scrooge. Presented December 23, 1954, in color, this classic ran well over the usual *Shower of Stars* budget, backed by Chrysler. March wrote an article to appear before the December 23 show, entitled "The Story That Can Never Die":

A century has passed and Dickens's masterpiece refuses to die. A literary Rock of Ages, it has probably, in its evolution from book to stage, movie, radio and TV, delighted more people than any other holiday story in the English language.

Naturally, I am thrilled that I've been chosen to play Scrooge on TV this coming week. In preparing for the role, I have pondered the qualities that have made this tale immortal. Whence comes its appeal, its unerring instinct for striking the keynote of Christmas?

The 'Christmas Carol' trumpets a message which all mankind hungers to hear: that by our good actions, no matter how belated, we can erase past errors, pave the way for redemption and reweave the pattern of our life. To my mind, it is this message of redemption that gives Dickens's work its everlasting life, and makes Christmas not only the birthday of Christ but the rebirth-day hope for all. (*This Week Sunday Magazine*, 1954, March Papers)

It was filmed in Hollywood in just five days. March wore two pounds of makeup topped off with an unkempt fright wig. This aided him in his compelling role as Scrooge, the bitter old man who hated Christmas. At the time it was thought that this particular show, for it was a resounding success, should be rerun every Yuletide. But it never gained the status of the 1951 English production with Alistair Sim, the movie that replayed every year rather than the Fredric March version.

March's one movie for 1954 was released to the public January 20, 1955, Paramount's *The Bridges at Toko-Ri,* the first movie that his new West Coast agent, Phil Gersh, obtained for him. March was still suffering the stigma of his former Communist label when Phil campaigned to win him as a client. It seems Leland Hayward dropped March because of the "pinko"charges. Mr. Gersh had no such qualms and remained the Marches' agent the rest of their lives. Phil was able to acquire for March the part of the admiral, at a reduced compensation, but at least it proved him employable. *Bridges* was March's second film with William Holden. The film, based on James Michener's novel, is a cut above the usual war drama, with impressive statements about fighting, comradeship, and family. Holden portrays an American flier whose family is caught up in the confusion of the Korean War. March's character has emotionally identified one of his pilots (Holden) with his own dead son. When interviewed, March asserted:

The size of the role does not interest me much—I'm the admiral commanding a task force of carrier-based jets. The admiral knows no war is a good war to be in and that it nearly always must be fought in the worst possible place at the worst possible time. He has seen two of his own sons killed in action. This affects the admiral's relationship with the young jet pilots he must send off to battle. In order to make the role as believable as possible I had to search my own personal life for some experience parallel to the admirals'. Only in such a way could I really know how such a man would feel and act. (March Papers)

Bosley Crowther, *New York Times*; "Fredric March as the paternalistic admiral fairly cracks with the tension of concern" (March Papers).   *Hollywood Reporter*: "Fredric March shows great acting skill, but not acting tricks, in the role of a patriotic admiral who finds more than his share of frustrations in the Korean War" (March Papers).

During August of 1954, March agreed to come out of what he insisted was semi-retirement to enact the role of a Midwest householder whose home was terrorized for several days when three escaped convicts (led by Humphrey Bogart) invaded his property. In fact, March's semi-retirement was halted entirely for the year 1955, for he made three pictures, one after another: *The Desperate Hours*, *Alexander the Great* on location in Spain, *The Man in the Gray Flannel Suit*.

19

The Horrors of a Successful Play

The following passage is taken from Fredric March's personal script for *The Desperate Hours*; the items enclosed in parentheses and boldfaced denote his added handwritten comments. In this film, Humphrey Bogart starred as the escaped convict menacing an all-American family headed by Fredric March and Martha Scott. March as Dan Hilliard and Martha as his wife, Eleanor, are seen conversing in their upstairs bedroom.

Dan:	Dan closes door and turns to face Eleanor. The following is quiet. Dan attempts to regain the hopeful manner, to reassure. **(firm)** "Ellie. When they leave **(hard to say—strong—don't argue with me)** . . . I'll have to go along." Seeing her face, he rushes on, "Oh, only for a short time. And only *me* . . . to make sure they get out of town safely."
Eleanor:	(Shaking head) "No, no, I won't let you."
Dan:	**(simple & firm)** "Listen to me—wait *four hours*—no longer."
Eleanor:	(Shocked—hysterical) "Four hours—??!!"
Dan:	"If you don't hear from me, call the police."
Eleanor:	"Dan, I'm . . ." She seems about to scream; Dan places a hand over her mouth.

Glenn's VOICE from below:
          "C'mon, *c'mon*!"

Dan: "Ellie, it's the only *way*.

Eleanor: (In whisper) "That man hates you. He'll kill you . . ."

Glenn's voice: (Closer) "Hilliard! That dough's waiting!"

Eleanor: "Darling . . . *we* are not saved if something happens to you. I won't let you." Dan is shaking her gently. Now he breaks out *forcefully*.

Dan: **(strong on 1st phrase with finality)** "That's the way it *is*, that's all! You do as I *say*!" **(look at her but no emotion in the look)**. After this apparent harshness, he pulls her to him and kisses her with some violence, his emotion overwhelming him. Then he goes to door, turns once . . . goes out. (March's Script, March Papers)

The Desperate Hours is the screen version of Joseph Hayes's Broadway play about a young punk leader of three escaped convicts. The young punk, played by Paul Newman on Broadway, was aged for the picture version because Bogart wanted to portray the gangster, an absolute heavy without a shred of humanity in him. So, Bogart oozes malevolence as he and his escaped convicts terrorize a typical middle American family of four headed by an anguished Fredric March. The terrorism continues until finally the slowly awakened, last ditch effort heroism of the father enables the daughter's fiancé and a methodical but far from slow detective to bring about a rescue. Bogart, as the convict leader, was, of course, chillingly evil. Yet it is March, as the father, who contributes the outstanding performance. March ultimately came out the best in the reviews, for Bogart was badly miscast and looked poor for perhaps the first time on film. Fred considered his role "as the most outstanding I have had the honor to play in my thirty years of professional acting" (*Desperate Hours Press Book*, 1955).

Wyler's first choice for the father character had been Spencer Tracy, who had almost taken the part when a dispute over who would get top billing arose. Phil Gersh, March's erstwhile agent, who also represented Bogart, then convinced Wyler to use Fredric March as the father. However, whenever

Wyler could not have his number one actor, he invariably gave the substitute actor a bad time, so bad that Phil had to be on the set most evenings at 6:00 p.m. to make sure Wyler let his two stars go for the evening.

One instance that highlights Wyler's poor treatment of March was related by Martha Scott, at his 1987 tribute. She portrayed his wife in *Desperate* (for a second time—the first in *One Foot in Heaven*). It was their first scene together and many notables were watching: Danny Kaye, Martin and Lewis, and others. It was a simple scene between the two, but Wyler made them do it over and over forty-five times.

"What's wrong?" Fred whispered to Martha.

"It's got to be me; you're wonderful," she replied.

So she asked Wyler, who told her, "It is Fred—he's projecting for the audience and I want him to find it for himself—a simple scene" (March Tribute Film, Jean Bickel Owen, 21 September, 1987).

Another actress on the film, Ann Doran, remembered a dedicated Mr. March who kept his mind on the characterization, maintaining that mood during working hours. Beverly Garland, another actress in *Desperate*, recalled that "Bogart and March played chess every day and no one took much notice of me (it was one of her first pictures). Mr. March did give me the eye now and then but I stayed far away" (Letter, Beverly Garland, 30 July 1990). She must have heard of his reputation.

Regardless of Wyler, March was powerful as head of the family never before noted for bravery, but bent on protecting them from the intruders. He conveyed with remarkable effect his initial fright and bewilderment and subsequently the cool-minded courage and wisdom that lead to Bogart's defeat. It was released October 5, 1955, and March came out best in the reviews. The *Hollywood Reporter*: "March makes the fathers courage seem monumental by showing how cowardly any man of sense has to be in a situation like this. He is great in the scenes of antagonism with his small son" (March Papers). The work of both March and Richard Eyer as his son was so compelling on the screen that the celebrated incident of the father's slapping his son had to be omitted. It was more than audiences could stand.

During work on *Desperate*, an informal poll of some thirty top stars, directors and producers was tabulated and announced. Fredric March was picked as Best Film Actor two to one, with runners-up Marlon Brando, William Holden, Ronald Colman, and Spencer Tracy. March's longevity in the movies had been unmatched by any star of his stature. When asked what his secret was, he answered, "I'll play any role—if it's a good one" (*Indianapolis Star*, 30 January 1955, March Papers). That explains the difference between a Personality (as are most movie stars) and a professional actor. The Personality, usually big at the box office, makes a career of playing only himself.

March's next film was *Alexander the Great*, personifying Philip of Macedon in Robert Rossen's mammoth historical undertaking, the result of three years of research and two years of writing. Because the terrain, people and climate of Spain were uniquely suited to portraying the lands and peoples along the route of conquest of Alexander, Rossen made his production headquarters in Madrid. He arranged to take over one of Madrid's major film headquarters, the Sevilla Film Studios, where the permanent staff of plasterers, carpenters, painters, and other Spanish technicians would be able to construct sets on three large sound stages to a total of sixty-five interior and location sets ranging from the amphitheater in Greece to palaces in old Persia.

After signing Richard Burton, a young Welsh stage and screen actor, for the part of the young conqueror who died at thirty-three years of age, Rossen went after Fredric March to portray Philip of Macedon. Rossen approached March to play the part because he wanted not just a star, but an actor of integrity to interpret a character to which he, as a writer, had become deeply attached. Philip was the fourth century B.C. Macedonian king who united Greece, paving the way for his son Alexander's astonishing conquests. Rossen felt that March would understand Philip. March had not acted in an historical epic since 1948's *Columbus* fiasco, and not in the "ancient" category since *The Sign of the Cross* in 1932.

From February 15 through July 1955, with Burton, March and Claire Bloom (as Philip's wife) in title roles, thousands of extras, including bareback riding horsemen, 100 dancers and 150 speaking actors, brought to life Rossen's screenplay. During the five months of the production's depiction of Alexander's rise to power and his drive to the east from Macedonia through Greece and Turkey, the Near East, Egypt, Persia and India, the film was photographed in and around Madrid's Sevilla Studios, then on to Manzanor, El Escorial, Segovia, and Toledo. The Spanish town of Rasacrifia was used to reenact the terrible siege of Granicus. The village of El Molar became the Macedonian city of Pella. The other Alexandrian battles were photographed in Spanish Morocco for seven weeks of cinematic wars of attrition and conquest.

During the filming, Peter Cushing (who portrayed Memnon) observed March's old-world charm, manners, and courtesies to all his fellow actors and the film crew. Cushing recalled that chairs with their name on the canvas backrest were provided for all film stars. He often saw Mr. March sit on an upturned box during the long hours of waiting while a scene was being lit, rather than disturb a tired extra who'd taken his seat. This evidently was a typical gesture of his kindness and thought for others. Cushing admired March and his work greatly.

While the Marches' (Florence was in attendance) had time off from the rigors of movie making, they made a lifelong acquaintance of an American assistant cultural attaché stationed in Madrid. As living at the Ritz was not much fun for the Marches, especially because they knew not a soul, the attaché and his wife took them to Toledo for a tour. While visiting one of those monstrous palaces with marble floors and high ceilings, the attaché explained how the Spaniards used brass braziers to keep warm, usually by placing them under a table around which everyone sat with a heavy cloth hanging down to the floor and covering everyone's lap. Olive pits were used as fuel. As ever, the comedic March remarked, with wry humor, when he felt a chill coming on, "Ask them to throw another olive pit on the fire, would you?" (March Papers).

It took Rossen 141 minutes to recount what should have been a most colorful epic, although it would take an avid ancient historian, indeed, to sit through this dour biography. Rossen's *Alexander* staggered to the screen March 28, 1956, in all its Technicolor epicness, and proceeded to delight audiences with battles, authentic sets and costumes and to bog them down with the confused scripting. Burton in blonde wig and ancient Macedonian battle dress, made many (too many) long speeches and threw himself and others into battle after battle after battle until he conquered what was then most commonly referred to as "the world." Rossen would one moment have the screen filled with spectacular fighting, and the next with characters standing around reflecting on the nature of glory. Unlike the film's hero, this lavish epic of life and love among ancient royalty from 356 to 323 b.c. failed to conquer the public eye in 1956 a.d. March, however, and as was usual, received good notices. *Los Angeles Herald and Express*: "Fredric March gives strength to this role as he plays the man with an unquenchable desire to unite all of Greece under his rule and then march against Greek's mutual enemy, Persia" (March Papers). The *New Yorker*: "Fredric March gives a credible portrayal of a mighty soldier slowly going to seed" (March Papers).

After *Alexander* was in the can, Fred remained in Europe with Florence to await the arrival of their first grandchild, their grandson Gianni, born in Florence, October 15 to the March's daughter and greatest source of joy, Penelope Fantacci. November of 1955 found him back in Hollywood, out of costume, playing the broadcasting executive Ralph Hopkins to Gregory Peck's corporate speechwriter in *The Man in the Gray Flannel Suit*, by novelist Sloan Wilson. Produced by Darryl Zanuck, *Man* recalls the lush days of all-star casts and all-star productions, with the cast including Jennifer Jones, Lee J. Cobb, Keenan Wynn and Arthur O'Connell. The story centers on the efforts of Peck, who is suffering a psychological hangover from the killings and dangers of war, to achieve integrity on his job and in his marriage. As the hero he wears the same uniform as thousands of other workers in his class, the gray flannel suit.

March portrays the broadcasting tycoon who has given all his energies to the building of a big business, neglecting wife and children in the process. His portrait is a masterful study of an older man who comes to realize that his life, given its objectives, could not have been otherwise, but that perhaps his wealth and power are not worth what they have cost him. It is up to March, as "the man in the gray flannel suit's" employer, to persuade Peck to forsake the twenty-four-hour executive ladder and devote more time to his family.

To assure authenticity, director Nunnally Johnson took his cast and crew to Westport, Connecticut, and New York to film location scenes, then returned to Hollywood, where the interiors were shot. Peck, in the gray flannels of the New York professional man, was widely covered in news and magazine pictures while riding the commuter train. Since the picture embraced both the present time and, in flashbacks, the period of World War II, a dozen sound stages were used during the two months of filming. Although the company approached its task of converting the best-seller into a movie with the utmost seriousness, a warmth and mutual respect colored the attitude of both cast and crew during the filming. For instance, spontaneous applause greeted March and his movie daughter, Gigi Perreau, when they finished a long and difficult scene in one take.

Released April 12, 1956, *Man* met with critical approval. Although March's role was overshadowed by Peck's, Lawrence Quirk felt March made his relatively few scenes count heavily, and Peck was hard pressed to keep up with him in the scenes they played together. Typical reviews read as follows: from *Variety*: "As the broadcasting tycoon, lonely in his power, Fredric March is excellent, and the scenes between him and Peck lift the picture high above the ordinary" (March Papers).

In late March 1956, March again hosted the Academy Awards before starting his new television project for NBC, *Dodsworth*. March and Claire Trevor were to portray Sam and Fran Dodsworth in the *Producer's Showcase* presentation, directed by Alex Segal. March, admittedly not very fond of working for the home screen, had to be talked into it by agent Phil Gersh, who argued that he should do TV now and then and especially try a ninety-minute show. *Dodsworth*, by Sinclair Lewis, was rehearsed for three days, then presented April 30, 1956. The story is about a Midwestern businessman who succumbs to his younger wife's pleas and sells his business to take the grand European tour. On the tour, she reveals her abiding fear of growing old, takes up with assorted shallow Continental lovers, and finally reaps the consequences of her vanity and selfishness when she is discarded. The husband, in his unpolished sincerity, sees through both the European veneer and his wife's superficiality and finally leaves her for a sane life with a civilized widow. *Variety* felt that television's constant flirtation with hits of yesteryear had resulted in another casualty, however, The *New York Times* wrote: "Fredric March was altogether ideal as the businessman. It is a part that requires a broad emotional range—a boyish elation on the first sight of a foreign shore, the uncomprehending irritability that accompanies loneliness, the inner hurt of a ruthlessly broken partnership and the intoxicating relief of being one's self again. He put all the pieces together" (March Papers).

March was interviewed while rehearsing *Dodsworth*. He explained:

I'm 58. When you get as old as I am, you want to enjoy life. Mostly that means traveling to me. I couldn't face another long run in a Broadway show. We've had some pretty long runs in shows like *Skin of Our Teeth*, *The American Way*, and *Bell For Adano*. It was fun doing them but I wouldn't want to stick in a show for a year or two again. That's for the kids, the ones with stardust in their eyes. If your play's a hit, you're stuck with it. If it's a flop it's no fun. (March Papers)

For all his protestations that he and Florence would not do another stage production, Fred had to backpeddle fast when the plum role of James Tyrone, Sr., in Eugene O'Neill's autobiographical play *Long Day's Journey into Night* was deposited into his lap. When interviewed in 1964 for WTIC-Hartford, Fred commented, "I first went out to Hollywood in 1928, from the stage—they had some idea they needed people in the movies who could talk. For years I liked the stage better, but then I began to switch. Then something like *Long Day's Journey into Night* comes along and suddenly—'Oh God, here I am trapped in a hit.' Of course, you want to be in a hit, but Mrs. March and I did *Long Day's Journey* for sixty-nine weeks, four hours a night!" Florence continued, "Just think that a man of Freddie's reputation, a man as much in demand as he is, had to wait five years to find O'Neill's *Long Day's Journey*. In that five years there was not one script that came our way that seemed worth doing." Fred responded, "And we're not all that choosy." Florence: "Well, I hope we are." Fred: "But I shouldn't have to wait five years" (*Yale Reports*, 17 May 1964, 6, March Papers).

Long Day's Journey is a telling and recognizable portrait of the O'Neill family (renamed Tyrone) circa 1912, revolving around the story of O'Neill's real life miserly thespian father, James O'Neill, Sr. James Tyrone, Sr. (Fred), the sixty-five-year-old head of the household, is a onetime matinee idol with a weakness for drink and real estate. Penny-wise to the point of stinginess, preferring to buy worthless land rather than spend his money for proper doctors to attend his family, he is constantly at odds with his cynical elder son, also an actor, though considerably less successful. Fred once remarked, "Another thing about the old boy, James Tyrone, it wasn't too far away from my natural bent, because he was an old-time ham actor, too, you know" (March Papers). James Tyrone was to be March's most famous and important stage role, winning his second Antoinette Perry Award as Best Actor.

Other characters included Tyrone's drug addicted wife, Mary (Florence), a sad, haunted, and sick woman forced to spend her life in second-rate hotels as the wife of a trouper; their sons, James Tyrone, Jr. (Jason Robards, Jr.), and the younger son, Edmund Tyrone (Bradford Dillman). Edmund conspicuously suffers from a "summer cold" that everyone realizes is really consumption (tuberculosis). He is sensitive and studious and the idol of his mother, even though it was his birth that caused a quack doctor summoned by Tyrone first to administer the drugs to which Mary has since been addicted.

The play starts in the very early morning of a "long day," a day that brings the realization that Mary, indeed, is slipping back to her old morphine addicted past; James, Jr., is a bum; Edmund must go away to state hospital for his "cold"; and James, Sr., faces his enormous failure with his wife and his sons, although denying them vehemently to the last minute of the play. As the day passes James, Jr., and Tyrone drink heavily, and James, Jr., foresees that in destroying himself he may also destroy Edmund. Mary, lost in her memories, appears carrying her wedding gown in her arms, still attempting to find the past. It is, in fact, a most depressing and disheartening play, eliciting, literally wrenching, an audience response.

O'Neill had requested that this particular play not be done until twenty-five years after his death, but his widow released it in 1957 to producers Leigh Cornell, Theodore Mann and José Quintero, deciding there was no good reason to keep it locked up anymore. Quintero was slated to direct. This play runs three and three-quarter hours each performance, even though the Marches' tried and failed to get O'Neill's widow to shorten it. Indeed, the four acts are long and not easily sustained except by actors of unusual ability. *Long* opened in Boston October 16, 1956, on Broadway at the Helen Hayes Theater November 7, 1956, running through to June 29, 1957, with a hiatus in Paris to take part in the United States Cultural Exchange program; reopened on Broadway August 25, 1957, and ran through March 26, 1958, when the Marches' finally quit before the play went to London. *Long* became a Pulitzer and Tony Award winning play—in other words, a hit! So much for the semi-retirement, traveling, etc. monologue.

March, the perfectionist, made a fervent effort to "know" the great romantic actor of the 1890s and early 1900s, both as an actor and in his personal life. It was difficult because all of the elder O'Neill's colleagues and most of his friends had long since passed on. However, March managed to make James Tyrone a dignified, patient figure, even a man of compassion. March lifted him, without the audience being aware of it, above the petty disputes and the battle, to the friendly sympathy of the audience at final curtain. The role brought March not only a challenge, but great personal satisfaction. He remarked, "I am enjoying it tremendously. It is a most rewarding experience" (March Papers).

Bradford Dillman acted the difficult Edmund role, a role that gave him tremendous critical acclaim. When interviewed in 1990, he had many memories of his tenure in *Long Day*'s, memories about Fredric March. "It took me the better part of a year before I could bring myself to call him

Freddie, although he invited me to do so. To me he was either Mr. March or Sir. I was really in awe of the man" (Interview, Bradford Dillman, 11 August 1990). Dillman first met the Marches' when he and José Quintero were invited to Firefly for the first readings of the play. Dillman and Quintero spent the night in the made-over barn imbibing from the fully stocked bar the Marches' kept, when they stumbled upon a doorstop to one of the closets. The door stop happened to be Fredric March's 1931 Oscar. When looking higher up on the shelf they found the second, the 1946 Oscar. This gave Dillman insight into Mr. March, "Although he was a proud man, he was cognizant of his great talent; he was not a vain man at all" (Interview, Bradford Dillman, 11 August 1990).

Dillman learned a valuable theatrical lesson on the second night in Boston, during a twenty-minute tense scene that involved March and Dillman. Opening night had been cancelled because Florence had ruptured a vocal cord and understudy Ruth Cromwell had not yet learned her part. Also, Ruth was a "method" actress and Fred was not, so even before the twenty-minute scene between him and Dillman, he had difficulties keeping time opposite Ruth. It was climaxed by a five-minute speech by James Tyrone, Sr.—the greatest opportunity for the actor playing that part to score a lot of heavy points. March successfully launched the first sentence, and then went blank, totally forgetting his five minute speech. He looked to Dillman for help. Dillman felt he had two options open to him. First, save Mr. March by cutting all the way to the end of the long speech, but if he did that, cut out that great moment in the play, March had every right to cut up Dillman's Actors Equity card. Dillman chose what he deemed a safer course, the second option that came to his mind. Thinking, "He's a secure actor, he will work his way out," Dillman just sat staring at Fred, waiting. Once Fred realized this, he lurched (he was playing drunk) to the side of the stage calling for the stage manager, who whispered the beginning line. Fred, in his panic, could not hear him.

Dillman remembered, "By the time Freddie heard the *shouted* cue, anyone in the last row in the second balcony could tell him what the line was" (Interview, Bradford Dillman, 11 August 1990).

Fred finished the rest of the play flawlessly. After several curtain calls, Dillman cheerfully made his way toward his dressing room, when, all of a sudden, he was levitated into the air from behind and thrown up against the wall by a furious Fredric March.

Fred screamed at Dillman, "Where the FUCK were you?"

"Sir?" asked Dillman weakly.

"That wasn't my sweat you saw out there, kid, that was my *blood*. I was wading in *blood* on that stage and you sit there like some simpering *ass*!" Fred roared. Dillman started to explain his actions, when Fred interrupted, "No! *No* excuse—don't you *ever* do that to an actor again!" (Interview, Bradford Dillman, 11 August 1990).

After a meek "Yes, sir" the two got on famously for the length of Dillman's stay on *Long*. He learned a valuable lesson, namely, that he should have cut through to his own speech, for no actor ever wants to be embarrassed, and Fredric March had been deeply embarrassed.

When questioned about the Marches' acting technique, Dillman said that they were from a different generation in terms of training.

> Their work was highly technical. What they established in rehearsals would be repeated every performance. Florence wouldn't vary by an inflection. Freddie a little but not much. Jason and I, we were trained to give our life's blood every night. It was crippling to me—I dreaded going to the theater. . . . I left right after Paris. They were trained to deal with this, they did not invest anything emotional, while we dredged up all this garbage from our own lives.

This point was confirmed by Fred who remarked during an interview, "A great many actors have said, and I'm sure mean it sincerely, that they take their roles home with them and that it makes a lot of difference with their life. I hope it's never happened to me. I don't think it has" (March Papers).

Dillman finished, "Everything that Freddie performed he always brought, not only the vitality but he brought intelligence. He had a great knack for making choices that were colorful and interesting. He had an element of danger—if I was sitting in the audience, I didn't dare take my eyes off him because I didn't know what he might be doing next that I might miss (Interview, Bradford Dillman, 11 August 1990).

Once they opened on Broadway, the cast all knew they were part of a special play, an *important* play. As the actor Tyrone, March created a masterful characterization: belligerent and tarnished, full of crumbling doubt. Richard Watts, Jr., *New York Post*: "A magnificent and shattering play. . . . It seems to me that Fredric March gives the finest and most penetrating performance of his career as the father. Florence Eldridge is touching and real as the mother. . . . This is a play that gives the entire season stature" (March Papers). Brooks Atkinson, *New York Times*: "As the aging actor who stands at the head of the family, Fredric March gives a masterful performance that will stand as a milestone in the acting of an O'Neill play. Petty, mean, bullying, impulsive and sharp-tongued, he also has magnificence—a man of stirring passions, deep loyalties and basic humility. This is a character portrait of grandeur" (March Papers).

One congratulatory letter, from a friend, Fred particularly treasured, and kept for posterity: "What do you say to the King? All the grand phrases have been salted off on actors who weren't within nine light years of you. I'd bring you myrrh, but you're probably up to your ass in myrrh. All Kings are. And opening night you proved again you're the only American actor of genius in our time" (March Papers).

The Drama Critics Poll results for the 1956–57 season disclosed Fredric March as the Best Male Lead in a Straight Play and Florence Eldridge as the Best Female Lead in a Straight Play. *Long* also won the Pulitzer and Tony awards, while Fredric March added to his stature with the Tony for Best Actor. Their successful representation at the Paris Festival of Plays of the American Contemporary Theater was dampened only by their knowledge that Bradford Dillman would soon be leaving the play.

On January 9, 1958, Fred and Florence were featured on Ed Sullivan's TV show with a gripping performance in the second scene of the second act, the scene in which the mother berated herself for giving birth to the consumptive Edmund. When questioned after the television show about losing interest while doing a play that ran two years, Fred replied, "Your interest may diminish, but your performances must not. *Long* is such a strict regime, like being in prison or the army. . . . That's a damned long hard grind but you mustn't let your performance show it. As the old saying goes, 'There's a different audience every night'" (March Papers).

Plans were soon under way to take the show to London, with the Marches' starring in their respective roles, however, the sons had not been cast as yet (Robards had left by this time, also). Then, to their dismay, they found that they were not to be consulted in the selection of the supporting cast. On March 9, 1958, Fred sent a letter to the London managing director of the Globe Theater, Hugh Beaumont, nicknamed Binky:

> For our part we must delay final commitment either approval of cast or have the firm knowledge of what other actors have been engaged. Having had to experience this part carrying two weak actors [he was *not* referring to Dillman or Robards, but to the second season replacements], we are more than ever convinced that it would be unfair to this wonderful play and to our own reputations to commit ourselves now with neither of the votes cast nor with the approval of cast, which has been elementary in our theater dealings for so long." (March Papers)

On March 19, 1958, the Marches contended that the producers felt it was no concern of theirs to approve the personnel in their supporting casts, therefore, they sent a telegram to Binky on March 19, 1958.

DEAR BINKY:
BECAUSE PRESENT PRODUCERS REFUSE OUR APPROVAL SUPPORTING PLAYERS WHICH IS ELEMENTARY IN THEATER PROCEDURE, WE REGRET WE MUST WITHDRAW FROM NEGOTIATIONS LONDON PRODUCTION.
HOPE HAPPIER SITUATION WILL ONE DAY BRING US TO

LONDON UNDER YOUR MANAGEMENT. FLORENCE, FREDDIE
MARCH. (March Papers)

This came as a complete bombshell to Binky, who had already signed
contracts for the Edinburgh Festival engagement, September 8, and had
flooded England with national newspaper publicity announcing that the
Marches' would both be at the festival in the O'Neill play. He straightaway
fired off a quick letter back to them: "Apart from contractual problems with
the Festival Committee, it would be a dreadful thing if, in point of fact, this
trip, which has been so carefully planned, all collapsed" (Letter from Binky,
21 March 1958, March Papers).

   The negotiations failed. March told newspaper reporters, "We feel this is
a play that has to do with four people, each of whose contribution is equally
important. We are most anxious to know who the two sons would be" (March
Papers). They quit the play by March 26, 1958. They next took an extended
vacation after the long haul of *Long Day's*, remaining on Firefly throughout
the summer. Phil Gersh, however, managed to convince Fred to try television
with Florence in the supporting role in Terrence Rattigan's play *The Winslow
Boy*. Done for the CBS "Du Pont Show of the Month," November 13, 1958,
Winslow was a television play of ninety minutes' duration. March accepted,
still bemoaning live television, finding it too frantic, but did admit he liked to
do one show a season because of its reaching so many people. He felt that
it was very difficult to get really deep into a characterization with such short
rehearsal time. If he was going to do television, he wanted to give a real
performance, not sloughing it off. He felt, also, that it was very difficult to
keep in character during a television rehearsal with all that yelling and
direction going on in one's ears. Once a year was more than enough for
March. In fact, he considered live television the invention of the devil for an
actor, explaining, "I'm a slow starter, I like to get to know the person I'm
playing. For live TV, you work like the devil for nineteen days but it's tough
to get under the skin of the character you're playing" (March Papers).

   "I hate it," he would mumble. "It's just like opening night on Broadway, I
always like to get past the first evening's performance so I can get into my
part and lines and work out the kinks." Shuddering, March continued, "In live
TV, you always come away feeling you'd like another chance at it. It's exciting
to everybody but the actor" (March Papers). (March may have, indeed,
detested television, but for his many appearances on the old television
entertainment show "What's My Line?" he garnered the honor of being the
most spectacular guest. His gimmick to disguise his voice was that of
switching accents and points of reference so that he had the panelists reeling.)
But he liked Sumner Locke Elliott's TV adaptation of *The Winslow Boy*,
thinking it more exciting than the original Broadway play. This, plus the fact
that Alex Segal, in whom he had complete trust, would direct, persuaded Fred

to endure the torture of live TV. The added advantage that Florence would be able to play his wife in this full-length TV play also induced him. He also reminded himself that there was still another very practical reason for going through the hellish business of live television. He got paid for it!

Terence Rattigan's play is based on an actual case, one that created a tremendous stir in England at the beginning of the century. A thirteen year old boy has been expelled from the Royal Naval College at Osborne for alleged theft and is denied a hearing or even a rebuttal. When he claims he is innocent, his father, a bank manager of modest means, believes him, launching a two-year litigation that exhausts the family's finances, ruins his daughter's love affair and compels his older son to leave Oxford to take a minor job in the bank. The *Los Angeles Times* reviewed DuPont's third "Show of the Month" with, "Fredric March as the father was superb—Freddy March is like the Good Housekeeping Seal of Approval—anything he's in is great!" (March Papers) *New York Times*: "Mr. March gave a towering performance as the father; he was human, understanding and fiercely determined. . . . Miss Eldridge was altogether right as the English mother living amid a problem that she never fully understood or approved" (March Papers).

Director Delbert Mann next recruited March for the picturization of the Paddy Chayevsky Broadway stage play *Middle of the Night*, filmed in New York, during January and February 1959. March portrayed the role Edward G. Robinson had on the stage, that of an older widower in love with a much younger woman (Kim Novak). He was the hard-working garment manufacturer, prepared to give up everything for her despite conventional objections to his love for a woman thirty years his junior. Delbert Mann frankly regarded his two stars as the most auspicious he had ever worked with. The heroine was a person who needed support and assurance. Mann felt Kim was the same way. The male character was a fellow who projects that for her. March, again, personified that sort of support.

March would only take on the part if Mann would shoot around his commitment to read the Gettysburg Address. March had been asked to read the famous Lincoln address to a joint session of Congress at a ceremony commemorating the 150th anniversary of Abraham Lincoln's birth. After taping was through, March watched himself on TV, shaking his head, "You want to do it over again, but it's the greatest thrill of an actor's life to address a joint session."

March, paunchy and looking every minute of those fifty-six years of his character (actually he was sixty-one at the time of filming), gave a memorable performance as the aging lover. His lined, weary face mirrored all the joy and pain of his need for love, being constantly reminded that 'there is no fool like an old fool.' It was released June 17, 1959; the reviews for *Middle of the Night* were mixed. Some despaired that, although Mr. March was an excellent actor when it came to showing joy and distress, he was not successful at pretending to be a Jewish father and businessman. For instance, *Saturday Review*: "Fredric March, fine actor though he is doesn't provide the appeal that Robinson brought to the role. . . . The embraces of the older man and the girl have a way of chilling the bone marrow, and worse, accentuating that tragic age difference" (March Papers). The better reviews included *Daily News*: "March proves again that he is a highly skilled actor who knows his craft A to Z. His characterization of the energetic, lonely widower is finely etched on the screen" (March Papers). *New York Herald Tribune*:

In the beginning March looks bedraggled, sloppy, chews slackly on an old cigar. The effect of a young woman's love on him is a visual thing. It stiffens his posture, lightens his eye, and makes him lean forward into the next minute. But when disappointment or doubts cut into him, March collapses intermittently into an aging man, possessive, jealous and afraid of death. His teeth tap together nervously. His back bows. His eyes turn frantic. From March one expects a good performance. This one is very solid. (March Papers)

On April 29, 1959, Fred and Florence attended a black tie dinner at Columbia University in order to recite three short poems by Mark VanDoren, who was presented the Alexander Hamilton Medal, given each year to some highly distinguished alumnus. The year 1959 was to be one of honors for Fredric March for he was to receive an Honorary Doctorate of Humanities from his alma mater, the University of Wisconsin at Madison, set for June 8. Both Fred and Florence had previously received an Honorary Doctorate of Letters from Elmira College in 1957. Before visiting Wisconsin, he and Florence flew to London in late April, in order to fulfill a prior commitment, another television series—Fred was to narrate *Tales from Charles Dickens*. Fortunately, this was to be taped for later showing. He also publicized his newest film, *Middle of the Night*, while in London. A press conference was given in Mr. March's honor and attended by other stars as well as nearly fifty English reporters. Some British reporters were a bit too sharp in interviewing Fred and he responded just as sharply. The conference began with questions more or less on this order:
"How old are you?"
"How much money have you in the bank?"
"Do you consider yourself an up-and-coming young actor?"
"When was the last time you had a press conference?"
"Why don't you retire?"
"What have you been doing for the last decade?"
March was shocked! He didn't know what to say or do, not knowing whether to try to be flip or whether he ought to be serious. He told them his

age—sixty-one on August 31—and said he didn't consider himself a newcomer
to the acting profession. After all, he was on Broadway for sixty-nine weeks
in *Long Day's Journey into Night* and he had averaged a film a year for many
years.

March closed the conference with, "I told them I'm loaded. I have money
enough to retire. I want to but I don't want to. I guess it was a mistake to
admit I save my money because in writing it up they were sneery about it.
Their attitude was terrible. I just don't understand what they were trying to
do. I've had it with the British press!" (*New York Herald Tribune*, Joe Hyams
Abroad, 26 May 1959, March Papers). Disgusted, he departed for the States
eager to start researching his next picture role, starring opposite an actor he
greatly admired, in his only appearance with Spencer Tracy.

20

Inherit the Wind

In the summer of 1959 Fredric March accepted one of the starring parts in *Inherit the Wind* from director-producer Stanley Kramer. Kramer had first contacted the Marches' in October of 1958 with a rough draft of the movie version of the Jerome Lawrence and Robert E. Lee play based on the famous 1925 Scopes "monkey trial" in Tennessee. March was to portray the prosecuting attorney Matthew Harrison Brady, a character based on the historical William Jennings Bryan, an oldtime religious fundamentalist and presidential hopeful. Fred was looking forward to this picture because the costar was one of his favorite actors, Spencer Tracy. Kramer, also, was ecstatic that he had managed to obtain two of America's most respected actors, feeling March and Tracy stood as giants in their field.

When interviewed in 1990, Kramer remarked,

There are very few Titans, those men who stood by themselves. I was rolling the dice with the best! Fred was adjustable, pliable and he obeyed co-workers rules often remarking, "Take the job seriously and yourself not at all." He tended to overworry and be moody at times. But he wanted it to be *right* and I respected that. In *Inherit the Wind*, I thought he played William Jennings Bryan [the Matthew Harrison Brady character] brilliantly. Bryan's political character and personal values were grabbed by March and flaunted as Bryan flaunted them. (Interview, Stanley Kramer, 10 August 1990)

March began researching William Jennings Bryan far in advance of actual filming. Some of the detailed research involved listening to Bryan's "Cross of Gold" speech, given when Bryan was thirty-six years old, an aggressive and eloquent spokesman of silver in America and soon to be Democratic presidential candidate for the election of 1896. The issues of sound money and free silver involved choosing between a deflationist monetary policy and an inflationist one for economic recovery from the most recent depression. Mckinly chose sound money, the gold standard and currency restriction as the safest course. For bankrupt farmers and Western miners, on the other hand, gold was a "Cross of Gold" forced on the honest laborer who was being crucified by the money lenders and wanted free silver. Bryan quickly emerged as the choice of the agrarian wing, but lost the election to William McKinley. The Democrats named Bryan again in the 1900 election campaign, hoping he would carry the banner of "No Imperialism." Instead, he insisted that silver was still the nation's chief concern, inspiring the negative "Bryan would rather be wrong than President" slogan. The Republicans held all the trump cards that year, too—McKinley won again with new Vice President Theodore Roosevelt and thereafter, America became a world power (reluctantly).

Bryan was the Democratic choice again in the 1908 election, defeated a third time by Roosevelt's successor, William H. Taft, he made the poorest showing of any Democrat since the party split in 1860. With the election of Democrat Woodrow Wilson to the White House in 1912, Bryan was named secretary of state, a job at which he was moderately successful. During the buildup to World War I in 1915, Bryan, who felt that Wilson's protest note to Berlin about their sinking of the *Lusitania* was perilously close to an ultimatum, resigned from the cabinet rather than sign the note. Bryan's solution had been to renounce responsibility for the lives of Americans who chose passage on belligerent ships. This was unpardonable to Wilson. Bryan went back to his law practice.

In the years after World War I the America of the Protestant, old-stock culture felt deeply threatened by the values of the thriving city and erected barriers against change. The census of 1920 revealed that for the first time most Americans lived in urban areas, a frightening statistic for those in small towns and on farms. They attributed to the metropolis all that was corrupt in American society: the revolution in morals, the corner saloon and the modern skepticism of the literal interpretation of the Bible. Their ideology of religious fundamentalism took an aggressive form after the war. Bryan liked to think he stood for this average man and relished his nickname of "The Great Commoner." So, into this atmosphere he charged, a self-proclaimed crusader for religious orthodoxy. Under his leadership, several states enacted laws forbidding the teaching of the newest doctrine of the "moderns" of that day—evolution. In 1925 the whole country became caught up in the fundamentalist controversy when a high school biology teacher, John T. Scopes, was tried for violating a Tennessee statute forbidding the teaching of evolution. Bryan joined the prosecution team while Clarence Darrow, social philosopher, agnostic, and free spirit, a great lawyer who habitually defended unpopular causes and persons, defended John T. Scopes (undertaken without pay and wholly in character).

To Dayton, Tennessee, swarmed armies of reporters to watch Darrow, the rebellious attorney, clash with Bryan in a savage examination that revealed the ignorance of the "silver-tongued orator." On the afternoon of July 20, 1925, in a Dayton, Tennessee, courtroom, the career of William Jennings Bryan ended with a whimper. The high point of the trial came when Darrow cross-examined Bryan about his religious beliefs. A golden orator, presidential candidate, and defender of the faith, Bryan had turned himself into the Don Quixote of a bygone rural American age, playing the role of Bible expert as a witness against evolution in the Scopes trial. For an hour and a half, sweating and shouting under the baiting of defense counsel Darrow, he spouted fundamentalisms and contradicted himself. Bryan affirmed his literal interpretation of the Bible—that the world was created in 4004 B.C., that Jonah was swallowed by a big fish, that Eve was made out of Adam's rib. When Darrow talked about geology, Bryan told him that he was more interested in the Rock of Ages than in the age of rocks. Darrow and Bryan battled it out, shaking their fists at each other. In essence, one answer of Bryan's stood for all: "The Bible states it; it must be so." He left the stand exhausted and discredited. Once he had one leg in the White House and the nation trembled under his roars. But, by the end of the trial, Bryan, then sixty-five years old, had visibly aged in front of his Bible Belt audience.

The court convicted Scopes and the Tennesseeans applauded Bryan. Even though he won the case (indeed, how could he have not with a Bible-bred judge), he retired to a friend's home in Dayton to read the clippings on the trial and what he read could not have cheered him for he found even his pearly tones under attack. The drama at Dayton had come out as a farce instead of a holy thing, as much of the world shook with laughter over the spectacle Bryan had made of himself. While Tennessee threw out the Scopes conviction because the "Jedge" erred in setting the sentence instead of letting the jury do it, the state supreme court upheld the evolution law itself. But by then it was too late for Bryan to savor his victory. He was dead. He died of apoplexy on July 26, five days after his ordeal on the stand against the wily Darrow. With him died much of the older America.

This, then, was the intricate man Fredric March was to portray: a Bible-thumping orator, self-righteous in his beliefs, indeed, old-fashioned, representing an America that was on the losing end of historical change. Brady was a vulnerable man, as was the real Bryan, and March knew that, knew that his character would have to break down in the courtroom at the climax of *Inherit the Wind*. He found out soon that Bryan, in a word, was a "ham," something March had often been accused of. What a part this would be! What marvelous things he could do (and did) with it not to mention the possibilities of makeup. There was never any question in March's mind, nor in director Kramer's, that he would portray this flamboyant character from the early twentieth century as close to type as possible. Part of the research took

March to a commerce instructor, Max Otto, at his former university. While he was in Madison to receive his Honorary Doctorate of Humanities, Otto reminded him of the recording made at the University of Bryan's speech to the students in 1921 on the first leg of his crusade against the doctrine of evolution. He gave March tips on how Bryan gave this speech.

Initially, March was a little hesitant to visit Madison, for once the university had announced that he was to receive the Honorary Doctorate, former students looked up his scholastic record and deluged him with letters complaining, "Why would the university give an honorary degree to a member of the Ku Klux Klan?" Fred had been a member of said named organization as a junior in 1919, but at that time it represented the Junior Honor organization. The title was changed to TUMAS during the twenties because of the new connotation of the Ku Klux Klan. The university flooded newspapers with this explanation and Fredric March went to Madison to receive his degree on June 8, 1959, as planned and without incident. Florence accompanied him and in the afternoon following the graduation ceremonies they were entertained at an informal reception given by the alumni. They then headed back to Firefly for a summer with daughter Penny and her two sons, Gianni and Michael. The quiet of the redone barn provided him the necessary atmosphere in which to "break the back" of perhaps one of his best characterizations, that of Matthew Harrison Brady.

So it was, in October of 1959, that producer-director Kramer set the stage for the most explosive clash of personalities in the Hollywood annals when he cast a pair of two-time Best Actor Oscar winners for the court contest. In another sample of his penchant for offbeat casting, Kramer signed dance star Gene Kelly for the straight role as the cynical newspaperman. Kelly was grateful for a chance to appear with the two formidable talents, whom he admired. He tried to learn as much as he could about the style and technique of Tracy and March. "I could understand and see what Fred was doing. He was like Olivier. A wonderful technician. You could *see* the characterization taking shape—the cogs and wheels beginning to turn. If you studied his methods closely, it was all there, like an open book" (Hirschborn 1984, 229).

Florence was to play Mrs. Brady, marking her seventh appearance opposite her husband; Dick York was cast in the Scopes part, and a young Claude Akins (aged for this role) was cast as the Brady-supporting minister Reverend Brown. In 1925, the "Monkey Trial" lasted nine days. In 1959, its replay took twenty-two days for Kramer to film the supercharged, highly emotional but often hilarious trial before 300 spectators in a set exactly duplicating the Dayton courtroom. The nondescript American small town of Hillsboro was built for the film and 1,750 extras, all in attire of the mid-1920s and some vintage vehicles, were employed to pack its streets for parade, torchlight procession and carnival sequences.

Claude Akins, too, was thrilled to be included in the "clash of the giants!"

Contacted in 1990 for his memories, Akins described March as a triple threat: young leading man, character actor, and elderly character actor. Akins remembered many March techniques, "Mr. March included small things in his characterizing —such as the rolling gait of a fat man, the store bought teeth that don't catch, and dispelling the heat with his fan." He also remembered that Florence hovered around Fred, holding herself and Fred at a distance, as if protecting him. Akins found Fred warm and friendly when he had a chance to chat with him (seldom) but he always felt Florence was thinking "How dare he (Akins) get up on the stage and act with my Freddie" (Telephone interview, Claude Akins, 17 July 1990). Agent Phil Gersh recalled that this was typical Florence behavior. She thought she was protecting Fred, but in reality she was a snob, and probably thought Akins not of her class. Many agreed with Akins's assessment of Florence; one New Milford neighbor commented; "Towards the end of the Marches' stay in New Milford there was rift between our families . . . Florence could be a very difficult person. When Dad was running for Judge of Probate Court, Florence decided that she would not let the 'March name' be used for political reasons . . . which did not amount to much in a small town like New Milford. Anyhow there was virtually no contact from 1960 on" (Letter, Michael Bradbury, 5 July 1991).

For *Inherit* March made himself up to resemble closely the legendary Bryan, complete with bald pate, thick midsection, and flamboyant mannerisms, and became the personification of bigotry and intolerance. Tracy portrayed Henry Drummond, the character molded after Clarence Darrow, as Tracy, not Darrow. Each achieved his own well-thought-out effects without infringing on the other's territory. Kramer recalled, "Tracy admired March as much as March admired Tracy—they had a mutual admiration society" (Interview, Stanley Kramer, 10 August 1990). Yet, as the filming progressed, the two men became highly competitive. Kramer continued:

> March and Tracy were quite a couple—quite a match-up. It was a delight to watch . . . during the filming we had them nose to nose for long courtroom battles in dialogue and assorted histrionics. The stage was filled with people from every office and company on the lot. And how these two luxuriated in the applause of the audience. Every take brought down the house, and their escapades were something to see. March would fan himself vigorously with a large straw fan each time Tracy launched into an oration. Tracy had no props, but he got even. He sat behind March and picked his nose during a three-and-one-half-minute summation. (Swindell 1969, 248)

When asked how he liked working with Spencer Tracy, March responded:

> It was grand, just grand. I'm nuts about Spence. Working with him was

a real joy. The truth is, I *enjoyed* making *Inherit the Wind*. Spence and I, we were so diametrically opposed in our methods. I was so flamboyant. And Tracy—so good, so quiet. Actually, I went overboard a bit. I was determined to make a buffoon out of Bryan, but I couldn't stop clowning. I'd get going in a scene and get a few laughs from the crew and keep at it. (March Papers)

Spencer Tracy's biographer, Larry Swindell, related at length about March's technique, commenting that there was not a "typical" March style. He stated that March could convey a strength through understatement or inflation about equally well, but when he confronted Tracy in the courtroom, he knew he could not beat Tracy at the underplaying game, so he acted up a storm for a contrast:

What a treat that was! They were jealous of one another, for each rated the other as the best American actor on stage or screen. They didn't deny that they were staging a duel and it was fitting that it sort of ended in a draw. Look at his performance: It's outrageously big, but thoroughly disciplined; true enough, no doubt, of its William Jennings Bryan prototype. (Swindell, Inquirer Book Editor, 1975, March Papers)

The movie portrayed the confrontation between the two men when Drummond crucifies Brady on the witness stand: March's Brady as an authority on the Holy Bible, ready to combat Spencer Tracy's characterization of the defense attorney, Henry Drummond. The courtroom favored Brady until Drummond holds up an innocuous rock, asking Brady how old the rock might be. In response, Brady fans his face furiously (the temperature was in the nineties) with a funeral parlor advertisement fan, stating that he is "more interested in the 'Rock of Ages' than . . . in the age of rocks." Drummond tries again with various questions about the rock in order to place Brady off his guard. He begins by explaining that the rock is the fossil remains of a marine prehistoric creature, found in that very county, that had lived there millions of years ago when the mountain ranges were submerged in water.

Brady next makes a grave error, which Drummond will eventually pounce on: "I know. The Bible gives a fine account of the flood." He waves his fan in the air with emphasis and counters Drummond on his dates, affirming that the rock is not more than six thousand years old. Brady then recites from "a fine biblical scholar" who has determined that the exact date and hour of the creation occurred in the year four thousand B.C.! Drummond responds by stating firmly that that was only an opinion and how did he know that the creation occurred in a specific year? Brady states flatly, "Not an opinion—a literal fact. Which the good Bishop arrived at through careful computation of the ages of the prophets as set down in the Old Testament." He continues excitedly, "In fact, he determined that the Lord began the creation on the twenty-thrid of October, four thousand four B.C. at . . . ahh . . . (he pauses to think). Nine a.m." At this revelation, Drummond knows he has the upper hand and continues to batter away at Brady, asking, "That Eastern Standard time? (the audience picked up on his train of thought) Or Rocky Mountain time? It wasn't Daylight Savings time, was it?" Drummond allowed himself a slow grin. "Because the Lord didn't make the sun until the fourth day."

Brady agrees, as Drummond presses, "That first day, well, what do ya think it was . . . ahh . . . twenty-four hours long?" Brady frowns, "Bible says it was a day." Drummond asks, "Well, there was no sun out, how do you know how long it was? Brady responds emphatically, "The Bible says it was a day!" Drummond drills, "But was it a normal day, a literal day, a twenty-four hour day?" The audience is hushed during this encounter, apprehensive that their hero, Brady, might not make a good show of himself. He does not disappoint them, as he continues to dig a deeper hole for himself, sweating profusely as Drummond refuses to drop the Bible "day"questioning. "I don't know."

"What do ya think?" Drummond asks.

"I do not think about things . . . I do not think about." Brady is visibly uncomfortable.

Drummond raises his voice, "Do you ever think about things that you *do* think about? Isn't it possible it could have been twenty-five hours—no way to measure, no way to tell. Could it have been twenty-five hours?"

"It's possible."

Almost shouting, Drummond hammers, "Then you interpret that the first day is recorded in the book of Genesis could have been a day of indeterminate length?"

"I mean to state, that, it is not necessarily a twenty-four hour day!"Brady fires back.

"It could have been thirty hours, could've been a week, could've been a month, could've been a year, could've been a hundred years . . . or (yelling) it could've been *ten million years*!"

The assistant prosecuting attorney leaps to his feet demanding, "I protest. This is not only irrelevant, immaterial, it is illegal! I demand to know the purpose of Mr. Drummond's examination . . . What's he trying to do?"

Brady answers, "I'lltell you what he's trying to do! He wants to destroy everybody's belief in the Bible . . . and in God!"

Drummond states, "That's not true and you know it. The Bible is a book—it's a good book, but it is not the only book."

"It is the revealed word of the Almighty God, spake to the man who wrote the Bible," counters Brady.

"How do you know that God didn't spake to Charles Darwin?"

Importantly, Brady answers, "I know, because God tells me to oppose the evil teachings of that man!"

"Oh, God speaks to you?"

"Yes."

"He tells you what is right and wrong?"

"Yes."

"And you act accordingly?"

"*YES!*"

Drummond has Brady now, falling into his trap neatly as the audience sways away from the elder statesman they had previously treasured. "So, you, Matthew Harrison Brady, through oratory or legislature or whatever, you pass on God's orders to the rest of the world! Well, meet the prophet from Nebraska!" It is all over for Brady at this point. Drummond, dismissing the old man, walks away. The audience erupts into action by talking and shouting and are not at all interested in what Mr. Brady has to say. Brady continues to recite all the books from the Bible as the courtroom dissolves into confusion. The Judge bangs his gavel and Brady's wife comes forward to help her husband down from the witness stand. Brady looks old as he and his wife walks out of the courtroom that had once held him in religious awe. (Nathan Douglas and Harold Smith)

It is to director Kramer's credit that he was concerned not only for the ideas at stake, but for what these ideas do to people in private as well as in public. In a brief and tender scene between Brady and his wife, after the tense courtroom battle, the elder statesman cries, "Mother, they laughed at me. I can't stand it when they laugh at me." He starts to weep, his head on her shoulder, as she comforted him, much as she might a young child. However, Florence's one big scene was cut by Kramer as he felt it was not needed; this always bothered her.

Released October 12, 1960, *Inherit the Wind* was recognized critically but not at the box office. "The film got extravagant reviews," said Kramer, "but it died at the box office. United Artists said this was just a silly story about two old men, so they didn't distribute it properly. Then the fundamentalists called me the Antichrist, so there were some local problems in booking the film too. It just died" (Lorentz 1975, 220). The actual reviews were excellent with Tracy endowing his character with strength and stature from the outset. But Mr. Tracy had to share the acting honors with Fredric March, who gave a shattering performance as Brady, a man who proudly believed in himself and his own righteousness, indifferent to the opinions of the rest of the world.

March emphasized the clownish side of the Bryan character, traits that probably had become uppermost in Bryan'old age, portraying the monumental hulk of a man who had Biblical catchwords and phrases ready for every occasion. *New York Times*, Bosley Crowther: "With the dramatic face-off between Spencer Tracy and Fredric March, the two unsurpassable actors persuaded to play the roles, Mr. Kramer has wonderfully accomplished not only a graphic fleshing of his theme but he also has got one of the most brilliant and engrossing displays of acting ever witnessed on the screen" (March Papers). *Motion Picture Daily*: "March is superb in his characterization, having the more challenging chore of wearing special makeup and delineating the suffering change in a great historical figure, whose victory through moral defeat in the trial, ends in a fatal stroke" (March Papers). *New York Post*, Archer Winsten:

It should be noted that seldom in the history of cinema or theater had a performer shown such a miraculous capacity for growth in his [March's] later years. All through the early and middle years of his career March got by on personal charm and a capability that was studious and intelligent, never inspired. Now, at last in this picture he seems to have risen to an entirely different level of characterization than anything that went before. It has taken him forty years to do it, but he is now consistently conquering the heights . . . Spencer Tracy makes a solid lawyer, not another Clarence Darrow, but a good Tracy-type lawyer just the same." (March Papers)

After Tracy received his Oscar nomination for *Inherit,* March was nominated for the German Silver Bear Award for Best Acting for the same picture. Tracy lost and March won. The Germans liked the March portrayal more and in the 1960 Berlin Film Festival March was awarded the Silver-Bear Emblem as Best Actor, July 6, 1960. Tracy sent him a congratulatory telegram: "Some say you are in Italy Others New York Others Wisconsin Wherever you are congratulations and love to you both. Spence" (March Papers). In the Fredric March Papers, their rivalry is most apparent, for March kept a poster of *Inherit the Wind* displaying the two characters battling head to head; under Tracy a statement that he had been nominated for the Oscar. March wrote alongside the statement, "And he *did not* get it! F. M."

After the conclusion of filming, Fred and Florence planned a trip around the world via the Orient. Leaving January 4, 1960, they visited Israel, Iran, India, Ceylon, Singapore, Thailand, Hong Kong, Japan, and Honolulu, arriving home by May 15. Dr. and Mrs. Burrill Crohn, Firefly neighbors, accompanied them. Fred was requested to read over the radio the Gettysburg Address on Lincoln's birthday because Abraham Lincoln was greatly admired in India. Also while in India, the Marches' ran into a spot of trouble; the four friends were arrested for violating India's liquor prohibition laws. Four ounces of liquor were found in their luggage during a search at a roadblock. A travel agency representative posted bail and Fred and his companions continued on their Far Eastern tour assured that the charges were to be dropped, but the affair aroused criticism in India that tourists were being harassed at a time when the government sought to attract more visitors. An Indian government official extended his unqualified apologies, wishing the whole incident had not happened. He also expressed hope that the U.S. Congress, where demands were made for an investigation of the incident, would accept the apology and they did. Florence, a gifted writer, recorded her memories of this occurrence, at the border of the Indian states of Karalla and Madras, during a routine inspection.

At last, in Burrill's medical bag they discovered about two ounces of Bourbon. Madras is a dry State. The bottle was waved triumphantly. The officer removed the cork, sniffed, rolled his eyes, shuddered with disgust and looked at all of us as though we'd been caught in an indecent act. In addition to the bottle, they decided to confiscate Burrill's bag. Burrill, needless to say, decided that whither he went, the bag went. So we were ushered back to the car—I sitting on Freddie's lap in order to accommodate the Police Officer who had been too long in the sun to make a pleasant companion on a long, hot drive.

We were asked to sign statements in duplicate and triplicate. The Indians adore paperwork. We had, of course, no idea what we were signing, but the young man said that it was a confession that we had two ounces of liquor in our possession. When we protested that only one person had possessed the liquor, we were told that all shared the responsibility. "Guilt by association" is a fiendish doctrine wherever one meets it.

Burrill, who had clutched his bag throughout the entire incident endeavoring to prove that the whiskey was a medicine and only one item in his well-stocked bag, proceeded to unearth the antibiotics and other talismans he carried against any illness we might succumb to on our journey. This was a mistake as now the interrogation took the form of "Why do you carry all these drugs?" With the sinister implication that they had cornered Lucky Luciano himself. (March Papers)

The Marches' and Crohns left India posthaste and wiser. Fred wrote to Dore Schary (head of MGM) while on this junket to the Orient, commenting, "It is a great experience. Israel nine days (tea with Abba Eban); Iran nine days (dinner with the Shah and his bride and Princess Shanna); lunch two days ago in Delhi with Nehru. How fortunate can we be!" (March Papers).

Another New Milford neighbor met the foursome in Hong Kong. It was perhaps the only time that this neighbor ever saw Fredric March get angry and lose his temper. During lunch an American tourist set up a tripod with camera right next to him and commenced picture taking. Fred got livid and grabbed the camera, handing it back to the tourist. "Madam, you could have at least had the decency to ask my permission! Now, go *away*!" In another incident the philanderer in Fred came to the fore. At a state dinner in Hong Kong, Fred was seated next to a young princess with her young prince husband seated across. She could not get far enough away from Fred because he was constantly grabbing at her beneath the table.

Upon their arrival home Fred received two more awards to add to the Silver Bear for Best Acting in *Inherit the Wind*. The first was the *Man of the Year* award granted by the New York based University of Wisconsin Alumni Club. The second was an even more important degree than the one granted to him by the University of Wisconsin one year prior. He was to receive another Honorary Doctorate of Fine Arts from Ripon College, Ripon, Wisconsin. This was a meaningful award for Fred because Ripon was Spencer Tracy's former college. Tracy attended in 1920–22, dropping out to pursue his acting career rather than finish his education. Of course, Tracy had already been granted the degree, and it bothered Fred that he had not. Fred flew to Madison in order for old college friend Larry Hall to drive him to Ripon to receive the award. Afterward, a small dinner party was arranged, allowing Fred to reminisce with Jack Ramsey (who drove in from Racine) and Larry.

It was back to New Milford for the remainder of 1960; Fred's next picture commitment would not start filming until January 9, 1961. He was to portray a doctor, a new challenge for him.

21

The Great Orator Plays God

Newsweek interviewed March about his latest movie, *The Young Doctors*. "I was a little leery about *The Young Doctors* at first. I got concerned that it wasn't such a good idea to throw out to the public that doctors disagree among themselves. Then I said the hell with it, they probably do. I was astounded when the AMA gave it their recommendation. Damn good . . ."

"Did you consciously hold down your acting in *The Young Doctors*, after your flamboyant characterization of Bryan in *Inherit the Wind*?"

"Oh sure, I learned from Spence," Fred said with a smile. "But I must be honest, it wasn't all me. I was going to play it scruffy and broad and the director said, 'Aw, Freddie, no. Play yourself, play it like *The Best Years of Our Lives*.' I thought, what the heck was that? I guess this is the most held down I've been in a long time. This Fall I'm going to do *Gideon*, this Paddy Chayefsky play in which I play God, but only for six months. There's a lot of humor in this Chayefsky play . . . God's going to get some laughs, I think."

The interviewer next asked about what medium Fred preferred, films, TV, or stage. Fred sat down across from the reporter, the dining table between them, assuming the grim visage that had become his trademark. Remaining warm and friendly, he took on the mannerisms of his familiar "man with a problem" characterization, drumming his fingers on the table, repeatedly adjusting his sleeves and shirt cuffs, smoking as if each cigarette were his last and giving frequent non-speaking exercise to the muscles of his mouth.

Finally, he answered, "I prefer films. You can do a picture ineight or ten weeks and get it over with and then do what you want to do. You reach many millions and you get a Hell of a lot more dough."

Relaxing, just a bit, but making a face, "Live television is the hardest acting to do. Tape is less frightening. I don't have too many years left in my life, and I like to travel, and I'd rather do a picture and get it over with than do a play."

The interviewer continued, "What about your old movies that are being shown on television—do you see any of them, make a point of it, I mean?"

"No, I never watch my own movies on television; in fact, I make a point *not* to. I don't stay up late, for one thing, and, for another, I'd find it depressing."

The interviewer continued, "What is your 'method' or technique of acting?"

"What I enjoy, is working on a scene until I finally get it right (he drove his right fisted hand into his left palm for emphasis). It's fun to know you're hitting it. When I first consider a part, I find myself judging the script as a whole. Simultaneously, I try to decide whether I can play the part, whether it's dramatically interesting, whether I feel I can make it make sense."

"It's a mistake, I think to go for parts, as some actors do, instead of the play as a whole." Shrugging, "But then, in a way, I've liked everything I've been in. I'm kind of a dimwit. I just like to act."

When the *Newsweek* article came out September 4, 1961 the review went as follows:

A generally low-keyed study of several staffers at a small Eastern hospital, *The Young Doctors* is a critic's nightmare — a movie whose faults are more apparent, but less important, than its virtues. What counts more, though, is that the movie has a bedrock honesty and, in the performance of Fredric March, one of the neatest acting jobs of the year.

The Young Doctors has a powerful simplicity, but its chief distinction is March. Chewing his way through cigar after cigar and scene after scene, this country's most talented impersonator gives a rare kind of performance —the kind that, while clearly a performance, is so right that one feels like cheering every time he merely walks on the screen.

Stuart Millar, co-producer on *The Young Doctors*, recruited March September 1960 by sending the script and convincing him that scriptwriter Joe Hayes, whom March knew well, had expressly written the character Dr. Joseph Pearson, a crusty old pathologist, with Fredric March and only March in mind for the part. Accepting, Fred started researching at a local New York hospital before Thanksgiving 1960. *The Young Doctors* was to be filmed in New York, starting in January 1961 to end by the first week in March.

Doctors is a typical medical soap opera full of the usual operating theater histrionics. Scripted from Arthur Hailey's novel *The Final Diagnosis*, it contains, briefly, an old doctor versus a young doctor personality clash, romantic involvements between medics and nurses, a baby's life saved, and a leg amputated.   Ben Gazzara portrays the young doctor of the new order, brought into a small hospital to assist an aging pathologist, Dr. Pearson (March), and the battle begins. Dr. Pearson is a well-intentioned humanist striving hopelessly to keep abreast of his work in an era when good intentions and human warmth alone are insufficient to the challenges of medicine. Negligent, stubborn, lonely, he is destined from the outset of the story to surrender his work to the younger generation. By the film's end, they end up respecting one another.

Another staff intern was portrayed by a young Dick Clark, who commented,

The one thing that impressed me most about working with Fredric on *The Young Doctors* was his consistency of performance. If he scratched his nose in the master shot, he scratched his nose in the close-up in the exact same way. Things that appeared to be so natural and unstudied were obviously meticulously planned by him. His tone of voice, his physical movements, his bits of business were all crafted to perfection. In addition to his professionalism, I appreciated how kindly he dealt with me, knowing I was scared to death. (Letter, Dick Clark, 24 May 1990)

Arthur Hill portrayed Tomaselli, the hospital's administrator, and recalled an unusual if not surprising incident that happened during the production phase of the film. The particular scene involved an instructional episode for five student nurses. Part of Pearson's duties as head pathologist was to perform an autopsy with the nurses watching. The following quote is from Fredric March's actual script on file with the March Papers in the University of Wisconsin's Sources for Mass Communications, Film and Theater Research collection. His written comments are represented in parentheses and bold-faced.

The scene is in the autopsy room: As the nurses enter, we see each face—reactions to the corpse, which is out of view, but which each is forced to stare at, with varying reactions reflected on faces. Dr. Shawcross, the intern, is with them wondering who will faint first.

The door opens, and Dr. Pearson enters—swiftly (**cigar lighted**), all business. As he speaks, during the following, he slips into an operating room-type scrub suit, and the intern ties the strings of the apron at back. He goes to a washbasin where the intern shakes powder over his hands and holds a pair of gloves for him. By the end of the speech he has moved to the autopsy table and examined the papers which another doctor hands him. The whole proceeding has the air of a polished theatrical performance which Dr. Pearson enjoys to the hilt!

He faces the nurses, taking a deep drag on his cigar, then moves to the table. Pearson speaks (**eyes flickering over the girls**):

"You often hear people ask: What does a pathologist do? You never hear anyone ask: What does a surgeon do? (**with acid meaning**) Well, a pathologist is the one who examines the surgeon's mistakes—when it's too late."

He continues along this vein, eventually takes a knife from the instrument panel and proceeds offscreen with the autopsy. "Now that we have established that—in this specific case—the medical diagnosis was correct—we move to the cranial area."

Pearson holds up to the camera's view a sponge like object representing the cadaver's brain, continues, "I hold in my hand a human brain. Yet—what do you see—only a mass of tissue. Only a few hours ago this was the thinking center of a human being. (**long pause**) A human being." (**eyes down then up**) "Not only the *thinking center*—the coordinator of the senses—(**eyes down**) touch, smell, sight, taste.   It held *thoughts—hopes—dreams*—(**eyes up**) memories —(**eyes down**) told the eyes to cry, the mouth to speak." (**eyes up**) "This man was an engineer. (**eyes down**) This, then, was a brain that used mathematics, understood stresses, devised constructions, perhaps built houses, or highways, or *dams*, a (**eyes up**) *cathedral*—(**eyes down**) legacies from this brain to other human beings . . . to (**eyes up**) you and me. This white, male, aged 53—was a person. A human *being*." (Joseph Hayes)

March had been practicing with a counterfeit brain at rehearsals, assuming that would be used during the take. Not so. The powers that be arranged to buy an indigent's brain from another hospital on the morning that this scene was to be shot. Therefore, with the real brain carefully in place, director Phil Karlson casually mentioned to Fred, seconds before Action was to be shouted, that the brain, was, in fact, real. Arthur Hill recalled, "If you don't think *that* had an electric effect on Fredric March" (Telephone interview, Arthur Hill, 3 June 1990). Carrying on, trouper March proceeded to say his lines with more conviction than he had shown at rehearsals.

When it was released to satisfactory reviews August 23, 1961, March, again, received the lion's share. The *New York Times*, Bosley Crowther: "This aging and waning physician—played so finely by Fredric March that you have more regard and sympathy for him than anyone else in the film" (March Papers). *Los Angeles Times Calendar*: "March gives a sustained, completely un-mannered performance as the unyielding, opinionated old pro who has been at it too long; he is tired." *New York Herald Tribune*: "Fredric March gives a memorable performance as Dr. Pearson, the super annuated man at the head of a metropolitan hospital's pathology department" (Quirk 1971, 229).

While working on *The Young Doctors*, March received good news from the

American Academy of Arts and Letters. On May 24, 1961, he was to receive
the Award for Good Speech on the Stage for the year 1961. Awarded since
1924, it had recognized the most exemplary artists in American speech, the
men and women of the stage who belonged to the royal family of fine
speakers. This medal had in the past been awarded to such notables as
Walter Hampden, Judith Anderson, Otis Skinner, Julia Marlowe, George
Arliss, Ina Claire, Ethel Barrymore, Claude Rains, and Katharine Cornell.
The program involved annual ceremony and informal luncheon. The
ceremonial speech: "Fredric March, as both an actor and a man, has great
integrity—and it is, therefore, not coincidental, that so many of the vehicles in
which he has starred have had a strong social message. To Fredric
March—our gold key" (March Papers).

The summer was spent at Firefly with daughter Penny, husband Bert, and
their three children; a girl had been added, Cristina. One unfortunate event
that spring had been the death in May of Fred's college and boyhood friend
Jack Ramsey. The College Avenue gang now consisted of Fredric March;
Vinnie Hood, still of Racine; and Chuck Carpenter, of New York. The death
of such a dear friend placed a damper on their summer activities. Fred wrote
a special letter to Jack's widow, Helen (Huguenin) Ramsey, ending, "And
keep praying dear. Believe me it works—*I know*" (Letter, Fredric March to
Mrs. Ramsey, c. 1960, Jackie Ramsey Macaulay).

Toward August, March repaired to his barn in order to start memorizing a
new part in what was to be his last appearance on Broadway. He had been
cajoled out of his semiretirement (again) in order to portray the Angel of the
Lord in Paddy Chayefsky's *Gideon*. *Gideon* is the story of a farmer, Gideon,
chosen by God to become a military hero. Against his will, but with the
Angel of the Lord's help—he conquers 120,000 Midianites with only 300
Israelites. So, at age sixty-four, March played God. (Coincidentally, in his
last motion picture, *The Young Doctors*, his aging doctor character, confronted
by a difficult medical decision, turned to a colleague and said, "Who wants to
play God?") March had signed to do six months and the ribbing started
before he set foot on the rehearsal stage. "My friends have kidded me a bit.
They say things like, 'Well, where do you go from here?' or, 'So you finally
made it, Freddie, you're playing God at last'" (March Papers). Fred took a
little advantage himself, sending a birthday telegram to his goddaughter, Jane
Carpenter Post. "When you and Bob [Jane's husband] next come to New
York please let me get you seats to *Gideon* so that you can see your devoted
Godfather play God" (Telegram, Fredric March to Jane Carpenter Post, April
1962). Whether he would be in the play for six months was doubtful, for
March did not like to play the same part many times (he had given that up
after *Long Day's Journey into Night*).

Douglas Campbell, a distinguished Canadian actor, was signed for the part
of Gideon with Tyrone Guthrie directing. Rehearsals started September 11,

1961, with a three-week pre-Broadway stand at the New Locust Theater in Philadelphia October 14 through November 4, before previewing at the Plymouth on Broadway on November 7 and 8, then opening officially on November 9. Rehearsals went well once Fred gave up wearing the sandals necessary when portraying an ancient character. The stage was sharply tilted, designed to give an impression of the barren, hilly landscape of Israel and to provide a place above man for the Angel of God. Campbell played it barefoot, while Fred kept stumbling in sandals so much that they finally got him some ballet slippers. Also, one of Fred's robes weighed about fourteen pounds and got pretty hot under the lights. The makeup for the Angel was elaborate, modeled after the Michelangelo painting in the Sistine Chapel, involving a long flowing wig with beard. The whole effect managed to render Fred a fierce and forbidding figure, enough to strike terror into the heart, a godlike and awesome deity.

Gideon opened and was immediately hailed as a hit. Philadelphia reviews were typical: "In patriarchal beard and long black robes, Fredric March lends all his stentorian authority to the role of the Angel. He is sardonically impatient with the mere mortal who questions the power of the Almighty and needs reassuring signs" (March Papers). March, however, was more impressed with the portrayal of Gideon by Douglas Campbell. After the first few nights March went to the producers, Fred Coe and Arthur Cantor, and said that he had never seen a performance such as Douglas Campbell had just given, commenting that he should be starred!

"Well, that's big of you to say so, Freddie," Cantor said. "Do you mind if I pass the compliment on to Campbell?"

"But, I'm serious! I want his name to go up with mine."

March's contract read that he was to have star billing. That meant that a comparatively unknown actor in America would open on Broadway with his name on the marquee. What a Christmas present! When they told Campbell he at first looked stunned and then turned to his generous benefactor and said just, "Thank you, Lord!" (March Papers)

When *Gideon* opened November 9 on Broadway at the Plymouth, it enjoyed a packed audience and more excellent reviews. *New York Times*: "Although it has so much inherent majesty, the part of the Angel of God is subtly difficult, for it must shift constantly between human and divine dimensions. Fredric March manages these transitions and achieves a totality both warm and imposing" (March Papers). *New York Journal American*: "In his constantly assured and powerful portrayal of the deity, Fredric March displays an engaging sense of humor coupled with a fierce and unrelenting awareness of his omnipotence" (March Papers).

Before *Gideon*'s special Thanksgiving matinee, March granted an interview to *Theater Arts*. His publicist had warned the interviewer that March as he grew older, hated interviews, always feeling foolish when he read what he said to a reporter. He felt his work ought to speak for itself. The reporter managed a few quotes out of March, but not much, filling the article with his own impressions. For example, that March put on a role much as a man fit himself into a Grafton Street suit. He got the script letter perfect in his head, memorizing every last line before his first rehearsal call. Then he let the outer garment settle around him and adjusted himself to its wrinkles and creases. For instance, a Paul Newman seemed to wear his suits awkwardly, straining at the seams. March, the faultless old pro, wore them with a nonchalant attitude that never revealed his careful preparation. March did comment, "I think it's almost physically impossible to give a well-rounded performance without knowing it beforehand. To try and rehearse eight hours a day and then go home at night and knock more lines into your head—it just doesn't work. You *know* it first, then try to polish as you go along" (*Theater Arts*, 18 December 1961, March Papers).

During early spring, although still in *Gideon*, March managed to squeeze in a half hour taping of *The American Bell* by Archibald MacLeish at the Phoenix Theater to be televised April 5, 1962. By early April, he had accepted a role in a foreign film, *The Condemned of Altona*, produced by Carlo Ponti. In order to participate, he had to buy up his contract with *Gideon* then spend the summer in Germany, Italy and Greece to film the Jean-Paul Sartre play about a German shipbuilder with a hidden insane older son, reliving all his war crimes in the father's attic. March left *Gideon* by April 29 so that he could start memorizing his new role for director Vittorio de Sica. *Condemned*, poorly scripted and directed, took six weeks of filming in Hamburg and four weeks in Pisa, Italy. When it was released, a little over a year later, October 30, 1963, Bosley Crowther of the *New York Times* summed it up best: "The industrial magnate father played sternly by Fredric March . . . I am afraid the *Condemned of Altona* must be condemned to the fate of a disappointing film" (March Papers).

After production ended in early September of 1962, Fred flew with son-in-law Bert Fantacci to Greece where Florence, daughter Penny and the three grandchildren had already been vacationing for three weeks. The whole group then flew back to the Fantacci household in Florence in order for Fred and Florence to take "the waters" at Montacantini. The Marches set sail for home soon after, the best part, they felt, of any trip.

March's next film obligation was not until May of 1963, *Seven Days in May*, a screenplay by Rod Serling for Paramount. He was set to play a future president from the best-seller about an attempted takeover of the country by a military coup. Before production began, March managed to keep busy in a variety of activities. November 29, he and Florence were part of a televised program that kicked off a fund-raising campaign for the National Cultural Center on the east bank of the Potomac in Washington. With the idea that culture should be everyone's business, the two-hour televised program was broadcast from five locations: Washington, New York, Chicago, Los Angeles, and Augusta, Georgia.   Viewers in sixty-five cities saw President Kennedy enter Washington's National Armory, amid a flourish of ceremonial trumpets, and heard him give a brief talk.   The program involved dancers, instrumentalists, three orchestras, comedy routines, excerpts from dramas and singers. In New York, the main event and longest part of the entire telecast consisted of a twenty-minute segment during which Fred, Florence, Jason Robards Jr., Bradford Dillman and Colleen Dewhurst appeared in scenes and speeches from the works of Eugene O'Neill, under the direction of José Quintero.   Certain O'Neill excerpts were chosen to show his impact on American theater. Of course, Fred and Florence presented scenes from *Long Day's Journey Into Night*.

Another obligation for both Marches involved the Capitol Records series of twelve records *Life*'s History of the United States. The Marches' narrated the series, taping December 1962 until March 1964. Advertised by *Life* as the Sounds of History, each bound volume of a *Life* History was complemented by a twelve-inch 33-1/3 rpm record. On one side you hear great documents and speeches read by Fred and Florence, on the other side the great music of the various periods. Fred also participated in CBS Reports' *Storm over the Supreme Court*, parts I (February 20, 1963) and II (March 13, 1963). The program examined the court and its record; in a sense, the Supreme Court itself was on trial, with arguments for and against the high tribunal presented by three leading literary men—Carl Sandburg, Mark Van Doren, and Archibald MacLeish, all Pulitzer Prize winners in poetry and history—and actor Fredric March. They read into the record judgments and opinions by many of the great jurists who had sat on the court, as well as verbal attacks by illustrious presidents who challenged its power and authority. The second part of the documentary dealt with the court's controversial school-prayer decision. On a smaller scale, Fred recorded The Declaration of Independence April 2, 1963, for Colpix Records, then participated in the NBC television broadcast of *American Landmark: Lexington—Concord*, April 21, 1963. This NBC Special presentation of the dramatic events that sparked the Revolutionary War, narrated by March, was filmed on the historic sites of the happenings.

In early May, March proceeded to Hollywood to fulfill his picture commitment, *Seven Days in May*, which was finished in time for him to meet Penny, her husband, and the grandchildren by July 2 in New York, for it was the Fantaccis' turn to visit Firefly. *Seven Days in May* was March's first film with John Frankenheimer (director and co-producer), theirs was to remain a long and enduring friendship. March portrays the ineffectual president of the United States in this film, based on the best-selling novel by Fletcher Knebel and Charles W. Bailey II. The plot centers around a military attempt to overthrow the United States government with March finally facing up to what he has to do to stop it. Burt Lancaster and Kirk Douglas star as military leaders confronting March's president. Lancaster was cast as a reactionary general who plots a military takeover in Washington. Army Colonel Douglas suspects right-wing General Lancaster is plotting to dispose of President March and take over the government. Douglas alerts March, who then attempts to thwart the coup. Fortunately, it works. Richard Anderson (who portrayed Colonel Murdock) enjoyed watching March, remembering that, after a particularly grueling scene, March took off his suit jacket and handed it to the costumer for the next days shooting, instructing him *not* to press it but to keep it in its current state of crumple. John Frankenheimer recalled at the 1987 tribute, "He was an inspiration for everyone in that film. He held the picture together. He came beautifully prepared. He set a tone for that movie that everybody felt they had to follow. The movie went well because of that, because of him" (Fredric March Tribute, 21 September 1987, Jean Bickel Owen).

During the movie one is always aware of the eyes of Fredric March. He used his eyes in this and all his films as extraordinary actor's weapons, prompting the *Christian Science Monitor* article "The Eyes of March."

The special distinction of Mr. March's eyes is that they are not simply an efficient signaling system. They are part of the man. They burn from within. Almost against the owner's will, or so it seems, they betray a passionate hate, a rather tense love, an inordinate will, a self-consuming pain. He can stare motionlessly at an overstuffed chair, and our spines will crawl with the conflict. (March Papers)

Released February 19, 1964, *Seven* won the March 1964 Box Office Blue Ribbon Award, given each month by the National Screen Council on the basis of outstanding merit and suitability for family entertainment. Council membership comprised motion picture editors, radio and TV film commentators, representatives of better films councils, civic, educational and exhibitor organizations. March's personal reviews were, as always, matchless. *New York Times*, Bosley Crowther: "Fredric March's performance as the President is the firmest and the best. In it is reflected an awareness of the immensity of the anguish of this man" (March Papers). Judith Crist in the *New York Herald Tribune* thought he should actually run for president, "the way he wheeled and dealed this country cautiously and successfully out of crisis" (March Papers).

For the balance of 1963, March was in demand for various television projects, readings, tributes, etc. He narrated *The Saga of Western Man* for ABC, which involved a program on the year 1492, when Columbus discovered America, broadcast October 16; Rome, broadcast during November; and 1776, broadcast December 8. He joined in an International Tribute to

Eleanor Roosevelt at Lincoln Center October 16, again as narrator, marking the high point of the opening of United Nations Week. However, his most important speech was on November 24, 1963. Fredric March opened the Tribute from the Arts to the recently assassinated President John F. Kennedy. He spoke these words from his archive notes:

The wind is cold and crisp in New York this night. And outside this door, it tumbles and pursues the fallen leaves along the streets. It is what we would call "A fine fall day." If it were not the most terrible november day in history.

In any normal november, we would on this night begin to turn our thoughts, our hearts, to giving thanks to God, for the goodness of life and land. But this year instead of life there is death, instead of thanks, tragedy, in place of goodness, grief.

A president, a friend, has been struck down, our friend. As he was a friend of freedom, so he was a friend of the arts.

It was as natural to him that poets take part in his inauguration as politicians.

That the White House should echo with the sounds of music as well as those of diplomacy.

That not only the voice of the statesman but the voice of the actor be heard there. That those who write, as well as those who rule, be welcome there.

Yet, now, he is gone from us. Suddenly, swiftly. And we of the arts have come to say farewell. What wreats or gifts can we lay at the feet of the fallen hero? What can we give him in farewell more than our respect, our sorrow, our love? Those gifts he asked of us in life, the word. And what ability we have to speak it. The song. And our voices to sing it. Music. And our skill and heart to play it. These we bring him now.
(March Papers)

Nineteen sixty-four consisted of much the same type activity for Fred and Florence. They finished *Life*'s History of the United States. With his fine speaking voice March was in great demand to speak and narrate; it seemed he had reversed and gone back to the early century, when he entertained his parents' friends by "speaking pieces."

The rundown for 1964 included the following (March Papers).

January 18—Dramatic reading, Salute to Denmark Ball at the New York Hilton Hotel.
January 19—Dramatic reading *Lights On* benefit for the Fight for Sight Carnegie Hall.
January 27—Dramatic reading, Tribute to Arts, Madison Square Garden.

March 2—record 11—taped *Life*'s History.

March 13—Record 12—taped *Life*'s History.

April—five days—Both Marches' visited Yale University as Visiting Arts and Letters Fellows.

May 4—Taped a television special on the *Pieta*.

May 11—Taped for ABC-TV *The Supreme Court Decision*.

May 14—Appeared in support of the NAACP observation of its tenth anniversary of the United States Supreme Court ruling on school segregation, reading extracts from the Supreme Court decision.

May 17—"Five Days in April." Both went to Yale University as Visiting Arts and Letters Fellows.

May 23-24—Taping in Cimarron, Kansas, for NBC's Special Projects Department, Fred narrated on site, *Smalltown USA: A Farewell Portrait* to be broadcast September 18.

May 26—Taped a statement for American Heart Association 1965 Heart Fund Campaign.

May 30—Memorial Day speech in New Milford which Fred wrote: "Just as we strive with eternal vigilance to contain the enemy without—let us look into our own hearts and strike out all hatred and violence so that in this fateful summer ahead we may come closer here at home to achieving the true Brotherhood of Man!"

June/July/August —trip to Florence, Italy, to visit daughter's family.

August 31—Fredric March's 67th birthday.

September 9—Taped several messages at his New York apartment about the U.S. Treasury coin shortage for the American Bankers Association.

September 20—Participated in Lincoln Center Day, the opening of the Lincoln Center of Performing Arts.

September 21—Narrated *The Presidency: A Splendid Misery* for CBS.

October 16—Guests at the First Public Nobel Dinner at the Americana Hotel. Fred was asked to read William Faulkner's Nobel Prize acceptance speech, because no other artist of that time had been more identified with the bridge between the arts and society than had Fredric March.

November 11—Fred, via radio, spoke for hemophilia, calling for donations to the various local chapters of the National Hemophilia Foundation.

November/December —*The Artist's Eye*; Fred walked through the White House discussing the various paintings (aired January 15, 1965).

December 17—January 10—Beverly Hills to visit Bickel relatives.

January, 1965—Fred narrated *Power for a Nation* for the Department of Interior. The half hour special portrayed the importance of the power industry in the United States emphasizing the relationship of federal power production and marketing to the industry.

February 23—Fred narrated ABC-TV's special on Leonardo da Vinci.

In January of 1965, both Marches' had been recruited by the State Department (Office of Cultural Presentations) to tour eight Near Eastern countries April 2 through May 13, presenting recitations of poetry and excerpts from plays in which they had appeared in the American theater. They were to be the first husband-and-wife acting team to go abroad under the auspices of the State Department's division of cultural presentations. Given a choice of places to visit, they selected Greece, Iran, Turkey, Italy, Egypt, Afghanistan, Lebanon and Syria. In setting up their tour, someone suggested that showings might be arranged along the way of some of the films in which Fred had appeared. At this, Florence teased, "They'll come look at you and say, 'You used to be a glamour boy.'" Fred responded, "I resent the past tense!" ("Entertainment and the Arts," *Tulsa World*, 28 March–3 April 1965, March Papers).

Their itinerary covered a dozen bookings, giving twenty-three performances, entitled "An Evening with Fredric March and Florence Eldridge," beginning April 4 in Cairo and ending May 13 in Naples. A program of an hour and twenty minutes without an intermission included excerpts from three plays the couple had performed in, *Long Day's Journey into Night*, *The Skin of Our Teeth*, and *The Autumn Garden*; poems by Robert Frost as well as Alan Seeger's *I Have a Rendezvous with Death*, and Longfellow's *The Building of the Ship*. The Marches' opened at Cairo's Pocket Theater, April 5, to a spellbound audience. For the first time, most of the audience was hearing American literature and American poetry presented live. Many went out of curiosity to see Fredric March. But from the first moment, the curiosity was replaced by a response to the magic of their art.

The rest of the tour was just as successful. They arrived in New York to a heartfelt "thank you" cable sent them by Dean Rusk, the former secretary of state: "Please advise Mr. and Mrs. Fredric March that the Department congratulates and thanks them sincerely for having initiated with outstanding success a new phase in the cultural presentations program. Their highly effective performance ... has made a real contribution to the program's basic purpose of building respect for our artistic achievements and thereby to the cause of improved international understanding" (March Papers). Gratified, the Marches' quickly repaired to Firefly for a long overdue rest.

Fall encompassed various readings and speeches. On October 7, Fred introduced President Lyndon Johnson for his "Salute to Congress" speech, given at the White House. Then on October 24, as part of United Nations Day, both Fred and Florence recited quotations of Adlai Stevenson at a tribute for him. November involved a taping for the Protestant Council Show for ABC. On November 23 the Marches' were honored at the State Dinner of the Lotus Club.

December of 1965, March contemplated another movie role, to be filmed in the summer of 1966. An entirely different role presented itself: a pitiful and greedy Indian agent. The role interested him, because the closest he had gotten to a Western in all his movies had been in his characterization of Mark Twain. Although he was not in the best of health (he was sixty-eight years old), he decided to trust director Martin Ritt's judgment and try out this Western called *Hombre*, starring Paul Newman.

22

Fredric March in a Western?

May of 1966 found Fredric March in Arizona on the set of director and coproducer Martin Ritt's Western film *Hombre*. Filmed February through July of 1966, *Hombre*, physically, was not an easy film for March to make, for not only the heat of Tucson, Arizona, but the rough terrain that the little band of stagecoach passengers had to clamber about on made for a difficult environment. *Hombre* centers around a young white man (Paul Newman) brought up by Apaches. When he boards a stagecoach full of passengers he runs into two-faced Professor Favor, played by Fredric March, an old codger who laments the evils done to the Indians but has swindled a fortune as their government agent. The stagecoach is attacked by bandits (led by Richard Boone) intent on stealing Favor's loot. Newman leads them to safety in the hills, defending them from the marauders and dying gallantly.

At the 1987 tribute, Martin Ritt, *Hombre*'s capable director, was present, relating some comic anecdotes that happened on the set of *Hombre* for the audience.

One day, I went to him, "Freddie, I think this performance would be extraordinary if you play it without your teeth." And he looked at me and he said, 'That must have been an awful tough thing for you to ask.' [the tribute audience laughed] And, I've never been the recipient of too much generosity from actors. And the fact that he thought of that at that moment really sorta kinda wiped me out. And in the course of that film, I was having trouble with one of the actors. I was just about ready to tell him off . . . when up stepped Freddie and told him off right in front of me! At this, the audience again erupted into laughter. (March Tribute Movie, 27 September 1987, Jean Bickel Owen)

Hombre was not released until March 21, 1967, and received good reviews.

Variety: "Fredric March, essaying an Indian agent who embezzled food appropriations for his charges . . . scored in a strong, unsympathetic —but eventually pathetic —role" (March Papers).

Fred turned sixty-nine August 31, 1966, while enjoying his fourth grandchild, Marie, in Florence. Not many people are lucky enough to continue working most of their lives at what they enjoy, but at sixty-nine Fredric March was still active in the medium he loved. In September, he was off to Rome to narrate an ABC television special, *The Legacy of Rome*, to be broadcast November 25. After this, Fred settled back into semiretirement with Florence at Firefly. Both Marches announced that they would star in a CBS Playhouse drama, *Do Not Go Gentle into the Good Night* for a fall release, but Fred's health prevented it. Traveling when they could, they both still read an occasional script, but mainly enjoyed the company of their New Milford neighbors and the many visits by their California nieces and nephews; Fred's godchild, Jane Carpenter Post; and Penny and Bert and family from Italy.

On January 30, 1968, Fred starred with Helen Hayes, Henry Fonda, Robert Ryan, and Andy Williams in the Inaugural Program for Ford's Theater in Washington, D.C.   The theater had not been open since the fateful assassination of Lincoln on April 14, 1865. After this he was involved with a Tribute to Pablo Casals at the 28th Anniversary Dinner of Freedom House, April 8. As he had cut down dramatically on his speaking appearances and television, the Marches planned to give up their New York apartment in fall 1968 and move completely to Firefly.

In December of 1967, Fred was informed that he was to receive the 1968 Distinguished Service Award from the University of Wisconsin.   The committee chose from 200 nominees who had served the university well and loyally, those who gave back to the institution throughout their careers. The award was to be conferred May 18, 1968, and wild horses could not stop Fredric March from attending. So plans were made for him by his Madison friends, Larry and Virginia Hall, to stay at the Governor's Mansion in Madison, where he would meet his brother, Jack.

When Fred and Florence arrived in Madison to receive his Distinguished Service Award, his brother Jack had already arrived. They were a day early, so the brothers left Florence in Madison, rented a car and drove to their old home-town of Racine to discover whether anything was still familiar. They decided to pop in on Fred's boyhood friend, Vinnie Hood, who still worked at a bank in Racine as a vice president. They had not seen Vinnie since their father's funeral in 1941. Vinnie reminisced, "I left the bank early, but told the guard I'd be back at 4:00 p.m. When I arrived, the guard told me I had a couple visitors to see me, so I walked further into the hall looking for them. I stopped just inside the door and my hat was grabbed off my head, then I heard Fred Bickel exclaim, 'My God! He's got all his hair!'" (Interview, Vinnie Hood, 27 January 1990).

With salutations all around, the trio toured the town, all their old haunts and their College Avenue homes. After a pleasant late afternoon gab session, the Bickels said their good-byes and drove back to Madison. Vinnie would never see either of them again. That night after a dinner with Virginia and Larry Hall, the two brothers headed to the governor's residence but did not go to bed until the early morning hours reflecting on their university days. Jack went downstairs for some reason, and on his return, fell up the stairs breaking his arm in the process. He yelled for Fred, and the two managed to get him back to his room. Fred, not knowing what he should do, at 5:00 a.m. called Larry Hall, who drove right over with their neighbor, who was a doctor. Therefore, Jack attended the ceremonial dinner with his arm in a cast and an uncharacteristically solemn Fred occasionally winked at him from behind his wine glass. Normally, the inductees did not speak, but Fred wanted to respond. There happened to be a large crowd at the dinner particularly because of the presence of Fredric March and the audience was quite in awe of him. His speech was a thoughtful, slow, carefully measured presentation, not laborious, though. He received a standing ovation.

A party was held in March's honor that evening. All at the party were aware that Fred was never left alone by Florence for any length of time. As she had during the filming of *Inherit the Wind*, Florence hovered around Fred and generally dominated conversations. He was quiet, not the Fred that the group knew when she was around. Larry Hall's wife, Virginia, recalled a severe Mrs. March:

Florence was very hard to know. She was a very difficult person. You didn't feel folksy with her at all. Fred was obviously very afraid of Florence it seemed to me. She never had much to offer to the group. When she did talk, she talked about world problems. My husband discussed something, I don't remember what, and she put him in his place in a hurry! It was terrible, my husband was quiet immediately. I was amazed. She was very rude and unkind. Fred didn't do anything. (Interview, Virginia Hall, 18 May 1990)

The minute Florence left the room, he miraculously reverted to the old Fred Bickel the group remembered. After Fred's return to Firefly, he did send Larry and Virginia a personal thank you (3 December 1968):

Dear Virginia & Larry:
  It's impossible to thank you enough for your *many* kindnesses. It was grand to have Jack but I do wish Florence might have been with me. (Oh! The fun I've had recounting to her the whole great experience).
  You are two of the grandest people I know. And I am deeply grateful to you. Much love, Freddie

March's next film commitment was a result of not being able to resist the script. Filming on MGM's *tick . . . tick . . . tick* started in February 1969, ending in May. At seventy-one, he hadn't been in a film for three years. "My wife has had great fun kidding me about becoming unretired. But I just couldn't resist this script. I've never said, like Cagney, 'Boom—I'm finished'" (March Papers). In *tick*, March portrays a Southern small town mayor who is forced to examine his lifelong beliefs when his community elects a black sheriff. March remarked, "This old mayor I'm playing is determined there's not going to be any trouble. The NAACP or Federal troops or anybody is not going to be called in." March compared the situation with the election of civil rights leader Charles Evers as mayor of Fayette, Mississippi. The key players, the new sheriff (Jim Brown), the outgoing sheriff (George Kennedy), and March as mayor were sitting on a racial time bomb, thus the title.

Released February 17, 1970, it revealed a still spirited Fredric March performance. Lawrence Quirk: "An alert, sharp March was plainly in top form, and his interpretation of Mayor Parks was filled with the creative insights and individual touches which have always distinguished his performances. The year the film was released, 1970, saw March celebrating his 50th year as an actor and his 41st in films" (March Papers). Richard Schickel, *Life*: "The best thing about the film is the presence of Fredric March, too long away and certainly deserving of something more interesting to play than the crusty major of a dusty small town" (March Papers).

At this time of his life, Fredric March started experiencing some health problems: a slight hearing loss, need for a cane for balance, prostate surgery, and a few small strokes. The strokes and consequences, their continued presence in his life, eventually were to cause his death in 1975. From 1970 on, Fred needed to slow down and was content with his life at Firefly with Florence. However, he still traveled, managing Mexico for two months in the winter of 1969-70, and planned to attend the fifty year class reunion at his university on May 15, 1970. Virginia and Larry Hall made all the arrangements for the Marches' visit. Chuck Carpenter and his wife were also to attend. In advance of the time honored event, Fred and Chuck corresponded, scheming their return to the reunion via the reintroduction of their last Union Vodvil act, presented in spring 1920. Naturally, the act was the highlight of the reunion—brought down the Maple Bluff Country Club's roof on the hundred or so remaining classmates and their spouses. During the alumni luncheon, Fred delighted his audience with a few quips about being "survivors,"and said he liked to think of the University of Wisconsin as "On Wisconsin." "I think we need the "on,"and believe that this, too, shall pass [referring to campus anti–Viet Nam War demonstration disturbances], and that we'll come back for our 60th reunion for an on-on-on Wisconsin!" (March Papers). It was at this reunion that Fred asked Virginia whether his college sweetheart and first (if not only) love, Aline, was present. Unfortunately, she did not attend any of their reunions, possibly afraid of seeing Fred and her reaction to him. Aline died in 1984. She never saw Fred after June 1920.

Perhaps the greatest honor ever bestowed on Fredric March was the naming of a five-hundred–seat theater after him on October 15, 1971, at the University of Wisconsin branch in Oshkosh, Wisconsin. He considered it the "Thrill of my life. Many have gotten Oscars, but not many have had a theater named after them" (March Papers). A $7,000,000 million Arts and Communication Center was to be named after and dedicated to Fredric March. Dr. James Hawes, coordinator of theater in 1971, said, "The staff desired to name the theater after Fredric March because they wanted to honor a Wisconsin theater luminary and he seemed the logical choice since he has not been so honored. March was at the head of the list and there were no other real contenders" (Telephone interview, Dr. James Hawes, 29 December 1990). Two others had been mentioned —Don Ameche, a native of Kenosha, and Spencer Tracy, born in Milwaukee. Tracy, however, achieved fame almost entirely in motion pictures and had little stage experience.

Before opening night, the Marches' held a press conference followed by an informal question and answer session with students. When Fred and Florence arrived, he had his ever present cane, walked slowly and often cupped his hand behind his ear to hear better, puffing on an occasional pipe. The coordinator of theater at Oshkosh was present and noted that it was obvious during his stay that he was physically quite frail. The press conference featured reflections on his long career, and the question and answer student period revealed an exceedingly intelligent Fredric March. He was friendly and warm to interviewers and students who asked him questions. At the beginning, he told the audience to speak up, remarking, "For example, we don't go to movies too often, anymore. I'm a little hard of hearing and I don't get what it's all about sometimes, so I ask my wife to explain it on the way home" (March Papers).

Florence said, "What I can't explain, I make up" (March Papers).

Fred often turned his comments into script he remembered from his movies and plays. His eyes bulged when he spoke of Mr. Hyde and his mouth would twist.

About *Inherit the Wind*: "I think I did overplay that part a bit," Fred admitted. He blamed his overacting on Spencer Tracy. He said Tracy and he always tried to outact each other "just for fun" (March Papers). Now that Tracy was dead, the only actor left good enough for Fred to upstage was himself.

In answering one student's question about his style, he contrasted his methods with those of fellow actors. "Gary Cooper, Clark Gable, Cary Grant . . . even Bogart . . . all played themselves. I always played the character" (March Papers).

When asked his opinion of the Oscar, March said he felt the meaning of the award had diminished. "It's become more of a circus thing today. It's very political, I think, because the studios and the actors realize that there's more money in an Oscar-winning film." Fred added that actors who were nominated often took out ads in newspapers asking the Academy to vote for them. "We *never* did anything like that."

When asked which he preferred making, movies or live theater, he remarked, "Pictures are physically tiring; the theater is mentally tiring. Pictures last, the theater is built on sand. But I am grateful for my theater experience" (March Papers).

He singled out *The Best Years of Our Lives* as his favorite movie role and *Long Day's Journey into Night* as his favorite stage play. He considered work in television "an awful experience" (March Papers).

When asked what his next picture would be, he said, "I like to think I'm retired, that I quit while I was ahead. I had an awful good run for my money" (March Papers).

A student raised his hand, asking one final question: "What do you think of our theater?"

March smiled warmly, "It is magnificent. It's just beyond words" (March Papers).

He left a recent photograph of himself with the theater to display. The inscription read, "You have a marvelous theater. Fill it with work and joy. Good Luck, Fredric March, October 14, 1971" (March Papers).

The Marches' were to be honored guests for the opening night production of Friedrich Duerrenmatt's *The Visit*. Opening night would be by invitation only. After the final curtain, there would be a dedication ceremony and a reception for the audience and cast. At the dedication, Dr. Hawes stood alone on the stage in front of a packed audience, introducing the honoree with, "I need only say two words to introduce our distinguished guest—Fredric March." The audience erupted with cheers and applause while Fred walked proudly, without the aid of his cane, onto the stage to join Dr. Hawes. Florence, who was in the audience with Dr. Hawes's wife, turned to her in astonishment, "He walked without his cane. Freddie is never without his cane!" (March Papers). The reception was held in the small Experimental Theater, which was decorated with large photographs of plays and films in which Fred had appeared.

Well, March may have thought he retired, but after prodding by Florence and longtime friend John Cromwell, he accepted a part in the American Film Theater's production of *The Iceman Cometh*. *Iceman* was the first of in the eight play series. Also, Fred's respect for John Frankenheimer's directorial ability was a major factor in the actor's decision to leave his beloved Firefly Farm for Hollywood to work in an adaptation of Eugene O'Neill's play about the frequenters of a Manhattan bar, circa 1912. March was to portray the tough old bar owner, Harry Hope, in this four-hour version of the play starring Lee Marvin as Hickey. Hope, proprietor of a saloon and rooming house, is sixty, white-haired, so thin the description "bag of bones" is made for him. He has the face of an old balky family horse, prone to tantrums. Hope is one of those men whom everyone likes on sight, a soft-hearted slob, without malice, feeling superior to no one, a born easy mark for any appeal. He attempts to hide his defenselessness behind a testy belligerent manner, but this has never fooled anyone. He is a little deaf, but not half as deaf as he sometimes pretends. His sight is failing but is not as bad as he complains. He wears five-and-ten-cent-store spectacles which are so out of alignment that one eye at times peers half over one glass while the other eye looks half under the other. He has badly fitting store teeth, which click when he begins to fume. He is dressed in an old coat from one suit and pants from another. March was perfect for the role.

To John Frankenheimer's mind, Fredric March *was* the only Harry Hope for his film, enough to insure the frail actor out of his own pocket. Shooting was to start January 2, 1973, with principal photography ending by February 23. March accepted the part, but suffered another stroke just before Christmas landing him in the hospital. At the 1987 tribute, John Frankenheimer revealed,

I came by to see him and the thing I dreaded more than anything was the fact that Freddie couldn't do it, that he would be too sick to do the part. And I went there hoping to convince him that, above all, that I would hold the picture back, I just wanted him so desperately to do it. We walked into the Hospital and there was Freddie sitting up in bed. He said, "Now look! I know these lines. I can do it. I'll be there whenever you want. I just want to *do* the picture!" (Fredric March Tribute Movie, 21 September 1987, Jean Bickel Owen)

The Iceman Cometh was an ordeal for Fredric March. He was physically deteriorating before the camera's eyes. It was painful for him to walk, so he shuffled—even did a small jig (when asked why he let himself do that painful jig, he replied, "Because it was in the script"). The part of Harry Hope called up the consummate actor, for he may not have been well, but he knew every speech and would not cause delays on the set although the production catered to him, working around him.

Once actual filming got under way, Bradford Dillman, who played Willie Oban in this production, was shocked when he saw the extraordinary actor who had once played James Tyrone, Sr. Dillman commented,

A giant had suddenly become a rather frightened, frail old man. He had absolutely no energy. When he came in—you could hardly hear him—zero energy. He would sit by himself and the members of the cast, without being told, were sensitive enough to know you don't go over and engage in pleasantries, just leave him alone. But once Frankenheimer would call ACTION—Freddie would get to his feet, take a deep breath and all that old energy would come pouring out—then CUT—and he would sink into his chair exhausted. What a courageous man he was. (Interview, Bradford Dillman, 11 August 1990)

Because of the exceptional circumstances, many considered *Iceman* Fredric March's best performance in his long life of performances. When it was released October 31, 1973, Frankenheimer's choice for Harry Hope had not let him down. The *Baltimore Sun*: "Mr. March has repeatedly proved himself to be one of this country's most dependable actors. And here, in the role of a flabby, slack-jawed old man, he again displays those superlative qualities that made his portrayal of the elder Tyrone in the original Broadway version of O'Neill's *Long Day's Journey into Night* so remarkable" (March Papers). Pauline Kael, The *New Yorker*:

Fredric March can let the muscles in his face sag to hell to show a character falling apart. He interprets Harry Hope (who could be a dismal bore) with so much quiet tenderness and skill that when Harry regains his illusions and we see March's muscles tone up we don't know whether to smile for the character or for the actor. March is such an honorable actor; he's had a long and distinguished career. On the stage since 1920, in movies since 1929, and at 76 he goes on taking difficult roles; he's not out doing TV commercials or grabbing a series. (March Papers)

Phil Gersh, Fred's agent, was contacted by Jim Beam when they heard Fredric March was at the Beverly Wilshire Hotel during the making of *Iceman*. They wanted to hire Mr. March for a half hour's photographic session. Phil picked Fred up at the hotel and waited for him while he had his picture taken seated next to Mike Connors, of *Mannix* fame, both holding glasses of, presumably, Jim Beam whiskey. The ad was to appear in several magazines over the summer months of 1973. At the end of the shooting, JIM BEAM personnel handed Fred a check for $10,000. Phil recalled Fred shaking his head, not believing anyone would pay that much for a half hour of work. This was Fredric March's last job. Frail and spent from *Iceman*, he flew gratefully back to Firefly, heartsick though, because he knew he must sell the forty-acre place he and Florence loved dearly.

23

Illness

June 7 1973, Fred wrote to high school and college friend Chuck Carpenter about his health difficulties: "I had another inner-ear attack 2 months ago & cannot get over my constant dizziness. Some friends said not to worry that nearly everyone goes thru life a bit dizzy!"

The months of August and September were spent on the Incres Luxury Cruise Lines HMS *Victoria* on a two-week fjord cruise to the North Cape—Helsinki, Leningrad, etc. Daughter Penny and her husband Bert, and their four children were along, and of course, Florence. Fred wrote to his brother Jack often while on this voyage, for Jack had cancer and was expected to die soon. (Jack Bickel letters courtesy of daughter Jane Morris):

August 3, 1973—Bert is a real angel and always has a strong right arm to help me shuffle along. This a.m. he got me a wheel chair and pushed me around Bergen (Norway). Tomorrow is Oslo.

August 6, 1973—I'm alone in our cabin waiting for the 1:30 lunch bell. All the other 7 were off by under an hour ago to see Denmark. They'll be back after 5:00 as we sail for Helsinki at 6:00.

By August 16, the Marches' ended their cruise and checked into the Hotel President Terme in Abano (near Padua), Italy. Fred continued to write to Jack.

August 16, 1973—This is what I would call "My Last Trip." I'm too old for this (almost 76) shuffling-along business—wheel chairs at every stop business, etc. Bert and the boys have been wonderful. Gianni wheeled me thru the Hermitage at Leningrad and Michael thru the Frognes Park at Oslo (in the rain). All of them—& Flo—have been so damn kind to me, but it's a trip I should have taken 10 or 12 years ago.

August 24, 1973—I got driven to Verona and saw a *superb* ballet of "Cinderella" 2 nites ago. We leave here for Milan on the 5th and fly home on the 6th. We'll be at the Westbury that nite and back to N. Milford on 9/8.

September 1, 1973—The kids (6) all drove up from Florence yesterday and I had a wonderful B/day. They brot me a tie and shirt and 2 fine magnifying glasses w. lights (battery) in them so I can read the paper. Can hardly wait to talk to you.

September 9, 1973—Back home at Firefly—Golly!! Do I have a desk full of stuff—(not *all* B/day cards). I'll catch up slowly. Found your envelope of old pics and articles, some of which are great—especially my letter to you of 1907. I was only 10 and you were 15.

Fred's letters were a delight for his brother Jack during his declining days. Fred visited Jack and wife Mary at their Myrtle Beach home at the end of September. Fred's letter to Chuck Carpenter revealed the grave situation.

October 15, 1973—Flo and I are back from Wash DC after a 4 day convention on our Foreign Policy sponsored by the Santa Barbara Think tank of Robert Hutchins (an Alpha Delt). It was very interesting, but I have a hard time hearing. Before that we flew to So. Carolina where Jack & Mary are at Myrtle Beach. He is almost through poor devil. Phoned Mary yesterday and find he's in the Infirmary with a short time to go. So glad we visited him 10 days ago. Flo & I leave for our little condominium in Cal on Nov. 1st. Come see us. We love you. Fred

John (Jack) Bickel died November 3, at the age of 81. Jack's death was exceptionally hard on Fred, possibly leading to the debilitating stroke he suffered soon after moving to Los Angeles. This stroke left him extremely weak and partially paralyzed. He went steadily downhill from that point on. In a letter to Chuck with poor handwriting on May 11, 1974.

Dear Chuck,
Excuse mistakes in this letter but it's the 1st I've written since last November. That's when I had my stroke. Just after we got here last November I had my stroke and I still have nurses day and nite. Flo is a dream-boat and loves to cook. Thank God. My brother Jack died of Cancer a couple months ago. It hit me very hard. He and Harold both went of cancer. Hell! Can't I give you any good news!! Yes I can—you've still got Joy and I've got Florence. As Ever, Fred

Summer at Firefly, 1974, was an impossibility because of Fred's failing health so their beloved Connecticut farm that they had called home since 1939 was sold to Lady Keith, the former Slim Hawks Hayward. By July, Fred was in the hospital again, undergoing treatment for the cancer that had claimed both his brothers. Christmas was spent in their Los Angeles condo on South Barrington. Normally, Fred and Florence would have spent it with his niece, Jean Bickel Owen, in Pasadena, but because of suffering yet *another stroke* in late November, forcing him into the hospital for three weeks, Jean and husband David necessarily visited the Marches. It was Fredric March's last Christmas. A letter to Chuck Carpenter reveals his dejection.

January 11, 1975—Dear Chuck, You're the only one I write to. Hope you can read me. Saw the Vikings play and lost money on them. What I call a lousy game. So much love to you & all of yours. Ever, Fred.

Fredric March's final letter, in response to a letter from steadfast college friend, Larry Hall concerned their upcoming sixty year class reunion.

> 241 So. Barrington
> Los Angeles, Cal
> 90049
> Feby 1, 1975

Dear ole Larry—

Such a good letter from you—enclosing Sunnys.

I've had a stroke & write very *seldom*. At times I drop Chuck a line once in a while & hear from him quite often. He'd like me to write more but it's a real chore. No more films for me I fear, but I hope I'll be able to go to our next Reunion. At the moment, I doubt it, but I'm going to hope. Who is our Vice-President? Was it Phyllis Hale & is she still living? Maybe you'll have to take over.

We've moved out here but I certainly cannot do any more films!! I write Chuck & you but I don't know if you can read me. Give my love to your beautiful wife & please *stay well.* Ever yours in 1920. (My best to Sunny Ray.)

Please stay well.

> Aye
> *Freddie*

Fred entered Mt. Sinai Hospital on April 4, 1975; he died of kidney failure ten days later, April 14, 1975, at 10:30 a.m. with Florence by his side. He had previously specifically requested that no funeral or memorial service be held for him (he was cremated and buried on Firefly Farm, where a tree was planted to mark his grave—"Freddie's Tree" marked the plaque). The newspapers across America carried his death to millions on April 15. There were the usual accolades, two-time Oscar winner, two-time Tony winner, brief career history, survivors and quotes such as "He often was considered the archetypal American family man caught in the crises of modern life," or typically, "Fredric March, the magnetic actor renowned for his many film and stage appearances, an actor equipped with physical charm and intelligence, is dead at 77" (March Folder).

Current Biography listed Fredric March as born August 31, 1897; died April 14, 1975, a prolific, versatile, and highly skilled star of stage and motion pictures. But phrases such as these, though accurate, do nothing to recreate the vibrant, brilliant actor that Fredric March was. As Stanley Kramer remarked, "My God . . . he was a Titan!" (Interview, Stanley Kramer, 10 August 1990). Whether he had us laughing or crying, Fredric March truly touched many lives in all his roles. By far the best obituary was written by Larry Swindell (for *Inquirer*, 1975). Marjorie Main, Larry Parks and Richard Conte died within days of Fredric March at the time of Swindell's article:

> We mourn the Parkses and Contes and the Marjorie Mains but we adjust to their absence — we're adjusted already, for their replacements if not their counterparts were already long on the scene.
> But then a Fredric March dies and there can be no adjustment. The loss is permanent because the man was a giant of his profession, and indeed is irreplaceable.
> Fredric March was one of the verities of the screen. He always seemed to be there when we needed him, and we never stopped needing him. It was a comfort just to know he was still around.
> He's gone now . . . we can say of Fredric March what Damon Runyon once said of the jockey Earl Sande, 'Maybe there'll be another . . . maybe in a hundred years . . . and maybe not. (March Folder)

The man and the actor were special and especially talented.

Florence sent a photo of her "Freddie" taken just before his death to friends and relatives, with the following inscription:

> He wore his jaunty neckerchief to the end, as gallantly as ever Cyrano his white plume. Once, before his last two days of quiet, peaceful sleep, his spirit faltered for a moment, but even then, he thought of others as was his wont, and his prayer was, "God, help us *All*. (Courtesy Jean Bickel Owen).

Fredric March never made it to his university's sixtieth reunion. However, his friends from college days were not about to let his greatness be forgotten.

Epilogue

Scene: The Old Play Circle Theater at the University of Wisconsin, Madison, October 5, 1978, at the memorial union that Frederick Bickel helped raise funds for in 1920. The Play Circle Theater had just been renovated with funds raised by members of Fred's class of 1920 and renamed the "Fredric March Play Circle" in his honor. The atmosphere was emotional, as Porter Butts, Union Director emeritus, stood behind the podium before the small audience gathered in the rechristened theater, an audience that included many March relatives, in particular, Florence Eldridge and Penelope March Fantacci.

Porter scanned the audience,

Welcome. I came to the campus as a freshman in the fall of 1920, just three months after Fredric March left. But he was already a legendary figure—active member of our Union Board; manager of the football team; president of the Class of 1920, leading the first of all the class campaigns to raise funds for the Union; actor in many campus plays; a founder of National Collegiate Players; and the star of the Union Vodvil show, winning three silver cups for his performances, the first in 1918, a one-man act called "Where Has the Coal Bin?" (March Dedication Speech, 5 October 1978, introduction by Porter Butts, March Papers)

The audience laughed appreciatively. Waiting for them to quiet down, Porter continued,

In those days, the University administration at the time couldn't have cared less about providing theater facilities. I found that out because I also was in Union Vodvil and when I got the chance to change things in the 1930s, I and my Union associates, with universal support from the student body, planned for this theater wing of the Union. All we needed was money. And Fredric March was one of our best helpers by contributing enough funds, personally, to equip this Play Circle with a lighting system. In 1959 this University awarded Fredric March an Honorary degree and that citation read at his award means even more, now. (March Dedication Speech, 5 October 1978, introduction by Porter Butts, March Papers)

Porter cleared his throat and read:

Always identified with plays and pictures of the highest quality, he has achieved many unforgettable artistic triumphs . . . His versatile acting career spanning four decades of American stage, screen, radio and television, is without parallel in the entertainment world. Long ago, he achieved the immortality of universal recognition as a star of the first magnitude. (March Dedication Speech, 5 October 1978, introduction by Porter Butts, March Papers)

Applause broke out over the audience. After the commotion died down, Porter introduced the other speakers, each of whom had fond remembrances of Fredric March. March's daughter, Penny, donated a copy of an oil painting of her father as Major Joppolo featured in the stage setting of *A Bell for Adano* to hang outside the Play Circle. Florence presented $15,000 to the University to set up the Fredric March Scholarship fund for the Department of Theater and Drama. The first recipient was Merilee Wertlake.

The final curtain had come down on Fredric March. Lawrence Quirk, author of *The Films of Fredric March*, wrote that March's power to lose himself in a characterization, and yet retain the distinctive March personality magic, was characteristic of the acting gift he brought to the screen. March stamped his screen performances with naturalness of interpretation and effortlessness in character delineation, acting so artful and subtle, so skillfully underplayed, that it hardly seemed like acting at all. In other words, March was not just an actor; he was *too* good an actor, submerging himself so into the various characters, that he was not recognizable, or remembered —only the portrayals, those wonderful portrayals. And what better praise for an actor, than that of creating for his audience so perfect a characterization that they remember only, Dr. Harry Jekyll, Mr. Hyde, Death, Count Vronsky, Anthony Adverse, Jean Valjean, Bothwell, Norman Maine, Dr. Spence, Mark Twain, Al Stephenson, Willy Loman, Dan Hilliard, James Tyrone, Matthew Harrison Brady, and, finally, Harry Hope.

March never retired fully, prompting Bradford Dillman, who appeared with March in *Long Day's Journey into Night*, to comment, "I thought my career would be like Freddie's. You just grow older and take on more character parts, but such is not the case. No one today wants actors like that" (Interview, Bradford Dillman, 11 August 1990).

Once asked about typecasting in Hollywood of the thirties, March replied, "For a while I was tired of costume parts . . . no, I never *really* worried about typecasting. I always wanted to characterize. To me, it's the whole fun of acting. I like to imitate, maybe too much at times. These young actors, you don't find them fiddling around, putting on beards and so forth—and damn it, I think it takes a lot of the fun out of it. Every part is a character part" (March Papers).

Although March regularly outclassed his costars without upstaging them, he did represent an element of danger, seldom yielding to his fellow players the right to do more than respond to his performances. Therefore, many of his best lines were delivered into the air, with audience attention focused of necessity on his face and not on those to whom he was speaking. His was a talent of small touches combined to create a performance, his genius depending on his appreciation of the nature of small details to a screen actor. No one understood better than he that madness was best indicated by an almost undetectable tic, that a quick and sly smile could suggest more than what was actually said, and that one must relax into the role even when great intensity was required. Another of his special abilities was to suggest genuine mental pain, for, as a portrayer of tortured and distressed men, he had no equal. The complete physical control that allowed him to depict these traits convincingly was assisted by a face suggesting both intelligence and sensitivity. He had no master in the art of the disenchanted and rueful smile.

John Simon, writing for *Esquire* in December 1980:

March understood beautifully that less is more, that one must relax into the role even when—perhaps especially when—great intensity is required. . . . Most important, March had no discernible mannerisms, vocal, facial, or gestural. He simply—but this is no easy simplicity—poured himself into the role until the role said "When." Whether in romantic leads or in modern dress, March was easily, manfully in command. He made the transitions from juvenile to leading man to character actor with elegant facility and was just as good in the lower-and middle-class world of *The Best Years of Our Lives* as in the uppermost reaches of *Executive Suite*. "A fine and constantly growing actor" is how Stanley Kauffmann described him at an age when other actors have long since solidified into a mold; thanks to reruns of his movies, March keeps growing even after death. (March Folder)

His daughter, Penny, wrote in 1990, "As for his fame, I presume that it gave him pleasure because he certainly worked at his profession as diligently as he could. And the consequent fame was a gratifying return on a job well done.

But he never was anything but modest and when he received VIP treatment which, of course, he (then) did, he was always very appreciative and *never* asked for it himself" (Letter, Penelope March Fantacci, 26 September 1990).

When recalling favorite male actors of the "Golden Years," such as Bogart, Gable, Cooper, and Tracy, all were screen heroes who shaped their careers by projecting an image, in other words, projecting their own personality. If they were to continue to be popular, they routinely ended up portraying themselves in film after film. For example, one went to a Tracy film and expected Tracy to be Tracy in every film—that was his popularity. March, however, endeavored to create a new characterization for each role by concealing his own personality. He needed to become the individual he was portraying so that reviewers and audiences could not say, "March is doing a wonderful job as Mark Twain," but say, instead, "God, this really *is* Mark Twain; I hardly recognize March in the part." In 1957, during his long Broadway run as James Tyrone, Sr., in Eugene O'Neill's *Long Day's Journey into Night* (his second Tony), March commented, "To give an adequate performance, an actor must cast off his own identity and become the person he is portraying; that is, at least while on stage. That has been my compelling concern; to lose my own self in the role I am playing" (*Hartford Times*, 26 June 1957, March Papers).

March never became the folk hero that Tracy and Gable and Cooper and Bogart had been; however, he was their equal in prestige but not in personality. Why? Because, Fredric March was a craftsman. He might have settled for superstardom, but instead sought to become a renowned actor. Knowing that in achieving this he must forsake the other, he never regretted his choice.

José Quintero, director of *Long Day's Journey into Night*, wrote a memorial in the form of a personal letter that appeared in *Playbill*, August 1975. This letter is Fredric March's epitaph:

Dear Freddie,
  I remember our first reading of the play in the barn which you had converted into a large, spacious apartment. It was during that reading that I got the first clue to your genius. You asked me whether I wanted James Tyrone to have a slight brogue all the way through the play. I answered, "I don't know."
  "Neither do I," you said "but we mustn't forget that he was pure potato-famine Irish, and regardless of how he tried to disguise it, he wouldn't really forget anything, not even his brogue." I had never seen anybody work so intensively and relentlessly on a part. You began the play impeccably dressed, speaking in pure, perfect stage-English. Then slowly, every day a little more, I saw you, I felt you, peel away all facade until we got to the last act, when all facade had been peeled off, that you used the

sad, remembered song of an Irish brogue. And that's why Freddie, the
fortunate people who saw your monumental creation cried for you, tears
for the joy lost, tears for the happiness wasted.

I have seen other great, great actors perform James Tyrone in other
productions of *Long Day's Journey into Night*. And with all due respect,
I will have to tap them on the shoulder and say, "Excuse me, your
lordship. Let's step aside and let the one and only James Tyrone pass by."

So long Freddie.
José (Playbill, "On Stage," José Quintero, August 1975, 23)

Fredric March was honored posthumously at a joint tribute to the actor
from the Academy of Motion Picture Arts and Sciences and the American
Cinematheque, September 21, 1987. Moderator Norman Corwin closed the
ceremony with "Fredric March was an actor for all time, a citizen of the
world, a man who wore stardom lightly, in short, an American classic."
Hollywood, at last, had paid a long overdue homage to one of its classiest,
most underrated giants. The stature, the grace, the power of Fredric March:
craftsman first, star second.

Appendix A

Selected Plays

PLAYS ON BROADWAY

Debura. December 23, 1920. A tragicomedy in four acts adapted by Granville Barker from the French of Sacha Guitry. Produced by David Belasco at the Belasco Theater.

Cast: Lionel Atwill, Elsie Mackay, Bernard A. Reinold, Hubert Druce, Joseph Herbert, Rowland Buckstone, Margot Kelly, Pauline Merriam, Marie Bryar, Isabel Leighton, Edmund Gurney, Sidney Toler, Helen Reimer, Lydia Burnand, St. Clair Bayfield, Eden Gray, Rose Coghlan, John Roche, Sallie Bergman, Georgie Ryan, Morgan Farley, John L. Shine, **Frederick Bickel**, Robert Roland.

The Lawbreaker. February 1, 1922. A melodrama in four acts by Jules Eckert Goodman. Produced by William A. Brady at the Booth Theater.

Cast: Frank Sheridan, Clifford Dempsey, John Cromwell, **Frederick Bickel**, William Courtenay, Morgan Wallace, Frank Sylvester, John Milton, Herbert Rathke, Blanche Yurka, Marguerite Maxwell.

The Melody Man. May 13, 1924. A comedy in three acts by Herbert Richard Lorenz. Staged by Lawrence Marston and Alexander Leftwich at the Ritz Theater.

Cast: Eleanor Rome, Jerry Devine, Fred Starwer, Joe Lindwurm, Dave Stryker, Al Schenck, Bill Tulker, Louise Kelley, Eva Pulk, Donald Gallaher, Sam White, Renee Noel, Betty Weston, **Fredric March**, Lew Fields, Jules Jordan, Joseph Torpey, Sara Chapelle, Jimmy Kapper.

Puppets. March 9, 1925. A melodrama in three acts by Frances Lightner. Produced by Brock Pemberton at the Selwyn Theater, New York.

Cast: Ralph J. Locke, **Fredric March**, Michelette Buroni, Frank McDonald, Remo Bufano, Ascanio Spolidaro, Florence Koehler, Dwight Frye, C. Henry Gordon, Elizabeth Taylor, Miriam Hopkins, Stanley Grand, Charles D. Brown, Alexis M. Polianov.

Harvest. September 19, 1925. A play in three acts by Kate Horton. Produced by Messrs. Shubert in association with John Cromwell at the Belmont Theater, New York.
Cast: Louise Closser Hale, Elmer Cornell, Augustin Duncan, Ethel Taylor, Hilda Sprong, Wallace Erskine, **Fredric March**, Ronald Savery.

The Half-Caste. March 29, 1926. A play in three acts by Jack McClellan. Produced at the National Theater, New York.
Cast: John Gray, William Ingersoll, Isabel O'Madigan, Helenka Adamowska, Gertrude Moran, John O'Meara, Charles Lawrence, **Fredric March**, Veronica, Morris Armor, William Herring, Mabel Morgan, Bernice Hampshire, Leone Merriam, Virginia Bedford, Silvia Stoll, Henry Clark, David Munson, Charles Opunul, David Manaku, Gordon St. Cloud, James Kulalia, Frederick Perry, John O'Meara.

The Devil in the Cheese. December 29, 1926. A fantastic comedy in three acts by Tom Cushing. Produced by Charles Hopkins at the Charles Hopkins Theater, New York.
Cast: **Fredric March**, Dwight Frye, Robert McWade, Catherine Calhun Doucet, Linda Watkins, George Riddell, Bela Lugosi, Earl MacDonald, Frank Norman Hearn, Earl MacDonald Hooper Bunch, Joseph Hazel.

Yr. Obedient Husband. January 10, 1938. A comedy in three acts by Horace Jackson. Produced by Marwell Productions, Inc. (March/Cromwell) at the Broadhurst Theater. Staged by John Cromwell. Settings by Jo Mielziner.
Cast: **Fredric March**, Florence Eldridge, Dame May Whitty, Brenda Forbes, Frieda Altman, Martin Wolfson, Marilyn Jolie, Harold Thomas, Walter Jones, Helena Glenn, Leslie Austin, John Pickard, Ethel Morrison, A.J. Herbert, Katherine Stewart, Montgomery Clift.

The American Way. January 21, 1939. A spectacle play in two acts by George S. Kaufman and Moss Hart. Music by Oscar Levant. Produced by Sam H. Harris and Max Gordon at the Center Theater, New York. Staged by George S. Kaufman. Lighting and technical direction by Hassard Short. Settings by Donald Oenslager. Costumes by Irene Sharaff.
Cast: **Fredric March**, Florence Eldridge, James MacDonald, Eileen Burns, Jean Shelby, John Lorenz, Hugh Cameron, Le Roi Operti, Allen Kearns, Mary Brandon, Adrienne Marden, Alan Hewitt, David Wayne, Walter Kelly,

Stephen Sands, Dora Sayers, Alex Courtney, Edward Elliott, Dicky Van Patten, Elinor Pittis, Claire Howard, Richard Lloyd, Walter Beck, Barbara Woodall, Gretchen Davidson, Witner Bissell, Jack Arnold, George Herndon, Ward Tallman.

Hope for a Harvest. November 26, 1941. A drama in three acts by Sophie Treadwell. Produced by the Theater Guild at the Guild Theater, New York. Staged by Lester Vail. Supervised by Lawrence Langner and Theresa Helburn. Settings by Watson Barratt.
   Cast: Helen Carew, Judy Parrish, **Fredric March**, Florence Eldridge, John Marny, Arthur Franz, Shelley Hull, Edith King, Alan Reed, Doro Merande.

The Skin of Our Teeth. November 18, 1942. A fantastic comedy in three acts by Thornton Wilder. Produced by Michael Myerberg at the Plymouth Theater, New York. Staged by Elia Kazan. Settings by Albert Johnson. Costumes by Mary Percy Schenck.
   Cast: **Fredric March**, Florence Eldridge, Tallulah Bankhead, E.G. Marshall, Reno Buffano, Andrew Ratousheff, Dicky Van Patten, Frances Heflin, Montgomery Clift, Arthur Griffin, Ralph Kellard, Joseph Smiley, Ralph Cullinan, Edith Faversham, Emily Lorraine, Eva Mudge Nelson, Stanley Prager, Harry Clark, Elizabeth Scott, patricia Riordan, Florence Reed, Earl Sydnor, Carroll Clark, Stanley Weeds, Seumas Flynn, Aubrey Fossett, Stanley Prager, Harry Clark, Stephan Cole, Morton Da Costa, Joseph Smiley, Ralph Kellard, Eula Belle Moore, Viola Dean.

A Bell for Adano. December 16, 1944. A drama in three acts by Paul Osborn, based on a novel by John Hersey. Produced by Leland Hayward at the Cort Theater, New York. Staged by H.C. Potter. Setting and costumes by Motley. Lighting supervised by William Richardson.
   Cast: **Fredric March**, Everett Sloane, Gilbert Mack, Tito Vuolo, Silvio Minciotti, Joe Verdi, Leon Rathiu, Miriam Goldine, Alma Ross, Florence Aquino, Harold J. Stone, Margo, Bruce MacFarlane, Jack Arnold, Fred Barton, Harry Selby, Michael Vallon, Mario Badolati, Doreen McLean, Albert Raymo, Charles Majer, J. Scott Smart, Rolfe Sedan, Clark Poth, Alexander Granach, Phil Arthur, Rex King.

Years Ago. December 3, 1946. A comedy in three acts by Ruth Gordon. Produced by Max Gordon at the Mansfield Theater, New York. Staged by Garson Kanin. Setting by Donald Oenslager. Costumes by John Boyt.
   Cast: **Fredric March**, Florence Eldridge, Patricia Kirkland, Bethel Leslie, Jennifer Bunker, Richard Simon, Seth Arnold, Fredric Persson, Judith Cargill.

Now I Lay Me Down to Sleep. March 2, 1950. A comedy in three acts by

Elaine Ryan. Based on the novel by Ludwig Bemelmans. Produced by Nancy Stern and George Nichols III at the Broadhurst Theater, New York. Staged by Hume Cronyn. Settings by Wolfgang Roth. Costumes by John Derro.

Cast: **Fredric March**, Florence Eldridge, Lili Valenty, Ray Poole, Charles Chaplin, Jr., Henry Guertel, Charles Mayer, Stefan Schnabel, Henry Lascoe, Norman Barrs, Richard Abbott, Helen Seaman, Rick Jason, Rene Paul, Booth Colman, Philip Gordon, Gregory Morton, Thomas E. Noyes, Robert McCahon, Harold E. Gordon, Sally Anne Parsons, Jacqueline Dalya, Hope Miller, Rene Paul, Helen Scamon, Rudy Bond.

An Enemy of the People. December 28, 1950. A play in three acts by Henrik Ibsen. Adapted by Arthur Miller. Produced by Lars Nordenson at the Broadhurst Theater. Staged by Robert Lewis. Sets and costumes by Aline Bernstein. Production stage manager, Robert F. Simon.

Cast: **Fredric March**, Florence Eldridge, Morris Carnovsky, Art Smith, Michael Strong, Martin Brooks, Ralph Robertson, Richard Trask, Ralph Dunn, Anna Minot, Fred Stewart, Lon Gilbert.

The Autumn Garden. March 7, 1951. A comedy in three acts by Lillian Hellman. Produced by Kermit Bloomgarden at the Coronet Theater. Staged by Harold Clurman. Settings by Howard Bay. Costumes by Anna Hill Johnstone. Production supervisor, Dee Hughes.

Cast: **Fredric March**, Florence Eldridge, Ethel Griffies, Colin Keith-Johnston, Kent Smith, James Lipton, Margaret Barker, Joan Lorring, Maxwell Glanville, Carol Goodner, Jane Wyatt, Louise Holmes.

Long Day's Journey into Night. November 7, 1956. A play in four acts by Eugene O'Neill. Produced by Leigh Cornell, Theodore Mann and Jose Quintero at the Helen Hayes Theater, New York. Staged by Jose Quintero. Setting by David Hays. Lighting by Tharon Musser; costumes by Motley. Production Stage Manager, Elliott Martin. Stage manager, George Petrarca.

Cast: **Fredric March**, Florence Eldridge, Jason Robards, Jr., Bradford Dillman, Katherine Ross.

Gideon. November 9, 1961. A play by Paddy Chayefsky. Produced by Fred Coe and Arthur Cantor at the Plymouth Theater, New York. Staged by Tyrone Guthrie. Settings and lighting by David Hays. Costumes by Daningo Rodriguez. Production Stage Manager, Porter Van Zandt. Stage Manager, J. George Thorn.

Cast: **Fredric March**, Douglas Campbell, Martin Garner, Victor Kilian, Robert Weiss, Eric Berry, David Hooks, Alan Manson, Mark Lenard, George Segne, Alan Bergmann, Paul Marin, Edward Holmes, David Hooks, L. Egypt.

OTHER PLAYS

Dates		Name	Location
May 15,	1914	The County Chairman	Racine High School
May 23,	1919	The Romancers	Junior Play—University of Wisconsin
Dec. 07,	1920	Deburau	Boston
	1921	The County Chairman	Off-Broadway
	1921	Shavings	Road Company
Spring Fall	1922- 1923	Brownell/Storck Stock Co.	Dayton, Ohio
Dec. 07,	1923	Zeno	Chicago
August Jan.	1924- 1925	Tarnish	Midwest Tour
Feb. 02,	1925	The Knife in the Wall	Providence
Nov. 13,	1925	The Balcony Walkers	Off-Broadway
Jun. 12,	1926	The Swan	Elitch's, Denver
Jun. 20,	1926	Love 'Em and Leave 'Em	Elitch's, Denver
Jun. 27,	1926	Dancing Mothers	Elitch's, Denver
Jul. 04,	1926	The Music Master	Elitch's, Denver
Jul. 11,	1926	Craig's Wife	Elitch's, Denver
Jul. 18,	1926	The Poor Nut	Elitch's, Denver
Jul. 25,	1926	Icebound	Elitch's, Denver
Aug. 01,	1926	Not Herbert	Elitch's, Denver
Aug. 08,	1926	Liliom	Elitch's, Denver
Aug. 15,	1926	Easy Come Easy Go	Elitch's, Denver
Aug. 22,	1926	Hell-Bent fer Heaven	Elitch's, Denver
Aug. 29,	1926	These Charming People	Elitch's, Denver
Jun. 11,	1927	Quality Street	Elitch's, Denver
Jun. 19,	1927	The Butter and Egg Man	Elitch's, Denver
Jun. 26,	1927	Pigs	Elitch's, Denver
Jul. 03,	1927	The Ghost Train	Elitch's, Denver
Jul. 10,	1927	The Dove	Elitch's, Denver
Jul. 17,	1927	Gentlemen Prefer Blondes	Elitch's, Denver
Jul. 24,	1927	Sure Fire	Elitch's, Denver
Jul. 31,	1927	Loose Ankles	Elitch's, Denver
Aug. 07,	1927	The Last of Mrs. Cheyney	Elitch's, Denver
Aug. 14,	1927	The Shame Woman	Elitch's, Denver
Aug. 21,	1927	Spread Eagle	Elitch's, Denver
Aug. 28,	1927	The Cradle Snatchers	Elitch's, Denver
Sep.	1927-	Arms and the Man	Theater Guild Tour
Feb.	1928	Mr. Pim Passes By	Theater Guild Tour

Dates		Name	Location
		The Guardsman	Theater Guild Tour
		The Silver Cord	Theater Guild Tour
Jun. 09,	1928	Baby Cyclone	Elitch's, Denver
Jun. 17,	1928	The Springboard	Elitch's, Denver
Jun. 24,	1928	The Outsider	Elitch's, Denver
Jul. 01,	1928	Tommy	Elitch's, Denver
Jul. 08,	1928	Behold the Bridegroom	Elitch's, Denver
Jul. 15,	1928	Nightstick	Elitch's, Denver
Jul. 22,	1928	The Second Mrs. Tanqueray	Elitch's, Denver
Jul. 29,	1928	Saturday's Children	Elitch's, Denver
Aug. 05,	1928	The K Guy	Elitch's, Denver
Aug. 12,	1928	The Command to Love	Elitch's, Denver
Sep. 13,	1928	The Royal Family	Santa Barbara
Oct.	1928	The Royal Family	San Francisco
Oct. 29,	1928-	The Royal Family	Los Angeles
Dec.	1928		
Oct.	1951	The Autumn Garden	Tour

Appendix B

Narration/Radio/ Television

Dates		Name	Medium
Mar. 22,	1937	Death Takes a Holiday	Lux Radio Theater
Mar. 29,	1937	Bury the Dead	Speech/play
Dec.	1937	A Farewell to Arms	NBC's Star Playhouse Radio
	1938	Take the Stand	Ed Sullivan Interview
	1939	The 400,000,000	Narration
Jan. 22,	1940	Bachelor Mother	Lux Radio Theater
Apr. 15,	1940	Lights Out in Europe	Narration
Jul. 04,	1940	Call to America Pledge	Radio-WJZ —N.Y.
Jul. 15,	1940	Gentleman from Indiana	Radio
Apr. 12,	1943	The Lengthening Shadow	Calvacade of America Radio Play
Apr. 13,	1943	This Is America	Radio
May. 22,	1943	Opening Season	New York Philharmonic Symphony Series
Jun.	1943	Black Sea Fighters	Documentary
Jul. 04,	1943	One World	Radio
Jan.	1944	Radio interviews—USO	Radio
Jan. 03,	1944	Michael and Mary	Gertrude Lawrence Radio Theater
Jan. 16,	1944	A Star Is Born	Gertrude Lawrence Radio Theater
Feb. 05,	1944	Dark Victory	Gertrude Lawrence Radio Theater
Feb. 13,	1944	Citation	Philco Radio Hall of Fame

Dates		Name	Medium
Apr. 10,	1944	Information Please	Talk Show
Apr.	1944	Untitled	Columbia Presents
Mar. 17,	1944	Salute to Freedom	Narration
Jan. 26,	1947	Atlantic Charter Speech	Radio-WJZ —N.Y.
Oct. 7,	1949	Twentieth Century	Television Ford Theater
Jan.	1950	The Titan—Michelangelo	Documentary
Oct.	1950	Crusade for Freedom Broadcast	CBS Radio
Mar. 25,	1954	Hosted Academy Awards	NBC Century Theater Television
Sep. 17,	1954	The Royal Family	CBS Television The Best of Broadway
Dec. 23,	1954	A Christmas Carol	Shower of Stars
Mar.	1956	Hosted Academy Awards	Television
Apr. 30,	1956	Dodsworth	Producers Showcase
Jan. 09,	1958	Excerpts from Long Day's Journey into Night	Ed Sullivan Show
Nov. 13,	1958	The Winslow Boy	CBS DuPont Show of the Month
Apr.	1959	Tales from Charles Dickens	British Television
Mar. 02,	1961	Biography of War *Life*	Magazine Television
Apr. 05,	1962	The American Bell	Phoenix Theater—N.Y.C. Television
Nov. 29,	1962	Kick Off Program	National Cultural Center Television
Feb. 20,	1963	Storm Over the Supreme Court	CBS Reports Television
Mar. 13,	1963	Storm Over the Supreme Court	CBS Reports Television
Apr. 21,	1963	American Landmark — Lexington and Concord	NBC Television
Oct. 16,	1963	The Saga of Western Man	ABC Television
Nov.	1963	The Saga of Western Man	ABC Television
Nov. 24,	1963	Tribute to President Kennedy	All Stations Television
Dec. 08,	1963	The Saga of Western Man	ABC Television
May 04,	1964	Narrated "Pieta"	Television Special
May 11,	1964	The Supreme Court Decision	ABC Television
Sep. 18,	1964	Smalltown USA: A Farewell	NBC Television
Sep. 21,	1964	The Presidency: A Splendid Misery	CBS Television
	1964	Life's History of the United States	Record Narration
Jan.	1965	Power for a Nation	Television Special
Jan. 15,	1965	The Artist's Eye	Television Special

Dates	Name	Medium
Feb. 23, 1965	Leonardo da Vinci	ABC Television Special
Nov. 25, 1966	The Legacy of Rome	ABC Television Special

Appendix C

Motion Pictures

The Dummy. Paramount / 1929. Cast List: Mr. March was Trumbell Meredith; Ruth Chatterton (Agnes Meredith); John Cromwell (Walter Babbing); Fred Kohler (Joe Cooper); Mickey Bennett (Barney Cook); ZaSu Pitts (Rose Gleason); Richard Tucker (Blackie Baker); Eugene Pallette (Madison).

Other: Robert Milton (director); Herman J. Mankiewicz (adaptation and screenplay); based on the stage comedy by Harvey J. O'Higgins and Harriet Ford; J. Roy Hunt (photography); Hector Turnbull (supervisor); George Nichols (film editor); Morton Whitehill (assistant director).

Opened at the Paramount Theater, New York, March 3, 1929. Running time, 70 minutes.

The Wild Party. Paramount / 1929. Cast List: Mr. March was Gil Gilmore; Clara Bow (Stella Ames); Shirley O'Hara (Helen Owens); Marceline Day (Faith Morgan); Joyce Compton (Eva Tutt); Adrienne Dore (Babs); Virginia Thomas (Tess); Jean Lorraine (Ann); Kay Bryant (Thelma); Alice Adair (Maisie); Renee Whitney (Janice); Amo Ingram (Jean); Marguerite Cramer (Gwen); Jack Oakie (Al); Phillips R. Holmes (Phil); Ben Hendricks, Jr. (Ed); Jack Luden (George); Jack Raymond (Balaam).

Other: Dorothy Arzner (director); E. Lloyd Sheldon (screenplay); adapted from an original story by Warner Fabian; Victor Milner (photography).

Opened at the Rialto Theater, New York, March 30, 1929. Running time, 77 minutes.

The Studio Murder Mystery. Paramount / 1929. Cast: Mr. March was Richard Hardell; Neil Hamilton (Tony White); Florence Eldridge (Blanche Hardell); Warner Oland (Rupert Borka); Doris Hill (Helen MacDonald); Eugene Pallette (Detective Dirk); Chester Conklin (Gateman); Lane Chandler

(Martin); Gardner James (Ted MacDonald); Guy Oliver (MacDonald); E. H. Calvert (Grant); Donald MacKenzie (Captain Coffin).

Other: Frank Tuttle (director); Frank Tuttle (adaptation and dialogue); from the *Photoplay* Magazine serial of the same name, written by the Edingtons. Ethel Doherty (screenplay); Victor Milner (photography).

Opened at the Paramount Theater, New York, June 9, 1029. Running time, 62 minutes.

Paris Bound. Pathe / 1929. Cast: Mr. March was Jim Hutton; Ann Harding (Mary Hutton); George Irving (James Hutton, Sr.); Leslie Fenton (Richard Parrish); Hallam Cooley (Ptere); Juliette Crosby (Nora Cope); Charlotte Walker (Helen White); Carmelita Geraghty (Noel Farley); Ilka Chase (Fanny Shipmath).

Other: Arthur Hopkins (producer); Edward H. Griffith (director); Horace Jackson (adaptation); from the play by Philip Barry. Frank Reicher (dialogue co-director). Josia Zuro (music score).

Opened at the Paramount Theater, New York, September 20, 1929. Running time, 73 minutes.

Jealousy. Paramount / 1929. Cast: Mr. March was Pierre; Jeanne Eagels (Yvonne); Halliwell Hobbes (Rigaud); Blanche Le Clair (Renee); Henry Daniell (Clement); Hilda Moore (Charlotte).

Other: Jean De Limur (director); Garret Fort (screen adaptation); John D. Willimas (dialogue); based on the play by Louis Verneuil and the translation and stage adaptation by Eugene Walter.

Opened at the Paramount Theater, New York, September 13, 1929. Running time, 66 minutes.

Footlights and Fools. First National / 1929. Cast: Mr. March was Gregory Pyne; Collene Moore (Betty Murphy-Fifi D'Auray); Raymond Hackett (Jimmy Willet); Virginia Lee Corbin (Claire Floyd); Mickey Bennett (call boy); Edward Martindell (Chandler Cunningham); Adrienne D'Ambricourt (Jo); Frederick Howard (treasurer); Sidney Jarvis (stage Manager); Cleve Moore (press agent); Andy Rice, Jr. (song plugger); Ben Hendricks, Jr. (stage doorman); Larry Banthim (Bud Burke).

Other: William A. Seiter (director); John McCormick (producer); Carey Wilson (screenplay); adapted for the screen from a story by Katherine Brush. Stage numbers directed by Max Scheck. Oliver Garretson (sound recording); James Dunne (assistant director). Songs by Alfred Bryan and George W. Meyer: "You Can't Believe My Naughty Eyes," "If I Can't Have You," "Pilly Pom Plee." "If I Can't Have You" rendered by Earl Bartnett's Biltmore Trio. Part Technicolor.

Opened at the Mark Strand Theater, New York, November 8, 1929.

Running time, 78 minutes.

The Marriage Playground. Paramount / 1929. Cast: Mr. March was Martin Boyne; Mary Brian (Judith Wheater); Lilyan Tashman (Joyce Wheater); Huntley Gordon (Cliff Wheater); Kay Francis (Lady Wrench); William Austin (Lord Wrench); Seena Owen (Rose Sellers); Philippe de Lacy (Terry); Anita Louise (Blanca); Little Mitzi (Zinnie); Billy Seay (Bun); Ruby Parsley (Beatrice); Donald Smith (Chip); Jocelyn Lee (Sybil); Maude Turner Gordon (Aunt Julia Langley); David Newell (Gerald); Armand Kaliz (Prince Matriano); Joan Standing (Miss Scopey); Gordon Demain (Mr. Delafield).

Other: Lothar Mendes (director); J. Walter Ruben and Doris Anderson (screenplay); based on the novel *The Children* by Edith Wharton; Victor Milner (photography).

Opened at the Paramount Theater, New York, December 13, 1929. Running time, 70 minutes.

Sarah and Son. Paramount / 1929. Cast: Mr. March was Howard Vanning; Ruth Chatterton (Sarah Strong); Fuller Mellish, Jr. (Jim Gray); Gilbert Emery (John Ashmore); Doris Lloyd (Mrs. Ashmore); William Stack (Cyril Belloc); Philippe de Lacy (Bobby).

Other: Dorothey Arzner (director); Zoe Akins (adaptation and screenplay); based on the novel by Timothey Shea; Charles Lang (photography); Earl Hamen (sound recording).

Opened at the Paramount Theater, New York, March 14, 1930. Running time, 86 minutes.

Ladies Love Brutes. Paramount / 1930. Cast: Mr. March was Dwight Howell; George Bancroft (Joe Forziati); Mary Astor (Mimi Howaell); Margaret Quimby (Lucille Gates); Stanley Fieldss (Mike Mendino); Ben Hendricks, Jr. (Slattery); Lawford Davidson (George Winham); Ferike Boros (Mrs. Forziati); David Durand (Joey Forziati); Freddie Burke Frederick (Jackie Howell); Paul Fox (Slip); Claude Allister (tailor); Crawford Kent, E. H. Calvert (committeemen).

Other: Rowland V. Lee (director); Waldemar Young, Herman J. Mankiewicz (screenplay); based on Zoe Akins's play *Pardon My Glove*. Harry Fischbeck (photography).

Opened at the Rivoli Theater, New York, May 15, 1930. Running time, 80 minutes.

Paramount on Parade. Paramount / 1930. Cast: Mr. March was one of the doughboys in a sequence with Ruth Catterton in a cast that included (alphabetically): Iris Adrian, Richard Arlen, Jean Arthur, Mischa Auer, William Austin, George Bancroft, Clara Bow, Evelyn Brent, Mary Brian, Clive

Brook, Virginia Bruce, Nancy Carroll, Maurice Chevalier, Gary Cooper, Cecil Cunningham, Leon Errol, Stuart Erwin, Henry Fink, Kay Francis, Skeets Gallagher, Harry Green, Mitzi Green, Robert Greig, James Hall, Phillips Holmes, Helen kane, Dennis King, Jack Luden, Abe Lyman and His Band, Nino Martini, David Newell, Jack Oakie, Warner Oland, Zelma O'Neal, Eugene Pallette, Joan Peers, Jack Pennick, William Powell, Charles "Buddy" Rogers, Jackie Searle, Lillian Roth, Rolfe Sedan, Stanley Smith, Fay Wray.

Other: Dorothy Arzner, Otto Brower, Edmund Goulding, Victor Heerman, Edwin H. Knopf, Rowland V. Lee, Ernst Lubitsch, Lothar Mendes, Victor Schertizinger, Edward Sutherland, Frank Tuttle (directors); Albert A. Kaufman (producer); Elsie Janis (supervisor); Harry Fischbeck, Victor Milner (photography); Merrill White (film editor); John Wenger (production design); David Bennett (choreography). In some sequences, color by Technicolor.

Opened at the Rialto Theater, New York, April 19, 1930. Running time, 101 minutes.

True to the Navy. Paramount / 1930. Cast: Mr. March was Gunner McCoy; Clara Bow (Ruby Nolan); Harry Green (Solomon Bimberg); Rex Bell (Eddie); Eddie Fetherston (Michael); Eddie Dunn (Albert); Ray Cooke (Peewee); Harry Sweet (Artie); Adele Windsor (Maizie); Sam Hardy (Grogan); Jed Prouty (dancehall manager).

Other: Frank Tuttle (director); Keene Thompson, Doris Anderson and Herman Mankiewicz (screenplay); Victor Milner (photography).

Opened at the Paramount Theater, New York, May 23, 1930. Running time, 70 minutes.

Manslaughter. Paramount / 1930. Cast: Mr. March was Dan O'Bannon; Claudette Colbert (Lydia Thore); Emma Dunn (Miss Bennett); Natalie Moorhead (Eleanor); Richard Tucker (Albee); Hilda Vaughn (Evans); G. Pat Collins (Drummond); Gaylord Pendleton (Bobby); Stanley Fields (Peters); Arnold Lucy (Piers); Ivan Simpson (Morson); Irving Mitchell (Foster).

Other: George Abbott (director); George Abbott (screenplay and adaptation); based on the *Saturday Evening Post* story of the same name by Alice Duer Miller; A. J. Stout (photography); Otto Lovering (editor).

Opened at the Rivoli Theater, New York, July 23, 1930. Running time, 82 minutes.

Laughter. Paramount / 1930. Cast: Mr. March was Paul Lockridge; Nancy Carroll (Peggy Gibson); Frank Morgan (C. Mortimer Gibson); Glenn Anders (Ralph Le Saint); Diane Ellis (Marjorie Gibson); Leonard Carey (Benham); Ollie Burgoyne (Pearl).

Other: Harry D'Abbadie d'Arrast (director); Donald Ogden Stewart (dialogue); based on a story by Harry D'Abbadie d'Arrast and Douglas Doty;

George Folsey (photography); Ernest F. Zatorsky (sound recording); Helene Turner (editor); Song, "Little Did I Know" by I. Kahal, P. Norman and S. Fain.

Opened at the Paramount and Brooklyn Paramount Theaters, New York, November 14, 1930. Running time, 99 minutes.

The Royal Family of Broadway. Paramount / 1930. Cast: Mr. March was Tony Cavendish; Ina Claire (Julia Cavendish); Mary Brian (Gwen Cavendish); Henrietta Crosman (Fanny Cavendish); Charles Starrett (Perry Stewart); Arnold Korff (Oscar Wolff); Frank Conroy (Gilbert Marshall); Royal G. Stour (Joe); Elsie Edmond (Della); Murray Alper (McDermott); Wesley Stack (a hall boy); Herschel Mayall (the doctor).

Other: George Cukor and Cyril Gardner (directors); Herman Mankiewicz and Gertrude Purcell (screenplay); based on the play *The Royal Family* by George S. Kaufman and Edna Ferber; George Folsey (photography).

Opened at the Rivoli Theater, New York, December 22, 1930. Running time, 82 minutes.

Honor among Lovers. Paramount / 1931. Cast: Mr. March was Jerry Stafford; Claudette Colbert (Julia Traynor); Monroe Owsley (Philip Craig); Charles Ruggles (Monty Dunn); Ginger Rogers (Doris Blake); Avonne Taylor (Maybelle); Pat O'Brien (Conroy); Janet McLeary (Margaret); John Kearney (inspector); Ralph Morgan (Riggs); Jules Epailly (Louis); Leonard Carey (butler).

Other: Dorothy Arzner (director); Austin Parker and Gertrude Purcell (screenplay); adapted for the screen from a story by Austin Parker; George Folsey (photography). Photographed at the Astoria Studios, Long Island, New York.

Opened at the times Square Paramount and the Brooklyn Paramount Theaters, New York, February 27, 1931. Running time, 76 minutes.

The Night Angel. Paramount / 1931. Cast: Mr. March was Rudek Bekem; Nancy Carroll (Yula); Alan Hale (Bical); Alison Skipworth (Countess de Martini); Katherine Emmett (Mrs. Berkem); Phoebe Foster (Theresa); Otis Sheridan (Schmidt); Hubert Druce (Vincent); Lewis Waller (Kafka); Clarence Derwent (Rosenbach); Charles Howard (clown); Doris Rankin (matron); Francine Dowd (Mitzi).

Other: Edmund Goulding (director); Edmund Goulding (screenplay); from a story by Edmund Goulding; William Steiner (photography).

Opened at the Rivoli Theater, New York, June 10, 1931. Running time, 75 minutes.

My Sin. Paramount / 1931. Cast: Mr. March was Dick Grady; Tallulah

Bankhead (Carlott; Ann Trevor); Harry Davenport (Roger Metcalf); Scott Kolk (Larry Gordon); Anne Sutherland (Mrs. Gordon); Margaret Adams (Paula Marsden); Lily Cahill (Helen Grace); Jay Fassett (James Bradford).

Other: George Abbott (director); Owen Davis and Adelaide Heilbron (screenplay); George Abbott (adaptation); from the story by Fred Jackson; George Folsey (photographer); photographed at the Astoria Studios, Long Island, New York.

Opened at the Paramount Theater and the Brooklyn Paramount, New York, September 11, 1931. Running time, 77 minutes.

Dr. Jekyll and Mr. Hyde. Paramount / 1931. Cast: Mr. March was Dr. Henry Jekyll-Mr. Hyde; Miriam Hopkins (Ivy Parsons); Rose Hobart (Muriel Carew); Holmes Herbert (Dr. Lanyan); Halliwell Hobbes (Brig. Gen. Carew); Edgar Norton (Poole); Arnold Lucy (Utterson); Colonel MacDonnell (Hobson); Tempe Piggott (Mrs. Hawkins).

Other: Rouben Mamoulian (director); Samuel Hoffenstein and Percy Heath (screenplay); adapted from the novel by Robert Louis Stevenson; Karl Struss (photography).

Opened at the Rivoli Theater, New York, December 31, 1931. Running time, 98 minutes.

Strangers in Love. Paramount / 1932. Cast: Mr. March was Buddy Drake-Arthur Drake; Kay Francis (Diana Merrow); Stuart Erwin (Stan Keeney); Juliette Compton (Muriel Preston); George Barbier (Mr. Merrow); Sidney Toler (McPhail); Earle Foxe (J.C. Clarke); Lucien Littlefield (Professor Clark); Leslie Palmer (Bronson); Gertrude Howard (Snowball); Ben Taggart (Crenshaw); John M. Sullivan (Dr. Selous).

Other: Lothar Mendes (director); William Slavens McNutt and Grover Jones (adaptation and screenplay); based on the novel *The Shorn Lamb* by William J. Locke; Henry Sharp (photography).

Opened at the Paramount Theater and the Brooklyn Paramount, New York, March 5, 1932. Running time, 68 minutes.

Merrily We Go to Hell. Paramount / 1932. Cast: Mr. March was Jerry Corbett; Sylvia Sidney (Joan Prentice); Addrianne Allen (Claire Hempstead); Richard "Skeets" Gallagher (Buck); Florence Britton (Charicle); Esther Howard (Vi); George Irving (Mr. Prentice); Kent Taylor (Dick Taylor); Charles Coleman (Damery); Leonard Carey (butler); Milla Davenport (housekeeper); Robert Greig (baritone); Rev. Neal Dodd (minister); Mildred Boyd (June); Cary Grant (stage leading man).

Other: Dorothy Arzner (director); Edwin Justus mayer (screenplay); based on the novel *I Jerry, Take Thee, Joan* by Cleo Lucas; David Abel (photography).

Opened at the Paramount Theater, New York, June 10, 1932. Running time, 82 minutes.

Make Me a Star. Paramount / 1932. Cast: Mr. March was a guest star, playing himself. The other guest starts included: Tallulah Bankhead, Clive Brook, Maurice Chevalier, Claudette Colbert, Gary Cooper, Philips Holmes, Jack Oakie, Charlie Ruggles, Sylvia Sidney. All played themselves.

Other: William Beaudine (director); Sam Wintz, Walter De Leon, Arthur Kober (adaptation); Allen Siegler (photography); based on the book *Merton of the Movies* by Harry Leon Wilson and the play by George S. Kaufman and Moss Hart; Leroy Sonte (editor); Earle S. Hayman (sound recording).

Opened at the Paramount Theater, New York, July 1, 1932. Running time, 83 minutes.

Smilin' Through. Metro-Goldwyn-Mayer / 1932. Cast: Mr. March was Jeremy Wayne-Kenneth Wayne; Norma Shearer (Moonyean Clare; Kathleen Clare); Leslie Howard (John Carterett); O.P. Heggie (Doctor Owen); Ralph Forbes (Willie Ainley); Beryl Mercer (Mrs. Crouch); David Torrence (gardener); Margaret Seddon (Ellen); Forrester Harvey (orderly); Cora Sue Collins (young Kathleen).

Other: Sidney Franklin (director); Ernest Vajda and James Bernard Fagan (adaptation and screenplay); based on the play by Jane Cowl and Jane Murfin; Lee Garmes (photography); Margarte Booth (film editor).

Opened at the Capitol Theater, New York, October 14, 1932. Running time, 96 minutes.

The Sign of the Cross. Paramount / 1932. Cast: Mr. March was Marcus Superbus; Claudette Colbert (Poppaea); Elissa Landi (Mercia); Charles Laughton (Nero); Ian Keith (Tigellinus); Harry Beresford (Favius); Arthur Hohl (Titus); Tommy Conlon (Stephanus); Vivian Tobin (Dacia); Ferdinand Gottschalk (Giabrio); Joyzelle Joyner (Ancaria); Nat Pendleton (Strabo); William V. Mong (Licinius); Harold Healy (Tyros); Robert Alexander (Viturius); Robert Manning (Philodemus); Joe Bonomo (The Mule Giant.) Also included in the cast were: Otto Lederer, Lillian Leighton, Lane Chandler, Wilfred Lucas, Jerome Storm, Gertrude Norman, Florence Turner, Horace B. Carpenter, Ynez Seabury, Carol Holloway.

Other: Cecil B. DeMille (producer and director); Waldemar Young and Sidney Buchman (adaptation and screenplay); from the play by Wilson Barrett; Karl Struss (photography); Anne Bauchens (film editor); Rudolph Kipp (music).

Opened at the Rialto Theater, New York, November 30, 1932. Running time, 124 minutes.

Tonight Is Ours. Paramount / 1933. Cast: Mr. March was Sabien Pastal; Claudette Colbert (Nadya); Alison Skipworth (Grand Duchess Emilie); Paul Cavanaugh (Prince Keri); Arthur Byron (General Krish); Ethel Griffies (Zana); Clay Clement (Seminoff); Warburton Gamble (Alex); Edwin Maxwell (leader of the mob).

Other: Stuart Walker (director); Mitchell Leisen (associate director); Edwin Justus Mayer (screenplay); adapted from the play *The Queen Was in the Parlor* by Noel Coward; Karl Struss (photography).

Opened at the Paramount Theater, New York, January 21, 1933. Running time, 75 minutes.

The Eagle and the Hawk. Paramount / 1933. Cast: Mr. March was Jerry Young; Cary Grant (Henry Crocker); Jack Oakie (Mike Richards); Carole Lombard (the beautiful lady); Sir Guy Standing (Major Dunham); Forrester Harvey (Hogan); Kenneth Howell (John Stevens); Leyland Hodgson (Kingsford); Virginia Hammond (Lady Erskine); Crauford Kent (general); Douglas Scott (Tommy); Robert Manning (Major Kruppman); Russell Scott (flight sergeant).

Other: Stuart Walker (director); Screenplay by Bogart Rogers and Seton J. Miller; based on a story by John Monk Saunders; Harry Fischbeck (photographer); Mitchell Leisen (associate director).

Opened at the Paramount Theater, New York, May 12, 1933. Running time, 86 minutes.

Design for Living. Paramount / 1933. Cast: Mr. March was Tom Chambers; Gary Cooper (George Curtis); Miriam Hopkins (Gilda Farrell); Edward Everett Horton (Max Plunkett); Franklin Pangborn (Douglas); Isabel Jewell (stenographer); Harry Dunkinson (Egelbauer); Helena Phillips (Mrs. Egelbauer); James Donlin (fat man); Vernon Steele (first manager); Thomas Braidon (second manager); Jane Darwell (housekeeper); Armand Kaliz (Burton); Adrienne D'Ambricourt (cafe proprietress); Nora Cecil (Tom Chambers' secretary); Wyndham Standing (Max Plunkett's butler); Grace Hayle (woman on staircase); Olaf Hytten (Englishman at train); Mary Gordon (theater attendant); Lionel Belmore, Charles K. French (patron of theater); Rolfe Sedan (salesman).

Other: Ernst Lubitsch (producer and director); Ben Hecht (screenplay); Victor Milner (photography); Hans Dreier (art direction); Travis Banton (costumes); based on the play by Noel Coward; M. M. Paggie (sound recording); Francis Marsh (editor).

Opened at the Criterion Theater, New York, November 22, 1933. Running time, 90 minutes.

All of Me. Paramount / 1934. Cast: Mr. March was Don Ellis; Miriam

Hopkins (Lyda Darrow); George Raft (Honey Rogers); Helen Mack (Eve Haron); Nella Walker (Mrs. Darrow); William Collier, Jr. (Jerry Halman); Gilbert Emery (the Dean); Blanche Frederici (Miss Haskell); Kitty Kelly (Lorraine); Guy Usher (district attorney); John Marston (Nat Davis); Edgar Kennedy (guard).

Other: James Flood (director); Louis Lighton (producer); Sidney Buchman and Thomas Mitchell (screenplay); Thomas Mitchell (dialogue direction); adapted from Rose Porter's play *Chrysalis*;Ralph Rainger and Leo Robin (music and lyrics); Victor Milner (photography).

Opened at the Paramount Theater, New York, February 4, 1934. Running time, 70 minutes.

Death Takes a Holiday. Paramount / 1934. Cast: Mr. March was Prince Sirki/Death; Evelyn Venable (Grazia); Sir Guy Standing (Duke Lambert); Katherine Alexander (Alda); Gail Patrick (Rhoda); Helen Westley (Stephanie); Kathleen Howard (Princess Maria); Kent Taylor (Corrado); Henry Travers (Baron Cesarea); G.P. Huntley Jr. (Eric); Otto Hoffman (Fedele); Edward Van Sloan (Doctor Valle); Hector Sarno (Pietro); Frank Yaconelli (vendor); Anna DeLinsky (maid).

Other: Mitchell Leisen (director); Maxwell Anderson and Gladys Lehman (screenplay); based on a play by Alberto Casella; Charles Lang (photography); Hans Dreier and Ernst Figte (art direction).

Opened at the Paramount Theater, New York, February 23, 1934. Running time, 79 minutes.

Good Dame. Paramount / 1934. Cast: Mr. March was Mace Townsley; Sylvia Sidney (Lillie Taylor); Jack LaRue (Bluch Brown); Noel Francis (Puff Warner); Russell Hopton ("Spots" Edwards); Bradley Page (Regan); Guy Usher (Fallon); Kathleen Burke (Zandra); Joseph J. Frazer (Scanlon); Miami Alvarez (Cara); Walter Brennan (Elmer Spicer).

Other: Marion Gering (director); William R. Lipman, Vincent Lawrence, Frank Partos, Sam Hellman (screenplay); from a story by William R. Lipman. Leon Shamroy (photography).

Opened at the Paramount Theater, New York, March 16, 1934. Running time, 72 minutes.

The Affairs of Cellini. Twentieth Century United Artists Release / 1934. Cast: Mr. March was Benvenuto Cellini; Constance Bennett (Duchess of Florence); Frank Morgan (Alessandro, Duke of Florence); Fay Wray (Angela); Vince Barnett (Ascanio); Jessie Ralph (Beatrice); Louis Calhern (Ottaviano); Jay Eaton (Polverino); Paul Harvey (emissary); John Rutherford (captain of guards).

Other: Gregory LaCava (director); Bess Meredyth (screenplay); adapted from Edwin Justus Mayer's play *The Firebrand*, Charles Rosher (photography).

Opened at the Rivoli Theater, New York, September 5, 1934. Running time, 90 minutes.

The Barretts of Wimpole Street. Metro-Goldwyn-Mayer / 1934. Cast: Mr. March was Robert Browning; Norma Shearer (Elizabeth Barrett); Charles Laughton (Edward Moulton Barrett); Maureen O'Sullivan(Henrietta Barrett); Katherine Alexander (Arabel Barrett); Una O'Connor (Wilson); Ian Wolfe (Harry Bevan); Marion Clayton (Bella Hedley); Ralph Forbes (Captain Surtees Cook); Vernon Downing (Octavius Barrett); Neville Clark (Charles Barrett); Matthew Smith (George Barrett); Robert Carleton (Alfred Barrett); Alan Conrad (Henry Barrett); Peter Hobbes (Septimus Barrett); Ferdinand Munier (Dr. Chambers); Leo Carroll (Dr. Ford-Waterlow).

Other: Sidney Franklin (director); Claudine West, Ernest Vajda and Donald Ogden Stewart (screenplay); adapted from the play by Rudolph Besier; William Daniels (photography); Herbert Stothart (musical score).

Opened at the Captiol Theater, New York, September 28, 1934. Running time, 110 minutes.

We Live Again. Samuel Goldwyn United Artists / 1934. Cast: Mr. March was Prince Dmitri Nekhilyudov; Anna Sten (Katusha Maslova); Jane Baxter (Missy Kortchagin); C. Aubrey Smith (Prince Kortchagin); Ethel Griffies (Aunt Marie); Gwendolyn Logan (Aunt Sophia); Jessie Ralph (Matrona Pavlovna); Sam Jaffe (simonson); Cecil Cunningham (Theodosia); Jessie Arnold (Korablova); Fritzi Ridgeway (the redhead); Morgan Wallace (the colonel); Davison Clark (Tikhon); Leonid Kinskey (Kartinkin); Dale Fuller (Botchkova); Michael Visaroff (judge); Edgar Norton (judge).

Other: Rouben Mamoulian (director); Preston Sturges, Maxwell Anderson and Leonard Praskins (screenplay); adapted from Leo Tolstoy's novel *Resurrection*. Gregg Toland (photography); Sergei Soudeikin (settings); Alfred Newman (music); Robert Lee (assistant director).

Opened at Radio City Music Hall, November 1, 1934. Running time, 85 minutes.

Les Miserables. Twentieth Century United Artists / 1935. Cast: Mr. March was Jean Valjean; Charles Laughton (Javert); Cedric Hardwicke (Bishop Bienvenu); Rochelle Hudson (Big Cosette); Marilyn Knowlden (Little Cosette); Frances Drake (Eponine); John Beal (Marius); Jessie Ralph (Madame Magloire); Florence Eldridge (Fantine); Ferdinand Gottschalk (Thenardier); Jane Kerr (Madame Thenardier); Eily Malyon (Mother Superior); Vernon Downing (Brissac); Lyons Wickland (Lamarque); John Carradine (Enjolras); Charles Haefeli (Brevet); Leonid Kinskey (Genflon);

John Bleifer (Chenildieu); Harry Semels (Cochepaille); Mary Forbes
(Madame Baptiseme); Florence Roberts (Toussaint); Lorin Baker (Valain);
Perry Ivins (M. Devereax); Thomas Mills (L'estrange); Lowell Drew (Duval);
Davidson Clark (Marchin); Ian McClaren (head gardener).

Other: Richard Boleslawski (director); Darryl F. Zanuck (producer);
adapted from the novel by Victor Hugo; W. P. Lipscomb (screenplay); Gregg
Toland (photography); Alfred Newman (musical director); Barbara McLean
(film editor).

Opened at the Rivoli Theater, New York, April 20, 1935. Running time,
109 minutes.

Anna Karenina. Metro-Goldwyn-Mayer / 1935. Cast: Mr. March was
Vronsky; Greta Garbo (Anna Karenina); Freddie Bartholomew (Sergei);
Maureen O'Sullivan(Kitty); May Robson (Countess Vronsky); Basil Rathbone
(Kerenin); Reginald Owen (Stiva); Reginald Denny (Yashvin); Phoebe Foster
(Dolly); Gyles Isham (Levin); Buster Phelps (Grisha); Ella Ethridge (Anna's
maid); Joan Marsh (Lili); Sidney Bracey (Vronsky's valet); Cora Sue Collins
(Tania); Joe E. Tozer (butler); Guy D'Ennery (tutor); Harry Allen (Cord);
Mary Forbes (Princess Sorokino); Ethel Griffies (Madame Kortasoff); Harry
Beresford (Matve); Sarah Padden (governess).

Other: Clarence Brown (director); David O. Selznick (producer);
Clemence Dane and Salka Viertel (screenplay); S. N. Behrman (dialogue);
adapted from the novel by Count Leo Tolstoy; Herbert Stothart (musical
director); Marguerite Wallmann, Chester Hale (dances); Russian Symphony
Choir (choral effects); William Daniels (photography); Count Andrei Tolstoy
(story consultant); Robert J. Kearn (film editor).

Opened at the Capitol Theater, New York, August 30, 1935. Running
time, 85 minutes.

The Dark Angel. Samuel Goldwyn United Artists / 1935. Cast: Mr. March
was Alan Trent; Merle Oberon (Kitty Vane); Herbert Marshall (Gerald
Shannon); Janet Beecher (Mrs. Shannon); John Halliday (Sir George Barton);
Henrietta Crosman (Granny Vane); Frieda Inescort (Ann West); Claude
Allister (Lawrence Bidley); George Breakston (Joe); Fay Chaldecott (Betty);
Denis Chaldecott (Ginger); Douglas Walton (Roulston); Sarah Edwards (Mrs.
Bidley); John Miltern (Mr. Vane); Olaf Hytten (Mills); Lawrence Grant (Mr.
Tanner); Helena Byrne-Grant (Hannah); Ann Fielder (Mrs. Gallop); David
Torrence (Mr. Shannon); Cora Sue Collins (Kitty as a child); Randolph
Connolly (Lawrence as a child).

Other: Sidney Franklin (director); Samuel Goldwyn (producer); Lillian
Hellman and Mordaunt Shairp (screenplay); adapted from the play by Guy
Bolton; Gregg Toland (photography); Alfred Newman (musical direction);
Hugh Boswell (assistant director).

Opened at the Rivoli Theater, New York, September 5, 1935. Running time, 105 minutes.

Mary of Scotland. RKO Radio / 1936. Cast: Mr. March was the Earl of Bothwell; Katharine Hepburn (Mary Queen of Scots); Florence Eldridge (Elizabeth I of England); John Carradine (David Rizzio); Douglas Walton (Lord Darnley); Robert Barrat (Morton); Ian Keith (Moray); Gavin Muir (Leicester); Moroni Olsen (John Knox); Ralph Forbes (Randolph); William Stack (Ruthven); Alan Mowbray (Throckmorton); Frieda Inescort (Mary Beaton); Donald Crisp (Huntley); David Torrence (Lindsay); Molly Lamont (Mary Livingston); Anita Colby (Mary Fleming); Lionel Pape (Burghley); Jean Fenwick (Mary Seton); Alec Craig (Donal); Mary Gordon (nurse); Monte Blue (messenger); Brandon Hurst (Avian); Leonard Mudie (Maitland); D'Arcy Corrigan (Kirkcaldy); Wilfred Lucas (Lexington); Doris Lloyd (fisherman's wife); Lionel Belmore (fisherman); Cyril McLaglen (Faudoncide); Frank Baker (Douglas); Bobby Watson (fisherman's son); Robert Warwick (Sir Francis Knellys); Walter Byron (Sir Francis Walsingham); Wyndham Standing (sergeant); Earle Foxe (Duke of Kent); Paul McAllister (Du Croche); Gaston Glass (Chatelard); Neil Fitzgerald (nobleman); Ivan Simpson, Lawrence Grant, Nigel DeBrulier, Murray Kinnell, Barlowe Borland (the five judges).

Other: Pandro S. Berman (producer); John Ford (director); Dudley Nichols (screenplay); based on the play by Maxwell Anderson; Joseph H. August (photography); Van Nest Polglase (art direction); Carroll Clark (associate art director); Jane Loring (editor); Darrell Silvera (set Decorations); Robert Parrish (assistant editor); Hugh McDowell, Jr. (sound); Nathaniel Shilkret (music); Maurice de Packh (orchestration); Walter Plunkett (costumes); Mel Burns (makeup); Vernon L. Walker (special photographic effects); Edward Donahur (assistant director).

Opened at Radio City Music Hall, New York, July 30, 1936. Running time, 123 minutes.

The Road to Glory. Twentieth Century-Fox / 1936. Cast: Mr. March was Lieutenant Michael Denet; Warner Baxter (Captain Paul LaRoche); Lionel Barrymore (Papa LaRoche); June Lang (Monique); Gregory Ratoff (Bouffiou); Victor Killian (Regnier); Paul Stanton (Lieutenant Tannen); Theodore Von Eltz (major); paul Fix (Rigaud); Leonid Kinskey (Ledoux); Jacques Vanoire (courier); Edyth Raynore (nurse); George Warrington (old soldier).

Other: Howard Hawks (director); Darryl F. Zanuck (producer); Joel Sayre and William Faulkner (screenplay); from a story by Joel Sayre and William Faulkner; Gregg Toland (photography); Hans Peters (art direction); Thomas Little (settings); Louis Silvers (music); Edward Curtiss (editor); Ed O'Fearna (assistant director).

Opened at the Rivoli Theater, New York, August 5, 1936. Running time, 103 minutes.

Anthony Adverse. Warner Bros. / 1936. Cast: Mr. March was Anthony Adverse; Olivia de Havilland (Angela Guessippi); Edmund Gwenn (John Bonnyfeather); Claude Rains (Don Luis); Anita Louise (Maria) Louis Hayward (Denis Moore); Gale Sondergaard (Faith Paleologue); Steffi Duna (Neleta); Billy Mauch (Anthony Adverse, age 10); Donald Woods (Vincent Nolte); Akim Tamiroff (Carlo Cibo); Ralph Morgan (Debrulle); Henry O'Neill (Father Xavier); Pedro de Cordoba (Brother Francois); George E. Stone (Sancho); Luis Alberni (Tony Guessippi); Fritz Leiber (Ouvrard); Joeseph Crehan (Captain Elisha Jorham); Rafaela Ottiano (Signora Bovino); Rollo Lloyd (Napoleon Bonaparte); Leonard Mudie (De Bourienne); Marilyn Knowlden (Florence as a child); Mathilde Comont (Cook Guessippi); Eily Malyon (Mother Superior); J. Carroll Naish (Major Dounet); Scotty Beckett (Anthony as a small boy); Paul Sotoff (Ferdinando); Frank Reicher (coach driver to Paris); Clara Blandick (Mrs. Jorham); Addison Richards (Captain matanoza); William Ricciardi (coachman in Leghorn); Grace Stafford (Lucia); Boris Nicholai (courier).

Other: Mervyn LeRoy (director); Sheridan Gibney (screenplay); adapted from the novel by Hervey Allen; Tony Gaudio (photographer); Erich Wolfgang Korngold (music); Leo Forbstein (musical director); Dwight Franklin (technical consultant on eighteenth-century customs and costumes).

Opened at the Strand Theater, New York, August 26, 1936. Running time, 140 minutes.

A Star Is Born. Selznick-International United Artists / 1937. Cast: Mr. March was Norman Maine; Janet Gaynor (Esther Blodgett-Vicki Lester); Adolphe Menjou (Oliver Niles); May Robson (Lettie); Andy Devine (Danny McGuire); Lionel Stander (Libby); Elizabeth Jenns (Anita Regis); Edgar Kennedy (Pop Randall); Owen Moore (Casey Burke); J.C. Nugent (Theodore Smythe); Clara Blandick (Aunt Mattie); A.W. Sweatt (Esther's brother); Peggy Wood (Miss Philips, a clerk); Adrian Rosely (Harris); Arthur Hoyt (Ward); Guinn (Big-Goy) Williams (posture coach); Vince Barnett (Otto Friedl); Paul Stanton (Academy Awards speaker); Franklin Pangborn (Billy Moon).

Other: William A. Wellman (director); David O. Selznick (producer); Dorothy Parker, Alan Campbell and Robert Carson (screenplay); from a story by William A. Wellman and Robert Carson; Max Steiner (music); color by Technicolor; Eric Stacey (assistant director); Lansing C. Holden (color designer); W. Howard Greene (photography); Lyle Wheeler (art direction); Omar Kiam (costumes); James E. Newcom (film editor); Edward Boyle (interior decoration); Natalie Kalmus (color supervision).

Opened at Radio City Music Hall, New York, April 22, 1937. Running time, 98 minutes.

Nothing Sacred. Selznick-International United Artists / 1937. Cast: Mr. March was Wally Cook; Carole Lombard (Hazel Flagg); Charles Winninger (Dr. Downer); Walter Connolly (Stone); Sig Rumann (Dr. Eggelhoffer); Frank Fay (master of ceromonies); Maxi Rosenbloom (Max); Margaret Hamilton (drug store lady); Troy Brown (Ernest Walker); Hattie McDaniel (Mrs. Walker); Olin Howland (baggage man); George Chandler (photographer); Claire Du Brey (Miss Rafferty); John Qualen (Swede fireman); Charles Richman (mayor); Alex Schoenberg (Dr. Kochinwasser); Monte Woolley (Dr. Vunch); Alex Novinsky (Dr. Marachuffsky); Aileen Pringle (Mrs. Bullock); Hedda Hopper (dowager); Dick Rich (Moe); Katherine Shelton (Dr. Downer's nurse); A. W. Sweatt (office boy); Clarence Wilson (Mr. Watson); Betty Douglas ("Helen of Troy"); Eleanor Troy ("Catherine of Russia"); Monica Bannister ("Pocahontas"); Jinx Falkenberg ("Katinka"); Margaret Lyman ("Salome"); Shirley Chambers ("Lady Godiva").

Other: William A. Wellman (director); David O. Selznick (producer); Ben Hecht (screenplay); from a story by James H. Street; W. Howard Greene (photography); color by Technicolor; Natalie Kalmus (color supervision).

Opened at Radio City Music Hall, New York, November 25, 1937. Running time, 75 minutes.

The Buccaneer. Paramount / 1938. Cast: Mr. March was Jean Lafitte; Franciska Gaal (Gretchen); Margot Grahame (Annette deremy); Akim Tamiroff (Dominique You); Walter Brennan (Ezra Peavey); Anthony Quinn (Beluche); Ian Keith (Senator Crawford); Douglas Dumbrille (Senator Claiborne); Beulah Bondi (Aunt Charlotte); Robert Barrat (Captain Brown); Fred Kohler (Gramby); Hugh Sothern (Andrew Jackson); John Rogers (Mouse); Hans Steinke (Tarsus); Stanley Andrews (collector of port); Spring Byington (Dolly Madison); Montagu Love (Admiral Cockburn); Louise Campbell (Marie deremy); Eric Stanley (General Ross); Gilbert Emery (Captain Lockyer); Evelyn Keyes (Madeleine); Holmes Herbert (McWilliams); Francis J. McDonald (Camden Blount); Frank Melton (Lieutenant Shreve); Jack Hubbard (Charles); Richard Denning (Captain Reid); Lina Basquette (Roxane); John Patterson (young blade); Other cast members: Reginald Sheffield, Barry Norton, John Sutton, Mae Busch, Philo McCullough, Ralph Lewis, E.J. LeSaint, Ed Brady, Charlotte Wynters, Crauford Kent, James Craig, Stanhope Wheatcroft, Charles Morton, Ethel Clayton, Maude Fealy, Jane Keckley.

Other: Cecil B. De Mille (producer and director); William LeBaron (executive producer); William H. Pine (associate producer); Edwin Justus

Mayer, C. Gardner Sullivan, Harold lamb (screenplay); adaptation by Jeanie MacPherson of Lyle Saxon's *Lafitte the Pirate*; George Antheil (music); Victor Milner (photography); Anne Bauchens (film editor); Boris Morros (musical director); Farciot Edouart and Dewey Wrigley (special effects); Edwin Maxwell (dialogue supervision); Harry Lindgren (sound).

Opened at the Paramount Theater, New York, February 16, 1938. Running time, 124 minutes.

There Goes My Heart. Hal Roach United Artists / 1938. Cast: Mr. March was Bill Spencer; Virginia Bruce (Joan Butterfield); Patsy Kelly (Peggy O'Brien); Nancy Carroll (Dorothey Moore); Alan Mowbray (Pennypacker); Eugene Pallette (editor Stevens); Claude Gillingwater (Cyrus Butterfield); Arthur Lake (Flash Fisher); Harry Langdon (minister); Etienne Girardot (secretary); Robert Armstrong (Detective O'Brien); Irving Bacon (floorwalker); Irving Pichel (attorney); Sid Saylor (Robinson); Mary Field (Mrs. Crud).

Other: Norman Z. McLeod (director); Milton H. Bren (producer); Jack Jevne and Eddie Moran (screenplay); based on an original story by Ed Sullivan; Norbert Brodine (photography); Marvin Hatley (musical director); William Terhune (editor).

Opened at Radio City Music Hall, October 13, 1938. Running time, 91 minutes.

Trade Winds. Walter Wanger United Artists / 1939. Cast: Mr. March was Sam Wye; Joan Bennett (Kay Kerrigan); Ralph Bellamy (Blodgett); Ann Sothern (Jean); Sidney Blackmer (Thomas Bruhm II); Thomas Mitchell (Chief of Detectives); Robert Elliott (Detective Faulkner); Patricia Fair (Peggy); Wilma Francis (Judy); Phyllis Barry (Ruth); Dorothy Tree (Clara); Kay Linaker (Grace); Linda Winters (Ann); Walter Byron (Bob); Wilson Benge (butler); Harry Paine (captain).

Other: Tay Garnett (director); Walter Wanger (producer); Dorothy Parker, Alan Campbell, Frank R. Adams (screenplay); based on a story by Tay Garnett; Rudolph Mate (photography); James B. Shackleford (special photography); Dorothy Spencer, Walt Reynolds (editors).

Opened at Radio City Music Hall, January 12, 1939. Running time, 93 minutes.

Susan and God. Metro-Goldwyn-Mayer / 1940. Cast: Mr. March was Barrie Trexel; Joan Crawford (Susan Trexel); Ruth Hussey (Charlotte); John Carroll (Clyde); Rita Hayworth (Leonora); Nigel Bruce (Hutchie); Bruce Cabot (Michael); Rita Quigley (Blossom); Rose Hobart (Irene); Constance Collier (Lady Wigstaff); Gloria De Haven (Enid); Richard O. Crane (Bob); Norma Mitchell (Paige); Marjorie Main (Mary); Aldrich Bowker (Patrick).

Other: George Cukor (director); Hunt Stromberg (producer); Anita Loos (screeeenplay); based on the play by Rachel Crothers; Robert Planck (photography); Cedric Gibbons (art direction); Herbert Stothart (music); Adrian (costumes); William H. Terhune (editor).

Opened at the Capitol Theater, New York, July 11, 1940. Running time, 117 minutes.

Victory. Paramount / 1940. Cast: Mr. March was Hendrik Heyst; Betty Field (Alma); Sir Cedric Hardwicke (Mr. Jones); Sig Rumann (Mr. Schomberg); margaret Wycherly (Mrs. Schomberg); Jerome Cowan (Ricardo); Fritz Feld (Signor Makanoff); Rafaela Ottiano (Madame Makanoff); Lionel Royce (Pedro); Chester Gan (Wang).

Other: John Cromwell (director); Anthony Veiller (producer); John L. Balderston (screenplay); based on the novel by Joseph Conrad; Leo Tover (photography); William Shea (editor); Joseph Youngerman (assistant director).

Opened at the Rivoli Theater, New York, December 21, 1940. Running time, 77 minutes.

So Ends Our Night. Loew-Lewin United Artists / 1941. Cast: Mr. March was Josef Steiner; Margaret Sullavan (Ruth Holland); Frances Dee (Marie Steiner); Glenn Ford (Ludwig Kern); Anna Sten (Lilo); Erich Von Stroheim (Brenner); Allan Brett (Marcel); Joseph Cawthorn (Patzlock); Leonid Kinskey (The Chicken); Alexander Granach (The Pole); Roman Bohnen (Mr. Kern); Sig Rumann (Ammers); William Stock (Professor Meyer); Lionel Royce (Barnekrogg); Ernst Deutsch (Dr. Behr); Spencer Charters (Swiss policeman); Hans Schumm (Kabel).

Other: John Cromwell (director); David L. Loew and Albert Lewin (producers); Talbot Jennings (screenplay); based on the novel *Flotsam* by Erich Maria Remarque; William Daniels (photography); Louis Gruenberg (music); Stanley Kramer (production assistant); William Reynolds (editor).

Opened at Radio City Music Hall, New York, February 27, 1941. Running time, 120 minutes.

One Foot in Heaven. Warner Bros. / 1941. Cast: Mr. March was William Spence; Martha Scott (Hope Morris Spence); Buelah Bondi (Mrs. Lydia Sandow); Gene Lockhart (Preston Thurston); Elizabeth Fraser (Eileen Spence at eighteen); Harry Davenport (Elias Samson); Laura Hope Crews (Mrs. Preston Thurston); Grant Mitchell (Clayton Potter); Moroni Olsen (Dr. John Romer); Ernest Cossart (John E. Mavis); Jerome Cowan (Dr. Horrigan); Hobart Bosworth (Richard Hardy Case); Frankie Thomas (Hartzell Spence at ten); Casey Johnson (Fraser Spence at ten and seven); Virginia Brissac (Mrs. Jellerson); Olin Howland (Zake Harris); Roscoe Ates (George

Reynolds); Clara Blandick (Sister Watkins); Paula Trueman (Miss Peabody); Harlan Briggs (druggist MacFarlan).

Other: Irving Rapper (director); Casey Robinson (screenplay); based on the biography by Hartzell Spence; Dr. Norman Vincent Peale (technical adviser); a Hal B. Wallis Production; Max Steiner (music); Charles Rosher (photography); Hugh MacMullin (dialogue director); Warren Low (editor).

Opened at Radio City Music Hall, November 13, 1941. Running time, 106 minutes.

Bedtime Story. Columbia / 1942. Cast: Mr. March was Lucius Drake; Loretta Young (Jane Drake); Robert Benchley (Eddie Turner); Allyn Joslyn (William Dudley); Eve Arden (Virginia Cole); Helen Westley (Emma Harper); Joyce Compton (Beulah); Tim Ryan (Mac); Olaf Hytten (Collins); Andrew Tombes (Pierce).

Other: Alexander Hall (director); B. P. Schulberg (producer); Richard Flournoy (screenplay); based on a story by Horace Jackson and Grant Garrett; Joseph Walker (photography); William Mull (assistant director); Viola Lawrence (editor).

Opened at Radio City Music Hall, March 19, 1942. Running time, 85 minutes.

I Married a Witch. Cinema Guild United Artists / 1942. Cast: Mr. March was Wallace Wooley; Veronica lake (Jennifer); Robert Benchley (Dr. Dudley White); Susan Hayward (Estelle Masterson); Cecil Kellaway (Daniel); Elizabeth Patterson (Margaret); Robert Warwick (J.B. Masterson); Eily Malyon (Tabitha); Robert Greig (town crier); Helen St. Rayner (vocalist); Aldrich Bowker (Justice of the Peace); Emma Dunn (his wife).

Other: Rene Clair (director); Robert Pirosh and Mark Connelly (screenplay); based on a story by Thorne Smith completed by Norman Matson; a Rene Clair Production; Ted Tetzlaff (photography); Eda Warren (editor).

Opened at the Capitol Theater, New York, November 19, 1942. Running time, 82 minutes.

The Adventures of Mark Twain. Warner Brothers / 1944. Cast: Mr. March was Samuel Clemens (Mark Twain); Alexis Smith (Olivia Langdon); Donald Crisp (J.B. Pond); Alan Hale (Steve Gillis); C. Aubrey Smith (Oxford chancellor); John Carradine (Bret Harte); William Henry (Charles Langdon); Robert Barrat (Horace E. Bixby); Walter Hampden (Jervis Langdon); Joyce Reynolds (Clara Clemens); Whitford Kane (Joe Goodwin); Percy Kilbride (Billings); Nana Bryant (Mrs. Langdon); Jackie Brown (Sam Clemens at twelve); Dickie Jones (Sam Clemens at fifteen); Russell Gleason (Orrin Clemens); Joseph Crehan (General Grant); Douglas Wood (William Howells).

Other: Irving Rapper (director); Jesse L. Lasky (producer); Alan LeMay (screenplay); Alan LeMay and Harold M. Sherman (adaptation); Harry Chandlee (additional dialogue). All biographical material based on works owned or controlled by the Mark Twain Company and the play *Mark Twain* by Harold M. Sherman. Sol Polito, Laurence Butler, Edwin Linden, Don Siegel, James Leicester (photography); Max Steiner (music); Herschel Daugherty (dialogue director); Leo F. Forbstein (music director); Bernaud Kaun (arrangements); Ralph Dawson (editor).

Opened at the Hollywood Theater, May 3, 1944. Running time, 130 minutes.

Tomorrow the World. Lester Cowan United Artists / 1944. Cast: Mr. March was Mike Frame; Betty Field (Leora Richards); Agnes Moorehead (Jessie); Skippy Homeier (Emil Bruckner); Joan Carroll (Pat Frame); Edith Argold (Frieda); Rudy Wissler (Stan); Boots Brown (Roy); Marvin Davis (Dennis); Patsy Ann Thompson (Millie); Mary Newton (school principal); Tom Fadden (mailman).

Other: Leslie Fenton (director); Lester Cowan (producer); Ring Lardner, Jr., and Leopold Atlas (screenplay); adapted from the play by James Gow and Armand D'Usseau.

Opened at the Globe Theater, New York, December 21, 1944. Running time, 86 minutes.

The Best Years of Our Lives. Samuel Goldwyn RKO / 1946. Cast: Mr. March was Al Stephenson; Myrna Loy (Milly Stephenson); Dana Andrews (Fred Derry); Teresa Wright (Peggy Stephenson); Virginia Mayo (Marie Derry); Harold Russell (Homer Parrish); Cathy O'Donnell (Wilma Cameron); Hoagy Carmichael (Butch Engle); Gladys George (Hortense Derry); Roman Bohnen (Pat Derry); Ray Collins (Mr. Milton); Steve Cochran (Cliff); Minna Gombell (Mrs. Parrish); Walter Baldwin (Mr. Parrish); Dorothy Adams (Mrs. Cameron); Don Beddoe (Mr. Cameron); Erskine Sanford (Bullard); Marlene Ames (Luella Parrish); Michael Hall (Rob Stevenson); Charles Halton (Prew); Howland Chamberlin (Thorpe).

Other: William Wyler (director); Samuel Goldwyn (producer); Robert E. Sherwood (screenplay); from the novel *Glory for Me* by MacKinlay Kantor; Gregg Toland (photography); Daniel Mandell (editor); Joseph Boyle (assistant director); Julia Heron (set decorator); Hugo Friedhofer (music); Emil Newman (music director); Sharaff (costumes).

Opened at the Astor Theater, New York, November 21, 1946. Running time, 165 minutes.

Another Part of the Forest. Universal-International / 1948. Cast: Mr. March was Marcus Hubbard; Ann Blyth (Regina Hubbard); Edmond O'Brien

(Ben Hubbard); Florence Eldridge (Lavinia Hubbard); Dan Duryea (Oscar Hubbard); Betsy Blair (Birdie Bagtry); Fritz Leiber (Colonel Isham); Whit Bissell (Jugger); Don Beddoe (Penniman); Wilton Graff (Sam Taylor); Virginia Farmer (Clara Bagtry); Libby Taylor (Cora); Smoki Whitfield (Jake).

Other: Michael Gordon (director); Jerry Bresler (producer); Hal Mohr (photography); Vladimir Pozner (screenplay); from a play by Lillian Hellman; Daniele Amfitheatrof (music); Milton Carruth (editor).

Opened at the Rivoli Theater, New York, May 18, 1948. Running time, 106 minutes.

Live Today for Tomorrow. Universal-International / 1948. Cast: Mr. March was Judge Calvin Cooke; Florence Eldridge (Catherine Cooke); Geraldine Brooks (Ellie Cooke); Edmond O'Brien (David Douglas); Stanley Ridges (Dr. Walter Morrison); John McIntire (Judge Ogden); Frederic Tozere (Charles Dayton); Will Wright (Judge Jim Wilder); Virginia Brissac (Mrs. Russell); Francis McDonald (Mr. Russell); Mary Servoss (Julia); Don Beddoe (Peterson); Clarence Muse (Mr. Pope).

Other: Michael Gordon (director); Michael Blankfort and Robert Thoeren (screenplay); based on the novel *The Mills of God* by Ernst Lothar; Jerry Bresler (producer); Hal Mohr (photography); Daniele Amfitheatrof (music); Ralph Dawson (editor).

Opened at Loew's Criterion Theater, New York, December 5, 1948. Running time, 91 minutes.

Christopher Columbus. J. Arthur Rank Universal-International / 1949. Cast: Mr. March was Christopher Columbus; Florence Eldridge (Queen Isabella of Spain); Francis L. Sullivan (Francisco de Bobadilla); Kathleen Ryan (Beatriz); Derek Bond (Diego de Aranas); Nora Swinburne (Joanna de Torres); Abraham Sofaer (Luis de Santangel); Linden Travers (Beatriz de Peraza); James Robertson Justice (Martin Pinzon); Dennis Vance (Francesco Pinzon); Richard Aherne (Vincente Pinson); Felix Aylmer (Father Perez); Francis Lister (King Ferdinand of Spain); Edward Rigby (Pedro); Niall McGinnis (Juan de la Cosa); Ralph Truman (captain); David Cole (Columbus's son).

Other: David MacDonald (director); A. Frank Bundy (producer); Cyril Roberts and Muriel and Sydney Box (screenplay); a Sydney Box Production and a Gainsborough Picture; Stephen Dade and David Harcourt (photography); V. Sagovsky (editor); color by Technicolor.

Opened at the Victoria Theater, New York, October 12, 1949. Running time, 104 minutes. (Originally opened at the Odeon, London, June 14, 1949.)

Death of a Salesman. Columbia / 1951. Cast: Mr. March was Willy Loman; Mildred Dunnock (Linda Loman); Kevin McCarthy (Biff Loman); Cameron Mitchell (Happy Loman); Howard Smith (Charley); Royal Beal (Ben); Don

Keefer (Bernard); Jesse White (Stanley); Claire Carleton (Miss Francis); David Alpert (Howard Wanger); Elisabeth Fraser (Miss Forsythe); Patricial Walker (Letta).

Other: Laslo Benedek (director); Stanley Roberts (screenplay); based on the play by Arthur Miller; a Stanley Kramer Company Production; Frank F. Planer (photography); Alex North (music); Morris Stoloff (musical director); William Lyon (editor).

Opened at the Victoria Theater, New York, December 20, 1951. Running time, 115 minutes.

It's a Big Country. Metro-Goldwyn-Mayer / 1952. Cast: Mr. March was Papa Esposito; Ethel Barrymore (Mrs. Brian Riordan); Keefe Brasselle (Seargeant Klein); Gary Cooper (Texas); Nancy Davis (Miss Coleman); Van Johnson (Adam Burch); Gene Kelly (Icarus Xenophon); Janet Leigh (Rosa Szabo); Marjorie Main (Mrs. Wrenley); George Murphy (Callaghan); William Powell (Professor); S. Z. Sakall (Stefan Szabo); Lewis Stone (Sexton); James Whitmore (Stacey); Keenan Wynn (Michael Fisher); Leon Ames (Secret Service operative); Angela Clarke (Mama Esposito); Sharon McManus (Sam Szabo); Elizabeth Risdon (woman); Bill Baldwin (Austin).

Other: Clarence Brown, Don Hartman, John Sturges, Richard Thorpe, Charles Vidor, Don Weis, William A. Wellman (directors); Robert Sisk (producer); Helen Deutsch, Dorothy Kingsley, Isobel Lennart, William Ludwig, Allen Rivkin, Dore Schary, George Wells (screenplays); John Alton, Ray June, William Mellor, Joseph Ruttenberg (photography); Ben Lewis, Frederick Y. Smith (film editing); Johnny Green (music supervisor); Alberto Colombo, Adolph Deutsch, Lennie Hayton, Bronislau Kaper, Rudolph G. Kopp, David Raksin, David Rose, Charles Wolcott (musical arrangements); Douglas Shearer (sound recording); Malcolm Brown, William Ferrari, Cedric Gibbons, Eddie Imazu, Arthur Lonergan, Gabriel Scognamillo (art direction); based in part on stories by Edgar Brooke, Claudia Cranston, John McNulty, Ray Chordes, Joseph Petracca, Lucille Schlossberg.

Opened at the Trans-Lux 52nd Street Theater, New York, January 8, 1952. Running time, 90 minutes.

Man on a Tightrope. Twentieth Century-Fox / 1953. Cast: Mr. March was Karel Cernik; Terry Moore (Teresa Cernik); Cameron Mitchell (Joe Vosdek); Gloria Grahame (Zama Cernik); Adolph Menjou (Fesker); Robert Beatty (Barovic); Alex D'Arcy (Rudolph); Richard Boone (Krofta); Hansi (Kalka the Dwarf); Pat Henning (Konradin); Paul Hartman (Jaromir); John Dehner (the chief); Philip Kennelly (the sergeant); Dorothea Wieck (duchess); Edelweiss Malchin (Vina Konradin); Margaret Slezak (Mrs. Jaromir); William Castello (the captain); and the Birnbach Circus.

Other: Elia Kazan (director); Robert E. Sherwood (screenplay); Robert

L. Jacks (producer); based on a story by Neil Peterson; filmed entirely in Bavaria; Georg Kraus (photography); Franz Waxman (music); Earle Hagen (orchestration); Hans Tost (assistant director).

Opened at the Mayfair Theater, New York, June 4, 1953. Running time, 105 minutes.

Executive Suite. Metro-Goldwyn-Mayer / 1954. Cast: Mr. March was Loren Phineas Shaw; Barbara Stanwyck (Julia O. Tredway); William Holden (McDonald Walling); June Allyson (Mary Walling); Walter Pidgeon (Frederick Alderson); Shelley Winters (Eva Bardeman); Paul Douglas (Josiah Dudley); Louis Calhern (George Nyle Caswell); Dean Jagger (Jesse Q. Grimm); Nina Foch (Erica Martin); Tim Considine (Mike Walling); William Phipps (Bill Ludden); Lucile Knoch (Mrs. George Nye Caswell); Edgar Stehli (Julius Steibel); Mary Adams (Sara Grimm); Virginia Brissac (Edith Alperson); Harry Shannon (Ed Benedeck).

Other: Robert Wise (director); John Houseman (producer); Ernest Lehman (screenplay); adapted from the novel by Cameron Hawley, Jud Kinberg (associate producer); George Folsey (photography); Cedric Gibbons and Edward Carfagno (art directors); George Rhein (assistant director); Douglas Shearer (recording supervisor); Edwin B. Willis and Emil Kuri (set decorators); Helen Rose (gowns); Sydney Guilaroff (hairstyles); William Tuttle (makeup); Ralph E. Winters (editor).

Opened at Radio City Music Hall, New York, May 6, 1954. Running time, 115 minutes.

The Bridges at Toko-Ri. Paramount / 1955. Cast: Mr. March was Rear Admiral George Tarrant; William Holden (Lieutenant Harry Brubaker, USNR); Grace Kelly (Nancy Brubaker); Mickey Rooney (Mike Forney); Robert Strauss (Beer Barrel); Charles McGraw (Commander Wayne Lee); Keiko Awaji (Kimiko); Earl Holliman (Nestor Gamidge); Richard Shannon (Lieutenant Olds); Willis B. Bouchey (Captain Evans); Nadene Ashdown (Kathy Brubaker); Cheryl Lyn Calloway (Susie); James Jankins (Assistant C.L.C. officer); Marshall V. Beebe (pilot); Charles Tannen (M.P. major); Teru Shimada (Japanese father).

Other: Mark Robson (director); William Perlberg (producer); a Perlberg-Seaton production; Valentine Davies (screenplay); adapted from the novel by James A. Michener; Loyal Griggs (photography); Charles G. Clarke (aerial photography); Lyn Murray (music); Alma Macrorie (editor); Wallace Kelley and Thomas Tutweiler (second unit photography); Hal Pereira and Henry Bumstead (art directors); Edith Head (costumes); Wally Westmore (makeup); Hugo Grenzbach and Gene Garvin (sound); Commander M. U. Beebe, USN (technical advisor); color by Technicolor.

Opened at Radio City Music Hall, New York, January 20, 1955. Running time, 102 minutes.

The Desperate Hours. Paramount / 1955. Cast: Mr. March was Dan Hilliard; Humphrey Bogart (Glenn Griffin); Martha Scott (Eleanor Hilliard); Arthur Kennedy (Jesse Bard); Dewey Martin (Hal Griffin); Gig Young (Chuck); Mary Murphy (Cindy Hilliard); Richard Eyer (Ralphie Hilliard); Robert Middleton (Sam Kobish); Alan Reed (detective); Bert Freed (Winston); Ray Collins (Masters); Whit Bissell (Carson); Ray Teal (Fredericks); Michael Moore (detective); Don Haggerty (detective); Ric Roman (Sal); Pat Flaherty (Dutch); Beverly Garland (Miss Swift); Louis Lettieri (Bucky Walling); Ann Doran (Mrs. Walling); Walter Baldwin (Patterson).

Other: William Wyler (producer and director); Robert Wyler (associate producer); Joseph Hayes (screenplay) based on his novel and play. Lee Garmes (photography); Gail Kubik (music); Hal Pereira and Joseph MacMillan Johnson (art directors); Sam Comer and Grace Gregory (set decorations); Edith Head (costumes); Robert Swink (film editor); Wally Westmore (makeup artist); John P. Fulton and Farciot Edouart (special effects); Hugo Grenzbach and Winston Leverett (sound recording).

Opened at the Criterion Theater, New York, October 5, 1955. Running time, 112 minutes.

Alexander the Great. United Artists / 1956. Cast: Mr. March was Philip of Macedonia; Richard Burton (Alexander); Claire Bloom (Barsine); Danielle Darrieux (Olympias); Harry Andrews (Darius); Stanley Baker (Attalus); Niall MacGinnis (Parmenio); Peter Cushing (Memnon); Michael Hordern (Demosthenes); Barry Jones (Aristotle); Marisa de Leza (Eurydice); Gustavo Rojo (Cleitus); Ruben Rojo (Philotas); William Squire (Cachinos); Helmut Dantine (Nectanebus); Friedric Ledebur (Antipater); Peter Wynngarde (Pausanius); Virgilio Texeira (Ptolemy); Teresa Del Rio (Roxane); Julio Pena (Arsites); Jose Nieto (Spithridates); Carlos Baena (Nearchus); Larry Taylor (Perdiccas); Jose Marco (Harpacus); Ricardo Valle (Hephaestion); Carmen Carulla (Stateira); Jesus Luque (Aristander); Ramsey Ames (drunken woman); Mario de Barros (messenger); Ellen Rossen (Apites); Carlos Acevedo (Orchas).

Other: Robert Rossen (writer, producer and director); Robert Krasker (photographer); CinemaScope; color by Technicolor; Mario Nascimbene (music); Ralph Kempler (editor); Andre Andrejew (set design); Gordon S. Griffith (production executive); Cliff Richardson (special effects); David Ffolkes (costumes); Prince Peter of Greece (technical adviser); shot in Spain and Italy.

Opened at the Capitol Theater, New York, March 28, 1956. Running time, 143 minutes.

The Man in the Gray Flannel Suit. Twentieth Century-Fox / 1956. Cast: Mr. March was Hopkins; Gregory Peck (Tom Rath); Jennifer Jones (Betsy Rath); Marisa Pavan (Maria); Ann Harding (Mrs. Hopkins); Lee J. Cobb (Judge Bernstein); Keenan Wynn (Caesar Gardella); Gene Lockhart (Hawthorne); Gigi Perreau (Susan Hopkins); Portland Mason (Janie); Arthur O'Connell (Walker); Henry Daniell (Bill Ogden); Connie Gilchrist (Mrs. Manter); Joseph Sweeney (Edward Schultz); Sandy Descher (Barbara); Mickey Maga (Pete); Kenneth Tobey (Mahoney); Ruth Clifford (Florence); Geraldine Wall (Miriam); Alex Campbell (Johnson); Jerry Hall (Freddie); Jack Mather (police sergeant); Frank Wilcox (Dr. Pearce); Nan Martin (Miss Lawrence); Tris Coffin (Byron Holgate); William Philips (Bugala); Leon Alton (Cliff); Phyllis Graffeo (Gina); Dorothy Adams (Mrs. Hopkins' maid); Dorothy Phillips (maid); Mary Benoit (secretary); King Lockwood (business executive); Lomax Study (elevator operator); John Breen (Walter); Renato Vanni (Italian farm wife); Mario Siletti (carriage driver); Lee Graham (crew chief); Michael Jeffries (Mr. Sims); Roy Glenn (Master Sergeant Matthews).

Other: Nunnally Johnson (director); Nunnally Johnson (screenplay); Darryl F. Zanuck (producer); adapted from the novel by Sloan Wilson; CinemaScope; color by DeLuxe; Charles G. Clarke (photography); Dorothy Spencer (editor); Bernard Herrmann (music); Alfred Bruzlin, Harry M. Leonard (sound); Walter M. Scott, Stuart A. Reiss (set decoration); Lyle R. Wheeler, Jack Martin Smith (art directors); Hal Herman (assistant director).

Opened at the Roxy Theater, New York, April 12, 1956. Running time, 152 minutes.

Middle of the Night. Columbia / 1959. Cast: Mr. March was Jerry Kingsley; Kim Novak (Betty Preisser); Lee Philips (George Preisser); Glenda Farrell (Betty's mother); Martin Balsam (Jack); Albert Dekker (Lockman); Lee Grant (Marilyn); Edith Meiser (Evelyn Kingsley); Joan Copeland (Lillian); Betty Walker (the widow); Rudy Bond (Gould); Effie Afton (Mrs. Carroll); Jan Norris (Alice Mueller); Anna Berger (Caroline); Audrey Peters (Elizabeth); Lou Gilbert (Sherman); Dora Weissman (Lockman's wife); Lee Richardson (Lockman's son); Alfred Leberfeld (Ellman); Nelson Olmsted (Erskine).

Other: A Sudan Production. George Justin (producer); Delbert Mann (director); Paddy Chayefsky (screenplay); from the play by Mr. Chayefsky as presented on Broadway by Joshua Logan; Joseph Brun (photography); Frank L. Thompson (costumes); Jean Louis (Miss Novak's clothes); Edward S. Haworth (art director); Jack Wright, Jr. (set decorations); George Bassman (music composer and conductor); Richard Gramaglia and Richard Vorisek (sound); Irving Temaner (production coordinator); Everett Chambers (casting and dialogue supervision); Carl Lerner (film editor); Charles H. Maguire (assistant director); George Newman (makeup); Marguerite James (script supervisor); Lionel Kaplan (technical advisor); Stephen Bono (production manager); Flo Transfield (wardrobe); filmed in New York.

Opened at the Odeon and Trans-Lux Theaters, New York, June 17, 1959. Running time, 118 minutes.

Inherit the Wind. United Artists / 1960. Cast: Mr. March was Matthew Harrison Brady; Spencer Tracy (Henry Drummond); Gene Kelly (E.K. Hornbeck); Florence Eldridge (Mrs. Brady); Dick York (Bertram T. Cates); Donna Anderson (Rachel Brown); Harry Morgan (judge); Elliott Reid (Davenport); Philip Coolidge (major); Claude Akins (Reverend Brown); Paul Hartman (Meeker); Jimmy Boyd (Howard); Noah Beery, Jr. (Stebbins); Gordon Polk (Sillers); Ray Teal (Dunlap); Norman Fell (radio announcer); Hope Summers (Mrs. Krebs); Renee Godfrey (Mrs. Stebbins).

Other: Stanley Kramer (producer and director); Nathan Douglas and Harold Smith (screenplay); based on a play by Jerome Lawrence and Robert E. Lee; Ernest Laszlo (photography); Clem Beauchamp (production manager); Rudolph Sternad (production design); Ernest Gold (music); Frederic Knudtson (editor); Joe Lapis and Walter Elliott (sound); Bud Westmore (makeup); Anne P. Kramer (assistant to the producer); Ivan Volkman (assistant director).

Opened at the Astor and Trans-Lux 85th Street Theaters, New York, October 12, 1960. Running time, 127 minutes.

The Young Doctors. United Artists / 1961. Cast: Mr. March was Dr. Joseph Pearson; Ben Gazzara (Dr. David Coleman); Dick Clark (Dr. Alexander); Ina Balin (Cathy Hunt); Eddie Albert (Dr. Charles Dornberger); Phyllis Love (Elizabeth Alexander); Edward Andrews (Bannister); Aline MacMahon (Dr. Luxy Grainger); Arthur Hill (Tomaselli); Rosemary Murphy (Miss Groves); Barnard Hughes (Dr. Ken O'Donnell); Joseph Bova (Dr. Shawcross); George Segal (Dr. Howard); Matt Crowley (Dr. Rufus); Dick Button (operating intern); William Hansen (x-ray technician); Addison Powell (board physician).

Other: A Drexes-Miller-Turman Production. Stuart Miller and Lawrence Turman (producers); Phil Karson (director); Joseph Hayes (screenplay); based on the novel *The Final Diagnosis* by Arthur Hailey; Arthur J. Ornitz (photography); Elmer Bernstein (music); Jimmy Di Gangi and Angelo Laiacona (art direction); Richard Sylbert (production designer); Robert Swink (editor); Ruth Morley (costumes); filmed in New York City.

Opened at the Astor and Trans-Lux 85th Street Theaters, New York, August 23, 1961. Running time, 100 minutes.

The Condemned of Altona. Titanus-S.G.C. Twentieth Century-Fox / 1963. Cast: Mr. March was Gerlach; Sophia Loren (Johanna); Maximilian Schell (Franz); Robert Wagner (Werner); Franscoise Prevost (Leni); Alfredo Franchi (groundskeeper); Lucia Pelella (groundskeeper's wife); Roberto Massa (driver); Carlo Antonini (police official); Armando Sifo (policeman); Antonia Cianci (maid); Aldo Pecchioli (cook).

Other: Vittorio de Sica (director); Carlo Ponti (producer); Abby Mann and Cesare Zavittini (screenplay); based on a play by Jean-Paul Sartre; a co-production of Titanus Films (Rome) and S.G.C. Films (Paris); Robert Gerardi (photography); Music: *Symphony Number 11, Opus 203*, by Dmitri Shostakovich, conducted by Franco Ferrara; Ezio Frigerio (art director); Renato Guttuso (drawings); Manuel Del Campo and Adriana Novelli (editors); Ennio Sensi (sound); Pier Luigi Pizzi (wardrobe); Luciano Perugia (production manager); Luisa Alessandri and Giuseppe Menegatti (assistant directors); filmed in CinemaScope in Italy and Germany.

Opened at the Astor and 34th Street East Theaters, New York, October 30, 1963. Running time, 114 minutes.

Seven Days in May. Seven Arts-Joel Productions Paramount / 1964. Cast: Mr. March was President Jordan Lyman; Burt Lancaster General James M. Scott); Kirk Douglas (Colonel Martin "Jiggs"Casey); Ava Gardner (Eleanor Holbrook); Edmond O'Brien (Senator Raymond Clark); Martin Balsam (Paul Girard); George Macready (Christopher Todd); Whit Bissel (Senator Prentice); John Houseman (Admiral Barnswell); Hugh Marlowe (Harold McPherson); Bart Burns (Arthur Corwin); Richard Anderson (Colonel Murdock); Jack Mullaney (Lieutenant Howe); Andrew Duggan (Colonel "Mutt" Henderson); John Larkin (Colonel Broderick); Malcolm Atterbury (White House physician); Helen Kleeb (Esther Townsend); Colette Jackson (bar girl).

Other: John Frankenheimer (director and co-producer); Edward Lewis (producer); Rod Serling (Screenplay); based on a novel by Fletcher Knebel and Charles W. Bailey II; Ellsworth Fredricks (photography); Cary Odell (art direction); Edward Boyle (set decorations); Jerry Goldsmith (music); Ferris Webster (editor); Joe Edmondson (sound); Hal Polaire (production manager and assistant director).

Opened at the Criterion and Sutton Theaters, New York, February 19, 1964. Running time, 120 minutes.

Hombre. Twentieth Century-Fox / 1967. Cast: Mr. March was Alexander Favor; Paul Newman (John Russell); Richard Boone (Cicero Grimes); Diane Cilento (Jessie Brown); Cameron Mitchell (Sheriff Frank Braden); Barbara Rush (Audra Favor); Peter Lazer (Billy Lee Blake); Margaret Blye (Doris Blake); Martin Balsam (Henry Mendez); Skip Ward (Steve Early);Frank Silvera (Mexican bandit); David Canary (Lamar Dean); Val Avery (Delgado); Larry Ward (soldier); Linda Cordova (Mrs. Delgado); Pete Hernandez (Apache); Merrill C. Isbell (Apache).

Other: Martin Ritt and Irving Ravetch (producers); Martin Ritt (director); Ray Kellogg (second unit director); Irving Ravetch and Harriet Frank, Jr. (screenplay); based on the novel by Elmore Leonard; James Wong Howe (photography); David Rose (music composed and conducted); Frank Bracht (editor); Jack Martin Smith and Robert E. Smith (art direction); Jack R. Carter and David Dockendorf (set decorations); Walter M. Scott and Raphael Bretton (set decorations); Leo Shuken and Jack Hayes (orchestration); Don Feld (costumes); Ben Nye (makeup); Margaret Donovan (hairstyles); Harry A. Caplan (production manager); William McGarry (assistant director); location scenes filmed in Arizona; DeLuxe Color; Panavision.

Opened at the Astor and 68th Street Playhouse, New York, March 21, 1967. Running time, 111 minutes.

tick . . . tick . . . tick . . . Metro-Goldwyn-Mayer / 1970. Cast: Mr. March was Mayor Parks; Jim Brown (Jimmy Price); George Kennedy (John Little); Lynn Carlin (Julia Little); Don Stroud (Bengy Springer); Janet MacLachlan (Mary Price); Richard Elkins (Brad Wilkes); Clifton James (D.J. Rankin); Bob Random (John Braddock); Mills Watson (Deputy Warren); Bernie Casey (George Harley); Anthony James (H.C. Tolbert); Dub Taylor (Junior); Karl Swanson (Braddock, Sr.).

Other: Ralph Nelson (director); Ralph Nelson and James Lee Barrett (producers); James Lee Barrett (screenplay); Loyal Griggs (photography); Jerry Styner (music; George W. Davis, Bill Glasgow (art direction); Alex Beaton (film editor); Robert R. Benton, Don Greenwood, Sr. (set decoration); Franklin Milton (sound); Mike Curb (music supervision); Michael S. Glick (assistant director); Panavision; MetroColor.

Opened at Radio City Music Hall, New York, February 12, 1970. Running time, 96 minutes.

The Iceman Cometh. American Film Theater / 1973. Cast: Mr. March was Harry Hope; Lee Marvin (Hickey); Robert Ryan (Larry Slade); Jeff Bridges (Don Parritt); Martyn Green (The Captain); George Voskovec (The General); Moses Gunn (Joe Mott); Tom Pedi (Rocky Pioggi); Evans (Cora); Bradford Dillman (Willie Oban); Sorrell Brooke (Hugo Kalmar); John McLiam (Jimmy Tomorrow).

Other: John Frankenheimer (director); Ralph Woolsey (director of photography); Harold Kress (editor); Ely A. Landau (producer). American Film Theater adaptation of a Eugene O'Neill play.

Opened at selected theaters, October 31, 1973. Running time, 239 minutes.

Bibliography

BOOKS

Agee, James, *Agee on Film, Reviews and Comments by James Agee*, Beacon Press, Boston, 1968.

Anobile, Richard J., Rouben Mamoulian's *Dr. Jekyll and Mr. Hyde Starring Fredric March*, Darien House, Inc., New York, 1975.

Astor, Mary, *A Life on Film*, Delacorte Press, New York, 1971.

Atkinson, Brooks, *Broadway*, The Macmillan Co., New York, 1970.

Bailyn, Bernard, *The Great Republic: A History of the American People*, Little, Brown and Company, Boston, 1977.

Baxter, John, *Hollywood in the Thirties*, Paperback Library, New York, 1970.

Beck, Calvin, *Scream Queens, Heroines of the Horrors*, Macmillan Publishing Co., New York, 1978.

Behlmer, Rudy and Thoman, Tony, *Hollywood's Hollywood, The Movies about the Movies*, The Citadel Press, Secaucus, NJ, 1975.

Berg, A. Scott, *Goldwyn*, Alfred A. Knopf, New York, 1989.

Bowers, Ronald, *The Selznick Players*, A. S. Barnes and Co., New York, 1976.

Brooks, T. and Marsh, E., *Complete Dictionary to Prime Time Network TV Shows 1946–Present*, Ballantine, New York, 1985.

Brown, Jared, *Zero Mostel: A Biography*, Atheneum, New York, 1989.

Brown, Peter Harry, *Kim Novak, The Reluctant Goddess*, St. Martin's Press, New York, 1986.

Canham, Kingsley, *The Hollywood Professionals*, A. S. Barnes & Co., New York, 1976.

Clurman, Harold, *All People Are Famous*, Harcourt Brace Jovanovich, New York, 1974.

Corliss, Richard, *Greta Garbo*, Pyramid Publications, New York, 1974.

Dale, R. C., *The Films of Rene Clair*, The Scarecrow Press Inc., Metuchen,

NJ, 1986.

Dooley, Roger, *From Scarface to Scarlett: American Film in the 1930s*, Harcourt Brace Jovanovich, New York, 1981.

Douglas, Kirk, *The Ragman's Son: An Autobiography*, Simon & Schuster, New York, 1988.

Edmonds, I. G., *Paramount Pictures and the People Who Made Them*, Mimura, Reiko, A. S. Barnes & Company, New York, 1980.

Edwards, Anne, *A Remarkable Woman: A Biography of Katharine Hepburn*, William Morrow and Co., New York, 1985.

Everson, William K., *Classics of the Horror Film*, The Citadel Press, Secaucus, NJ, 1974.

Flamini, Roland, *Scarlett, Rhett, and a Cast of Thousands*, Macmillan Publishing Co., New York, 1975.

Freedland, Michael, *Cagney*, Stein and Day, New York, 1975.

Freedland, Michael, *Jack Lemmon*, St. Martin's Press, New York, 1985.

Gardner, Gerald and Harriet Modell, *The Tara Treasury*, Arlington House Publishers, Westport, Connecticut, 1980.

Goodman, Walter, *The Committee: The Extraordinary Career of the House Committee on Un-American Activities*, Farrar, Straus and Giroux, 1968.

Griffith, Richard Mayer, Arthur, *The Movies*, Bonanza Books, New York, 1957.

Halliwell, Leslie, *Halliwell's Hundred*, Granada, New York, 1982.

Hardy, Forsyth, *Grierson on the Movies*, Faber and Faber, Boston, 1981.

Harris, Warren G., *Gable and Lombard*, Simon and Schuster, New York, 1974.

Harvey, James, *Romantic Comedy in Hollywood*, Alfred A. Knopf, New York, 1987.

Hayne, Donald, *The Autobiography of Cecil B. DeMille*, Prentice-Hall, Inc., Englewood Cliffs, NJ, 1959.

Higham, Charles, *Errol Flynn: The Untold Story*, A Dell Book, New York, 1981.

Higham, Charles, *Sisters: The Story of Olivia De Havilland and Joan Fontaine*, Coward-McCann, New York, 1984.

Hirschborn, Clive, *Gene Kelly*, St. Martin's Press, New York, 1984.

Hochman, Stanley, editor, *From Quasimodo to Scarlett O'Hara: A National Board of Review Anthology 1920–1940*, Frederick Ungar Publishing Co., New York, 1982.

Hunter, Allen, *Walter Matthau*, St. Martin's Press, 1984.

Israel, Lee, *Miss Tallulah Bankhead*, G. P. Putnam's Sons, New York, 1972.

Kael, Pauline, *Reeling: An Atlantic Monthly Pressbook*, Little, Brown, and Company, Boston, Toronto, 1976.

Katsilibas, Davis and Loy, Myrna, *Myrna Loy: Being and Becoming*, Alfred A. Knopf, New York, 1987.

Kazan, Elia, *Elia Kazan: A Life*, Alfred A. Knopf, New York, 1988.

Keyes, Evelyn, *Scarlett O'Hara's Younger Sister*, A Fawcett Crest Book, New York, 1977.

Klein, Michael and Gilliun, Parker, *The English Novel and the Movies*, Frederick Ungar Publishing Co., New York, 1981.

Kobal, John, *People Will Talk*, Alfred A. Knopf, New York, 1985.

Kobler, John, *Damned in Paradise: The Life of John Barrymore*, Atheneum, New York, 1977.

Lambert, Gavin, *On Cukor*, G. P. Putnum's Sons, New York, 1972.

Langer, Lawrence, *The Magic Curtain*, E. P. Dutton & Company, New York, 1951.

Lenburg, Jeff, *Peekaboo: The Story of Veronica Lake*, St. Martin's Press, New York, 1983.

Leonard, William, *Theater: Stage to Screen to Television*, Scarecrow Press, New York, 1981.

Leroy, Mervyn, *Mervyn Leroy: Take One*, Hawthorn Books, New York, 1974.

Levin, Martin, *Hollywood and the Great Fan Magazines*, Arbor House Publishing Co., Inc., New York, 1970.

Leyda, Jay, *Voices of Film Experience*, Macmillan Publishing Co., New York, 1977.

Lorentz, Pare, *Lorentz on Film*, Hopkinson and Blake, Publishers, New York, 1975.

Madson, Axel, *William Wyler*, Thomas Y. Crowell Co., New York, 1973.

Maney, Richard, *Fanfare*, Harper & Brothers Publishers, New York, 1957.

Marx, Arthur, *Goldwyn: A Biography of the Man behind the Myth*, Ballantine Books, 1977.

McGilligan, Patrick, *Cagney: The Actor as Auteur*, A. S. Barnes & Co., San Diego, 1982.

Meyer, William, *Warner Brothers Directors: The Hard-Boiled, The Comic, and The Weepers*, Arlington House Publishers, New Rochelle, NY, 1978.

Milne, Tom, *Mamoulian*, Indiana University Press, Bloomington, London, 1969.

Mordenn, Ethan, *Movie Star: A Look at the Women Who Made Hollywood*, St. Martin's Press, New York, 1983.

Myrick, Susan, *White Columns in Hollywood*, Mercer University Press, Macon, GA, 1982.

Ogden, August, *The Dies Committee*, The Catholic University of America Press, Washington, DC, 1945.

Parish, James Robert, *The Paramount Pretties*, Arlington House, New Rochelle, NY, 1972.

Parish, James Robert, *The RKO Gals*, Arlington House, New Rochelle, NY, 1974.

Quirk, Lawrence J., *The Films of Fredric March*, The Citadel Press, New

York, 1971.

Quirk, Lawrence J., *The Great Romantic Films*, The Citadel Press, Secaucus, NJ, 1974.

Quirk, Lawrence J., *Claudette Colbert: An Illustrated Biography*, Crown Publishers, New York, 1985.

Quirk, Lawrence J., *Child of Fate: MargaretSullavan*, St. Martin's Press, New York, 1986.

Quirk, Lawrence J., *Norma: The Story of Norma Shearer*, St. Martin's Press, New York, 1988.

Ringgold, Gene and Bodeen, Dewitt, *The Films of Cecil B. DeMille*, The Citadel Press, New York, 1969.

Ronald, Bruce and Ronald, Virginia, *Now Playing: An Informal History of the Victoria Theater*, Landfall Press, Dayton, OH, 1989.

Ross, Lillian and Ross, Helen, *The Player: A Profile of an Art*, Simon and Schuster, New York, 1962.

Russell, Harold, *The Best Years of My Life*, Paul S. Eriksson Publisher, Middleburg, VT, 1981.

Samuels, Charles, *Encountering Directors*, G. P. Putnam's Sons, New York, 1972.

Shank, Theodore J., *A Digest of 500 Plays*, Crowell-Collier Press, New York, 1963.

Sheppard, Dick, *Elizabeth: The Life and Career of Elizabeth Taylor*, Doubleday and Co., Garden City, NY, 1974.

Shipman, David, *The Great Movie Stars: The Golden Years*, DaCapo Press, New York, 1982.

Sinclair, Andrew, *John Ford*, The Dial Press/James Wade, New York, 1979.

Spoto, Donald, *Stanley Kramer: Film Maker*, G. P. Putnam's Sons, New York, 1978.

Stenn, David, *Clara Bow Runnin' Wild*, Doubleday, New York, 1988.

Stott, William and Stott, Jane, *On Broadway*, University of Texas Press, Austin, 1978.

Sumners, Anthony, *Goddess: The Secret Lives of Marilyn Monroe*, Macmillan Publishing Co., New York, 1985.

Swindell, Larry, *Spencer Tracy*, The World Publishing Company, New York, 1969.

Swindell, Larry, *Screwball*, William Morrow & Co., New York, 1975.

Thomas, Bob, *Selznick*, Doubleday & Co., Garden City, New York, 1970.

Thomas, Bob, *Golden Boy: The Untold Story of William Holden*, St. Martin's Press, NY, 1983.

Thomas, Tony, *Cads and Cavaliers: The Gentlemen Adventurers of the Movies*, South Brunswick, NY, 1973.

Timberlake, Craig, *The Life & Work of David Belasco*, Bishop of Broadway, Library Publishers, New York, 1954.

Warren, Doug and Cagney, James, *Cagney: The Authorized Biography*, St. Martin's Press, New York, 1983.

Wiley, Mason and Bona, Damien, *Inside Oscar, The Unofficial History of the Academy Awards*, Ballantine Books, New York, 1987.

Wray, Fay, *On the Other Hand: A Life Story*, St. Martin's Press, New York, 1989.

Young, William, *Famous Actors and Actresses on the American Stage*, Documents of American Theater History, Volume 2 K–Z, R. R. Bowker Co., New York, 1975.

Zierold, Norman, *Garbo*, Stein and Day, New York, 1969.

Zierold, Norman, *The Hollywood Tycoons*, Hamish Hamilton, London, 1969.

Zierold, Norman, *The Moguls*, Coward-McCann, Inc., New York, 1969.

TAPED INTERVIEWS

Hood, J. Vincent. Interview with author. Racine, WI. 1–13–90, 1–27–90.
Perkins, Lillian Dufour. Interview with author. Racine, WI. 1–27–90.
Jones, Alice Cahoon. Interview with author. Racine, WI. 2–10–90.
Peters, Oswald. Interview with author. Grafton, WI. 2–18–90.
Macaulay, Jackie Ramsey. Interview with author. Madison, WI. 2–24–90.
Macaulay, Stewart. Interview with author. Madison, WI. 2–24–90.
Nevins, Alice Wright. Interview with author. Racine, WI. 3–4–90.
Bundesen, Dorothy. Interview with author. Brown Deer, WI. 4–1–90.
Mucks Jr., Arlie. Interview with author. Madison, WI. 4–12–90.
Hall, Virginia. Interview with author. Madison, WI. 5–18–90.
Brickley, Julie Ramsey. Interview with author. Green Bay, WI. 6–9–90.
Hobart, Rose. Interview with author. Beverly Hills, CA. 8–9–90.
Bellamy, Ralph. Interview with author. Beverly Hills, CA. 8–9–90.
Kramer, Stanley. Interview with author. Beverly Hills, CA. 8–10–90.
Wise, Robert. Interview with author. Beverly Hills, CA. 8–10–90.
Lang, June. Interview with author. Beverly Hills, CA. 8–11–90.
Dillman, Bradford. Interview with author. Beverly Hills, CA. 8–11–90.
Brown, Martha. Interview with author. Beverly Hills, CA. 8–10–90.
Owen, Jean Bickel. Interview with author. Pasadena, CA. 8–10–90.
Davis, Kathryn. Interview with author. Shorewood, WI. 9–17–90. 9–24–90.
Post, Jane Carpenter Post. Interview with author. Mantoloking, NJ. 5–3–91.
Leon, Eleanor. Interview with author. Kent, CT. 5–4–91.
Legere-Binns, Marsha. Interview with author. New Milford, CT. 5–4–91.

TELEPHONE INTERVIEWS

Sheratsky, Dr. Rodney, scholar. Called author. Burlington, WI. 12–6–89.
Sheratsky, Dr. Rodney, scholar. Telephone interview by author. NJ.

12–16–89.

Kerdasha, Phyllis, daughter of Aline Ellis. Telephone interview by author. Burlington, WI. 3–25–90.

Butts, Porter, Director Emeritus Memorial Union, University of Wisconsin, Madison. Telephone interview by author. Burlington, WI. 5–5–90.

Hepburn, Katharine, actress. Telephone interview by author. Burlington, WI, 5–5–90.

Stander, Lionel, actor. Called author. Burlington, WI. 5–17–90.

Hobart, Rose, actress. Telephone interview by author. Burlington, WI. 5–7–90.

Quirk, Lawrence J., author. Telephone interview by author. Burlington, WI. 5–25–90.

Hill, Arthur, actor. Called author. Burlington, WI. 6–3–90.

Anderson, Richard, actor. Called author. Burlington, WI. 6–3–90.

Mann, Delbert, director. Telephone interview by author. Burlington, WI. 6–4–90.

Post, Jane Carpenter Post, goddaughter of Fredric March. Called author. Burlington, WI. 6–11–90.

Bickel, John H., nephew of Fredric March. Telephone interview by author. Milwaukee, WI. 7–17–90.

Akins, Claude, actor. Telephone interview by author. Milwaukee, WI. 7–17–90.

Gersh, Phil, agent. Telephone interview by author. Burlington, WI. 8–19–90.

Leon, Eleanor, New Milford neighbor. Telephone interview by author. Burlington, WI. 8–19–90.

Rodgers, Mrs. Richard (Dorothy), New York friend. Telephone interview by author. Burlington, WI. 8–28–90.

Knopf, Christopher, Producer. Telephone interview by author. Milwaukee, WI. 8–22–90.

Knopf, Mildred, Los Angeles friend. Telephone interview by author. Milwaukee, WI. 8–24–90.

Mader, Roland, Business Agent. Telephone interview by author. Burlington, WI. 8–27–90.

Hartley, Elizabeth, neice of Fredric March. Telephone interview by author. Burlington, WI. 8–27–90.

Davis, Kathryn, first cousin of Fredric March. Telephone interview by author. Burlington, WI. 9–2–90.

Binns, Marsha, owner of the March "Barn," New Milford. Telephone interview by author. 9–25–90.

Quirk, Lawrence J., author. Called author, New York. 9–18–90.

Hawes, James, director of theater. Telephone interview by author. 12–29–90.

LETTERS

Gallagher, Mary. Letter to Charles Carpenter. 10–6–61.
Sheratsky, Dr. Rodney. Letter to author. 12–11–89, 2–3–90, 2–21–90,
  3–24–90, 4–20–90, 7–7–90.
Hymer, Esther Wanner. Letter to author. 4–23–90.
Craig, Isabel McLay. Letter to author. 4–11–90.
Ferguson, Mary Ella. Letter to author. 4–11–90.
Wilson, Helen Harper. Letter to author. 1–25–90.
Chandler, Arthur. Letter to author. 1–25–90.
Taylor, H. Gordon. Letter to author. 1–25–90.
Peters, Oswald. Letter to author. 2–12–90.
Taylor, Fanny. Letter to author. 5–1–90.
Lidden, Charles P. Letter to author. 5–2–90.
Eidam, Elizabeth Sehon. Letter to author. 2–5–90.
Mortimer, Iva Rankin. Letter to author. 3–15–90.
O'Sullivan, Maureen. Letter to author. 5–8–90.
Hepburn, Katharine. Letter to author. 5–1–90.
Bellamy, Ralph. Letter to author. 5–10–90.
Hobart, Rose. Letter to author. 5–1–90.
Kazan, Elia. Letter to author. 5–17–90.
Wise, Robert. Letter to author. 5–18–90.
Doran, Ann. Letter to author. 5–20–90.
Lang, June. Letter to author. 5–9–90.
Kerdasha, Phyllis. Letter to author. 3–20–90.
Link, Gloria. Letter to author. 3–29–90.
Fantacci, Penelope March. Letter to author. 4–21–90.
Fantacci, Penelope March. Letter to author. 5–17–90.
Falkenburg, Jinx. Letter to author. 5–21–90.
Swinburne, Nora. Letter to author. 5–21–90.
Clark, Dick. Letter to author. 5–24–90.
Keefer, Don. Letter to author. 5–20–90.
Beddoe, Don. Letter to author. 5–25–90.
Mauch, Billy. Letter to author. 5–30–90.
Dillman, Bradford. Letter to author. 5–23–90.
Cushing, Peter. Letter to author. 5–29–90.
Mann, Delbert. Letter to author. 5–31–90.
Akins, Claude. Letter to author. 6–1–90.
Moore, Terry. Letter to author. 6–15–90.
Wyatt, Jane. Letter to author. 7–2–90.
Fantacci, Penelope March. Letter to author. 7–25–90 thru 7–29–90.
Garland, Beverly. Letter to author. 7–30–90.
Morris, Jane. Letter to author. 8–23–90.

Fantacci, Penelope March. Letter to author. 8–27–90.
Fantacci, Penelope March. Letter to author. 9–12–90.
Fantacci, Penelope March. Letter to author. 9–26–90.
Barton, Robert. Letter to author. 10–5–90.
Morris, Jane. Letter to author. 11–3–90.
Quinn, Anthony. Letter to author. 11–27–90.
Fantacci, Penelope March. Letter to author. 2–18–91.
Gersh, Phil. Letter to author. 6–28–91.
Bradbury, Michael. Letter to author. 7–5–91.
Parrish, Vicki. Letter to author. 9–6–92.

LETTERS FROM FREDRIC MARCH

Bickel, Frederick. Letter to mother. 6–23–12.
Bickel, Frederick. Letter to mother. 7–11–12.
Bickel, Frederick. Letter to Jack Bickel. 3–12–13.
March, Fredric. Letter to Paul Osborn. 5–30–63.
March, Fredric. Letter to Dore Schary. 1–29–60.
March, Fredric. Letter to Vinnie Hood. 2–25–72.
March, Fredric. Letter to Vinnie Hood. 4–1–72.
March, Fredric. Letter to Jack Bickel. 7–1–40.
March, Fredric. Letter to Jack Bickel. 10–4–41.
March, Fredric. Letter to Jack Bickel. 9–1–43.
March, Fredric. Letter to Laurence Hall. 10–7–60.
March, Fredric. Letter to Laurence Hall. 12–6–60.
March, Fredric. Letter to Laurence Hall. 2–16–60.
March, Fredric. Letter to Laurence Hall. 5–18–63.
March, Fredric. Letter to Laurence Hall. 9–23–63.
March, Fredric. Letter to Laurence Hall. 1–8–65.
March, Fredric. Letter to Laurence Hall. 9–27–65.
March, Fredric. Letter to Laurence Hall. 12–3–68.
March, Fredric. Letter to Laurence Hall. 5–21–68.
March, Fredric. Letter to Laurence Hall. 3–19–70.
March, Fredric. Letter to Laurence Hall. 5–19–70.
March, Fredric. Letter to Laurence Hall. 5–21–70.
March, Fredric. Letter to Laurence Hall. 9–23–71.
March, Fredric. Letter to Laurence Hall. 2–1–75.
March, Fredric. Letter to Charles Carpenter. 10–6–61.
March, Fredric. Letter to Chuck Carpenter. 6–7–73.
March, Fredric. Letter to Chuck Carpenter. 10–15–73.
March, Fredric. Letter to Chuck Carpenter. 4–11–74.
March, Fredric. Letter to Chuck Carpenter. 1–11–75.
March, Fredric. Letter to Mrs. Jack Ramsey. c. 1960.

March, Fredric. Letter to Jack Bickel. 8–3–73.
March, Fredric. Letter to Jack Bickel. 8–6–73.
March, Fredric. Letter to Jack Bickel. 8–16–73.
March, Fredric. Letter to Jack Bickel. 8–24–73.
March, Fredric. Letter to Jack Bickel. 9–1–73.
March, Fredric. Letter to Jack Bickel. 9–9–73.
March, Fredric. Letter to Jack Bickel. 10–15–73.

ARCHIVE MATERIAL

March Papers: State Historical Society of Wisconsin, Sources for Mass
Communications, Film and Theater Research, The University of Wisconsin,
Madison, WI.
    Fredric March Papers—Record Group 123AN
    Gale Sondergaard Papers—Record Group 58AN
    Kermit Bloomgarden Papers—Record Group 8AN
    Arthur Cantor Papers—Record Group 85AN
    Paddy Chayefsky Papers—Record Group 26AN
    John Cromwell Papers—Record Group 139AN
    Edna Ferber Papers—Record Group 98AN
    David Ffolkes Papers—Record Group 177AN
    Paul Romaine Osborn Papers—Record Group 49AN
    Rod Serling Papers—Record Group 43AN
    Nedrick Young Papers—Record Group 132AN

March Folder: Racine County Historical Society and Museum—Fredric March
Folder and first film, Racine WI.

PERIODICALS

American Home, "On Location for 200 Years," March 1944.
American Magazine, "Papa Christmas," Dec. 1961, pp. 88.
American Magazine, "Those Incredible Barrymores," by John Barrymore, Feb.
    1933 (March Papers).
Boston Globe, July 1, 1949 (March Papers).
Esquire, "These Are a Few of My Favorite Things," Dec. 1980, pp. 46–48.
Hartford Times, "March Interview," June 26 1957 (March Papers).
Hollywood Citizen News, "Take the Stand Fredric March," by Ed Sullivan, June
    14, 1938 (March Papers).
Hollywood Studio Magazine, "Men Who Create Monsters; Some Memories of
    Wally Westmore," by Teet Carle, Oct. 1973, SS-1–SS-2.
Hollywood Then and Now, "Gregory Catsos' Hollywood—Sylvia Sydney," Feb.
    1991, p. 11.

Indianapolis Star, Jan. 30, 1955 (March Papers).

Life, "A Bell for Adano," Dec. 18, 1944 (March Papers).

Life, "A New Image of Bryan," Sept. 26, 1960, p. 77.

Los Angeles Daily News, "Cinematters," by Virginia Wright, Oct. 6, 1941 (March Papers).

Los Angeles Evening Herald and Express, Aug. 17, 1940 (March Papers).

Los Angeles Sunday Times, Dec. 26 1935 (March Papers).

Minneapolis Morning Tribune, Dec. 19, 1951 (March Papers).

Minneapolis Star, Dec. 18, 1951 March Papers).

The Mirror, June 8, 1949 (March Papers).

Movie Classic Magazine, "The Road to Glory," by James Reid, June 1936, p. 30.

New Movie Magazine, "Bright College Years," by J. Gunnar Back, March 1931, pp. 86–91.

New Republic, May 10, 1975 (March Papers).

Newsweek, "The March Story," Jan. 2, 1950, p. 49.

Newsweek, "Talk with the Stars," Sept. 4, 1961 (March Papers).

New York Herald Tribune, "Joe Hyams Abroad," May 26 1959 (March Papers).

New York Times Magazine, "Broadway Stars: Ten Years Ago and Today," Apr. 20, 1947, p. 24.

New York Times Magazine, "The March Man 'Cometh,'" by Guy Flatley, May 27, 1973, pp. 1, 3 (March Papers).

Photoplay, "Fred Marches On," by Philip Merton, June, 1930, pp. 86 and 151.

Photoplay, "Leaves of Absence: Excerpts from My Diary on My Trip to Glamorous Tahiti, Land of Phantasy," by Fredric March, March 1935, pp. 56–57, 98–99, 100–101.

Picture Play, "Her Ex," by Laura Ellsworth Fitch, Feb. 1937 (March Papers).

Playbill, "On Stage," by Jose Quintero, Aug. 1975, p. 23.

Saturday Review of Literature, "Portrait of Major Joppolo," Dec. 23, 1944, pp. 18–19.

Screenland, "The Real Life Story of Fredric March," as told to Margaret Reid, June/July 1932 (March Papers).

Screenplay, 1932 (March Papers).

Silver Screen, "The Far East Comes to Hollywood," by Gladys Babcock, Feb. 19, 1939, pp. 26.

This Week Sunday Magazine, 1954 (March Papers).

Time, Sept. 1, 1941, p. 86.

"March-to-the-Altar." Unpublished article (c. 1932) by Mary Bickel, (March Papers).

Larry Swindell article, Inquirer Book Editor (March Folder).

Sheila Graham interview with Fredric March, Dec. 24 1936 (March Papers).

OTHER

Badger, University of Wisconsin annual, 1917–1921.

Current Biography, 1943.

Daily Cardinal, University of Wisconsin, Madison, 1916–1920.

Death Takes a Holiday Press Book, 1934.

Desperate Hours Press Book, 1955.

Desperate Hours, personal script of Fredric March (March Papers).

ENICAR, Monthly High School paper, Racine High School, 1913–1914.

KIPIKAWI, Racine High School annual, 1911–1914.

Letter to Fredric March, Feb. 26, 1942, from Clara Clemens Gabrilowitsch (March Papers).

March tribute Movie, Jean Bickel Owen, 21 September 1987.

Milwaukee Journal, various.

New York Times Film Reviews, 1929–1972.

New York Times, May 27, 1973.

Playbill, Aug. 1975.

Racine Journal Times, various.

Wisconsin Alumnus, Jan. 1962, "Fredric March—An Appreciation," pp 22–23. University of Wisconsin, Grade Transcripts of Frederick Bickel. Racine Schools, Grade Transcripts of Frederick Bickel.

Levy, Edwin Lewis, "Elitch's Gardens, Denver, Colorado: A History of the Oldest Summer Theater in the United States (1890–1941)." Ph.D. dissertation, Columbia University, 1960.

Yale Broadcast, May 17, 1964, WTIC Hartford, 7:30 p.m., "Five Days in April."

Yale Reports, WTIC-Hartford, Sunday 7:30 p.m., May 17, 1964, #326 pp 1–10, "Five Days in April."

Index

Academy Awards, 53, 63, 68, 103, 156, 159, 175-176
An Act of Murder, 160-161
The Adventures of Mark Twain, 129, 130-131, 135-138, 147, 149
The Affairs of Cellini, 75-79, 88
Akins, Claude, 202-203
Alexander the Great, 182, 185-187
All of Me, 75-77
Alpha Delta Phi, 8-9, 12
The American Way, 118-119, 189
Anderson, Richard, 219
Anna Karenina, 86, 89-90
Another Part of the Forest, 159, 163
Anthony Adverse, 98-100
Anti-Nazi activity, 119
The Autumn Garden, 173, 175

Baker, Ellis, 27, 29-33, 35-38, 41, 62, 65
The Balcony Walkers, 31
Bankhead, Tallulah, 54, 139-141
The Barretts of Wimpole Street, 80-81, 88
Barrymore, Ethel, 43, 215
Barrymore, John, 23, 43-44, 2-53,

62, 64, 101-102, 148, 169
Baxter, Warner, 96-97
Bedtime Story, 128-129
Beery, Wallace, 68
Belasco, David, 25-25
A Bell for Adano, 149-151, 169, 189, 238
Bellamy, Ralph, 47, 63, 92, 113, 117, 120, 149
Benchley, Robert, 133
Benedek, Laslo, 174
Bennett, Constance, 76, 80
Bennett, Joan, 118
Berman, Pandro, 91
The Best Years of Our Lives, 2, 153-157, 177, 230
Bickel, Cora (mother), 2-4, 12, 23, 28, 30, 41, 48, 50
Bickel, Fred, 18, 21-28
Bickel, Frederick McIntyre, 2, 4-9, 11-19, 21
Bickel, Harold (brother), 2, 8, 12, 120, 180
Bickel, John F. (father), 2-3, 11-12, 30, 51, 97
Bickel, Mary (sister-in-law), 3, 22
Bickel, Rosina Elizabeth, 2-3, 5

Bloomgarden, Kermit, 166-167,
    173
Blyth, Ann, 159
Bogart, Humphrey, 176, 183-184,
    229, 240
Bow, Clara, 46-47, 50
Brian, Mary, 49
The Bridges at Toko-Ri, 170, 181
Broadway, 88, 100, 102, 109
Brown, Clarence, 89
Brownell-Stork Stock Company,
    26-27
The Buccaneer, 104-105, 107-112
Burke, Billie, 24
Burke, Melville, 33, 43
Burns, Julia, 7, 11-12
Burton, Richard, 186

Cagney, James, 98, 104, 114, 228
Campbell, Douglas, 215-216
Carpenter, Charles, 5-6, 11-13,
    15-16, 18, 22, 75, 120, 172,
    215, 228, 234-235
Carroll, Nancy, 46, 54
Chatterton, Ruth, 46, 50
Chayefsky, Paddy, 195, 211
A Christmas Carol, 180-181
Christopher Columbus, 161, 163,
    165-167, 186
Claire, Rene, 133-134
Clark, Dick, 213
Colbert, Claudette, 46, 51, 54,
    69-71, 116, 180
Colman, Ronald, 91, 185
Communist activity, accusations
    of, 117, 123-124, 167, 176,
    181
The Condemned of Altona, 217
Cooper, Gary, 1, 46, 73, 82, 102,
    229, 240
Coplon, Judith, case of, 168-169
Counterattack, charges of
    Communism, 114, 161-162,
    169-170

The County Chairman, 9, 26
Coward, Noel, 73
Crane, Vernon, 5, 11
Crawford, Joan, 121-122
Cromwell, John, 27, 29, 104,
    109, 114-115, 124-125
Cronyn, Hume, 171
Cukor, George, 102
Cushing, Peter, 186

The Dark Angel, 91
Davis, Bette, 92
Davis, Kathryn (cousin), 3, 16, 67
De Havilland, Olivia, 98-99
Death of a Salesman, 166,
    173-176
Death Takes a Holiday, 75, 77-78,
    88
Deburau, 25-26
DeMille, Cecil B., 68, 105,
    107-112
Design for Living, 73
The Desperate Hours, 182-185
The Devil and the Cheese, 38
Dies, Martin, 105, 113-114, 123,
    168
Dillman, Bradford, 108, 139, 148,
    189-193, 218, 231-232,
    238-239
Distinguished Service Award,
    226-227
Dodsworth, 188-189
Douglas, Kirk, 219
Dr. Jekyll and Mr. Hyde, 2, 31,
    57-64, 67
The Dummy, 46
Dunnock, Mildred, 174

Eagels, Jeanne, 48
The Eagle and the Hawk, 71, 103
Edwin Booth Society, 13-14, 17
Eisenhower Medal, 151, 169
Eldridge, Florence (second wife),
    33-35, 39, 47-48, 75, 86, 88,

91-92, 100-101, 108-109,
112-113, 118-120, 124,
139-143, 148, 157-163, 166,
169-173, 176-177, 186,
189192, 196, 202-203,
207-208, 217-218, 222, 226,
233, 235-238
Elitch's Gardens, 32-37, 40-41
Ellis, Aline Elizabeth (girlfriend),
15-16, 18-19, 21-23, 29-30,
38, 41, 228-229
An Enemy of the People, 172-173
Executive Suite, 178-180

Fantacci, Penelope March
(daughter), 65, 67,786, 120,
126, 130, 177, 180, 187, 215,
217-218, 233, 237-240
Fantacci, Umberto (son-in-law),
180, 215, 217, 233
Ferber, Edna, 43
Field, Betty, 124, 149
Firefly Farm, 120, 177, 194, 215,
218, 228, 232, 234-235
Flood, James, 76
Flynn, Errol, 79, 99, 116, 148
Fontanne, Lynn, 40, 73
Footlights and Fools, 49
Ford, Glenn, 125
Ford, John, 91-92
Frankenheimer, John, 218-219,
230-232
Frye, Dwight, 38

Gaal, Franciska, 110
Gable, Clark, 116, 229, 240
Gabrilowitsch, Clara Clemens,
135-136
Gallagher, Mary, 5
Garbo, Greta, 86, 89, 90-91
Garland, Beverly, 185
Garnett, Tay, 117
Garson, Greer, 147

Gazzara, Ben, 213
German Silver Bear award, 207
Gersh, Phil, 139, 181, 184, 194,
203, 232
Gideon, 211, 215-217
Gilbert, John, 89, 101
Goldwyn, Samuel, 82, 86, 91, 156
Good Dame, 75,78-80
Gordon, Ruth, 157-158
Grant, Cary, 71
Griffith, D. W., 24, 34
Guthrie, Tyrone, 215

The Half Caste, 32
Hall, Alexander, 128
Hall, Laurence, 18, 121, 172,
209, 226-228, 235
Hall, Virginia, 121, 172, 226-228
Harding, Anne, 48
Haresfoot (drama society), 13-14
Harvest, 31
Hawks, Howard, 96
Hayward, Leland, 149
Hellman, Lillian, 91, 104, 109,
159, 173
Hepburn, Katharine, 91-92
Hill, Arthur, 213-214
Hobart, Rose, 58, 61
Hodiak, John, 151
Holbrook, Hal, 137
Holden, William, 178, 181, 185
Hombre, 223, 225-226
Homeier, Skippy, 149
Honor Among Lovers, 54
Hood, J. Vincent, 5-6, 11, 22,
215, 226-227
Hope for Harvest, 125, 129-130
Hopkins, Miriam, 31, 58, 61, 73,
76
Houseman, John, 115, 178
Howard, Leslie, 91
HUAC, 105, 113, 123, 170-171
Huguenin, Jimmy, 5

The Iceman Cometh, 230-231
I Married a Witch, 133-135
Inherit the Wind, 199-207,
    209,211, 229
It's a Big Country, 173, 176-177

Jealousy, 48

Kanin, Garson, 157
Kaufman, George S., 43, 146
Kazan, Elia, 139-140, 142, 161,
    166, 170, 177
Keefer, Don, 174
Kelly, Gene, 202
Keyes, Evelyn, 107-108
The Knife in the Wall, 31
Kramer, Stanley, 173-174, 199,
    201-203, 206
Ku Klux Klan, 18, 202

Ladies Love Brutes, 50
Lake, Veronica, 133-135
Lancaster, Burt, 219
Landi, Elissa, 69
Lang, June, 97
Langer, Lawrence, 41
Lasky, Jesse, 129, 135-136
Laughter, 51-52
Laughton, Charles, 69, 81, 87-88,
    117
The Lawbreaker, 26, 28
Leech, John L., 123-124
Lei Aloha, 26
Leisen, Mitchell, 70, 77
LeRoy, Mervyn, 98-99
Les Miserables, 75, 82, 87-88
Lion of Venice Award, 175
Lombard, Carole, 71-72, 103-104
Long Day's Journey into Night,
    139, 189-194, 197, 215, 230,
    232, 238, 240-241
Loy, Myrna, 100-101, 116
Lubitsch, Ernst, 73

Lugosi, Bela, 38
Lunt, Alfred, 40, 68, 73, 142

Macauley, Jackie Ramsey,
    175-176, 215
Macauley, Stewart, 176
Mader, Roland, 116, 158
Make Me a Star, 64
Mamoulian, Rouben, 55, 57-60,
    82, 85
The Man in the Gray Flannel Suit,
    182, 187-188
Man on a Tightrope, 177-178
Mann, Delbert, 195
Manslaughter, 51
March, Anthony (son), 81, 86,
    120, 177
March, Fredric, 29-33, 35-38, 40-
    41, 43-54, 57-65, 67-93, 95-
    105, 107-114, 117-121, 123-
    131, 133-147, 149-151, 153-
    161, 163, 165-173, 175-197,
    199-209, 211-223, 225-236,
    241
The Marriage Playground, 49
Mary of Scotland, 91-93, 96, 108
Mauch, Billy, 99
Mayer, L. B., 90
McCarthy, Joseph, 161, 170, 172,
    175
The Melody Man, 29
Mendes, Lothar, 49
Merman, Ethel, 142
Merrily We Go To Hell, 64, 79
Metro-Goldwyn-Mayer, 63, 81,
    101, 121
Middle of the Night, 195-196
Millar, Stuart, 212
Miller, Arthur, 166, 173
Moore, Colleen, 48
Morgan, Frank, 80
Mulvihill, John, 32-34, 40, 77
My Sin, 54

Myerberg, Michael, 139, 141

Nagel, Conrad, 68
New Milford farm, 120
Newman, Paul, 217, 223, 225

The Night Angel, 54
Nothing Sacred, 103-104
Novak, Kim, 195
Now I Lay Me Down to Sleep,
    169, 171

Oberon, Merle, 91
Ommanney, Katharine, 37
One Foot in Heaven, 125-128
O'Neill, Eugene, 139, 189, 192,
    194, 218, 230, 232, 240
Oshkosh, theater at, 229-230

Palmer, Lilli, 169
Paramount contract, 45, 54
Paramount on Parade, 50
Paramount, 45, 54, 64, 75-76
Paris Bound, 48
Parsons, Louella, 115
Peale, Norman Vincent, 126
Peck, Gregory, 187,188
Perkins, Lillian, 3, 6
Peters, Oswald, 17, 22
Pi Epsilon Delta, 17
Pichel, Irving, 57
Post, Jane Carpenter, 215
Powell, Eleanor, 90
Powell, William, 154

Quinn, Anthony, 112
Quintero, José, 190, 218, 240-241
Quirk, Lawrence, 48, 50, 54, 64,
    71, 79-80, 87, 91, 100, 102,
    112, 116, 176-177, 188, 214,
    228, 238

Raft, George, 76

Rapper, Irving, 126, 130, 136
Rathbone, Basil, 104
Ritt, Martin, 223, 225
The Road to Glory, 95-98
Robson, Flora, 92
The Romancers, 16-17
Rossen, Robert, 186-187
The Royal Family (play), 40, 43,
    44, 180
The Royal Family of Broadway
    (film), 52, 81
Russell, Harold, 155-156

Sarah and Son, 50
Schary, Dore, 176, 208
Schulberg, B. P., 46, 57, 68
Scott, Martha, 126, 183, 185
Selznick, David O., 89, 101-103,
    116-117
Selznick, Myron, 46, 54
Seven Days in May, 217-218
Shavings, 26
Shearer, Norma, 65, 67, 80-81, 90
Sidney, Sylvia, 64, 78-79, 167
The Sign of the Cross, 68-79, 73,
    87, 186
The Skin of Our Teeth, 139-142,
    189
Smilin' Through, 65, 67-68
Smith, Alexis, 137
So Ends Our Night, 125
Stander, Lionel, 102, 104
Standing, Sir Guy, 77
Sten, Anna, 82-83, 86
Strangers in Love, 64
The Studio Murder Mystery, 47
Sullavan, Margaret, 125
Sullivan, Ed, 39, 61, 147, 193
A Summer Day in Racine, 12
Susan and God, 121
Swinburne, Nora, 167

Tamiroff, Akim, 111

Tarnish, 30
Theater Guild Tour, 40-41
There Goes My Heart, 116-117
tick...tick...tick, 228
Tolstoy, Leo, 82-85
Tomorrow the World, 149
Tone, Franchot, 114
Tonight Is Ours, 70
Tony Awards (Antoinette Perry
    Award), 159, 189, 193
Tracy, Spencer, 1, 63, 184-185,
    197, 199, 202-204, 206-207,
    209, 229, 240
Trade Winds, 117-118
True to the Navy, 50
Twentieth Century Pictures, 75,
    80, 82, 87-89, 95-96

Union Vodvil, 13-14, 16-18, 228
USO tour, 138, 143-147

Venable, Evelyn, 77-78
Victory, 124-125

Wanger, Walter, 117
Warner Brothers, 98, 129-130,
    135-136, 148
We Live Again, 82-86, 88-89
Wellman, William, 101, 103
Westmore, Wally, 60-62, 68, 111
The Wild Party, 46, 47
Wilder, Thornton, 138, 140-142
The Winslow Boy, 194
Winters, Shelly, 178-179
Wise, Robert, 178
World War I, 15
World War II, 104, 119-120, 124,
    130, 142,-143, 147-148
Wray, Fay, 80
Wright, Teresa, 154-155
Wyler, William, 153, 184

Years Ago, 156-159
The Young Doctors, 211-214
Young, Loretta, 128
Yr. Obedient Husband, 109,
    112-116

Zanuck, Darryl, 75-76, 96, 100,
    187
Zeno, 27-28

About the Author

DEBORAH C. PETERSON is Adjunct Professor for Cardinal Stritch College and Concordia University in Milwaukee, Wisconsin. Her primary research interests include film and Civil War history.

Recent Titles in
Contributions in Drama and Theatre Studies

Playwrights and Acting: Acting Methodologies for Brecht, Ionesco, Pinter, and Shepard
James H. McTeague

Israel Horovitz: A Collection of Critical Essays
Leslie Kane, editor

Jung's Advice to the Players: A Jungian Reading of Shakespeare's Problem Plays
Sally F. Porterfield

Where the Words Are Valid: T. S. Eliot's Communities of Drama
Randy Malamud

Greek Tragedy on the American Stage: Ancient Drama in the Commercial Theater,
1882–1994
Karelisa V. Hartigan

"Vast Encyclopedia": The Theatre of Thornton Wilder
Paul Lifton

Christopher Marlowe and the Renaissance of Tragedy
Douglas Cole

Menander and the Making of Comedy
J. Michael Walton and Peter D. Arnott

A History of Polish Theater, 1939–1989: Spheres of Captivity and Freedom
Kazimierz Braun

Theatre, Opera, and Audiences in Revolutionary Paris: Analysis and Repertory
Emmet Kennedy, Marie-Laurence Netter, James P. McGregor, and Mark V. Olsen

The Stage Clown in Shakespeare's Theatre
Bente A. Videbaek

Shadows of Realism: Dramaturgy and the Theories and Practices of Modernism
Nancy Kindelan

ISBN 0-313-29802-5

EAN

9 780313 298028

HARDCOVER BAR CODE

90000>